This Book Comes With Lots of
FREE Online Resources

Nolo's award-winning website has a page dedicated just to this book. Here you can:

KEEP UP TO DATE. When there are important changes to the information in this book, we'll post updates.

GET DISCOUNTS ON NOLO PRODUCTS. Get discounts on hundreds of books, forms, and software.

READ BLOGS. Get the latest info from Nolo authors' blogs.

LISTEN TO PODCASTS. Listen to authors discuss timely issues on topics that interest you.

WATCH VIDEOS. Get a quick introduction to a legal topic with our short videos.

And that's not all.
Nolo.com contains thousands of articles on everyday legal and business issues, plus a plain-English law dictionary, all written by Nolo experts and available for free. You'll also find more useful **books, software, online apps, downloadable forms,** plus a **lawyer directory.**

Get updates and more at
www.nolo.com/back-of-book/CHB.html

14th Edition

Chapter 13 Bankruptcy

Keep Your Property & Repay Debts Over Time

Attorney Cara O'Neill

FOURTEENTH EDITION   MAY 2018

Editor   CARA O'NEILL

Book Design   SUSAN PUTNEY

Proofreading   ROBERT WELLS

Index   THÉRÈSE SHERE

Printing   BANG PRINTING

ISSN 2576-7178 (online)
ISSN 2576-716X (print)

ISBN 978-1-4133-2515-7 (paperback)
ISBN 978-1-4133-2516-4 (ebook)

This book covers only United States law, unless it specifically states otherwise.

Please note

We believe accurate, plain-English legal information should help you solve many of your own legal problems. But this text is not a substitute for personalized advice from a knowledgeable lawyer. If you want the help of a trained professional—and we'll always point out situations in which we think that's a good idea—consult an attorney licensed to practice in your state.

Acknowledgments

This book wouldn't be possible without the original author, Stephen R. Elias. Steve wrote many Nolo books, including *The Foreclosure Survival Guide: Keep Your House or Walk Away With Money in Your Pocket* and *The New Bankruptcy: Will It Work for You?* and he was the coauthor of *How to File for Chapter 7 Bankruptcy*. Steve was a practicing attorney in California, New York, and Vermont before joining Nolo in 1980. Over his long career, he was featured in such major media as *The New York Times, The Wall Street Journal, Newsweek,* "Good Morning America," "20/20," *Money* magazine, and more. He has been missed since his passing in 2011.

Thanks must also go to attorneys Kathleen Michon and Patricia Dzikowski, both of whom have had a hand in significantly shaping this book over the years.

About the Author

Cara O'Neill is a bankruptcy attorney in Northern California and a legal editor with Nolo. She has been practicing law in California for over 20 years. Prior to joining Nolo, she served as an administrative law judge, litigated both criminal and civil cases, and taught law courses as an adjunct professor. She earned her law degree in 1994 from the University of the Pacific, McGeorge School of Law, where she served as a law review editor and graduated a member of the Order of the Barristers—an honor society recognizing excellence in courtroom advocacy. Cara has authored and coauthored a number of Nolo books, including *How to File for Chapter 7 Bankruptcy*, *The New Bankruptcy*, *Money Troubles*, and *Credit Repair*.

Table of Contents

Part I: Is Chapter 13 Right for You?

Part II: Filing for Chapter 13 Bankruptcy

Part III: Making Your Plan Work

Part IV: Help Beyond the Book

Appendixes

Is Chapter 13 Right for You?

How Chapter 13 Works

Chances are good that you've picked up this book because your debts have become overwhelming. Maybe you are facing foreclosure on your home or repossession of your car, or receiving letters and phone calls from debt collectors. Or perhaps, you've realized that your debts have grown far beyond your ability to repay them, and you're wondering if there's anything you can do to get control of your finances.

Chapter 13 bankruptcy could be the best way to resolve your debt problems. When you file for Chapter 13, you agree to repay all or a portion of your debts over time, under the supervision of the bankruptcy court. Chapter 13 allows you to keep your property while using your anticipated income to repay some or all of your debts.

This book opens up the world of Chapter 13 to anyone who wants to get a good idea of how Chapter 13 works and what it can do for you. The book stops short of giving you all the forms and instructions you would need to do your own Chapter 13 bankruptcy. That's because we believe that very few people can carry out this task without attorney representation. (See "Do You Need a Lawyer?" below.)

That said, times are changing, and filing for bankruptcy is getting easier—primarily because the official forms are now easier to use.

During the form revision process, it was hoped that an official Chapter 13 plan form would be created, but, after all of the revised forms made their debut, a national plan didn't materialize.

That all changed late last year. Now, anyone who files for Chapter 13 bankruptcy after December 1, 2017, will use either the official plan form or a local plan form that complies with newly adopted federal standards. And, for the first time, an official *Chapter 13 Plan* (Form 113) is included in this book.

This is a big deal for anyone tasked with drafting a plan. Not only does the new plan form provide helpful instructions, but the new federal requirements allow for consistency throughout the courts and lets us provide even more detailed help than we've been able to give readers in the past. (See Ch. 8.) Finally, we're hopeful that as the forms and instructions continue to improve, filing a Chapter 13 matter without an attorney will become more feasible for everyone. (Keep in mind that the forms don't explain bankruptcy law or procedure. You're responsible for learning the process and understanding how a filing will affect your income and assets.)

But we're jumping ahead. There's a lot to know before you get to the plan.

This first chapter gets you started with an overview of Chapter 13 bankruptcy.

It also explains other types of bankruptcy relief (including Chapter 7 bankruptcy) and options for dealing with your debts outside of bankruptcy.

> ### Online Companion Page: Get Legal Updates and More at Nolo.com
>
> You can find the online companion page to this book at:
> **www.nolo.com/back-of-book/CHB.html**
> There you will find important updates to the law.

An Overview of Chapter 13 Bankruptcy

Chapter 13 can be a good solution for people who need time to pay off certain debts and who have enough income to meet the Chapter 13 requirements. In Chapter 13, you get to keep all of your property, regardless of its value. But, you will have to pay your unsecured creditors (those to whom you owe credit card debts, medical debts, and most court judgments, for example) at least as much as they would have received had you filed for Chapter 7 bankruptcy. Typically, this amount would be the value of the property you would have lost in a Chapter 7 bankruptcy, minus sales costs. This is a minimum amount, however. Your monthly Chapter 13 payment might be higher, depending on your other bills. If you can afford to make the required payment over the course of three- to five-years, you can keep the property.

Chapter 13 has many other benefits (discussed below in "Reasons to Choose Chapter 13"), but some of the most powerful can help you save your home. Chapter 13 bankruptcy allows you to catch up on mortgage payments through your plan so that you can avoid foreclosure. (See Ch. 8.) And if you have second mortgages that are no longer secured by the equity in your property because your home's value has decreased (your home is significantly "underwater") you can eliminate them.

Costs

Like everyone who files for Chapter 13 bankruptcy, you have to pay the filing fee of $310, due either when you file your initial bankruptcy paperwork or in up to four installments (with the court's permission). You'll also have to pay a fee—typically less than $60 total—to a credit counseling agency for prefiling credit counseling and postfiling debt management counseling. If you decide to hire a lawyer to help you with your case, you can expect to pay an additional $3,000 or more in legal fees, depending on the prevailing rate in your area. In most cases, you won't have to come up with the entire legal fee all at once. Many attorneys will ask you to make an initial payment—which could be as low as $100 but likely more—and allow you to pay the rest over the course of your plan.

Do You Need a Lawyer?

For the vast majority of Chapter 13 filers, the answer is "yes." In fact, most bankruptcy courts strongly suggest that filers retain counsel.

It's not that people can't understand how Chapter 13 bankruptcy works. And most people can fill out the petition and accompanying schedules and forms. The problem is that Chapter 13 law can be tricky, and most people don't understand what will happen to their income and assets, how much they'll have to repay creditors, and other complicated Chapter 13 repayment plan requirements. Calculating plan payments is especially difficult without the assistance of computer software, which is expensive and generally requires bankruptcy knowledge to complete properly. It is also not uncommon for the trustee or creditors to challenge or object to various aspects of your plan. You may have to argue against objections, negotiate with creditors, or modify your plan. In fact, most Chapter 13 plans need at least one modification before the court approves them, even when prepared by an attorney. Experienced Chapter 13 bankruptcy lawyers have software to prepare your Chapter 13 plan and the expertise to handle objections and to modify your plan as needed.

We believe that most Chapter 13 filers benefit from legal representation. Having said that, it's still important to understand the Chapter 13 process, including options for dealing with debts and property, the possibility of reducing loan amounts (called cramdown), and what you can expect to pay in your Chapter 13 plan. This book also helps you identify various tricky issues that might arise in your bankruptcy case. Armed with this knowledge, you'll be in a better position to help your attorney represent you.

It's also helpful to run some preliminary numbers yourself to determine if Chapter 7 is an option for you or if funding a Chapter 13 plan is possible given your income and expenses. Chs. 4 and 5 take you through the means test (to see if you qualify for Chapter 7 bankruptcy) and provide step-by-step instructions on figuring out if you can fund a Chapter 13 plan.

To learn more about hiring and working with a bankruptcy lawyer, see Ch. 15.

Filing Your Papers

To begin a Chapter 13 bankruptcy, you fill out a packet of forms in which you disclose your property and debts, as well as your financial transactions for the years immediately before your filing. Many of the official forms for Chapter 13 bankruptcy are the same as those for Chapter 7.

In addition, you must prepare:
- two forms (Form 122C-1: *Chapter 13 Statement of Your Current Monthly Income and Calculation of Commitment Period* and Form 122C-2, *Chapter 13 Calculation of Your Disposable Income*) that determine whether your income is more or less than the median income in your state. The calculation determines how long your repayment plan must last. If your income is more than the median for your state, your plan, with a few exceptions, must last

five years; if your income is less than the median, you can propose a three-year plan. If your income is more than the median, Form 122C-2 calculates how much disposable income you will have available to pay your unsecured creditors over the five-year period.

- your Chapter 13 repayment plan, which shows how you propose to pay certain mandatory debts (child support, tax arrearages, and so on), secured debts on property you intend to keep, and, if you have sufficient income, at least a portion of your other unsecured debts over the three- to five-year period. (See Ch. 8.)
- a certificate showing you have participated in a credit counseling program during the 180-day period before filing for bankruptcy (this requirement is explained in Ch. 9). If the credit counseling agency comes up with a proposed repayment plan that would allow you to pay your debts outside of bankruptcy, you must submit this as well.
- a certificate regarding child support obligations and your residence.

You'll also have to submit documents that will verify the figures in your paperwork. You'll either file those documents with your paperwork or submit them to the bankruptcy trustee appointed to oversee your case, depending on the rules of your local jurisdiction. Such documents can include:

- pay stubs from the 60-day period before you file, along with a cover sheet.
- proof that you've filed your federal and state income tax returns for the previous four years.
- a copy of your most recent IRS income tax return (or a transcript of that return).
- if you're a sole proprietor, profit and loss statements.

Chs. 7 through 9 discuss in detail the bankruptcy forms, repayment plan, and filing process.

The Repayment Plan

The repayment plan you submit with your other bankruptcy papers (or shortly after your initial filing) shows the judge how you will devote your disposable income to pay off all or some of your debt over the life of your plan.

Which Debts Must Be Repaid

Chapter 13 requires you to pay particular, high-priority debts in full over the course of the life of the plan, including recent income tax debt, domestic support obligations, and mortgage and car loan arrearages (if you want to keep the car or home). You also must pay as much of your remaining debts as you can from the income you have available.

But that's not all. You'll have to show that you can keep up on your other obligations, too, such as a mortgage or car note and other monthly living expenses. And, as explained in Ch. 3, your plan also has to allow for total payments to your unsecured creditors that are at least as much as they would have received had you filed for Chapter 7 bankruptcy instead of Chapter 13. In other words, these payments must be at least equal to the value of the property you'd have to give up in a Chapter 7 case, less the costs, commissions, and fees that would have to be paid to sell that property.

Length of the Repayment Period

You must propose a repayment plan that lasts for either three or five years, depending on your income. As you'll learn in Ch. 4, a filer whose average gross monthly income over the six months before filing is more than the median income in their state must propose a five-year repayment plan unless the plan proposes to pay 100% of the filer's unsecured debt. For more information on how long your plan will last, see Ch 5.

Filers whose average gross monthly income for the six-month period is less than the median usually have the choice of filing for either Chapter 7 or Chapter 13 bankruptcy. If they use Chapter 13, these filers may propose a three-year repayment plan and may use their actual expenses to calculate how much income they will have to devote to that plan. Such filers sometimes opt to pay a smaller payment over five years if it will increase their chances of getting their plan approved by the court.

Filers must use certain standard expense amounts set by the IRS—rather than their actual expenses—to calculate their plan payments. This ensures that higher-income filers with excessive monthly expenses don't receive an advantage as the result of living a lavish lifestyle.

To learn more about how to calculate your income, find out whether your income is above or below your state's median, and figure out which expenses to use in calculating your plan payments, see Ch. 4.

Coming Up With a Plan the Judge Will Approve

You can't proceed with a Chapter 13 bankruptcy unless a bankruptcy judge approves (confirms) your plan. As mentioned, some creditors are entitled to receive 100% of what you owe them, while others may receive a much smaller percentage or even nothing at all if you have insufficient disposable income left over after the mandatory debts are paid. For example, a Chapter 13 plan must propose that any child support you owe to a spouse or child (as opposed to a government agency) will be paid in full over the life of your plan. If you can't prove that you have enough income to do so, the judge will not confirm it. On the other hand, the judge can confirm a plan that doesn't repay any portion of your credit card debts if you won't have any disposable income left after paying your child support obligations and other required debts.

> **TIP**
>
> **You may have more—or less— disposable income than you think.** Chapter 13 requires you to commit your "projected disposable income" to repaying your debts over the life of your plan. Initially, you calculate your projected disposable income by subtracting your allowable expenses from your average income during the six months before you file for bankruptcy. But if this does not give an accurate picture of your current income and expenses and given certain circumstances, you might be allowed to use your current income and expenses at the time you file, if those figures more accurately reflect your finances going forward. For more information on calculating your disposable income, see Ch. 5.

The Automatic Stay

When you file for Chapter 13 bankruptcy, the automatic stay goes into effect right away. The stay prevents most creditors from taking action to collect a debt against you or your property. So, for example, if a foreclosure sale of your home or a vehicle repossession is in the works, the stay stops the sale or repossession dead in its tracks. (However, the automatic stay doesn't apply if you've had two previous bankruptcy cases dismissed in the past year and it may be limited in time if you had one case dismissed.) The automatic stay is discussed in more detail in Ch. 2.

The Meeting of Creditors

As soon as you file your bankruptcy papers, the court will schedule a meeting of creditors (also called a 341 hearing) which will take place within 20 to 40 days after your filing date—and send notice of this meeting to you and the creditors listed in your bankruptcy papers. You (and your spouse if you have filed jointly) are required to attend. You'll each need to bring two forms of identification—a picture ID and proof of your Social Security number.

The creditors' meeting is conducted by the Chapter 13 bankruptcy trustee for your court. No judge is present, and the meeting is held outside of court, usually in the nearest federal building. Although the bankruptcy trustee is not a judge, you still have a duty to cooperate with the trustee as a condition of receiving a discharge.

Keep in mind that if your meeting will be held in a federal building, there may be restrictions on what you can and cannot bring with you, and those restrictions might include a cell phone. Check beforehand.

A typical creditors' meeting lasts less than 15 minutes. The trustee will briefly go over any questions raised by the information you entered in the forms. The trustee is likely to be most interested in the fairness and legality of your proposed repayment plan and your ability to make the payments you have proposed. (See Ch. 8 for more on Chapter 13 plans.) The trustee has a vested interest in your plan being approved because the trustee gets paid a percentage of all payments your creditors receive.

The trustee will also require proof that you have filed your tax returns for the previous four years. If you can't show that you filed returns, the trustee may continue the meeting to give you a chance to file these returns. Ultimately, you will not be allowed to proceed with a Chapter 13 bankruptcy unless and until you bring your tax filings up to date.

RESOURCE

Help if you are behind in tax payments. If you owe taxes, you may benefit from professional help in the form of a tax attorney, an enrolled agent (licensed by the IRS), or a tax preparer. For more information on getting current on taxes and getting professional help, read *Stand Up to the IRS*, by Frederick W. Daily and Erica Good Pless (Nolo).

When the trustee is finished asking questions, any creditors who show up will have a chance to question you. It's unlikely that a creditor will appear, but if one does, you'll be required to answer questions related to your past and present financial circumstances. The creditors most likely to show are often disgruntled and are either suing you (or are planning to sue you) or plan to fight the discharge of your debt on fraud grounds. Such creditors use the meeting to gather evidence in support of their case, much like litigants do in a deposition. They'll likely evaluate what they learn before deciding whether to proceed against you and, if they do, you can expect your answers to be used against you later.

By contrast, it's common to use the meeting to discover whether the trustee has an objection to your plan and why. You may be able to make changes to accommodate the trustee (which would require you to modify the plan). Keep in mind, though, that if you're unable to resolve the issue, the trustee (or creditors) will raise the objection and then the bankruptcy judge (who is not at the meeting) will make a decision.

Plan Objections

A creditor who has an objection to the plan you have proposed is unlikely to voice that objection at the meeting of creditors. Instead, the creditor will file a motion with the court. If you're unable to resolve a concern held by the trustee, you can expect the trustee to file a motion, as well.

A trustee or creditor might claim, for example, that your plan isn't feasible (you don't have enough income to make the required plan payment), that you're giving yourself too much time to pay your arrears on your car note or mortgage, or that your plan proposes to pay an amount that's less than what the creditor is entitled to receive.

An unsecured creditor who is scheduled to receive very little under your plan might object if that creditor thinks you should cut your living expenses and thereby increase your disposable income (the amount from which unsecured creditors are paid). This is more likely to happen if you are using your actual expenses to compute your disposable income (as filers whose income is less than the state median are allowed to do) instead of standard expense figures set by the IRS.

As a general rule, the judge will go along with the trustee unless your lawyer can make a good case that the trustee (or creditor) is wrong.

The Confirmation Hearing

Chapter 13 bankruptcy requires at least one appearance by you or your attorney before a bankruptcy judge. (In some districts, the judge comes into the courtroom only if the trustee or a creditor objects to your plan, and you want the judge to rule on the objection.) At this "confirmation hearing," which is usually held a few weeks after the creditors' meeting, the judge either confirms (approves of) your proposed plan or sends you back to the drawing board for various reasons—usually because your plan doesn't meet Chapter 13 requirements. For example, a judge might reject your plan because you don't have enough income to pay off your priority creditors (those creditors you're required to pay in full) while staying current on your secured debts, such as a car note or mortgage.

You are entitled to amend your proposed plan until you get it right or the judge decides that it's hopeless. During this time though, you must make payments to the trustee under your proposed plan. Each amendment requires a new confirmation hearing and appropriate written notice

to your creditors. (For more information on the confirmation hearing, see Ch. 10.) Once your plan is confirmed, it will govern your payments for the three- to five-year repayment period.

Possible Additional Court Appearances

If your plan is prepared perfectly from the beginning, your confirmation hearing will probably be the only time the bankruptcy judge deals with your case. However, additional appearances in court by you or your attorney may be necessary to:

- confirm your repayment plan if you need to modify or change your plan
- value an asset, if your plan proposes to pay less for a car or other property and the creditor objects to the valuation (this might happen if you try to cram down the debt to the item's current value)
- respond to requests by a creditor or the trustee to dismiss your case or amend your plan
- respond to a creditor who opposes your right to discharge a particular debt (perhaps claiming that you incurred the debt through fraud)
- discharge a type of debt that can be discharged only if the judge decides that it should be (for example, to discharge a student loan because of undue hardship)
- eliminate a lien on your property that will survive your Chapter 13 bankruptcy unless the judge removes it, or

- reaffirm a debt owed on a car or other secured property or that would otherwise not survive your bankruptcy.

Many of these procedures are explained in Ch. 11.

Making Your Payments Under the Plan

You are required to make your first payment under your proposed repayment plan within 30 days after you file for bankruptcy. If the bankruptcy court ultimately confirms your plan, your payment will be distributed to your creditors in accordance with the plan's terms. If your Chapter 13 bankruptcy never gets off the ground, in most instances, the trustee will return the money to you, less administrative expenses. If the judge has ordered the trustee to make payments to your secured creditors before the confirmation of your plan, the trustee will deduct the amount of these payments from the total returned to you.

Once your plan is confirmed, you will continue to make payments, usually monthly, to the bankruptcy trustee, an official appointed to oversee your case. In some jurisdictions, the trustee will require you to agree to an order that takes the payments directly out of your bank account or paycheck (this option isn't available everywhere, although many filers would like to take advantage of it). The trustee uses your monthly payments to pay the creditors in accordance with the payment order contained in your plan. The

trustee also collects a statutory fee (roughly 8% to 10% of the amount you will pay under your plan, but it might be less).

If you can show that you have a history of regular income spread out in uneven payments over the year—for example, quarterly royalty payments or predictable seasonal income fluctuations (for instance, if you do construction work in a location that has severe winters)—your plan may provide for payments when you typically earn income, rather than every month, but in most cases it will be monthly.

If Something Goes Wrong

Three to five years is a long time. What happens if you can't make a payment or it becomes apparent—perhaps because of a change in your income or life circumstances—that you won't be able to complete your plan? If you miss only a payment or two, you can usually arrange with the trustee to make up the difference. If you lose your income stream, however, and you definitely won't be able to complete the plan, you might be able to convert your bankruptcy to Chapter 7 (if that makes sense), obtain a "hardship" discharge from the court, or modify the plan. Whether one of these options will make sense will depend on several factors, such as the type of debt you have and whether you'd lose property if you converted to a Chapter 7 case. For that reason, in many cases, Chapter 13 bankruptcies that don't work out are dismissed entirely.

If your case is dismissed, you'll owe your creditors the balances on your debts from before you filed your Chapter 13 case, less the payments you made, plus the interest that accrued while your case was open. See Chs. 12 and 13 for more on what happens if you are unable to complete your plan.

Personal Financial Management Counseling

Before you make your last plan payment, you'll have to complete a personal financial management counseling course (called budget counseling)—and file an official form certifying that you did so—in order to get your discharge. This counseling covers basic budgeting, managing your money, and using credit responsibly. See Ch. 10 for more on this requirement.

After You Complete Your Plan

Once you complete your plan, certify that you've remained current on your ongoing child support or alimony obligations, and file proof that you've completed your personal financial management counseling, your remaining debts will be discharged, if they are the type of debts that can be discharged in Chapter 13. (See "Which Debts Are Discharged in Chapter 13 Bankruptcy," below, for more information.) For instance, if you have $40,000 in credit card debt, and you pay off $10,000 through your repayment plan, the remaining $30,000 will be discharged once you complete the plan. However, you will still owe whatever is left on the debts that you can't, by law, discharge in Chapter 13. Practically speaking, most people will emerge from Chapter 13 bankruptcy current on domestic support obligations and debt free otherwise, except for student loan and mortgage balances (you're not required to repay long-term obligations fully).

> **EXAMPLE:** Karen owes $60,000 in credit card debts, $60,000 in student loans, and $2,000 in alimony. Karen pays off the alimony in full (as required by law) and 10% of her credit card debts and student loans. The remainder of the credit card debts will be discharged, but she will still owe the rest of her student loan debt ($54,000) unless she can convince the judge to order it discharged because of undue hardship.

Which Debts Are Discharged in Chapter 13 Bankruptcy

Not all debts are discharged in Chapter 13 bankruptcy. Of course, if you will repay all of your unsecured debts in full over the life of your plan, no discharge is necessary. But if your plan provides for less than full repayment of your unsecured debts, whatever you still owe at the end of your plan may or may not be discharged.

Discharging Student Loans in Chapter 13 Bankruptcy: The *Brunner* Test

For the most part, student loans cannot be discharged in Chapter 13 bankruptcy. However, in rare circumstances, courts will discharge some or all of your student loans at the end of your Chapter 13 repayment period if paying them would cause undue hardship.

While there is some indication that courts are becoming more sympathetic to debtors saddled with student loan obligations and struggling to support their families, the bar to prove *undue* hardship (as opposed to *ordinary* hardship) is still set too high for most debtors.

Many courts use a three-factor test to determine if repaying your student loans would cause undue hardship, called the *Brunner* test (after a court case of the same name). Not all courts use this test, but even in those that don't, it's still difficult to discharge a student loan.

Under the *Brunner* test, a bankruptcy court looks at the following three factors to determine if repayment of your student loans would cause an undue hardship:

- Based upon your current income and expenses, you cannot maintain a minimal standard of living for yourself and your dependents if you are forced to repay your loans.
- Your current financial situation is likely to continue for a big part of the repayment period.
- You have made a good-faith effort to repay your student loans.

Debts That Are Discharged

As a general rule, whatever you still owe on most credit card debts, medical bills, and lawyer bills is discharged, as are most court judgments and loans. Also, under bankruptcy law, debts you owe to an ex-spouse arising from a divorce or separation agreement that are not for support are discharged in Chapter 13 (but not in Chapter 7), as are debts incurred for the purpose of paying taxes.

Debts That Are Not Discharged

Debts that survive a Chapter 13 bankruptcy (unless you pay them in full during the life of your plan) include:

- debts that you don't list in your bankruptcy forms
- court-imposed fines and restitution
- back child support and alimony
- student loans (unless you can show hardship)
- recent back taxes
- taxes for years in which you did not file a return (or, in some jurisdictions, for years in which you filed a late return), and
- debts you owe because of a civil judgment arising out of your willful or malicious acts, or for personal injuries or death caused by your drunk driving.

Debts That Are Not Discharged If the Creditor Successfully Objects

Some types of debts will survive your bankruptcy only if the creditor files papers and goes to court to prove that the debt shouldn't be discharged. For example, if a creditor successfully objects to a debt arising from your fraudulent actions or recent credit card charges for luxuries, those debts will be waiting for you after your bankruptcy, unless you managed to pay them all off during your repayment plan.

Chapter 13 Bankruptcy and Foreclosure

If you are behind on your mortgage payments or facing foreclosure, Chapter 13 bankruptcy might be able to help you keep your home. It can do this by allowing you to temporarily (or permanently) stop the foreclosure, catch up on back mortgage payments through your plan, get rid of certain junior liens thus freeing up more money to pay your first mortgage (although this option isn't being used much as real estate appreciates in value), and perhaps work out a foreclosure alternative with your lender through a bankruptcy foreclosure mediation program.

The Automatic Stay Can Stop a Foreclosure

If you are facing foreclosure, in most situations, filing a Chapter 13 bankruptcy will immediately stop the foreclosure process, at least temporarily. There are exceptions, however, if you filed bankruptcy within the previous two years, or if the bankruptcy court lifted the stay and allowed your lender to proceed with the foreclosure in a dismissed bankruptcy case. (See Ch. 2 for more on the automatic stay and home foreclosures.)

Catching Up on Mortgage Arrears Through Your Chapter 13 Plan

You must remain current on a secured debt, such as your house payment, if you want to keep the property. When you signed your loan documents, you agreed that the bank could take the house if you failed to live up to your obligation.

Your contract remains in place even if you file for bankruptcy. So, to stay in the home, you must continue paying for it. One of the benefits of Chapter 13 bankruptcy is that it allows you to include your past-due mortgage debt in your Chapter 13 plan. This means you can continue making your monthly payment, pay the arrears back over the length of your plan, and remain in the house.

The same is true of past due homeowners' association assessments—you can catch up through your plan. As long as you keep making your regular mortgage payments (and your ongoing HOA assessments) and your Chapter 13 plan payments, your lender cannot foreclose. Chapter 7 bankruptcy, on the other hand, does not provide a way to get current on mortgage arrears. For this reason, Chapter 13 bankruptcy is often the best avenue for saving your home if you are behind in your mortgage or HOA assessments.

Getting Rid of Second Mortgages, HELOCs, and Other Junior Liens

Chapter 13 bankruptcy has another helpful remedy—lien stripping. Lien stripping allows you to remove second mortgages, home equity lines of credit (HELOCs), and other junior liens from your home if they are wholly unsecured. (See "Lien Stripping: Getting Rid of Second Mortgages and Other Liens on Real Estate," below, to learn what wholly unsecured means.) By getting rid of some or all these payments, a homeowner is often better positioned to afford the remaining mortgages.

Foreclosure Mediation Programs in Bankruptcy

After the 2008 recession and subsequent foreclosure crisis, an increasing number of bankruptcy courts instituted programs to help debtors, particularly in Chapter 13, resolve foreclosure issues with their lenders. These programs (often called "loss mitigation programs") vary by district. Most involve some form of foreclosure mediation in which the homeowner and the lender meet in the presence of a neutral mediator

and try to work out an alternative to foreclosure. Possible workouts might include a loan modification, short sale, or deed in lieu of foreclosure. Most of these bankruptcy court programs apply only to residential property. But a few also include income-producing residential property (rental property) and second homes.

Deficiency balances are discharged in bankruptcy. A deficiency occurs when the amount you owe on your home exceeds the value of the home. In many states, after foreclosing on your home, the mortgage lender can sue you for the deficiency (in some states the lender can get the deficiency judgment through the foreclosure itself without filing a separate lawsuit). But Chapter 7 and Chapter 13 bankruptcies discharge all mortgage deficiencies. Knowing this provides an incentive for the mortgage lender to work out a deal with you if your property is worth less than the amount you owe.

Special Chapter 13 Features: Cramdowns and Lien Stripping

In Chapter 13 bankruptcy, you may be able to reduce the amount of a secured loan (for example, your car loan) to the actual value of the property; this is called a cramdown. And you might be able to get rid of second or third mortgages, HELOCs, or home equity loans if they are no longer secured by the equity in your home. This is called lien stripping.

Although these provisions are powerful, they don't apply to the first mortgage of your residential real property. Some people believe they can "modify" the first mortgage on their home through Chapter 13 bankruptcy. For the most part, this is a myth, although there are a few exceptions, such as for vacation and rental properties.

CAUTION

You lose the benefit of cramdown or lien stripping if your case is dismissed or converted to Chapter 7. Loan reductions or lien eliminations you get through cramdown or lien stripping are only good if you complete all of your payments under the Chapter 13 plan (or under a Chapter 11 bankruptcy). If your case is dismissed or converted to a Chapter 7, the secured creditors get their full lien amounts back, less any amounts you have paid through your plan.

TIP

You may be able to modify your mortgage through nonbankruptcy avenues. Although you can't modify a first mortgage on a residential home through bankruptcy, you may be able to negotiate with your lender directly to reduce your interest rate, payments, or more. Or, you might be able to take advantage of government programs designed to help homeowners modify their mortgages. For more information, check out Nolo's Foreclosure section at www.nolo.com or get *Your Foreclosure Survival Guide*, by Amy Loftsgordon (Nolo).

Cramdowns: Reducing Secured Loans to the Value of the Collateral

If the amount you owe on a secured loan is more than the value of the collateral (the collateral is the property you pledge to guarantee payment of the loan), you may be able to take advantage of Chapter 13 provisions that result in what is commonly known as a cramdown. When you cram down a loan, you reduce the amount owed to equal the value of the collateral—and this happens without having to get the lender's agreement.

While a cramdown sounds great, there's a catch—you have to pay off the entire reduced balance in your Chapter 13 repayment plan. So while it works well to reduce a car payment (assuming you meet the 910-day rule), only high-earning filers will be able to use a cramdown for property with high loan balances, such as a vacation home.

Property That Is Eligible for Cramdown

You can only use a cramdown on loans secured by certain types of property. Significantly, you cannot cram down mortgages on your personal residence. But you may be able to use it on a mobile home mortgage or a mortgage for a multiunit building if you live in one of the units. Mortgages on your investment properties, such as rental property, a second home, or commercial property, are eligible. A cramdown is also available, subject to certain limitations, for car loans and other personal property loans.

Car loans. Cramdowns are often used for car loans. There are a few restrictions to keep in mind, however. For cars, in order to cram down the loan, one of the following must apply:

- You incurred the debt at least 910 days before you filed for bankruptcy.
- The loan is not a purchase money loan (that is, you secured the debt with a car you already owned, not a car you bought with the loan).
- The car secured by the loan is not a personal vehicle (that is, you bought it for your business).

Other personal property loans. You may cram down debts for personal property (other than motor vehicles) only if you took out the loan at least a year before you filed for bankruptcy, or if the loan was not used to purchase the property that you pledged to secure repayment (that is, you owned the property before you took out the loan).

Real estate loans. You may be able to cram down mortgages secured by the following types of properties:

- multiunit buildings (even if you live in one of the units)
- vacation or rental homes
- buildings or lots adjacent to your home that are not likely to be considered part of your residence, such as farmland

- mobile homes (these are considered to be personal property), and
- property that is not your residence.

Cramming Down Negative Equity in the 9th Circuit

If you bought a car within 910 days of your bankruptcy filing (which means your loan is ineligible for cramdown), you might be able to cram down part of the loan if you traded in a car to buy the new car. You can only do this in the 9th Circuit (all other circuits have rejected this interpretation of the law). Here's how it works:

If, when you purchase a car, you trade in a car that is underwater (you owe more on the car than the car is currently worth), the lender often adds the difference between the trade-in value of your car and the remaining balance on the loan to your new car loan. For example, say your old car is worth $5,000 but you still owe $8,000 on the car loan. The lender for your current car purchase takes your old car as a trade-in, and adds $3,000 ($8,000 balance on loan minus the $5,000 value of car) to your new car loan. This amount is called negative equity.

In the 9th Circuit, if you file for bankruptcy, you can treat the $3,000 as unsecured debt, even if you bought the second car within 910 days of your bankruptcy filing. (*In re Penrod*, 611 F.3d 1158 (9th Cir. 2010).)

How Cramdown Works

In bankruptcy, when a loan is undersecured (which means the amount you owe is greater than the value of the property pledged to secure repayment), the debt can be broken down into secured and unsecured portions. The amount equal to the value of the property is the secured portion and any amount over the value of the property is unsecured.

The first step in a cramdown is coming up with an accurate value for the property. Under Rule 3012, you can ask the court to value your property through the plan or in a separate motion. (See Ch. 8 to learn about new notice requirements if you make your request in your plan.). If the creditor objects to your valuation, you'll present your proof of value, such as an appraisal, and the creditor is provided with an opportunity to present its own valuation. If the values are not the same and you are unable to reach a compromise with the secured creditor, the court will hold an evidentiary hearing. You and the creditor bring your appraisers to testify, and the bankruptcy judge makes a decision.

After the judge determines the value (and thereby the amounts of the secured and unsecured claims), in most cases, you must pay the entire amount of the secured portion through your plan, with interest. The appropriate interest is also determined as part of your motion and is generally set at prime plus one to three points. For example, if the prime rate is 3.25%, an appropriate interest rate may be between 4.25% and 6.25%.

The unsecured portion of the claim is lumped in with your other unsecured debts. Because of the way unsecured debt is treated in a Chapter 13 bankruptcy, many bankruptcy filers pay pennies on the dollar on the unsecured portion.

Here's an example of how this works: You owe $20,000 on a car you bought three years ago. The car is now worth $15,000 (which means only $15,000 of the car loan is secured by the property). You can cram down the loan to $15,000 and pay this amount through your Chapter 13 plan. The remaining amount—$5,000—will be added to your unsecured debt and treated like all of your other unsecured debt.

Determining the Value of the Property

The appropriate methods of valuation depend on the type of property you are valuing.

Real estate and mobile homes. For real estate and mobile homes, use the current market value of the property. This is best accomplished through a formal appraisal—especially if you think the value may be contested by the secured creditor. If you don't anticipate a fight, you may be able to use comparable sales in your area. This will be less expensive than paying for a full appraisal.

Personal property. For personal property, use the replacement value of the property. Replacement value is not the amount it would cost to replace the item with a new item. Rather, it's the amount a merchant could get for a used item of similar age and in a similar condition in a retail environment (as opposed to a fire sale or an auction). You can have the property appraised or use some other method to determine its replacement value.

For motor vehicles, you may be able to use an automotive industry guide, such as the *Kelley Blue Book*. Start with the retail value (rather than the wholesale value) and adjust that amount for the car's condition and mileage. If the car lender disputes the figure, you may need to have the vehicle appraised.

Lien Stripping: Getting Rid of Second Mortgages and Other Liens on Real Estate

With lien stripping, you may be able to eliminate certain second mortgages, HELOCs, and other liens on your real property. Unlike cramdowns, lien stripping can be used to reduce your secured debt payments on your personal residence as well as other real property. Like a cramdown, it involves valuing the property. Here's how it works.

If you have more than one mortgage on your property, you can ask the court to value the property and eliminate or "strip off" any mortgage that is determined to be wholly, or completely, unsecured. (See Ch. 8 for information on the procedure.) To figure out if a mortgage is completely unsecured, start with the value of the property and subtract the amount of any mortgages or liens that are more senior (meaning they must be paid off first) to the mortgage you are trying to strip. If the value of the property is *less* than the total amount of the senior mortgages and liens, then there is no equity left to secure the mortgage you are trying to strip. This means it's wholly unsecured and eligible for stripping. To get the lien stripped, you must file a motion with the court. If the court grants your motion, the lien is removed from your property and the debt will be treated as an unsecured debt.

Lien stripping is generally not available for first mortgages. A first mortgage, being the most senior lien on the property, will never be completely unsecured. A second or third mortgage, or a HELOC, is usually eligible for lien stripping if it is wholly unsecured. A mortgage is wholly unsecured if, after selling the property, the sales proceeds are insufficient to pay any portion of the junior mortgage.

If you have a homeowners' or condominium association lien, however, you might not be able to strip it, even if it's wholly unsecured. Whether you can depends on state law and the way the lien was created. (Consult with a local attorney to find out.)

EXAMPLE: John and Ellen own a home currently worth $100,000. They have three mortgages—the first is $80,000, the second is $27,000, and the third is $50,000. The first mortgage is entirely secured because it is less than the value of the home. The second mortgage is partially secured since the value of the house less the first mortgage ($100,000 − $80,000 = $20,000) is enough to cover part of the second mortgage. Since it is not completely unsecured, it cannot be stripped. John and Ellen have more luck with their third mortgage, which is completely unsecured. When you deduct the amount owed on the first two mortgages from the value of the house ($100,000 − $80,000 − $27,000 = -$7,000), the result is less than zero. There is no equity left to pay any portion of the third mortgage. John and Ellen can strip the entire $50,000 third mortgage.

Like a cramdown, when a mortgage is stripped, the underlying debt becomes unsecured and is paid in your Chapter 13 plan along with your other unsecured creditors, such as credit cards and medical bills. These creditors get paid out of your disposable income, which for most people is minimal. Therefore, a stripped mortgage is often paid very little through the plan. Once you've completed your plan, any remaining balance gets wiped out with other dischargeable unsecured debt.

> **CAUTION**
>
> **Lien stripping is not the same as lien avoidance.** In Chapter 13 bankruptcy, you may also be able to "avoid" liens, or get rid of them, if the property is exempt. Although the end result may be the same, or similar, lien avoidance is different from lien stripping because it hinges on property exemptions (the law that allows you to protect certain property in bankruptcy). To learn more about lien avoidance, see Ch. 11.

Is Chapter 13 Right for You?

For most people, the two choices for bankruptcy relief are Chapter 7 and Chapter 13. In Chapter 7 bankruptcy, you immediately wipe out many debts, but in exchange you must give up any property you own that isn't protected by state or federal exemption laws.

Some of you won't have a choice between Chapter 7 and Chapter 13 bankruptcy. If your income exceeds Chapter 7 bankruptcy qualifications, you will have to use Chapter 13 and repay some of your debt. (See Ch. 4 to find out whether you'll be limited to Chapter 13.) Likewise, if you don't have a steady income, your only bankruptcy choice is Chapter 7. Many people who can choose between the two decide to file under Chapter 7, but there are some situations when Chapter 13 will be the better option.

Upper-Income Filers Must Use Chapter 13

If your average monthly income during the six months prior to filing is higher than the state median, you won't qualify for a discharge if your total five-year disposable income would be:

- $77,000 or more and satisfy at least 25% of your unsecured debt, or
- $12,850 or more, regardless of the percentage of unsecured debt that amount would pay.

(See Ch. 4 for more on this "means" test.)

Reasons to Choose Chapter 7

Most people who have a choice traditionally have opted to file for Chapter 7 bankruptcy because it is relatively fast, effective, easy to file, and doesn't require payments over time. It also doesn't require you to be current on your income tax filings (although you might run into a problem if the trustee believes that you're not filing because you're entitled to a significant tax refund). In the typical situation, a case is opened and closed within three to four months, and the filer emerges debt free except for a mortgage, car payments, and certain types of debts that survive bankruptcy (such as student loans, recent taxes, and back child support).

If you have any secured debts, such as a mortgage or car note, Chapter 7 allows you to keep the collateral as long as you are current on your payments. However, if your equity in the collateral substantially exceeds the exemption available to you for that type of property—meaning that you have more equity than you're allowed to protect in bankruptcy—the trustee can sell the property, pay off the loan, pay you your exemption amount, and pay the rest to your unsecured creditor. If you are behind on your payments, the creditor can come into the bankruptcy court and ask the judge for permission to repossess the car (or other personal property) or foreclose on your mortgage. Or, the lender can wait until the bankruptcy is over to recover the property.

As a general rule, however, most Chapter 7 filers can keep all their property, either because they don't own much to begin with or because any equity they own is protected by an exemption. But this isn't always the case—especially as the economy improves and people regain equity in their homes.

Nevertheless, assuming you qualify, that you can protect all or most of your property, and that you have the type of debt that is wiped out in Chapter 7 bankruptcy, you likely will find it easier—and more effective—to file for Chapter 7 than to keep up with a long-term payment plan under Chapter 13.

Reasons to Choose Chapter 13

Although Chapter 7 is easier and doesn't require repayment, there are many good reasons why people who qualify for both types of bankruptcy choose Chapter 13 instead. Each chapter solves different problems.

Generally, Chapter 13 bankruptcy might make sense if you will have adequate, steady income to fund your plan, and are in any of the following situations (this isn't an exclusive list—additional situations exist):

- You are facing foreclosure on your home or your car is being repossessed, and you want to keep your property. Using Chapter 13, you can make up the missed payments over time and reinstate the original agreement. You cannot do this in Chapter 7 bankruptcy which means you'll likely lose the property.

- You owe more on vacation or investment property than the property is worth, and you can reduce the mortgage to the value of the property in Chapter 13. (This is possible only if you are not using the real estate as your primary residence and you can afford to repay the entire reduced mortgage balance through your plan.) (See "Special Chapter 13 Features: Cramdowns and Lien Stripping," above.)

- You have more than one mortgage and are facing foreclosure because you can't make all the payments. If your home's value is less than or equal to what you owe on your first mortgage, you can use Chapter 13 to change the additional mortgages into unsecured debts—which don't have to be repaid in full—and lower the amount of your monthly payments. (See "Special Chapter 13 Features: Cramdowns and Lien Stripping," above.)

- Your car is reliable and you want to keep it, but it's worth far less than you owe. You can take advantage of Chapter 13 bankruptcy's cramdown option (for cars purchased more than 2½ years before filing for bankruptcy) to keep the car by repaying its replacement value in equal payments over the life of your plan, rather than the full amount you owe on the contract. (See "Special Chapter 13 Features: Cramdowns and Lien Stripping," above.).

- You have a codebtor who will be protected under your Chapter 13 plan but who would not be protected if you used Chapter 7 (the creditor won't be able to collect against the codebtor while you're in Chapter 13) (see Ch. 2).

- You have a tax obligation, student loan, or another debt that cannot be discharged in bankruptcy, but can be paid off over time in a Chapter 13 plan (you can avoid a wage garnishment by paying in Chapter 13).

- You owe debts that can be discharged in a Chapter 13 bankruptcy but not in a Chapter 7 bankruptcy. For instance, debts incurred to pay taxes can't be discharged in Chapter 7 but can be discharged in Chapter 13.

- You have a sole proprietorship business that you would have to close down in a Chapter 7 bankruptcy but that you could continue to operate in Chapter 13.

- You have valuable personal property or real estate that you would lose in a Chapter 7 case, but could keep if you file for Chapter 13 (you'll need to have enough income to pay the unprotected value over the course of the plan).

Alternatives to Bankruptcy

By now, you should have a pretty good idea about what you can hope to get out of a Chapter 13 bankruptcy. Before you decide whether a Chapter 13 or Chapter 7 bankruptcy is the right solution for your debt problems, however, you should consider some basic options outside of the bankruptcy system. Although bankruptcy is the only sensible remedy for some people with debt problems, an alternative course of action makes better sense for others. This section explores some of your other options.

Do Nothing

Surprisingly, the best approach for some people who are deeply in debt is to take no action at all. You can't be thrown in jail for not paying your debts (with the exception of child support), and your creditors can't collect money from you that you just don't have. If you don't have income and property that a creditor could take, and you don't foresee having any in the future, you're likely considered "judgment proof." People who are judgment proof rarely file for bankruptcy. Here's why.

Creditors Must Sue to Collect

Except for taxing agencies and student loan creditors, creditors must sue you in court and get a money judgment before they can go after your income and property. The big exception to this general rule is that a creditor can take collateral—foreclose on a house or repossess a car, for example—when you default on a debt that's secured by that collateral. (Although in some states, mortgage servicers must file a lawsuit in order to foreclose on your house.)

Under the typical security agreement (a contract involving collateral), the creditor can repossess the property without first going to court. But the creditor will not be able to go after your other property and income for any "deficiency" (the difference between what you owe and what the repossessed property fetches at auction) without first going to court for a money judgment.

To get a money judgment, a creditor must have you personally served with a summons and complaint. In most states, you will have 30 days to file a response in the court where you are being sued. If you don't respond, the creditor can obtain a default judgment and seek to collect it from your income and property. If you do respond—and you are entitled to do so even if you think you owe the debt—the process will typically be set back several months until the court can schedule a trial where you can be heard. In most courts, you respond by filing a single document in which you deny everything in the creditor's complaint (or, in some courts, admit or deny each of the allegations in the complaint).

Much of Your Property Is Protected

Even if creditors get money judgments against you, they can't take away such essentials as:

- basic clothing
- ordinary household furnishings
- personal effects
- food
- Social Security or SSI payments necessary for your support
- unemployment benefits
- public assistance
- bank accounts with direct deposits from government benefit programs, and
- 75% of your wages (but more can be taken to pay child support judgments).

The general state exemptions described in Ch. 4 (and listed in Appendix A) apply whether or not you file for bankruptcy. Even creditors who get money judgments against you can't take these protected items. (However, neither the federal bankruptcy exemptions nor the state bankruptcy-only exemptions available in California and a few other states apply if a creditor sues you in state civil court.)

When You Are Judgment Proof

A judgment is good only if the person who has it—the judgment creditor—can seize income or property from the debtor. If you have no property or income that can be taken to pay the judgment, you are said to be "judgment proof." For example, if your only income is from Social Security (which can be seized only by the IRS and federal student loan creditors) and all your property is exempt under your state's exemption laws, your judgment creditor can't take your income. Your life will continue as before, although one or more of your creditors may get pushy from time to time. While money judgments last a long time and can be renewed, this won't make any difference unless your fortune changes for the better. If that happens, or is likely to happen, you might reconsider bankruptcy.

If your creditors know that their chances of collecting judgments from you any time soon are slim, they probably won't sue you in the first place. Instead, they'll simply write off your debts and treat them as deductible business losses for income tax purposes. After some years have passed (usually between four and ten), the debt will become legally uncollectible, under state laws known as statutes of limitation.

These statutes of limitation won't help you if the creditor sues or renews its judgment within the time limit. Lawsuits typically cost thousands of dollars in legal fees. If a creditor decides, on the basis of your economic profile, not to go to court at the present time, it is unlikely to seek a judgment down the line to extend its claims. In short, because creditors are reluctant to throw good money after bad, your poor economic circumstances might shield you from trouble.

You should take this with a grain of salt, however. Creditors have been known to change course and pursue more tenuous claims as the economy tightens. Before making your decision, it's a good idea to research the current collection climate.

CAUTION
Don't restart the clock. A creditor has only a set amount of time—known as the statute of limitations—to sue you on a delinquent debt. Be careful, however. The statute of limitations can be renewed (restarted all over again) if you revive an old debt by, for example, admitting that you owe it or making a payment. The specifics vary by state. Savvy creditors are aware of this loophole and may try to trick you into reviving the debt so they can sue to collect it. So unless you are planning to make good on the debt or try to negotiate a new payment schedule (perhaps with a local merchant you'd like to continue doing business with), you should avoid any admissions.

Stopping Debt Collector Harassment

Many people file for bankruptcy to stop their creditors from making harassing telephone calls and writing threatening letters. As explained above and in Ch. 2, the automatic stay stops most collection efforts as soon as you file for bankruptcy. However, you don't have to start a bankruptcy case to get annoying creditors off your back. Federal law forbids collection agencies from threatening you, lying about what they can do to you, or invading your privacy. And some state laws prevent original creditors from taking similar actions.

Under federal law, you can legally force collection agencies to stop phoning or writing you by simply demanding that they stop. (This law is the federal Fair Debt Collections Practices Act, 15 U.S.C. §§ 1692 and following.) For more information, see *Solve Your Money Troubles: Debt, Credit & Bankruptcy*, by Amy Loftsgordon and Cara O'Neill (Nolo). Below is a sample letter asking a creditor to stop contacting the debtor.

SEE AN EXPERT
Your debt collector may be putting money in your pocket. The Fair Debt Collection Practices Act places a number of restrictions on debt collector activity. The remedies provided by the act include damages and attorneys' fees. More and more attorneys are interested in using these remedies, because they can earn some money without taking it out of a client's recovery. If you are suffering debt collection abuses, consider consulting with a bankruptcy or consumer rights attorney to find out if this type of lawsuit might be worth your while. For more information on the act and its remedies, see *Solve Your Money Troubles: Debt, Credit & Bankruptcy*, by Amy Loftsgordon and Cara O'Neill (Nolo).

Sample Letter Telling Collection Agency to Stop Contacting You

Sasnak Collection Service
49 Pirate Place
Topeka, Kansas 69000

November 11, 20xx

Attn: Marc Mist

Re: Lee Anne Ito
    Account No. 88-90-92

Dear Mr. Mist:

For the past three months, I have received several phone calls and letters from you concerning an overdue Rich's Department Store account.

This is my formal notice to you under 15 U.S.C. § 1692c(c) to cease all further communications with me except for the reasons specifically set forth in the federal law.

This letter is not meant in any way to be an acknowledgment that I owe this money.

Very truly yours,

Lee Anne Ito

Lee Anne Ito

Negotiate With Your Creditors

If you have some income, or you have assets you're willing to sell, you may be better off negotiating with your creditors than filing for bankruptcy. Negotiation may buy you some time to get back on your feet, or you and your creditors may agree to settle your debts for less than what you owe.

Creditors don't like having delinquent debt on the books because it reflects poorly on the bottom line. They also don't like the hassle of instituting collection proceedings, either. To avoid the collection process, creditors sometimes will reduce the debtor's expected payments, extend the time to pay, drop their demands for late fees, or make similar adjustments. They're most likely to be lenient if they believe you are making an honest effort to deal with your debt problems.

Some creditors will even settle for less than what you owe. You'll want to be aware of a few things before deciding on this approach, however.

- Most creditors won't negotiate with you until you're late on your payments. The problem? If you fall behind and don't settle for less, you might have a difficult time bringing your account current.

- During the negotiation process, you'll likely be asked to provide proof that you're unable to pay the current balance, and the financial information you produce could be used to collect from you in the future. For instance, if you turn over a bank statement, the creditor might use the information to levy against (withdraw funds from) that account later.

- The Internal Revenue Service considers forgiven debt taxable. If you receive a Cancellation of Debt form (Form 1099-C), you'll likely need to include the amount as income on your yearly return (some exceptions apply). By contrast, you aren't taxed on debt that's discharged in bankruptcy.

You might be wondering whether you should tell your creditors that you are thinking about filing for bankruptcy. After all, shouldn't they be willing to negotiate for a lesser amount—that you can pay— if you can get rid of the debt entirely? Unfortunately, experience shows that this tactic often backfires. Why? Filing for bankruptcy doesn't concern a creditor until you actually file the paperwork, primarily because many people claim that they're going to file for bankruptcy when they have no intention of doing so. As a result, it's likely that the creditor won't believe you. And, just in case you do intend to file, the creditor will likely increase collection efforts in an attempt to get something before getting paid is no longer an option. Some creditors will call you every day demanding to know who your attorney is. When you tell them you don't have an attorney, they may well take the opportunity to berate you for not paying your debts and warn you to call them when you do get an attorney. In short, mentioning the "B" word is more likely to cause you grief than it is to produce a good result.

The Automatic Stay

One of the most powerful features of bankruptcy is the automatic stay: an injunction (a court order prohibiting an action) that goes into effect as soon as you file, prohibiting your creditors from taking certain actions against you. The automatic stay stops most debt collectors dead in their tracks and keeps them at bay for the rest of your case. Once you file, all collection activity (with some exceptions, explained below) must go through the bankruptcy court—and most creditors cannot take any further collection actions against you while the bankruptcy is pending.

This chapter explains how the automatic stay applies to typical debt collection efforts, including a couple of situations in which you might not get the protection of the automatic stay. It also explains how the automatic stay protects your codebtors from collection activities. And, it covers how the automatic stay works in eviction proceedings—vital information for any renter who files for bankruptcy.

> **TIP**
>
> **You don't need bankruptcy to stop your creditors from harassing you.** Many people begin thinking about bankruptcy when their creditors start phoning them at home and on the job. Federal law prohibits debt collectors from doing this once you tell the creditors, in writing, that you don't want to be called. And if you orally tell debt collectors that you refuse to pay, it is illegal for them to contact you except to send one last letter making a final demand for payment before filing a lawsuit. While just telling a creditor to stop usually works, you may have to send a written follow-up letter. (You can find a sample letter in Ch. 1.)

How the Automatic Stay Works

The automatic stay is "automatic" because you don't have to ask the court to issue it, and the court doesn't have to take any special action to make it effective: The stay goes into effect automatically, as soon as you file your bankruptcy case. The stay prohibits creditors and collection agencies from taking any action to collect most kinds of debts unless the law or the bankruptcy court says they can. In some circumstances, the creditor can file an action in court to have the stay lifted or modified (called a "Motion to Lift Stay" or a "Motion to Modify Stay"). In a few others, the creditor can simply begin collection proceedings without seeking advance permission from the court.

How Long the Stay Lasts

Unless it is lifted by the bankruptcy court, the stay will remain in effect until one of the following happens:

- The court confirms your Chapter 13 plan (see Ch. 10).
- Your case is dismissed.

When the court confirms your Chapter 13 plan, the automatic stay is replaced by an injunction in the order confirming your plan. If you are current on your payment obligations under the plan, the injunction prohibits creditors from taking action against you. Even if you do fall behind on plan obligations, most creditors must get bankruptcy court permission before they are permitted to take action. However, it's never a good idea to fall behind on plan payments because it could result in your case being dismissed.

How the Stay Affects Common Collection Actions

Most common types of creditor collection actions are stopped by the stay—including harassing calls by debt collectors, reporting debts to credit reporting bureaus, threatening letters by attorneys, and lawsuits to collect payment for credit card and health care bills.

Home Foreclosures

Many people file for Chapter 13 bankruptcy to prevent losing their homes in foreclosure. The automatic stay will temporarily prevent a foreclosure no matter which type of bankruptcy you file. However, in Chapter 7 bankruptcy, a creditor may be able to lift the stay and proceed with the foreclosure. The foreclosure can be permanently stopped in a Chapter 13 bankruptcy.

> EXAMPLE: Angel owns his home. He has been faithfully making his monthly mortgage payment of $900 for eight years and has incurred $50,000 worth of credit card debt. In May 20xx, Angel's job at a local

telecommunications company is outsourced as part of a monster layoff. He obtains another job at a much lower salary and slowly but surely falls two months behind on his mortgage payments. His lender sends him a notice of intent to foreclose on the mortgage.

Angel visits a bankruptcy lawyer, who explains that he can file for Chapter 7 bankruptcy to wipe out the credit card debt, but unless he can get current on his mortgage, the lender may be able to get permission from the bankruptcy court to proceed with the foreclosure. On the other hand, if Angel files for Chapter 13 bankruptcy, he can stop the foreclosure from proceeding and also buy some time to pay off the arrearage through his Chapter 13 plan.

> CAUTION
>
> **You cannot endlessly prevent foreclosure by filing a string of bankruptcies.** The automatic stay won't stop a foreclosure in a Chapter 13 bankruptcy if you filed another bankruptcy case within the previous two years and the court, in that proceeding, lifted the stay and allowed the lender to proceed with the foreclosure.

> EXAMPLE: Julie falls three months behind on her mortgage and receives a notice of intent to foreclose from her lender. Julie stops making any further payments and tries to sell her home to recover her remaining equity, but the market has slowed, and she can't find a buyer. Julie files for Chapter 7

bankruptcy to prevent her home from being sold at auction (the procedure used in about half the states). The auction is postponed because of the automatic stay, but the creditor moves to have the stay lifted. The judge grants the motion two months after Julie filed for bankruptcy. The lender sets a new date for the auction.

Julie now files for Chapter 13 bankruptcy, intending to keep her home by paying the arrearage over the life of the plan. Because the stay was lifted in a bankruptcy case that Julie filed within the last two years, the stay will not apply automatically to the mortgage creditor in Julie's Chapter 13 case. Instead, the lender will be allowed to proceed with the rescheduled auction unless she can convince the judge to reinstate the stay.

Even if you are in Julie's position, you may still be able to keep your home. As mentioned, the automatic stay in Chapter 13 cases lasts only until the court confirms the plan filed by the debtor. Once the plan is confirmed, it governs the behavior of debtor and creditor alike. For example, if Julie continues with her Chapter 13 case, and the court confirms a plan that provides for repayment of the arrearage before the lender completes the foreclosure, the lender will have to abide by the plan and allow her to catch up on her payments.

If your lender is able to proceed with the foreclosure because of the two-year rule or because it obtained an order lifting the stay, and it sells your home before your plan is confirmed, you may have trouble getting the home back. The law favors purchasers who qualify as "bona fide purchasers for value" (BFPs)—third-party buyers who have no idea there might be a problem with the foreclosure or mortgage. If a BFP buys your house at auction, that might be the end of the story. Although not always. It will depend on the law of your state. If you are in this situation, talk to a bankruptcy attorney right away.

Vehicle Repossessions

Vehicle repossessions work in much the same way as foreclosures except that there is typically no advance repossession notice. If you fall behind on your car note and really don't want your car repossessed, you can file for Chapter 13 bankruptcy and make up the back payments (or arrearage) as part of your plan. If you file your bankruptcy petition before the repossession, the automatic stay will protect your car up until the time the judge confirms a plan that proposes to pay the arrearage. You'll have to make "adequate protection" payments before your plan is confirmed to cover the depreciation that occurs between the date you file for bankruptcy and the date your plan is finally confirmed. Typically, this means paying the same amount that you would otherwise pay monthly on your car loan.

Even if your car is repossessed before you file, if the judge confirms a repayment plan that provides for payment of the arrearage and the amount you owe monthly on the note, you will be able to get your car back, unless the vehicle has already been auctioned off to a bona fide purchaser for value, in which case, it is gone forever.

Often, a car is worth much less than the debtor owes on it. If you're in this situation, it may not be a bad idea to let the repossession go forward, especially if you bought the car fairly recently.

However, if you bought the car at least 2½ years ago, Chapter 13 gives you an alternative: You can reduce the amount you owe to the replacement value of the car (taking its age and condition into account), plus interest at a relatively low rate. This is called a cramdown. Even if you can't make your payments under your current car note, your monthly bill might be much more affordable once the loan has been crammed down. (Ch. 1 discusses cramdowns in more detail.)

Credit Card Debts, Medical Debts, and Attorneys' Fees

Anyone trying to collect credit card debts, medical debts, attorneys' fees, debts arising from breach of contract, or legal judgments against you (other than child support and alimony) must cease all collection activities after you file your bankruptcy case. They cannot:

- file a lawsuit or proceed with a pending lawsuit against you

- record liens against your property
- report the debt to a credit reporting bureau, or
- seize your property or income, such as money in a bank account or your paycheck.

Public Benefits

Government entities that are seeking to collect overpayments of public benefits, such as SSI, Medicaid, or Temporary Assistance to Needy Families (welfare), cannot reduce or terminate your benefits to get the overpayment back while your bankruptcy is pending. If, however, you become ineligible for benefits for other reasons, bankruptcy doesn't prevent the agency from denying or terminating your benefits on those grounds.

Criminal Proceedings

Criminal proceedings are not stayed by bankruptcy. If a case against you can be broken down into criminal and debt components, only the criminal component will be allowed to continue; the debt component will be put on hold while your bankruptcy is pending. For example, if you were convicted of writing a bad check and have been sentenced to community service and ordered to pay money damages, your obligation to do community service will not be stopped by the automatic stay (but your obligation to pay money damages might be).

IRS Liens and Levies

As explained in "When the Stay Doesn't Apply," below, certain tax proceedings are not affected by the automatic stay. The automatic stay does, however, stop the IRS from issuing a lien or seizing (levying against) any of your property or income.

Utilities

Companies providing you with utilities (such as gas, heating oil, electricity, telephone service, and water) may not discontinue service because you file for bankruptcy. However, they can request a deposit and shut off your service 20 days after you file if you don't provide them with the deposit or another means to assure future payment.

How the Stay Affects Actions Against Codebtors

Many people file for Chapter 13 bankruptcy to protect their codebtors from liability. If your parent cosigned a loan with you and you file for Chapter 7 bankruptcy, the creditor can collect from your parent while the automatic stay is in place. In Chapter 13, with rare exceptions, the automatic stay also protects your codebtors unless the court lifts the stay. The court will lift the stay only in the following cases:

- Your codebtor received the item or services for which the debt was taken (for instance, the car obtained by the loan in question).

- Your repayment plan will not pay the debt.
- The creditor's interest would be irreparably harmed or is at risk if the stay were allowed to continue (for example, the collateral is not insured).
- The debt is a tax debt.

If your Chapter 13 case is closed, dismissed, or converted to Chapter 7 or 11, your codebtor loses the protection of the automatic stay. Also, the stay does not protect a codebtor whose liability for the debt arose in the ordinary course of the codebtor's business.

When the Stay Doesn't Apply

The stay doesn't put a stop to every type of collection action, nor does it apply in every situation. Congress has determined that certain debts or proceedings are sufficiently important to "trump" the automatic stay. In these situations, collection actions can continue just as if you had never filed for bankruptcy. And even in circumstances when the stay would otherwise apply, you can lose the protection of the stay through your own actions.

Actions Not Stopped by the Stay

The automatic stay does not prohibit the following types of actions from proceeding.

Divorce and Child Support

Almost all proceedings related to divorce or parenting continue as before: They are not affected by the automatic stay. These include actions to:

- set and collect current child support and alimony
- collect back child support and alimony from property that is not in the bankruptcy estate (for instance, postfiling income that isn't included in your plan)
- determine child custody and visitation
- establish paternity in a lawsuit
- modify child support and alimony
- protect a spouse or child from domestic violence
- continue to withhold income to collect child support
- report overdue support to credit bureaus
- intercept tax refunds to pay back child support, and
- withhold, suspend, or restrict drivers' and professional licenses as leverage to collect child support.

Tax Proceedings

The IRS can continue certain actions, such as conducting a tax audit, issuing a tax deficiency notice, demanding a tax return, issuing a tax assessment, demanding payment of an assessment, or pursuing a codebtor for taxes owed.

Pension Loans

The stay doesn't prevent withholding from a debtor's income to repay a loan from an ERISA-qualified pension (this includes most job-related pensions and individual retirement plans).

How You Can Lose the Protection of the Stay

Even if the stay would otherwise apply, you can lose its protection through your own actions. The stay may not protect you from collection efforts if you had one or more bankruptcy cases pending but dismissed within a year of your current bankruptcy filing.

The automatic stay will last only 30 days if you had one prior bankruptcy case that was dismissed within the year before you file. You can ask the court to extend the stay, but you have to file a motion and obtain an order before the 30 days expires. And if you had two cases dismissed within the last year, the automatic stay won't kick in at all (unless the court orders otherwise). There are two lessons here for debtors:

- Don't let your case be dismissed.
- If your case is dismissed and you want to file again within the year, you should definitely talk to an attorney before you decide to file.

One Dismissal in the Past Year

With a couple of exceptions, if you had a bankruptcy case dismissed during the previous year for any reason, voluntarily or involuntarily, the court will presume that your new filing is in bad faith, and the stay will terminate 30 days after your new case is filed. You, the trustee, the U.S. Trustee, or the creditor can ask the court to continue the stay beyond the 30-day period. Most likely it will have to be you. The court will extend the stay only if you (or whoever else makes the request) can show that your current case was not filed in bad faith.

The motion to extend the stay must be scheduled for hearing within the 30-day period after you file for bankruptcy and must give creditors adequate notice under local motion rules of why the stay should be extended. As a practical matter, this means the motion must:

- be filed within several days after you file for bankruptcy (unless you follow the procedures to get an "emergency" hearing on the motion, in which case you have a little more time to file the motion)
- be served on all creditors to whom you want the stay to apply (this is usually all of them), and
- provide specific reasons why your filing was not in bad faith and the stay should be extended.

When deciding whether to extend the stay beyond 30 days, the court will look at a number of factors to decide whether your current filing is in good faith. Here are some of the factors that will work against you:

- More than one prior bankruptcy case was filed by (or against) you in the past year.
- Your prior case was dismissed because you failed to file required documents

on time (for instance, you didn't give the trustee your most recent tax return at least seven days before the first meeting of creditors) or amend the petition on a timely basis when required to do so. If you failed to file these documents inadvertently or because of a careless error, that won't help you with the judge—unless you used an attorney in the prior case. Judges are more willing to give debtors the benefit of the doubt if their attorneys were responsible for the mistakes.

- The prior case was dismissed while a creditor's request for relief from the stay was pending.
- Your circumstances haven't changed since your previous case was dismissed.

Two Dismissals in the Past Year

If you had more than two cases dismissed during the previous year, no stay will apply in your current case unless you convince the court, within 30 days of your filing, that your current case was not filed in bad faith and that a stay should therefore be granted. The court will look at the factors outlined above to decide whether you have overcome the presumption of bad faith.

Evictions

A landlord may evict a tenant, despite the automatic stay, if:

- The landlord obtained a judgment for possession before the tenant filed for bankruptcy. (If the judgment was for failing to pay rent, there is a possible exception to this rule—see below.)
- The landlord is evicting the tenant for endangering the property or the illegal use of controlled substances on the property.

If the landlord does not already have a judgment when you file, and he or she wants to evict you for reasons other than endangering the property or using controlled substances (for example, the eviction is based on your failure to pay rent or violation of another lease provision), the automatic stay prevents the landlord from beginning or continuing with eviction proceedings. However, the landlord can always ask the judge to lift the stay—and courts tend to grant these requests.

> **TIP**
> **Different rules apply to evictions of an owner following foreclosure.** The law that allows evictions to proceed despite the automatic stay doesn't apply to evictions of the former owner of the home following a foreclosure sale. If a court has ordered you to leave your home following foreclosure and the sheriff is trying to evict you, filing for bankruptcy will legally postpone the eviction until you receive a bankruptcy discharge or until the judge lifts the automatic stay, whichever happens first.

If the Landlord Already Has a Judgment

If your landlord already has a judgment of possession against you when you file for bankruptcy, the automatic stay won't help you (with the possible exception described just below). The landlord may proceed with the eviction just as if you never filed for bankruptcy. Even if you intend to leave (or have already left), you'll still have to complete the top portion of Form 101A and file it along with your bankruptcy petition. (See Ch.7 for more on completing the bankruptcy forms.)

If the eviction order is based on your failure to pay rent, you may be able to have the automatic stay reinstated. However, this exception applies only if your state's law allows you to remain in your rental unit and "cure" (pay back) the rent delinquency after the landlord has a judgment for possession. Here's what you'll have to do to take advantage of this exception:

Step 1: If the law in your state allows you to remain in your rental property by paying the judgment amount, and you plan to stay in your residence for the 30 days following your bankruptcy filing, you need to fill out both the top and bottom portions of Form 101A. Complete the certification on the bottom half by checking both boxes and signing the form. The certification states that your state law allows you to stay in the property by paying the delinquent amount. If you are not sure if this is true in your state, consult with an attorney. Remember, you are signing under penalty of perjury so guessing is not good enough. You must also deposit with the bankruptcy court clerk an amount sufficient to cover rent for 30 days. The clerk may charge administrative fees and might not accept a personal check. You must serve a copy of Form 101A on your landlord and certify to the court that you have done this. It is usually sufficient to mail a copy of the form to your landlord as soon as it is filed. Check your local court rules to see if there are additional requirements in your area.

Once you have filed your bankruptcy petition and Form 101A and deposited the rent, you are protected from eviction for 30 days unless the landlord successfully objects to your initial certification before the 30-day period ends. If the landlord objects to your certification, the court must hold a hearing on the objection within ten days, so theoretically you could have less than 30 days of protection if the landlord files and serves the objection immediately.

Step 2: If you wish to stay in the rental property beyond 30 days, you must also complete and file Form 101B, and then serve it on the landlord. You can file this form along with your bankruptcy petition or within the 30-day period after you file for bankruptcy. In Form 101B, you certify that under state or other nonbankruptcy law, you are entitled to retain possession of the rental property as long as you pay the landlord the entire amount of the judgment and any other rents due, and that you have actually paid the landlord these amounts within the 30 days following your bankruptcy filing. Unlike Step 1 above, you cannot satisfy this requirement merely by paying the current month's rent, but instead must pay the entire judgment amount. Pay the money directly to your landlord. If your landlord refuses to accept your money, you can likely deposit the judgment amount with the clerk and file a motion asking the court to order the landlord to accept your money. You must also continue to make rent payments as they come due.

If your landlord successfully objects to the certification in Form 101A, the stay will no longer be in effect and the landlord may proceed with the eviction. As in Step 1, the court must hold a hearing within ten days if the landlord objects.

SEE AN EXPERT

If you really want to keep your apartment, talk to a lawyer. As you can see, the rules are complicated. If you don't interpret your state's law properly, file the necessary paperwork on time, and successfully argue your side if the landlord objects, you could find yourself put out of your home. A good lawyer can tell you whether it's worth fighting an eviction—and, if so, what tactics to use.

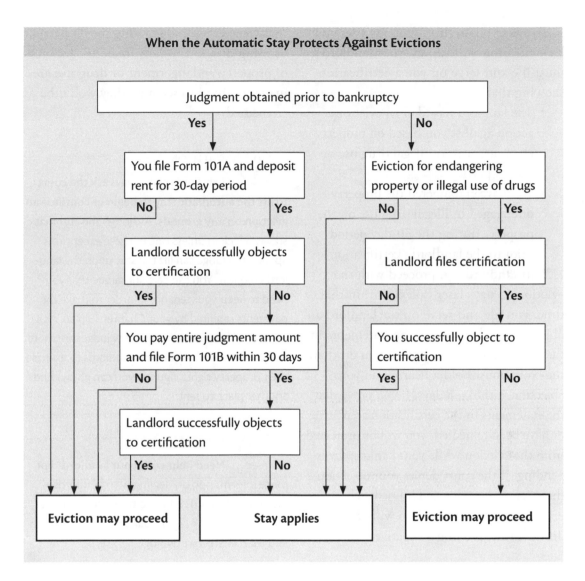

When the Automatic Stay Protects Against Evictions

Endangering the Property or Using Controlled Substances

An eviction action will not be stayed by your bankruptcy filing if your landlord wants you out because you endangered the property or engaged in the "illegal use of controlled substances" on the property. And your landlord doesn't have to have a judgment in hand when you file for bankruptcy: The landlord may start an eviction action against you or continue with a pending eviction action even after your filing date if the eviction is based on property endangerment or drug use.

To evict you on these grounds after you have filed for bankruptcy, your landlord must file and serve on you a certification showing that:

- The landlord has filed an eviction action against you based on property endangerment or illegal drug use on the property.
- You have endangered the property or engaged in illegal drug use on the property during the 30-day period prior to the landlord's certification.

Your landlord can proceed with the eviction 15 days later unless, within that time, you file and serve on the landlord an objection to the truth of the statements in the landlord's certification. If you do that, the court must hold a hearing on your objection within ten days. If you prove that the statements in the certification aren't true or have been remedied, you will be protected from the eviction while your bankruptcy is pending. If the court denies your objection, the eviction may proceed immediately.

As a practical matter, you will have a very difficult time proving a negative—that is, that you weren't endangering the property or using drugs. Similarly, once allegations of property endangerment or drug use are made, it's hard to see how they would be "remedied."

CAUTION

Landlords can always ask the court to lift the automatic stay to begin or continue an eviction on any grounds. Although the automatic stay will kick in unless one of these exceptions applies, the judge can lift the stay upon the land-lord's request. You can certainly argue that you need to keep your tenancy in order to make the payments required by your Chapter 13 plan. As a general rule, however, bankruptcy judges are more likely to lift the stay and allow landlords to exercise their property rights, figuring you can always find another place to rent.

RESOURCE

Need help with your landlord? For more information on dealing with landlords—including landlords who are trying to evict you—see *Every Tenant's Legal Guide*, by Janet Portman and Marcia Stewart (Nolo).

Are You Eligible to Use Chapter 13?

Before you can decide whether you should file for Chapter 13, you need to figure out whether you are legally eligible to do so. Not everyone can use Chapter 13: To qualify, you must meet certain eligibility requirements, and you must be able to propose a legally confirmable repayment plan. This chapter explains these requirements.

Prior Bankruptcy Discharges May Preclude a Chapter 13 Discharge

You can't get a Chapter 13 discharge if you received a discharge in a previous Chapter 13 case in the last two years or a discharge in a Chapter 7 case filed within the last four years. You aren't barred from filing for Chapter 13 bankruptcy in these circumstances, but you can't get a discharge. For instance, you can file for Chapter 13 bankruptcy the moment you receive a Chapter 7 discharge (you might do this to handle liens that survived your Chapter 7 case or debts that weren't discharged in that case), but you won't be able to discharge any debts that remain even if you complete your Chapter 13 repayment plan. (Filing for Chapter 13 immediately after filing for Chapter 7 is known colloquially as a "Chapter 20 bankruptcy.")

Business Entities Can't File for Chapter 13 Bankruptcy

To file a Chapter 13 bankruptcy case, you must be an individual (or a married couple filing jointly). You have to file the case in your own name because a business entity cannot file for Chapter 13 bankruptcy.

However, if you operate your business as a sole proprietorship, you are personally liable for the debts of the business and for bankruptcy purposes, you and your business are one and the same. So essentially, if the sole proprietorship generates income, you can use Chapter 13 to reorganize the debt and possibly remain open.

Also, you can include other types of business debts you're responsible for in your Chapter 13 bankruptcy case, too, such as a personal guarantee to make good on a corporate debt. Like credit card obligations, you'll likely pay a portion of the balance only. Keep in mind, however, that filing for bankruptcy can have a negative effect on existing business relationships (especially partnerships) so you'll want to seek counsel from a bankruptcy attorney before proceeding. Also, you should be aware that stockbrokers and commodity brokers cannot file a Chapter 13 bankruptcy case, even for personal (nonbusiness) debts.

Your Debts May Not Exceed Certain Limits

You do not qualify for Chapter 13 bankruptcy if your secured debts exceed $1,184,200 or your unsecured debts are more than $394,725. A secured debt is a debt secured by collateral (like your home or car). If you fail to pay, the creditor can take the collateral. Unsecured debts have no collateral guaranteeing payment.

For example, if you owe $2 million on your home, you can't file for Chapter 13 bankruptcy. The same would be true if you owed $100,000 on a student loan (unsecured), $100,000 on credit card debt (unsecured), and $200,000 on a court judgment due to injuries resulting from your negligent driving (unsecured). If you need help figuring out which of your debts are secured and which are unsecured, see "Classifying Your Debts" in Ch. 4.

When computing your debt load, include only debts that are both liquidated and noncontingent. A debt is liquidated if you know the exact dollar amount you owe; a debt is noncontingent if you owe it regardless of what happens in the future. For example, you don't have to include a debt that someone says you owe because you caused them property damage or personal injury, unless you have already settled the claim (or lost a lawsuit) for a set amount of money. Until that happens, you don't know how much you owe—and, if the person decides not to sue you, you might not owe anything at all.

Is Your Debt Contingent or Cosigned?

Many contingent debts involve a guarantee that you will cover a debt if someone else fails to pay. These can be hard to distinguish from debts you cosign. The difference is important, however, because you don't include contingent debts when you calculate

Chapter 13 debt limits, but you do include cosigned debts.

A contingent debt is one that you are not obligated to pay unless something (a contingency) happens. Your debt may be contingent if you "guarantee" another person's debt, but that person is still paying the debt according to the contract. In this situation, the creditor does not yet have a right to go after you for payment, but might in the future if the other person defaults.

This is different from cosigning an account or loan. Cosigned debts are equal and joint, and your obligation to pay does not rest on any contingency. Cosigned debts must be included in your debt limit calculation. Determining whether a debt is a contingent obligation or cosigned can be tricky. Check with a lawyer if you are not sure.

Debt Limits in Joint Bankruptcy Cases

The debt limits in order to file for Chapter 13 may be more flexible when you are filing jointly with your spouse. While some courts apply the same limits to both individual and joint filings, others have interpreted the law to allow for expanded limits if each spouse qualifies for Chapter 13 individually.

> **EXAMPLE:** Jane and Michael, a married couple, together have $400,000 in unsecured debts. This exceeds the $394,725 unsecured debt limit. However, as individuals, both Jane and Michael have regular income to fund a Chapter 13 plan and of the $400,000 in unsecured debt, only $50,000 is owed by

them together. Michael owes $300,000 from a failed business venture—so individually his total debt would be $350,000 ($300,000 individual debt plus $50,000 joint debt). Jane owes $50,000 in medical bills that are in her name only—her individual total debt would be $100,000. If they were to file Chapter 13 individually, each would meet the unsecured debt limit requirement and would be able to fund a Chapter 13 plan. If Jane and Michael live in a jurisdiction that allows for expanded debt limits in joint cases, their case can proceed.

You Must Be (and Stay) Current on Your Income Tax Filings

Within several months after you file for bankruptcy, you must prove that you have filed federal and state income tax returns for the four prior tax years. You can do this by submitting the returns themselves or transcripts of the returns obtained from the IRS. You are supposed to give the returns or transcripts to the trustee (the court official handling your case on behalf of the court) no later than the date set for your first meeting of creditors (about a month after you file). The trustee can keep the creditors' meeting "open" for an additional 120 days to give you time to file the returns and, if necessary, the court can give you an additional 30 days. Ultimately, if you don't produce your returns or transcripts of the returns for those four preceding years, the trustee will ask the court to dismiss your Chapter 13 case.

You can get a transcript of your tax records online at www.irs.gov, by calling 800-829-1040, or by submitting IRS Form 4506-T, *Request for Transcript of Tax Return*.

During the entire course of your plan, you must remain current on your tax filings and must provide the trustee—and any creditor who requests it—with copies of your returns. Failure to do so can result in your bankruptcy case being dismissed.

> **TIP**
> **If you can't get current on taxes, file for Chapter 7.** There is no requirement that you be current on your taxes in a Chapter 7 bankruptcy. If you need immediate bankruptcy relief and you know you won't be able to get current on your taxes within a relatively short period of time, Chapter 7 bankruptcy is your only practical option.

You Must Keep Making Your Child Support and Alimony Payments

You can file for Chapter 13 if you owe back payments for child support or spousal support (such as alimony), but you have to keep up with current support obligations while the case is pending or it will be dismissed. You can use the plan to catch up on the back payments but, in most cases, the past due amounts must be paid in full over the life of your plan.

You May Have to File Annual Income and Expense Reports

Whether you will be required to file annual income and expense reports in your Chapter 13 case will depend on local custom in your court, your bankruptcy trustee's procedures, or the terms of the order confirming your Chapter 13 plan. In most districts, at the very least you will be required to provide the Chapter 13 trustee with copies of your tax returns each year until your plan is completed.

Whatever the requirements are in your area, take them seriously. Failure to comply could result in the dismissal of your case. Many of the standing Chapter 13 trustees maintain websites which set out their procedures and the duties of the debtor during the case. Often you can find a link to the Chapter 13 trustee's website on your local bankruptcy court's website.

Your Proposed Repayment Plan Must Pay All Required Debts

Certain debts must be paid in full in a Chapter 13 plan. If your expected monthly income, less reasonable living expenses, won't allow you to pay off those debts within the required plan period, the court will not confirm your plan. Ch. 5 explains the process you must use to determine whether you can propose a confirmable Chapter 13 plan over the appropriate time period.

In addition to paying your mandatory debts in full, your plan must show that you'll be able to pay a commission to the trustee. The percentage varies by district and trustee but it's usually about 10% of your total monthly plan payment. For example, if you owe $50,000 in back income taxes (and the IRS has not recorded a lien) that would have to be paid in your Chapter 13 plan, your expected income must be sufficient to pay at least $10,000 a year for five years, toward that debt. You would also have to come up with another $1,000 each year for the trustee. And, you would have to be able to show that you could pay your living expenses while making these required payments. If the judge doesn't think you'll have enough income to cover all of your obligations, your plan won't be approved.

Debts That Must Be Paid in Chapter 13

Here are the types of debts that must be paid in full over the course of your Chapter 13 plan.

Priority Debts

Priority debts are unsecured debts (that is, debts for which you haven't pledged collateral and for which the creditor has not filed or recorded a lien) that are considered sufficiently important to jump to the head of the bankruptcy repayment line. The general rule is that priority debts must be paid in full over the course of a Chapter 13 case.

The most common priority debts that knock people out of Chapter 13 are back taxes and child support arrearages. (However, child support arrearages don't have to be paid in full during your repayment period if you owe the debt to a government agency rather than to your child or former spouse.) See "Classifying Your Debts" in Ch. 4 for a full list of priority debts.

Secured Debts That Will Outlive Your Plan

Your plan must provide that you will keep current on secured debts that are contractually scheduled to last longer than your repayment plan (such as mortgages). You must also pay off any arrearages you owe during the life of the plan, unless you are willing to surrender the collateral. If you do surrender the collateral and it is worth less than the amount you owe, the difference may be treated as unsecured debt and paid along with your credit cards and medical bills.

Other Secured Debts

All other secured debts must be paid in full under the plan, including tax liens secured by your property, loans secured by personal property collateral, and judgment liens that can't be removed for one reason or another.

Rough Calculation: Can You Repay Required Debts in Chapter 13?

To determine whether you could pay these mandatory debts during your repayment period, you must find out whether you will have enough income left over each month after paying your reasonable living expenses. (Remember, even though your income may be low enough to make you eligible for a three-year plan (see Ch. 1), you may propose a five-year plan if it will take you that long to pay off your mandatory debts.) Here's a quick way to figure out whether you can make these required payments:

Step 1: Compute your household's gross income over the past six months, divide it by six, and then multiply it by the number of months in your repayment period (60 for a five-year plan). (For help calculating your average monthly income, see Ch. 4.)

Step 2: Compute your actual monthly living expenses, including monthly installment payments on your car and other property necessary for your family's welfare, and multiply by the number of months in your repayment plan.

Step 3: Deduct your expenses computed in Step 2 from your income computed in Step 1.

Step 4: Add up all of your priority debts, secured debt arrearages for property you plan to keep, and secured debts, as described in "Debts That Must Be Paid in Chapter 13," above.

Step 5: Subtract your total mandatory debts, as calculated in Step 4, from the total amount of income you will have left over after paying expenses, as calculated in Step 3.

If this amount is a positive number, it means you may have enough income to pay your mandatory debts. If the amount is negative, you may have to make some adjustments, such as giving up property on which you are making payments or lowering your expenses, to propose a confirmable Chapter 13 plan. Remember, however, that your expenses must appear to be reasonable to the court. If your expenses look too low, the court may reject your plan as unreasonable.

RELATED TOPIC

See Ch. 5 for detailed instructions on calculating income, expenses, and repayment obligations. This quick test is intended to give you a rough idea of which debts have to be paid in full and whether you might be able to pay them, but the actual math is much more complicated (especially if your income exceeds the median income in your state for a household of your size). Ch. 5 takes you step by step through the required income and expense computations and helps you figure out whether you can propose a confirmable Chapter 13 plan.

Your Unsecured Creditors Must Get at Least as Much as They Would Have Received in a Chapter 7 Bankruptcy

In a Chapter 7 bankruptcy, the trustee liquidates your nonexempt property and distributes the proceeds to your unsecured creditors. In a Chapter 13 bankruptcy,

you can keep your property, whether or not it is exempt. Given this difference in the two types of bankruptcy, many people choose Chapter 13 rather than Chapter 7 because they want to hang on to some or all of their nonexempt property—that is, property they would have to surrender to the trustee in Chapter 7. For example, you may want to use Chapter 13 because you have a vacation home or valuable family heirlooms that you would lose if you filed for Chapter 7.

Although using Chapter 13 allows you to keep your property, it does not allow you to deprive unsecured creditors of the money they would have received if you had filed for Chapter 7. Your plan must propose payments to your nonpriority, unsecured creditors (those to whom you owe credit card debts, medical bills, lawsuit judgments, and so on) that are at least equal to what they would have received in a Chapter 7 case. In other words, your plan must show that they will be paid at least the value of your nonexempt property, less what it would cost to take that property and sell it (and less the trustee's fee for doing so). This is often called the liquidation analysis or liquidation test. Ch. 5 provides detailed information on how to run these numbers and come up with the minimum amount you must pay to these creditors through your Chapter 13 repayment plan.

You Must Participate in an Approved Personal Financial Management Course

You must also complete a postfiling personal financial management course before the court will discharge your debts. The agencies providing this service must be approved by the Office of the U.S. Trustee, a division of the Department of Justice that oversees bankruptcy proceedings. There are specific curriculum requirements that require about two hours of your time. Typically, the agency where you get your prefiling credit counseling will also offer this personal financial management course. For more information about the requirements for these agencies and how to find one, visit the Office of the U.S. Trustee's website at www.justice.gov/ust (select "Credit Counseling & Debtor Education" from the home page).

Do You Have to Use Chapter 13?

In October 2005, a massive change took place in the bankruptcy field. Believing that too many people were taking advantage of Chapter 7 bankruptcy to wipe out their debts, Congress passed the Bankruptcy Abuse Prevention and Consumer Protection Act of 2005 (BAPCPA). The stated purpose of this law is to force people who can afford to repay some of their debt to file for bankruptcy under Chapter 13 instead of under Chapter 7. To further this purpose, the BAPCPA makes it harder and more expensive to file under Chapter 7.

Because of the changes wrought by the BAPCPA, some debtors do not have the option to use Chapter 7: If they want to file for bankruptcy, they have to use Chapter 13. However, most people still have a choice. This chapter will help you figure out whether you have to use Chapter 13 or whether Chapter 7 is still an option for you.

> CAUTION
>
> **Don't skip this chapter, even if you know you will use Chapter 13.** Even if you have already decided to file for Chapter 13, make sure to read the instructions for Parts I, II, and III under "The Means Test," below. This information will help you compute your current monthly income and compare that figure to your state's median income. You will need these numbers to figure out the requirements of your repayment plan in Ch. 5.

What Is the Means Test?

There are two income tests that determine whether you are eligible for Chapter 7 bankruptcy:

- **The means test.** Debtors whose average household income over the previous six months exceeds the median income in their state for a family of the same size must take this test. These debtors must answer a series of questions about their income and expenses to determine whether they have enough extra income to fund a Chapter 13 plan. If they do, their Chapter 7 filing will be labeled a presumed "abuse" and they will be forced out of Chapter 7.

- **The "abuse under all the circumstances" test.** This test compares your actual income to your actual expenses to determine whether you have enough money coming in to repay some of your debts. Even if you pass the means test, you can be forced out of Chapter 7 if, under this test, you appear to be able to fund a Chapter 13 repayment plan.

If you fail the means test, you are presumed to be abusing the bankruptcy laws and will be forced into a Chapter 13 bankruptcy unless you can prove that the law shouldn't apply to you for some reason. You'll fail the "abuse under all the circumstances" test if the Office of the U.S. Trustee—the government agency responsible for policing the bankruptcy system—can prove that you are ineligible for Chapter 7 because you used inappropriate figures in your means test calculation.

The only way to know for certain whether your income is too high is to complete two forms that all Chapter 7 debtors must complete as part of their bankruptcy. These are Form 122A-1, *Chapter 7 Statement of Your Current Monthly Income* and Form 122A-2, *Chapter 7 Means Test Calculation.*

In the first form, you determine whether your gross income (for the previous six months) is more or less than the median income for your state for your household size.

If your income is less than your state's median income. If your income (not including Social Security) is less than your state's median, you pass the means test and won't be presumed ineligible to use Chapter 7. But, you might face another hurdle if you file under Chapter 7. If the U.S. Trustee believes that your actual income less your actual expenses leaves you with enough money to repay a reasonable portion of your debt over five years, it will ask the court to find that allowing you to use Chapter 7 would be an abuse. If the court agrees, you'll have to use Chapter 13.

Whether you choose or are required to use Chapter 13, you will have two advantages if your income is less than the state median: You may propose a three-year (rather than a five-year) repayment plan,

and you may use your actual expenses—not amounts approved by the IRS—to calculate how much disposable income you will have left to devote to your plan.

What Is Abuse Under All the Circumstances?

Generally, there are two situations in which the court is likely to find an abuse: if it looks like your income will be higher, or your expenses should be lower, than the figures you used in the means test.

For example, the court might find an abuse under all the circumstances if it looks like you will have significant extra income in the future that didn't show up in the means test. (The means test looks only at your income in the six months before you file for bankruptcy.) If your spouse just landed a high-paying job in the last month, for instance, the court might push you into Chapter 13 if you now appear to have enough extra income to pay a significant portion of your unsecured, nonpriority debt over the next five years.

The court might also find an abuse if your expenses look extravagant or it appears that you could spend less for the same necessities. For example, if you are making large payments on a home or a luxury car, the court might decide that some of that money should be going toward debt repayment.

If your income is more than your state's median income. If your income is more than the state median, you must take the means test—by completing Form 122A-2—to find out whether you'll have the option of using Chapter 7 or will have to use Chapter 13. The purpose of this form is to find out whether you would have enough income left over, after subtracting certain expenses and deductions, to pay a portion of your unsecured debts (credit card debts, medical bills, and the like) over a five-year period.

The Means Test

SKIP AHEAD

Those who initially filed for Chapter 7 bankruptcy can skip ahead. If you are using Chapter 13 because you initially filed under Chapter 7 and have already taken and flunked the means test, or if the Court has converted your case to Chapter 13, skip to "Forced Conversion to Chapter 13," below.

Pull up Official Forms 122A-1, 122A-1 Supp, and 122A-2 from www.uscourts.gov so that you can fill them out as we go along. Or use the blank forms in Appendix B and fill in the numbers by hand.

Getting the Official Bankruptcy Forms

Getting your hands on the most up-to-date forms required by the bankruptcy courts is easy. All the forms are on the website of the United States Courts (at www.uscourts. gov). You can complete the forms online, save, edit, and print at your convenience. Or, print out blank forms so you can review them as they are discussed in this book. The direct link to the forms is www. uscourts.gov/forms/bankruptcy-forms.

Many local bankruptcy courts require additional forms, called local forms. You can get these from your local bankruptcy clerk's office or download them from the court's website.

Are You Exempt From Taking the Means Test?

You do not have to take the means test if any of these situations apply to you:

- Your debts are primarily business or nonconsumer debts (explained below).
- You are a disabled veteran.
- You are or have been a military reservist or a member of the National Guard.

Instead, complete Form 122A-1 Supp, *Statement of Exemption from Presumption of Abuse Under §707(b)(2)* to determine if you qualify for an exemption from the means test.

Part 1. Identify the Kind of Debts You Have

Line 1. If the majority of your debts are categorized as "non-consumer" debts, check the "No" box. This means that if most of your debts come from running a business, or otherwise qualify as non-consumer debts, you don't have to take the means test and you are free to choose between Chapter 7 and Chapter 13 bankruptcy.

You may be surprised at how the law categorizes consumer and non-consumer debts. While business debts clearly fall under the definition of non-consumer debt, this category also includes debts for which there is no profit motive in incurring them. Here are some guidelines:

- Back taxes (even unpaid personal income taxes) are considered to be non-consumer debts even if you don't own a business.
- Mortgage debt on a rental home is considered to be non-consumer debt.
- In some areas medical debts and damages resulting from accidents are non-consumer debts.
- Your mortgage on your personal residence or your vacation home is considered to be a consumer debt, and often, this tips the scale, making your consumer debt outweigh your non-consumer debt.
- Courts are not in agreement on the treatment of student loans. Some courts have found them to be consumer debts while others have classified them as non-consumer debts.

If you are unsure about how to classify your debt, check with an experienced bankruptcy lawyer who is familiar with the law in your area.

If you were able to check the "No" box, you are done with Form 122A-1 Supp. You can move to Form 122A-1 and check Box 1 at the top to indicate that there is no presumption of abuse. If you must check the "Yes" box because your debts are primarily consumer debts, move on to Part 2 of the form.

Part 2. Determine Whether the Military Service Provisions Apply to You

Line 2. To qualify as a disabled veteran for purposes of bankruptcy, you must qualify for disability compensation at a 30% disability rating or higher, or you must have been discharged or released from active duty as a result of a disability incurred or aggravated in the line of duty. If you meet these qualifications, check the "Yes" box and answer the question next to that box. If you incurred your debt mostly while you were on active duty or while you were performing a homeland defense activity, check the "Yes" box. If you were able to answer Yes, you are finished with Form 122A-1Supp. Go to Form 122A-1, and check Box 1 at the top of the page.

If you do not qualify as a disabled veteran, or if you do but your debt was not incurred mostly while you were on active duty or performing a homeland defense activity, check the appropriate "No" boxes and move to Line 3.

Line 3. Check "Yes" if you are or have been a Reservist or a member of the National Guard. Then answer the question next to the "Yes" box. If you were called to active duty or you performed a homeland defense activity, check "Yes" and review the timeline questions to determine whether the dates of your service allow you to choose between Chapter 7 and Chapter 13 without completing the means test. If you can check any one of the dates of service boxes, the presumption of abuse does not apply to you at this time and you do not need to take the means test. Go to Form 122A-1 and check Box 3 at the top of the form.

If you were not a Reservist or a member of the National Guard, or if you were but you were not called to active duty and did not perform a homeland defense activity, or you were not on active duty within the time frames identified on the form, you must complete Form 122A-1.

Form 122A-1: *Chapter 7 Statement of Your Current Monthly Income*

If you did not qualify for an exemption from the presumption of abuse, you will need to fill out Form 122A-1 to determine whether you need to take the means test.

Part 1. Calculate Your Current Monthly Income

Line 1. If you are unmarried, check the "Not married" box and follow the instructions (complete Column A only, Lines 2 through 11).

If you are married but filing separately, check the "Married and your spouse is NOT filing with you" box. If you and your spouse are living separately or are legally separated, check that box as well and follow the instructions (complete Column A only, Lines 2 through 11). If you and your spouse are living in the same household and are not legally separated, check the appropriate box and follow the instructions to fill out both Columns A and B, Lines 2 through 11.

If you are married and your spouse is filing with you, check the "Married and your spouse is filing with you" box and fill out both Columns A and B, Lines 2 through 11.

CAUTION

Use monthly figures. All figures you enter in Lines 2 through 11 must be monthly averages of your actual income during the six months before you file for bankruptcy. The six-month period ends on the last day of the month before the month in which you file your bankruptcy. For instance, if you file on September 9, the six-month period ends on August 31. If your income is the same for each of those six months (for example, because you've held the same job and worked the same hours during that period), then use your monthly income. If your earnings vary, add them up for the six-month period, then divide the total by six to get a monthly average. You should include all income you actually received during the six-month period, even if you earned it or became entitled to receive it before the six-month period began. (*In re Burrell,* 399 B.R. 620 (Bkrtcy. C.D. Ill. 2008).)

Line 2. Enter your average monthly earnings over the last six months for gross wages, salary, tips, bonuses, overtime, and commissions. (Gross means before any deductions including taxes, Social Security, health insurance, or anything else that is withheld from your paycheck.)

Line 3. Enter the average monthly amount you receive as alimony and support, but do not include any funds received from your current spouse if your spouse's income is being reported on this form.

Line 4. Enter the average monthly amount that any person regularly contributes to the payment of your monthly expenses. But be sure not to list income twice. If the regular contribution comes from your spouse, and his or her income will be listed on this form, do not include it again here.

Line 5. If you operate a business, profession, or farm, you'll need to compute your average monthly ordinary and necessary business expenses over the six-month period and subtract them from your average monthly gross (before expenses) business receipts for that period, using the lines provided here. Then enter the net monthly income into the appropriate column. Do not enter a negative number. If your business lost money, enter 0.

Line 6. If you have rental property, calculate your average monthly rental income over the six-month period and enter it here, along with your average monthly ordinary and necessary operating expenses for the same period. Do not include mortgage expense here.

Line 7. Calculate your average monthly income from interest, dividends, and royalties over the last six months and enter it here.

Line 8. Your average monthly unemployment compensation over the six-month period goes into the appropriate column here. Any unemployment compensation benefit you receive which is a benefit under the Social Security Act should not be included under Column A or B, but should be listed on the separate lines provided.

Line 9. Pension and retirement income is entered here. Again, do not list Social Security benefits, and make sure the amounts are monthly averages based on the amount you received over the six-month period.

Line 10. Insert the average monthly amount you received over the six-month period from any other source, excluding Social Security and victim reparations from war crimes and terrorism. These types of benefits are not including in your current monthly income calculations. You must itemize for this section and identify the source of the income.

Line 11. Add the subtotals for Lines A and B together. This is your "current monthly income." Because it's a six-month average, it might not match your actual monthly income at the time you file, especially if you've had a job loss or become unable to work in the last six months.

Part 2. Determine Whether the Means Test Applies to You

Line 12. Using your current monthly income figure from Line 11, calculate your current annual income.

Courts have interpreted a number of other gray areas regarding income, such as:

- Should you count income you have earned but did not receive within the six-month period?
- Do loans from a retirement plan count as income?
- What other items that aren't included on the form might count as income?

Citations to court opinions on these income issues can be found at www. legalconsumer.com/bankruptcy/CH13; scroll down to the information for Ch. 4 of this book and look for the appropriate link.

Line 13. Determine the family median income that applies to you, comparing your current annual income to the median income for your state and family size. You can find your state's median income at www.justice.gov/ust/means-testing.

Line 14. Do the math. If your "current monthly income" exceeds the state median, check Box 14b and then Box 2 at the top of Form 122A-1 (unless you qualified for an exemption on Form 122A-1Supp) and continue to Form 122A-2 to find out whether you can choose between Chapter 7 and Chapter 13.

Determining Household Size

Determining your household size is not always straightforward. For example, you might share custody of children, pay support for children who don't live in your home, have roommates or extended family members who live with you, or live with someone as an unmarried couple. There are three commonly used methods for determining your household size. The method you use depends on what the court allows in your area and which is a better match for your situation.

Heads on beds. This method simply counts all the people who regularly live in your home and does not take into account whether or not those people are financially connected. It would not be the best method for someone who lives with roommates.

Income tax approach. Under this method, only your spouse and the dependents you claim on your income tax return are included. This may not be the most accurate approach for an unmarried couple who live together and commingle their finances.

Economic unit. This method is the most flexible approach and counts the people who are financially supportive or dependent on each other and live as one economic unit. It allows you to exclude roommates but include others who are financially dependent on you, or with whom you commingle finances.

If your income is equal to or less than the median, check Box 14a and Box 1 at the top of Form 122A-1. This means that you aren't banned from using Chapter 7. You don't need to proceed with the form any further. If you decide to proceed under Chapter 13, having an income that doesn't exceed the state median income offers you two big advantages: You can propose a three-year (rather than a five-year) plan, and you can calculate the income you must commit to the plan using your actual expenses rather than expense figures set by the IRS, which are often lower.

TIP

Consider postponing your filing if you want to qualify for Chapter 7. If you conclude, on the basis of your "current monthly income," that you'll have to complete the rest of Forms 122A-1 and 122A-2, think about whether your income will decrease in the next few months. If you recently lost a high-paying job or had a sudden decrease in commissions or royalties, for example, your average income over the past six months might look pretty substantial. But in a few months, when you average in your lower earnings, it will come down quite a bit—perhaps even to less than the state median. If so, and if Chapter 7 would provide you a better remedy than Chapter 13, you might want to delay your bankruptcy filing. If you can't wait and the change is certain and likely to be permanent, you may be able to qualify for Chapter 7 by filing an affidavit of change of circumstances. However, you will still have to fill out the means test form with your actual income figures and you should be prepared for a challenge to your Chapter 7 filing.

Form 122A-2: *Chapter 7 Means Test Calculation*

This is the beginning of the means test. With a couple of exceptions, the values you will be entering in the form are fairly straightforward. The purpose of the means test is to find out whether you have enough income to pay some of your unsecured, nonpriority debts over a five-year period. (See "Classifying Your Debts," below, for help figuring out which debts fall into this category.)

Part 1. Determine Your Adjusted Income

Line 1. Enter the total from Line 11 on Form 122A-1.

Line 2. Check the appropriate boxes based on your entries on Form 122A-1.

Line 3. Marital Adjustment. If you filled out Column B on Form 122A-1 and your spouse is not filing for bankruptcy with you, you can subtract the amount of your spouse's income (as listed in Line 11, Column B) that was not regularly contributed to your household expenses or those of your dependents. This is called the "Marital Adjustment." Maximizing this deduction by taking care to deduct all of your nonfiling spouse's expenses can lower your monthly income for means testing purposes and may reduce the amount you will be required to pay into your plan.

For example, if Line 11, Column B, shows that your nonfiling spouse has a monthly income of $2,000, but your spouse contributes only $400 a month to your household, you can enter $1,600 here.

You must identify what your spouse uses those funds for. Examples of a nonfiling spouse's income that might not be contributed to the filing spouse's household are mortgage payments on a separately owned house, payments on a separately owned car, life insurance payments, payments into a retirement plan, and payments on credit cards or other revolving debt owned solely by the nonfiling spouse.

Line 4. Subtract the amount on Line 3 from the amount on Line 1. Enter the total here.

SKIP AHEAD

If you know you will use Chapter 13. If you have already decided to file for Chapter 13 bankruptcy, you can skip the rest of this chapter and continue on to Ch. 5. If you still want to know whether you have a choice between a Chapter 7 and Chapter 13 bankruptcy, continue completing this form.

Part 2. Calculate Your Deductions From Your Income

In this part, you will figure out which expenses you can deduct from your current monthly income. After you subtract all allowed expenses, you will be left with your monthly disposable income—the amount you would have left over, in theory, to pay into a Chapter 13 plan for the benefit of your nonpriority, unsecured creditors.

CAUTION

National and local expense standards change every few years, or more often. Many of the IRS expense standards are adjusted every three years. The next adjustment will occur on April 1, 2019. Other standards (such as local standards for housing) change more frequently. Be sure to check the expense standards on the U.S. Trustee's website at www.justice.gov/ust (click on "Means Testing Information") for the most recent figures.

Subpart A: Deductions Under Standards of the Internal Revenue Service (IRS)

If you have to complete this form—that is, if your current monthly income exceeds the state median income—you are not allowed to subtract all of your actual expenses. Instead, you must calculate some of your expenses according to standards set by the IRS. (The IRS uses these standards to decide how much a delinquent taxpayer should have to give the agency each month to repay back taxes on an installment plan.)

If you eventually decide to file under Chapter 13, you will have to use these same expenses to determine the amount of disposable income you must devote to your plan. (See Ch. 5 for more information.)

Line 5. The number you enter here is not necessarily the same as the number of people living in your home. Enter the number of people you could claim as dependents on your tax return, plus any additional dependents whom you support.

Line 6. Enter the total IRS National Standards for Food, Clothing and Other Items for your family size and income level. This is the amount the IRS believes you should get to spend for food, clothing, household supplies, personal care, and miscellaneous other items. You can get these figures from www.justice.gov/ust. Click "Means Testing Information," then scroll down to find the right link. You also can get these figures from your court clerk.

Line 7. Enter the amount you are allowed to claim for health expenses from the IRS National Standards for Out-of-Pocket Health Care. You can find these figures at www.justice.gov/ust. Click "Means Testing Information," then scroll down to the appropriate link. As you'll see, you can claim more for household members who are at least 65 years old, which is reflected on the form. You'll also see that the total amount you can claim is quite small; if you spend more than you're allowed to claim here, you can claim it on Line 22.

Line 8. Enter the amount of the IRS Housing and Utilities Standards, nonmortgage expenses for your county and family size. Get these figures from www.justice.gov/ust. Click "Means Testing Information," choose the applicable date range, and then scroll down to "Local Standards, Housing and Utilities," and enter your state in the drop-down menu. Find the figures for your county and family size, then enter the figure that appears under the heading "Non-Mortgage."

Line 9. On Line a, enter the amount of the IRS Housing and Utilities Standards, Mortgage/Rent expenses for your county and family size. These figures appear on the U.S. Trustee's website, on the same chart as nonmortgage expenses; follow the instructions for Line 8, above.

On Line b, enter the average monthly payment for any debts secured by your home, including a mortgage, home equity loan, taxes, and insurance. The average monthly payment is the total of all amounts contractually due to each secured creditor in the five years after you file for bankruptcy, divided by 60.

On Line c, subtract Line b from Line a. This may turn out to be a negative figure— if so, enter a zero in the right-hand column. Later in the means test, you'll be able to deduct your average monthly mortgage payment. Most courts allow you to take the IRS expense even if your actual expenses are less; for more information on this issue, go to www.legalconsumer.com/bankruptcy/CH13, scroll down to the information for Ch. 4, and look for the appropriate link.

Line 10. If your actual rental or mortgage expense is higher than that allowed by the IRS for shelter, you can claim an adjustment here. For instance, if the IRS mortgage/rental expense for a family of two is $550, you pay an actual rent of $900, and that amount is average for the area in which you live, enter the additional $350 here and explain why you should be able to subtract it (that you couldn't possibly find housing in your area for less, for example).

Line 11. You are entitled to claim an amount for local transportation expenses even if you don't have a car. How you do it and the amount allowed depends on whether you own or claim an operating expense for a vehicle. If you don't have a vehicle, check the box for 0 and move directly to Line 14. If you have one or more cars, check the appropriate box and move to Line 12.

Line 12. You should only enter a figure on this line if you have at least one vehicle. You must use the IRS local standards for this response. You can find the figures at www.justice.gov/ust/meanstesting; follow the links to the transportation expense standards. Use only the operating standards here. You'll use the public transportation expense standards for another line.

Line 13. In this section, you will use the IRS local standards to calculate the net ownership or lease expense for up to two vehicles. You may claim this expense only if you make loan or lease payments on the vehicles. If you have a vehicle that you don't make payments on, do not include it here. You must list each vehicle separately. Identify the first vehicle and then enter the IRS local standard for ownership or leasing cost on Line 13a. In 13b, identify the creditor you make payments to on this vehicle and enter the average monthly payment, which may be different from your monthly car payment. To calculate the average monthly payment, add up all payments which will be due to the creditor for the 60 months after you file for bankruptcy and divide that amount by 60. If your car will be paid off after 36 months, for example, you will add up the 36 future payments, and divide that amount by 60. On the form, you subtract this amount from the IRS local standard and enter the result as the net ownership or leasing cost for that vehicle. If the number is negative, enter 0. You will list your vehicle payments later in the form. If you have a second vehicle, repeat these steps and calculations.

Line 14. If you do not have a vehicle, enter the IRS local standard public transportation expense here. You should not enter anything on this line if you claimed a vehicle on Line 12.

Line 15. If you have a vehicle and also use public transportation, you can deduct your actual public transportation expense here as long as it does not exceed the IRS local standard public transportation amount.

Other Necessary Expenses

Line 16. Enter the total average monthly expense that you actually incur for all taxes *other than property or sales taxes*. Examples of taxes that you should enter here are income taxes, self-employment taxes, Social Security taxes, and Medicare taxes. In some cases, these taxes will show up on your wage stub. You'll need to convert the period covered by your wage stub to a monthly figure. Once you have figured out how much you pay each month for each type of tax, add them all together and enter them in the column on the right.

Converting Taxes to a Monthly Figure

If you are paid weekly, biweekly, or twice a month, you will have to convert the tax amounts on your pay stubs to a monthly amount. And, if you pay quarterly taxes (estimated income taxes, for example), you'll need to convert that figure as well. Here's how to do it:

- Weekly taxes: Multiply by 4.3 to get a monthly amount.
- Biweekly taxes: Divide by 2 to get a weekly amount, then multiply by 4.3.
- Bimonthly taxes: Divide by 2.
- Quarterly taxes: Divide by 3.

Line 17. Enter all of your mandatory payroll deductions here, other than the taxes you entered on Line 16. Use the conversion rules set out above to arrive at average monthly deductions. Make sure you deduct only mandatory deductions (such as required retirement contributions, union dues, and uniform costs). Contributions to a 401(k) should not be included, for example, because they are voluntary.

Line 18. Enter any monthly payments you make for term life insurance. Do not enter payments for any other type of insurance, such as credit insurance, car insurance, renters' insurance, insurance on the lives of your dependents, or whole life insurance on your own life. (Whole life insurance is the type that allows you to borrow against the policy.)

Line 19. Enter the amount of any payments you make pursuant to a court order. Child support and alimony are the most common examples, but you may also have to pay to satisfy a court money judgment or a criminal fine. Do not include court-ordered payments toward a child support or an alimony arrearage; only the payments you need to make to stay current should be entered here.

Line 20. Enter the total monthly amount that you pay for education required by your employer to keep your job and the total monthly amount you pay for the education of a physically or mentally challenged dependent child for whom no public education providing similar services is available. Included in this amount would be the actual costs of after-school enrichment educational services for a physically or mentally challenged child and the actual educational expenses you are paying in support of an individual educational plan (IEP).

Line 21. Enter the average monthly cost of child care. If your employment (and therefore, your need for child care) is seasonal, add up your child care costs for the year and divide the total by 12. Do not equate education with child care. For instance, child care for a child who is of public education school age should cover only the hours before and after school.

Line 22. Enter the average monthly amount you pay for out-of-pocket health care expenses, but only to the extent it exceeds the amount you were allowed to claim on Line 7. Do not include health care expenses that are reimbursed by insurance or provided by an HMO or by Medicaid. Also, don't include premiums you pay for health insurance; you claim these on Line 25.

Line 23. Enter the average monthly expenses you pay for any communication devices that are necessary for the health and welfare of you or your dependents. Examples provided by the form are cell phones, pagers, call waiting, caller identification, and special long distance or Internet services. Virtually all of these devices arguably are necessary for the health and welfare of your family. However, some expenses might not be allowed (for example, a smartphone, cell phone you use for your business, or broadband Internet service). When in doubt, list the expense.

Line 24. Add the expenses you entered in Lines 6 through 23 and put the total in the column at the right.

Note: If your current monthly income, as calculated on Line 4, less the expenses totaled on Line 24, is less than $110, you can file for Chapter 7 if you desire. Remember, however, that you can still be forced out of Chapter 7 if the U.S. Trustee successfully argues that your actual income, less your actual expenses, would produce enough disposable income to pay off a significant portion of your unsecured debts over a five-year period. Just what percentage of your unsecured debts would have to be paid off to warrant pushing you into Chapter 13 varies from court to court, but 20% is a pretty good working minimum.

Additional Expense Deductions

The expenses in this section are allowed by the Bankruptcy Code, in addition to the IRS expenses. However, you can't list an expense twice; if you already claimed it in another part of this form, don't list it again here.

Line 25. Here, list your reasonably necessary monthly expenses for health insurance, disability insurance, and health savings accounts (HSAs) on the lines provided. You can list a "reasonable" expense whether you actually pay that amount each month or not. If, however, you pay less than the reasonable amount you list, you must indicate how much you actually spend each month on the additional line provided. If the U.S. Trustee or one of your creditors later wants to challenge your expense claims—for example, to argue that you really have more disposable income than the form indicates—they can use this information.

Line 26. Anything you will continue to spend to care for a member of your household or immediate family because of his or her age, illness, or disability can be deducted here. If your contributions are episodic—a wheelchair here, a vacation with a companion there—estimate your average monthly expense and enter it here.

> CAUTION
>
> **Your response here could affect eligibility for government benefits.** Expenses you list here could render the person you are assisting ineligible for Social Security or other government benefits. For example, if you state that you are spending $500 a month for the care of a relative, and that relative is receiving SSI, your relative might receive a lower benefit amount each month, to reflect your contribution. If you are making such expenditures, you are required to disclose them here. If you find yourself in this predicament, talk to a lawyer.

Line 27. The average monthly expense of security systems and any other method of protecting your family should be entered here.

Line 28. If your actual home energy costs exceed the figure you entered on Line 8, enter the extra money you spend here. As the form indicates, you may need to prove this extra expense to the trustee. Whether you need to prove this extra expense will depend on the results of the means test. If the amount you enter here is the deciding factor in determining that you don't have enough disposable income to fund a Chapter 13 plan, proof will definitely be required.

Line 29. This item is for money you spend on your children's education. If your average monthly expense is $147.92 or more, put $147.92 in this blank; that's the maximum you can deduct until the expense figures change in April 2019. Remember not to list an amount twice; if you already listed an expense on Line 20 or 26, for example, don't repeat it here. Education expenses for children with special needs may be deductible later as a "special circumstance," as (perhaps) can expenses required by individual education plans (IEPs). (Special circumstance claims are explained in Ch. 5.)

Line 30. Here, you can list the amount by which your actual expenses for food and clothing exceed the IRS allowance for these items as entered in Line 6. However, you cannot list more than 5% over the IRS allowance.

Line 31. If you have been making charitable contributions to an organization before your bankruptcy filing date, you can enter them here as long as the group is organized and operated exclusively for religious, charitable, scientific, literary, or educational purposes; to foster national or international amateur sports competition (but only if no part of its activities involve the provision of athletic facilities or equipment); or for the prevention of cruelty to children or animals. You can't take this deduction if the organization has been disqualified from tax exemption status because of its political activities.

Line 32. Enter the total of Lines 25 through 31 in the column on the right.

Deductions for Debt Payment

Here, you deduct average monthly payments you will have to make over the next five years. Once you've completed this section, you can put all the numbers together to figure out whether you pass the means test.

Line 33. List the average monthly payment you will have to make over the next five years to creditors that hold a secured interest in your property (for example, the mortgage holder on your house or the creditor that holds your car note). As explained in the instructions for Line 13, you can calculate this amount by figuring out the total amount you will owe over the next five years, then dividing that total by 60. Courts are divided as to whether you can include this deduction if you aren't making the payments and plan to surrender the property to the creditor. Some courts have found that allowing debtors to deduct payments they aren't making is contrary to the purpose of the means test; other courts have ruled that these "phantom" payments should be deducted because the purpose of the means test is to provide a snapshot of your financial situation. For a listing of the cases that have ruled on this issue, go

to www.legalconsumer.com/bankruptcy/CH13, scroll down to the information for Ch. 4, and look for the appropriate link.

Line 34. Here, list the average monthly payment you would have to make to pay off any past amounts due to creditors on property that you must keep for your support or support of your dependents. That would typically include a car, your home, and any property you need for your employment. (Come up with the monthly figure by dividing the total of the past-due amounts you would have to pay by 60.)

Line 35. List the average monthly amount you will have to pay for priority claims over the next five years. (See "Classifying Your Debts," below, for a list of priority claims.) Typical priority claims include back taxes and back child and spousal support. Divide the total of all priority claims by 60 to arrive at the monthly average. Don't include payments you've already listed on the form, such as current child support obligations. This line is only for amounts you owe at the time of filing.

Line 36. Here, you must calculate the fee that the trustee would charge if you ended up in Chapter 13 bankruptcy. The fee depends on how much you would be paying, through the trustee, to your secured and unsecured creditors. It's impossible to come up with a figure at this point in the form, so leave it blank for now. If you don't pass the means test with this line left blank, come back here when you've completed

Part 3 and follow these instructions to come up with a figure:

- Add Lines 33, 34, and 35.
- Divide the total on Line 41b by 60 (to calculate the average monthly payment you would have to make to pay down 25% of your unsecured debt over five years).
- Add this number to the total of Lines 33, 34, and 35, and put the result on Line 36. This is the average amount you would have to pay into a Chapter 13 plan to cover your secured debts, arrearages on those debts, priority debts, and 25% of your unsecured debts.
- Then enter the multiplier percentage from the U.S. Trustee's website for your state and district. Go to www.justice.gov/ust, click "Means Testing Information," choose the applicable date range, scroll down to the section called "Administrative Expenses Multipliers" and click "Schedules," then select your state and district to get the percentage.
- Multiply the numbers on the two lines and enter the result in the column on the right.

Line 37. Add Lines 33, 34, and 35 and the administrative expense amount you calculated in Line 36. Enter the total in the column on the right.

Total Deductions from Income

Line 38. Enter the total of Lines 24, 32, and 37 in the column at the right. This is the total amount you can subtract from your current monthly income to arrive at your disposable income.

Part 3. Determine Whether There Is a Presumption of Abuse

This is where you find out whether you received a passing grade on the means test.

Line 39a. Enter the amount from Line 4.

Line 39b. Enter the amount from Line 38.

Line 39c. Subtract Line 39b from Line 39a and enter the result in the column on the right.

Line 39d. Multiply the total from Line 39c by 60 (to find out how much disposable income you will have over the next five years, according to these figures). Enter the result in the column at the right.

Line 40. Here you must check one of three boxes. If the amount on Line 39d is less than $7,700, check the top box. This means that you don't have enough money left over to make a Chapter 13 plan feasible, so you have the choice of filing for Chapter 7. If the total on Line 39d is more than $12,850, you have enough income to make a Chapter 13 plan feasible, and you probably won't be allowed to use Chapter 7. If your total is at least $7,700 but no more than $12,850, you will have to do a few more calculations to figure out where you fall. Proceed to Line 41. These threshold amounts change every three years. The next adjustment is scheduled to occur in April 2019.

Line 41a. Enter the total of your nonpriority, unsecured debts. See "Classifying Your Debts," below, for help figuring out which of your debts qualify.

Line 41b. Multiply the amount on Line 41a by 0.25 and enter the result in the box on the right. This amount represents 25% of your total nonpriority, unsecured debt.

Line 42. Here, you determine whether the income you have left over (listed on Line 51) is sufficient to pay 25% of your unsecured, nonpriority debt (listed on Line 54). If Line 39d is less than Line 41b, you have passed the means test and may choose to file for Chapter 7 bankruptcy. (Remember, however, that you might still face a challenge if your actual income less your actual expenses would leave you with enough money to fund a Chapter 13 repayment plan.)

If Line 39d is greater than Line 41b, you have failed the means test. If you fail the means test, you can complete Part 4, in which you list additional expenses or adjustments to income that were somehow not included in the earlier parts of the form. Those expenses and adjustments would be taken into account by the U.S. Trustee if you file a Chapter 7 case, as long as they don't duplicate expenses or adjustments you already listed and are reasonably necessary for the support of you and your family.

> **TIP**
> **Make sure not to understate your expenses.** If you want to use Chapter 7 but have failed the means test, go back over the form and carefully examine the expenses you listed for categories that aren't mandated by the IRS. People often underestimate their actual expenses. If you underestimated one or more expenses or left an expense out that is provided for in the form, make the adjustments and see whether you can get a passing grade. Because this form is so complex, we recommend that you go through it at least twice before arriving at your final figures.

Classifying Your Debts

To complete the means test, you need to know how to categorize each of your debts. As explained above, you have to calculate what you owe on your priority debts and your secured debts for the next five years, and you have to add up all of your nonpriority, unsecured debts to figure out what portion of them you could repay in a Chapter 13 plan. This section will help you determine which debts are which. The classifications you make here will also help you draft your repayment plan and complete your bankruptcy forms.

Secured Debts

A debt is "secured" if you stand to lose a particular piece of property when you don't make your payments to the creditor. Most secured debts are created when you sign loan papers giving a creditor a security interest in your property—such as a home loan or car loan. But a debt might also be secured if a creditor has filed a lien (a legal claim against your property that must be paid before the property can be sold). Here is a list of common secured debts and liens:

- **Mortgages.** Called deeds of trust in some states, these are loans to buy or refinance houses or other real estate. If you fail to pay, the lender can foreclose on your house.
- **Home equity loans (second mortgages).** If you fail to pay, the lender (typically a bank or finance company) can foreclose on your house.
- **Loans for cars, boats, tractors, motorcycles, or RVs.** If you fail to pay, the lender can repossess the vehicle.
- **Store charges with a security agreement.** Almost all store purchases on credit cards are unsecured. Some stores, notably Sears and many furniture, appliance, and electronics stores, however, claim to retain a security interest in all hard goods (durable goods) purchased, or they make customers sign security agreements when they use their store charge card. If they are

careful with their paperwork, their claims may be properly secured.

Debts Secured Through "Cross-Collateralization"

Some debts which would otherwise be unsecured might be secured through "cross-collateralization." This can happen if a bank or credit union agreement states that any collateral you pledge to secure a loan you take out with the bank will serve as collateral for all loans due to that same bank or credit union. In other words, if you take out a car loan and a debt consolidation loan from the same credit union, you might have agreed to let the car secure both loans instead of just the car loan. If you think this may have happened, have your lawyer check the paperwork.

- **Personal loans from banks, credit unions, or finance companies.** Often, you must pledge valuable personal property, such as a paid-off motor vehicle, as collateral for these loans. The property can be repossessed if you don't make the payments.
- **Judicial liens.** A judicial lien can be imposed on your property only after somebody sues you and wins a money judgment against you. In most states, the judgment creditor then must record (file) the judgment with the county or state. The recorded judgment creates a lien on your real

estate and, in some states, on some of your personal property as well.

- **Statutory liens.** Some liens are automatic, by law. For example, in most states, when you hire someone to work on your house, the worker and the supplier of materials automatically gets a mechanics' lien (sometimes called a materialmen's or contractor's lien) on the house if you don't pay.
- **Tax liens.** If you owe money to the IRS or another taxing authority, the debt is secured if the agency has recorded a lien against your property. (See "Tax Debts," below, for more information.)

Priority Debts

Priority debts are unsecured debts that are considered sufficiently important to jump to the head of the bankruptcy repayment line. Priority debts that may come up in consumer bankruptcies include:

- wages, salaries, and commissions owed by an employer, up to $12,475 (until April 2019 when this figure will be adjusted)
- contributions to employee benefit plans
- money owed to certain farmers and fishermen
- up to $2,775 in deposits made for the purchase, lease, or rental of property or services for personal, family, or household use that were not delivered or provided (as of April 1, 2016—the dollar amount adjusts every three years)
- alimony, maintenance, or support

- claim for death or personal injury the debtor caused while intoxicated
- nondischargeable taxes (see "Tax Debts," below), and
- customs, duties, and penalties you owe to the federal, state, or local government.

Nonpriority, Unsecured Debts

Not surprisingly, nonpriority, unsecured debts are all debts that are neither secured nor priority. Debts in this category include:

- credit and charge card purchases and cash advances
- department store credit card purchases, unless the store retains a security interest in the items you buy or requires you to sign a security agreement
- gasoline company credit card purchases
- back rent
- medical bills
- certain tax debts (see "Tax Debts," below)
- student loans
- utility bills
- loans from friends or relatives, unless you signed a promissory note secured by some property you own
- money judgments for breach of contract or negligence
- health club dues
- lawyers' bills (unless there's a lien on your property to secure payment)
- church or synagogue dues, and
- union dues.

Classifying Your Tax Debt	
If ...	**Your tax debt is ...**
All of the following are true: • The taxes first became due at least three years before you filed for bankruptcy (taxes first become due for a particular year on April 15 of the following year, or on October 15 of the following year if you request an extension). • You filed your tax return at least two years prior to your bankruptcy filing date (tax returns filed after the due date and returns filed by the IRS for you do not qualify as filed returns). • The taxes have not been assessed by the IRS within the 240 days before you filed for bankruptcy. • The IRS is not arguing that you willfully intended to avoid paying the tax.	**dischargeable,** meaning you can completely eliminate your income tax debt, and the interest and penalties associated with it in a bankruptcy.
The IRS has recorded a Notice of Federal Tax Lien.	**secured,** meaning you may be able to discharge your personal liability in bankruptcy, but the lien remains. If you don't pay off the entire debt during your case, the IRS can seize property you owned before filing to cover the rest. Practically speaking, the IRS looks to collect from real estate, retirement plans, and bank accounts.
Your tax debt is not dischargeable or secured.	**priority,** which means that it must be paid in full in your Chapter 13 plan.
Both of the following are true: • Your tax debt is not dischargeable or secured. • The IRS has recorded a Notice of Federal Tax Lien, but your property won't cover what you owe the IRS.	**undersecured** (if you have no seizable assets) or partially undersecured (if you have some). The undersecured portion (the amount that exceeds the value of your assets) is dischargeable if the first three conditions listed above for dischargeable taxes are met.

Tax Debts

A tax debt can be secured, priority, or unsecured. If a taxing agency has placed a lien on your property, the debt is secured. If the tax debt is not dischargeable in bankruptcy, the debt is priority. And if the tax debt can be discharged, it is unsecured. The chart above will help you figure out what category particular tax debts may fall into.

If you are looking to discharge a significant amount of tax debt, consult with a tax attorney. Previous offers in compromise, prior bankruptcies, or other arrangements with taxing authorities could alter these time frames.

Forced Conversion to Chapter 13

If you already filed for Chapter 7 and flunked the means test, the U.S. Trustee, the trustee, or a creditor will have filed a motion under 11 U.S.C. § 707(b)(2) to have the court declare your filing "abusive." If the court agrees, it will give you the choice of having your case dismissed or converted to Chapter 13. If you consent to the conversion, the court will order it.

To remain in Chapter 13, you will have to file a confirmable plan within 15 days of the conversion, start making payments on the plan within 15 days after that, and otherwise comply with the eligibility requirements unique to Chapter 13 (see Ch. 3 for more on these requirements).

! CAUTION

You may not be eligible for either type of bankruptcy. It's entirely possible to be kicked out of Chapter 7 because your income is too high, then be unable to come up with a Chapter 13 repayment plan that's acceptable to the judge. In other words, there may be no bankruptcy remedy for you. For instance, you may get tossed out of Chapter 7 because your current monthly income was too high when you filed. If, however, you don't have a steady income by the time you convert to Chapter 13, your plan won't be confirmed. If you find yourself in this situation, talk to a lawyer right away.

Can You Propose a Plan the Judge Will Approve?

Before you are allowed to proceed with your Chapter 13 bankruptcy, the judge must approve your repayment plan. As explained briefly in Ch. 3, your plan will be approved only if it shows that you will have enough steady income to:

- pay certain types of debts in full over the life of your plan, and
- pay your nonpriority, unsecured creditors at least what they would have received if you had filed under Chapter 7.

The plan must also show that all of your "projected disposable income" (as defined by the bankruptcy laws) will go toward paying your remaining debts for the duration of your plan.

How long your plan must last and how much money you must devote to it depends on whether your current monthly income, which you calculated in Ch. 4, is more or less than your state's median income. If your current monthly income is less than the median income for your state, you can propose a three-year plan, and you may use your actual expenses to calculate your disposable income.

If your current monthly income is more than the median income for your state, your plan must last five years, and you must use expense amounts set by the IRS (which might differ from your actual expenses) to calculate your disposable income. In essence, this means that you will probably have to devote more money to your plan for a longer period of time.

RELATED TOPIC

If you haven't calculated your current monthly income, go back to Ch. 4. Ch. 4 explains how to come up with this figure and compare it to your state's median. You'll need to know your current monthly income—and whether it is more or less than your state's median—to figure out whether you can come up with a confirmable repayment plan.

This chapter will give you a fairly accurate idea as to whether you can propose a repayment plan that meets the legal requirements. If you decide to go ahead with a Chapter 13 bankruptcy, your attorney (or your attorney's software) will do the fine-tuning to come up with your repayment plan.

SEE AN EXPERT

Talk to a lawyer if you can't make the numbers work. This chapter will help you determine whether you can come up with a plan the judge will approve if you decide to file for Chapter 13. If the numbers don't work out, you may want to talk to a lawyer before you give up. An attorney may be able to provide a different slant on the numbers you provide in the form and the choices you make when completing this chapter.

Repayment Plan Calculations: An Overview

Upon first glance, this chapter might look intimidating. It asks you to fill in a long form and requires you to come up with numerous income and expense figures. Our advice: Don't sweat the details yet. The purpose of the chapter is to get a rough idea as to whether you have enough income, given your expenses and debts, to propose a plan that will work within the law. The forms are pretty self-explanatory (and we provide instructions). You'll eventually need to provide your attorney with this information, so it doesn't hurt to run through it here. If you don't have an exact figure for something, enter your best estimate.

Below, we've provided an overview of how these calculations work—so you can see the big picture as you go through the details. Or, you can use the overview below to rough out some numbers before you visit an attorney, and skip the details altogether.

Start with your current monthly income as you computed it in Ch. 4.

Subtract living expenses. This is where your income as it compares to your state median income comes into play. If your income is below the state median income (as determined in Ch. 4), you get to subtract your *actual* living expenses (as long as they are reasonable). If your income is above the state median income, you must use set dollar amounts dictated by national and local IRS standards. You are allowed to include certain

additional living expenses that are not covered by the IRS expense standards.

As part of your living expenses, you will also subtract installment payments on secured debts. These are your monthly payments on debts secured by property you plan to keep, like your mortgage or car note. Add up the monthly payments that will come due during your plan and divide the total by the number of months in your plan.

> **TIP**
>
> **Reduce installment payments with a cramdown.** You might be able to reduce the amount of a secured loan to the replacement value of the property. (See "Special Chapter 13 Features: Cramdowns and Lien Stripping" in Ch. 1 for details.) Doing so could significantly reduce the amount of your installment payments on that loan.

Subtract priority debts. Your priority debts (listed in Ch. 3) must be paid off in full through your plan. Total up the remaining balance on all priority debts and divide by the length of your plan (36 months if your income is less than the state median, 60 months if your income is more than the state median).

Subtract secured debt arrearages. Your plan must propose to pay 100% of arrearages on secured debts if you want to keep the property. For example, you must pay off mortgage arrears through the plan. Total up your arrearages and divide by 60 to get the monthly deduction if yours is a five-year plan, or 36 if yours is a three-year plan.

Subtract debts secured by liens. You have to pay off some liens by the end of the plan. To learn which ones, see Step 6 below. Total up these liens and divide by the length of your plan.

Subtract payments to unsecured creditors. You must pay your unsecured, nonpriority creditors at least what they would have received had you filed for Chapter 7 bankruptcy. To get a rough estimate of what this figure will be, start with the value of your nonexempt property, subtract the trustee's commission and costs of sale, and divide the total by your plan length.

Subtract the trustee's commission. You must pay the trustee a percentage of your plan payment, usually 10%. To get a rough estimate, add all of the above items in this list and multiply the total by 0.1 (10%) to get the commission.

TOTAL. The resulting number is a rough estimate of what you would have left after making your monthly plan payment under Chapter 13 bankruptcy. If you get zero or a negative number, you may not have enough income to fund a plan.

If Your Current Monthly Income Is Less Than Your State's Median Income

If your current monthly income is less than your state's median income, you can propose a plan that lasts for three years or less. However, the court can authorize a plan lasting up to five years, if necessary. Because certain debts must be paid off in full in a Chapter 13 plan, debtors often need a longer plan period so they can afford the monthly payments. For example, if you owe a $20,000 arrearage on your mortgage, a three-year plan would require monthly payments of at least $555. If you stretched out those payments over five years, you would owe only $333 each month.

SKIP AHEAD

This section is only for those whose current monthly income is less than their state's median income. If your income—as calculated in Ch. 4—is equal to or more than the state median, skip ahead to "If Your Current Monthly Income Is More Than Your State's Median Income," below.

Step 1: Calculate Your Base Income

Your base income is the amount you will use to determine whether you have sufficient income to fund a Chapter 13 plan. Your base income is simply your current monthly income (your average gross income over the six-month period before you filed for bankruptcy, as calculated in Ch. 4) less any child support payments, foster care payments, or disability payments you receive for a dependent child, as long as those amounts are necessary for the child's care.

Current monthly income
(from Ch. 4):   _____

Child support, foster care,
  or disability payments: –_____

Base income: =_____

If Your Actual Income Is Different From Your "Current Monthly Income": *Hamilton v. Lanning*

The income figure you use in this section, although labeled "current monthly income," actually describes your average monthly income over the last six months. (The same is true if you calculate your income under the next section, "If Your Current Monthly Income Is More Than Your State's Median Income.") And yet, bankruptcy law says you must put all of your "projected disposable income" toward your repayment plan (unless you plan to pay your unsecured creditors 100%). So what happens if your "currently monthly income" doesn't match your actual or projected income? For example, what if you recently lost your job or your hours were greatly reduced? Or what if you received a one-time bonus or payout in the previous six months that you won't receive again (which would inflate your "current monthly income")?

In 2010, the U.S. Supreme Court ruled on this issue in *Hamilton v. Lanning* (130 S.Ct. 2464 (2010)) and endorsed a "forward-looking approach." It held that when calculating a debtor's projected disposable income, the court may account for changes in the debtor's income or expenses that are "known or virtually certain at the time of [plan] confirmation."

If your income has changed substantially from your "current monthly income" calculation, the court can consider this in approving your plan payments. If you anticipate an income change, you'll have to convince the court that the change is "virtually certain." What constitutes "virtually certain" is likely to be the source of further litigation in the bankruptcy courts.

The Court in *Lanning* also noted that changes in projected expenses may be considered by the court in approving plan payments. This too, is likely to foster further litigation.

Is Social Security Income Included as "Disposable Income"?

Although Social Security income is not included when calculating current monthly income on Form 122C-1, some trustees believe that the decision in *Hamilton v. Lanning* (which allows courts to consider a debtor's actual income, rather than the debtor's income on Form 122C-2, when figuring out how much income is available for plan payments) means that Social Security income should be factored into plan payments. Some courts agree and consider Social Security income when determining plan payments. However, appellate courts that have considered the issue have ruled that Social Security income need not be included and most districts follow this as well.

Step 2: Subtract Your Expenses

When determining your disposable income, you can subtract only those expenses that are reasonably necessary for you and your dependents and any child support or alimony obligation that first arose after you filed your bankruptcy petition.

The best way to calculate these expenses is to use one of the official bankruptcy forms—*Schedule J: Your Expenses*—as a starting point, then add certain other expenses allowed by the Bankruptcy Code.

Use *Schedule J* to Determine Reasonably Necessary Expenses

Print out Official Form 106J from the United States Courts website at www.uscourts.gov and input the numbers by hand or complete it online (see "Getting the Official Bankruptcy Forms," in Ch. 4). Or you can fill in the numbers in the blank version of *Schedule J* in Appendix B. If you and your spouse have separated but are filing jointly, you must complete *Schedule J* and your separated spouse must complete *Schedule J-2* (Form 106J-2). Transfer the line 22 total from *Schedule J-2* onto Line 22b of the *Schedule J.*

For each listed item, fill in your monthly expenses for you and any dependents. Remember to include payments you make for your dependents' expenses in your figures only if those expenses are reasonable and necessary for the dependents' support.

If you make some payments biweekly, quarterly, semiannually, or annually, prorate them to show your monthly payment.

What's a Reasonable Expense?

When it comes to expenses, what is considered reasonable varies from debtor to debtor, court to court, and even region to region. In general, expenses for luxury items or services will not be allowed. If an expense seems particularly high, the court will look to see whether you can achieve the same goal by spending less; the court will let you live adequately, but not high on the hog. For example, if you are making payments of $800 per month on a Cadillac, the court may find only $500 per month for a less expensive car to be reasonable, freeing up another $300 per month of disposable income.

Your best approach when completing *Schedule J* is to enter your actual expenses. If you want to know whether your expenses will later be considered reasonable, compare them with the cost of living schedules published by the federal government and collected for your convenience by the U.S. Trustee's Office at www.justice.gov/ust. These are the same expenses you used in Ch. 4 if you completed the means test there. If you didn't, click "Means Testing Information" on the U.S. Trustee's website, choose the applicable date range, and check out the following categories:

- National Standards: Food, Clothing & Other Items
- Local Housing and Utilities Standards, and
- Local Transportation Expense Standards.

You can also find out the applicable IRS standards for your area by taking the free, online means test at www.legalconsumer.com.

Line 4. Rental or home ownership expenses. Here you put your rent or first mortgage payment. If your rent or mortgage payment is unusually high for your area, the court might suggest that you move in order to bring this expense down, if alternate housing is easily available. If you are facing foreclosure and will be surrendering your home in your Chapter 13 bankruptcy, what amount should you list for your rent or home mortgage payment? You can either hunt around the neighborhood where you plan to live and use an average rental amount or you can use the IRS figure for average rentals in your area. (To find them, go to www.justice.gov/ust and choose "Means Testing Information" from the side menu. Scroll down to "Data Required for Completing Form 122A-2 and Form 122C-2." Choose the appropriate date, scroll down to "Housing and Utilities Standards" and choose your state.)

If not already included in the above listed monthly payment, separately list:

- Real estate taxes
- Property, homeowners', or renters' insurance
- Home maintenance and repair. If your estimates of maintenance and upkeep are high, you may have to provide the court with documentation for the past years' expenses. Obviously, the court will want you to maintain your home's condition, but in a reasonably inexpensive manner.
- Homeowners' association (HOA) or condo dues.

Line 5. Additional mortgage payments. List payments on mortgages other than your first mortgage, such as HELOC payments and second mortgages.

Line 6. Utilities. List your monthly utility expenses. Be sure to take a monthly average of gas, heating fuel, and electricity if your bills vary month to month. Also under the utility category, put expenses for satellite TV, cellular telephone, pager, caller identification, and special long distance and Internet subscriptions necessary for the welfare of you or your dependents. An unusually high expense may be questioned and, if the expense is not necessary, you may have to take steps to reduce it.

Line 7. Food and housekeeping supplies. To determine whether or not your figure is reasonable, the court will most likely compare it to the federal cost of living figure for your area. (See "What's a Reasonable Expense?" above.) If your expenses are higher than average, be ready to explain them—for example, because a family member needs a special diet. If the expenses are high because you eat out a lot, you may have to adjust your lifestyle.

Line 8. Childcare and children's education costs. Courts are reluctant to allow private school tuition if it means that your creditors will not be paid in full through your Chapter 13 plan. You may be able to convince the court to allow it if your child has special needs, or other special circumstances exist that make private school tuition necessary. Courts will likely decide this on a case by case basis. The fact that the school provides a religious education for your child may be a factor, but is not determinative. College expenses for an adult child without special needs may also be allowed but are subject to even more scrutiny. Expensive private school tuition probably won't be permitted.

Line 9. Clothing, laundry, and dry cleaning. You are not expected to wear only secondhand clothing, especially if your employment has a high-end dress standard. But extravagant or frequent purchases may not be allowed. To get an idea of how much you spend now, total up the clothing purchases for which you have receipts, credit card statements, or an entry in your checkbook, and arrive at a monthly average. If you have to dress up for work, it is not unreasonable to include dry cleaning expenses.

Line 10. Personal care products and services.

Line 11. Medical and dental expenses. Don't list payments you're making on bills from medical providers and hospitals for services that you've already received. Those will be paid through your Chapter 13 plan. There may be special circumstances where the court might let you include 100% of the bill as part of your monthly expenses if you need ongoing medical treatment and the provider will not continue to treat you without full payment. If you are in this situation, include the expense on this worksheet but be prepared to address the matter before the court. Special circumstances are determined on a case by

case basis. Medical and dental insurance goes on Line 15, unless it is deducted from your pay, in which case it is reported on *Schedule I.*

Line 12. Transportation. The court will let you pay a reasonable amount to get to and from work and provide necessary transportation for your children. The court will allow expenses for gas, bus or train fare, maintenance, and registration. (Vehicle insurance goes on Line 15.) The IRS figures for a reasonable operating and public transportation expense vary from $200 to $400, depending on where you live and whether you have one or two cars. As mentioned on the form, you shouldn't put your car payments on this line: They come later.

Line 13. Entertainment, clubs, recreation, newspapers, magazines, and books. List your actual expenses, but keep in mind that if you are living extravagantly, you will probably have to cut back. The key to getting these expenses approved is their reasonableness. A trustee is not likely to approve a plan with a budget for Broadway shows, sailing once a week, a subscription to an expensive journal, or a country club membership. However, you can probably budget to rent movies, go bowling, get a daily newspaper, keep your membership at the local Y, and take care of your pet.

Line 14. Charitable contributions and religious donations. You can include donations to charity, in an amount up to 15% of your income for the year in which you make them. You can subtract charitable contributions even if you are paying your nonpriority, unsecured creditors only 1% of what you owe them. However, there are limitations. The amount you deduct must be in line with the amount you contributed to charity before filing for bankruptcy.

Line 15. Insurance. The court will want you to maintain your medical insurance coverage, so it will allow medical insurance for you and your dependents as an expense. This is also where you list vehicle insurance. Term life insurance is an allowable expense. And you may be able to deduct a reasonable amount of disability insurance. Payments on a whole life insurance policy are generally seen as an investment and are more likely to be disallowed by the court. Don't list insurance on your real estate on this line—it goes on Lines 4 or 20.

Line 16. Taxes. List the monthly average of all taxes other than real estate taxes that are not deducted from your wages. Taxes deducted from your wages are reported as part of your income on *Schedule I*. Real estate taxes are included on Lines 4 and 20.

Line 17. Installment payments. List car or lease payments. Don't list installment payments on secured debts, including car loans, that you will not be paying after you file (because you are surrendering the vehicle or rejecting the car lease, for example.)

Line 18. Alimony, maintenance, and support paid to others. List your current support obligations only. Don't list any back support you owe. And don't list amounts that are automatically deducted from your

paycheck. These go on *Schedule I*. If you are under court order to pay tuition, medical costs, or other expenses for a child as part of your support payments, you may want to list those items here as well. Private school tuition or other costs that might otherwise be seen as unreasonable will likely be allowed if they are part of your court-ordered support payments. Just make sure not to list them twice.

Line 19. Payments for support of additional dependents not living at your home. Your expenses listed so far have included expenses for your dependents living at home. You also are permitted to claim expenses for the support of other dependents not living at home, including your children. These expenses include child care, clothes, books, an occasional movie, and the like.

Line 20. Other real property expenses. List expenses for real property that are not already included on Lines 4 and 5 or that are business expenses (business expenses are part of your income calculation). If you own property other than your home, you would put the mortgage, taxes, maintenance, insurance and other costs of ownership here.

Line 21. Other. List any additional expenses here, except payments you are making on back income taxes and on unsecured installment debts, such as credit card accounts, and personal loans: These debts must be paid out of your disposable income through your Chapter 13 plan. If you have student loans, check with your attorney. Most courts do not allow student loan payments to be listed here. Some courts will allow them under special circumstances. Be ready to explain why the expenses you list here are reasonable. Other expenses not already listed might include:

- **Your or your spouse's educational expenses.** If either you or your spouse is currently in school, list your expenses here. The court may reject a portion of these expenses if you or your spouse could be working and increasing the family's income. Courts are more likely to allow educational expenses to maintain your employment and costs of professional licenses necessary to your employment rather than expenses for earning a degree so that you can change professions in the future.
- **Miscellaneous personal expenses.** Often, these are the expenses that your creditors, the trustee, and the court scrutinize the most.

Business Expenses

On *Schedule J*, you do not list expenses related to your operation of a business, profession, or farm. Instead, business expenses are included as part of your monthly income calculation—you subtract business expenses from business receipts in order to come up with your business income. (See Ch. 4, "Form 122A-1: *Chapter 7 Statement of Your Current Monthly Income.*")

Line 22. Add up all of the expenses you listed from Lines 4 through 21. If you completed *Schedule J-2*, add the monthly expenses from that schedule as well. The result is your total monthly expenses.

Subtract these expenses from your base income, as calculated above.

Base income (from Step 1):	_____
Schedule J and *J-2* expenses:	− _____
Total:	= _____

If you still have a positive number—that is, if it looks like you will have some money left over after paying the expenses listed on *Schedule J*—you may be able to propose a confirmable Chapter 13 plan. If the number is negative, you won't have anything left to put toward a repayment plan. If you find yourself in this situation, revisit your expenses. Some of them may not be necessary.

Step 3: Subtract Your Priority Debts

As mentioned in Ch. 3, you must pay certain debts in full over the life of your plan—three years, unless the court authorizes a longer time. Among the debts that have to be paid in full are priority debts. (You can find a list of priority debts in Ch. 4, "Classifying Your Debts.")

If you owe any priority debts, divide the total amount you owe by 36 to determine how much you would have to pay each month in order to pay off these debts in three years. Subtract this amount from what's left of your base income after subtracting expenses and installment payments, in Step 3, above.

> Base income less expenses
> (from Step 2, above):   _____
> Monthly priority debt
> payments: − _____
> Total: = _____

If you have a positive number, move on to the next section. If the number is negative, you still might propose a confirmable plan under the following conditions:

- If one of the priority debts was child support or alimony that was assigned to a government agency (rather than money you owe directly to your child or ex-spouse), you don't have to pay the full amount in your plan. However, you do have to include the debt in your plan and commit all of your disposable income to a plan for five years rather than three years, unless it won't take you that long to pay the child support debt in full. If some of the debt still remains when your repayment period is over, it won't be discharged. You'll still have to pay the remainder.

- As mentioned, if you could pay off all of your priority debts over a five-year period rather than a three-year period, you can ask the court to allow a five-year plan at your confirmation hearing.

Step 4: Subtract Secured Debt Arrearages

One of the main reasons people file Chapter 13 is to deal with arrearages— amounts past due—on their home or car note, to prevent a foreclosure or repossession. Chapter 13 allows you to keep your home or car while paying off the arrearages under your plan. If you owe an arrearage and your plan shows that you are keeping the collateral (your home, car, or the like), you'll have to pay 100% of the arrearage and stay current on the main debt.

Add up all arrearages on debts securing collateral you want to keep. Divide the total by the number of months in your plan to arrive at a monthly amount. Subtract this total monthly payment from your remaining income, from Step 3, above.

> Remaining income
> (from Step 3, above):   _____
> Monthly secured debt
> arrearage payments: − _____
> Total: = _____

If the number is positive, proceed to Step 5 below. If the number is negative, you may not be able to present a confirmable plan. If your calculations were based on a 36-month plan, try the calculations again using a 60-month plan. It might make a difference.

TIP

Giving up the property might help. If you surrender the collateral to the lender (and therefore, don't have to pay the full past-due amount), you might have some income left over. This means you may be able to come up with a confirmable plan.

Step 5: Subtract Debts Secured by Liens

In most cases, if you have a lien on your property other than a purchase money lien, you'll have to pay the lien off in full in your plan. For example, if the IRS has recorded a lien against your property for back taxes, or a contractor has placed a mechanics' lien on your property for work that you didn't pay for, your plan will not be confirmed unless it provides for payment of these liens in full.

TIP
What is a purchase money lien? Your property is encumbered by a purchase money lien if you took out the loan to buy the property that secures the loan. Typical examples include a car loan or a mortgage.

TIP
Different rules apply to judgment liens. If there is a lien on your property because you lost a lawsuit and owe someone money as a result, you might be able to remove the lien in a separate proceeding called "lien avoidance." If you use lien avoidance to remove a lien, you won't have to pay off the lien under your plan. See Ch. 11 for information on lien avoidance.

Add up all liens on your property (other than judgment liens and liens created when you obtained loans to purchase the property). Divide the total by 36 for a three-year plan (or by 60 if you are proposing a five-year plan) to obtain the monthly amount you will have to pay. Then, subtract this total from your remaining income from Step 4, above.

> Remaining income
> (from Step 4): _____
> Monthly lien payment: – _____
> Total disposable income: = _____

If you still have money left over, you can move on to Step 6. If your total disposable income is zero or less, your plan won't be confirmed.

Step 6: Compare Your Disposable Income to What Your Creditors Would Get If You Used Chapter 7

As explained briefly in Ch. 3, if you own nonexempt property, you will have to pay your nonpriority, unsecured creditors at least what they would have received if you had filed for Chapter 7: the value of your nonexempt property, less what it would cost for the trustee to take and sell that property, less the trustee's commission. To find out whether you have nonexempt property, skip to "Understanding Property Exemptions," below, for information on which exemptions you can use and how to apply them to your possessions.

If you find that all of your property is exempt, you don't have to worry about this step. As long as you came up with a positive number in Step 5, you should be able to propose a confirmable plan. If you do have nonexempt property, however, you will have to perform what's called a "liquidation analysis" to determine how much your unsecured creditors would actually receive if you used Chapter 7 (and therefore, how much they are entitled to receive under your Chapter 13 plan).

Start with the value of your equity in the property (see "Value Your Property," below, for tips on coming up with an estimated value). If a portion of the property is exempt, subtract the exempt amount. For example, many states exempt up to a certain amount of equity in a car. If you own a car outright that's worth $10,000, and the exemptions you are using allow you to exempt $4,000 of equity in a car, your total nonexempt amount is $6,000.

Next, subtract the trustee's commission. This amount represents what the trustee would get to keep if your property were taken and sold in a Chapter 7 case. Because this amount would not be distributed to your creditors, you can subtract it from the amount you have to pay them in a Chapter 13 case.

The trustee's commission on the money he or she collects and distributes to creditors is 25% of the first $5,000, 10% of the next $50,000, and 5% of the rest up to one million dollars. So, if you have a nonexempt bank account containing $25,000, the trustee gets to keep $1,250 (25% of

$5,000) plus $2,000 (10% of the remaining $20,000) for a total of $3,250. Put another way, your creditors would receive $21,750 instead of $25,000.

In addition to the trustee's commission, you can also subtract the costs of taking the property and selling it. For certain types of property, there are few (if any) costs of sale. Cash on hand, bank accounts, and investments that can easily be converted to cash fit within this category of property. However, other types of property—such as a home, a car, or furniture—have significant resale costs. Because your unsecured creditors wouldn't get any of this money in a Chapter 7 case, they also aren't entitled to it in your Chapter 13 case. And, because personal property (a piano or furnishings, for example) often sells at auction for significantly less than its replacement value, you might be able to argue for an even lower total.

EXAMPLE 1: Jane has a savings account containing $50,000, and none of it is exempt. She can subtract the trustee's commission: 25% of $5,000 ($1,250) plus 10% of the remaining $45,000 ($4,500) for a total of $5,750. If Jane were to file for Chapter 13, her unsecured creditors would be entitled to at least $44,250.

EXAMPLE 2: John owns his home, appraised at $100,000, free and clear. The exemption system he is using allows him to exempt $50,000 worth of equity, so his nonexempt equity is worth $50,000. From this amount, he can subtract the commission the trustee in a Chapter 7 case would earn from selling the property: 25% of $5,000 ($1,250) plus 10% of the remaining $45,000 of his equity ($4,500), or a total of $5,750. He can also subtract the costs of selling his house. Typically, sales costs come to about 8% of the sales price. If John's home sold for $100,000, he could subtract $8,000 in sales costs. So if John were to file for Chapter 13, his unsecured creditors would be entitled to at least $36,250: his nonexempt equity of $50,000, minus the trustee's commission of $5,750, minus $8,000 in sales costs.

EXAMPLE 3: Juan owns a car worth $10,000 free and clear. He can exempt $3,000 of his equity, so the value of his nonexempt amount is $7,000. From this amount, he can subtract the trustee's commission of $1,450 (25% of $5,000 plus 10% of $2,000), for a nonexempt total of $5,550. Then he can subtract the costs of sale, including the cost of picking up the car, storing it, and holding an auction at which the car will likely sell for well less than its replacement value. If Juan wants to play it safe, he could use the out-of-pocket expense rate typically agreed to by trustees, which is 5% of the car's value, or $500. This means his unsecured creditors in a Chapter 13 case would be entitled to $5,050. If Juan is willing to argue with the trustee, he could advocate for a higher expense rate, to account for the lower price the car is likely to fetch at auction.

Once you come up with the total amount your unsecured creditors would actually receive if you filed for Chapter 7, convert it to a monthly figure. For example, if

you find that your unsecured creditors are entitled to $7,200 and you are proposing a three-year repayment plan, divide $7,200 by 36 months to come up with the monthly amount you would have to pay: $200. Subtract this monthly total from the disposable income you calculated in Step 5.

Disposable income (from Step 5):	_____
Monthly amount for unsecured creditors:	− _____
Total:	= _____

Step 7: Subtract the Trustee's Fee

Your Chapter 13 trustee is entitled to roughly 10% of all payments you make under the plan, as a fee. It's hard to compute what that figure will be at this point; the total trustee's cut may depend on whether your mortgage (if you have one) and other secured debts will be paid through the plan by the trustee or directly to the creditor by you. For example, assume your mortgage payment is $2,000 a month, and you want to use Chapter 13 to cure an arrearage of $5,000. If you make your mortgage payment directly to the creditor, you will owe the trustee only $500 (10% of the arrearage). However, if you make your mortgage payment to the trustee as part of the plan, the trustee will be entitled to another $7,200 over the life of a three-year plan.

But will you be allowed to pay your mortgage outside of the plan? If you are current on your mortgage when you file for

Chapter 13, most courts will allow you to make the payments directly to the creditor, thereby avoiding the extra trustee's fee. However, if you are not current when you file, some courts require you to make your current mortgage payment through the plan along with the arrearage amount. In this situation, the court might allow you to take your mortgage payment out of the plan (and pay it directly) if and when you finish paying the arrearage amount before the plan is concluded. Other courts always allow the mortgage payment to be made directly as long as you are paying the arrearage through the plan. What is allowed varies by district and, sometimes, by judge or trustee. Often this information is posted on the Chapter 13 trustee's website. To find the website of the standing Chapter 13 trustee in your district, check the U.S. Trustee's website at www.justice.gov/ust (look for the private trustee locator under "Private Trustee Information").

> **CAUTION**
>
> **The court might lift the stay if you pay outside the plan.** Some courts will lift the stay for all secured debt you are paying outside of the plan. In these courts, paying outside the plan may save you money but, if you have any payment disputes with the creditor down the line, it will be able to proceed against you as if the bankruptcy had not been filed.

To get a rough figure, multiply the amount you came up with in Step 5 by 0.1 (10%), then subtract that amount from your total disposable income.

Remaining income (from Step 6):	_____
Monthly trustee's fee (remaining income x 0.1): –	_____
Total disposable income: =	_____

As long as your total is a positive number, you may be able to propose a confirmable plan. If your total is zero, this means you will have exactly enough money to meet your plan obligations, not a penny more or less.

If all of your property is exempt, and the disposable income you calculated in Step 5 was zero, your unsecured creditors won't get paid a cent. This is called a "zero-percent" plan. Before the bankruptcy law changed in 2005, many courts wouldn't confirm a plan that paid unsecured creditors less than a particular percentage (anywhere from 20% to 80%, depending on the court). Under the revised law, however, there is no legal reason why a zero-percent plan should not be confirmed, as long as your expenses are reasonable.

If Your Current Monthly Income Is More Than Your State's Median Income

If your current monthly income is more than your state's median income, you are required to use Form 122C-2, *Chapter 13 Calculation of Your Disposable Income*, to compute your disposable income. You'll find instructions for completing that form below.

You can print out Official Form 122C-2 from the United States Courts website at www.uscourts.gov and input the numbers by hand or complete it online (see "Getting the Official Bankruptcy Forms," in Ch. 4). Or you can fill in the numbers in the blank version of Form 122C-2 in Appendix B.

These calculations are essentially the same as the calculations you would perform if your income was below the state median income, with two exceptions:

- Instead of using your actual living expenses, you must use set amounts found in national and local IRS expense standards.
- For most people, the plan length will be 60 months instead of 36 months.

And as with below-median-income filers, you'll also have to determine whether you will be able, through your plan, to pay your unsecured creditors at least what they would have gotten had you filed for Chapter 7 bankruptcy instead of Chapter 13.

Step 1: Calculate Your Disposable Income

If your income is higher than the state median, you'll use Form 122C-2 to calculate your disposable income plus perform a few extra calculations that would otherwise be done by your lawyer's plan payment software in order to get a fairly accurate idea of what your plan payment would be. In order to complete Form 122C-2, you'll need to first calculate your current monthly income using Form 122C-1, *Chapter 13 Statement of Your Current Monthly Income and Calculation of Commitment Period*.

"Current Monthly Income" or Actual Projected Income: *Hamilton v. Lanning*

What if your "current monthly income" as calculated on Form 122C-1 (which is your average income over the past six months) does not match your actual income or the income you will receive during your repayment period? The U.S. Supreme Court has held that bankruptcy courts may account for changes in the debtor's income or expenses that are "known or virtually certain at the time of [plan] confirmation" when calculating projected disposable income for purposes of the plan payments. (*Hamilton v. Lanning*, 130 S.Ct. 2464 (2010).) For details, see "If Your Actual Income Is Different From Your 'Current Monthly Income': *Hamilton v. Lanning*," above.

TIP

Use information from forms you completed in Ch.4. Much of the information needed to complete Forms 122C-1 and 122C-2 has already been provided in several of the forms discussed in Ch.4. If you already filled out the forms in that chapter (specifically Forms 122A-1 and 122A-2), you can transfer that information onto Forms 122C-1 and 122C-2. If you haven't yet filled out the forms in Ch.4, we'll send you back to certain sections so that you can get instructions to fill out Forms 122C-1 and 122C-2 in this chapter.

Use Form 122C-1 to Calculate Your Current Monthly Income

Calculate your current monthly income by completing Lines 1 through 14 of Form 122C-1, *Chapter 13 Statement of Your Current Monthly Income and Calculation of Commitment Period* (for purposes of this chapter, you won't need to complete Lines 15 through 21). To do this, you'll transfer some of the information you included on Form 122A-1, *Statement of Your Current Income*, and Form 122A-2, *Chapter 7 Means Test Calculation*, both discussed in Ch. 4. Here's what to do:

- Transfer the information on Lines 1 through 11 of Form 122A-1 onto Lines 1 through 11 of Form 122C-1.
- Transfer the information from Lines 1 through 4 of Form 122A-2 onto Lines 12 through 14 of Form 122C-1.

If you haven't already filled out Forms 122A-1 and 122A-2, you can find the instructions that correspond to the above-mentioned Lines in Ch. 4, and enter the information directly onto Form 122C-1.

Use Form 122C-2 to Calculate Your Disposable Income

Part 1. Calculate Your Deductions From Your Income

The first part of Form 122C-2 consists of Lines 5 through 38 (there are no Lines 1 through 4). They correspond to the same lines in Form 122A-2, *Chapter 7 Means Test Calculation*. Transfer the information you included on Lines 5 through 38 of Form 122A-1 onto Lines 5 through 38 of Form 122C-2. If you have not yet completed Form 122A-2, use the corresponding instructions in Ch. 4 to complete Form 122C-2.

Part 2. Determine Your Disposable Income Under 11 U.S.C. § 1325(b)(2)

Here is where you subtract your expenses from your income to arrive at your total disposable income.

Line 39. Enter your current monthly income from Line 14 on Form 122C-1.

Line 40. Enter the monthly average of any child support payments, foster care payments, or disability payments for a dependent child, that:

- are necessary to spend on the child, and
- you included in Line 2 of Form 122C-1.

Line 41. Enter the monthly average of:

- all contributions or wage deductions made to qualified retirement plans, as specified in Section 541(b)(7) (these include virtually all defined-benefit pension plans arising from employment), and
- all repayments of loans from retirement plans, as specified in Section 362(b)(19) (employment pension plans and 401(k)s).

Line 42. Bring down the total expenses from Line 38.

Line 43. Special circumstances are situations that give rise to unexpected expenses that don't qualify as "additional expense claims" on Line 46. The law lists a serious medical condition (such as cancer, Alzheimer's disease, or Parkinson's disease) or a call to active duty in the armed forces as examples of special circumstances. It's not enough just to show that special circumstances exist: You must also show that they justify additional expenses or adjustments to your current monthly income "for which there is no reasonable alternative." And, you must be able to document the expenses. If you believe that something in your life—that is not already provided for in this form—will eat up part of your disposable income, list the expense here and line up your documentation.

Can You Make Voluntary Retirement Payments During Chapter 13?

Courts in different areas are divided on whether you may make voluntary payments to retirement plans during your Chapter 13 case. The majority of courts allow voluntary payments to retirement plans, but only if you were making the payments (in the same or greater amount) before you filed for bankruptcy. Some courts are even more liberal, allowing voluntary retirement plan payments even if they were not being made prior to your Chapter 13, while others do not allow contributions to retirement plans under any circumstances.

Line 44. Add Lines 40 through 43d, and enter the total.

Line 45. Subtract Line 44 from Line 39 and enter the result.

This is your first calculation of disposable income, but you're not through yet. (Remember, the purpose of using this form

in this chapter is to figure out your required plan payment, and we need to go through a few more acrobatics to get a fairly accurate payment amount. As discussed earlier, a lawyer will have software to do these calculations.) Now return to Line 36 and use the amount on Line 44 as the plan payment. Multiply the plan payment by the correct multiplier, which can be found on the U.S. Trustee's website (www.justice.gov/ust). Enter the result in the box and in the column on the right of Line 44. Recalculate Line 37 to include the average monthly administrative expense and then recalculate Line 38. Enter the new total for Line 38 onto Line 42 and using that new number, recalculate Lines 44 and 45.

Line 46. If you have changes in income or expenses that you couldn't include anywhere else on the form, you can enter them here, provided any expenses really are necessary for the health and welfare of you and your family. For a final disposable income figure, adjust Line 45 accordingly.

To find out whether you have enough disposable income to get a Chapter 13 plan confirmed, divide the total of any secured debts that weren't included in Line 33 by 60, to figure out how much you'd have to pay each month to pay off these liens in five years. Subtract the result from your disposable income. If this results in a negative figure, then you can't propose a confirmable plan, given your current expenses and property holdings. If your disposable income is zero or more, then you can propose a confirmable plan, as long as the total is at least equal to the value of your nonexempt property (see Step 2, below).

Cases on Special Circumstances

Here are some cases in which the court has allowed a particular special circumstance claim, but remember that courts in your area may see the issue differently:

- unusually high transportation expenses (*In re Batzkiel*, 349 B.R. 581 (Bkrtcy N.D. Iowa 2006); *In re Turner*, 376 B.R. 370 (Bkrtcy D. N.H. 2007))
- mandatory repayment of 401(k) loan (*In re Lenton*, 358 B.R. 651 (Bkrtcy E.D. Pa. 2006))
- reduction in income (*In re Martin*, 371 B.R. 347 (Bkrtcy C.D. Ill. 2007) (diminished future availability of overtime hours); *In re Tamez*, No. 07-60047 (Bkrtcy W.D. Tex. 2007) (reduction in income due to voluntary job changes))
- wife's pregnancy in a joint case (*In re Martin*, 371 B.R. 347 (Bkrtcy C.D. Ill. 2007))
- joint debtors who have two separate households (*In re Graham*, 363 B.R. 844 (Bkrtcy S.D. Ohio 2007); *In re Armstrong*, No. 06-31414 (Bkrtcy N.D. Ohio 2007))
- unusually high rent expenses (*In re Scarafiotti*, 375 B.R. 618 (Bkrtcy D. Colorado 2007))
- court-ordered child support payments (*In re Littman*, 370 B.R. 820 (Bkrtcy D. Idaho 2007)), and
- full monthly payments on student loans when necessary to avoid suspension of professional license (*In re Kalfayan*, 415 B.R. 907 (Bkrtcy S.D. Fla. 2009)).

Plan Length If You Have No Disposable Income

If your income is above the state median, you normally must propose a 60-month plan. However, if you don't have any disposable income left after deducting living expense and repayment of secured and priority debts, some courts will let you propose a 36-month plan. Other courts won't.

Step 2: Determine What Your Creditors Would Get If You Used Chapter 7

As explained in Step 6 in "If Your Current Monthly Income Is Less Than Your State's Median Income," above, your plan must pay your unsecured creditors at least what they would have received if you had filed under Chapter 7: the value of your nonexempt property, less what it would cost to take and sell it, less the trustee's commission for doing so. See Step 6, above, for information on how to make this calculation.

Once you come up with the total amount your unsecured creditors would actually receive if you filed for Chapter 7, convert it to a monthly figure. For example, if you find that your unsecured creditors are entitled to $7,200 and you are proposing a five-year repayment plan, divide $7,200 by 60 months to come up with the monthly amount you would have to pay: $120. Subtract this monthly total from the disposable income you calculated in Step 1.

Disposable income
(from Step 1): _____

Monthly amount for
unsecured creditors: – _____

Total: = _____

As long as your total is a positive number, you may be able to propose a confirmable plan. If your total is zero, this means you will have exactly enough money to meet your plan obligations, not a penny more or less.

If all of your property is exempt, and the disposable income you calculated in Step 1 was zero, your unsecured creditors won't get paid a cent. This is called a "zero-percent" plan. Before the bankruptcy law changed in 2005, many courts wouldn't confirm a plan that paid unsecured creditors less than a particular percentage (anywhere from 20% to 80%, depending on the court). Under the revised law, however, there is no legal reason why a zero-percent plan should not be confirmed, as long as your expenses are reasonable (that is, the court can't find any money you are paying for expenses that should go to your creditors instead).

Understanding Property Exemptions

This section covers exemptions—the rules that determine how much, if any, your Chapter 13 plan will have to pay to your nonpriority, unsecured creditors.

Your Bankruptcy Estate

When you file for bankruptcy, a bankruptcy estate is created. The estate consists of everything you own that cannot be claimed as exempt (protected) under the law. In Chapter 13, you are usually allowed to keep all of your property—whether it is exempt or not, but claiming property as exempt takes it out of the liquidation analysis (see "Step 2: Determine What Your Creditors Would Get if You Used Chapter 7," above). In addition, if you need to convert your case to Chapter 7, property that you have properly claimed as exempt will be protected there as well.

First, you need to determine what types of property become property of the bankruptcy estate. It's best to break this down into several broad categories:

- **Property you own and possess.** Everything in your possession that you own, whether or not you owe money on it—for example, a car, real estate, clothing, books, television, stereo system, furniture, tools, boat, artworks, or stock certificates—is included in your bankruptcy estate. Property that you have in your possession but belongs to someone else (such as the car your friend stores in your garage or the television you borrowed from your sister) is not part of your bankruptcy estate, because you don't have the right to sell it or give it away.

- **Property you own but don't possess.** You can own something even if you don't have physical possession of it. For instance, you may own a car that someone else is using. Other examples include a deposit held by a stockbroker, a security deposit held by your landlord or a utility company, or a business in which you've invested money.
- **Property you are entitled to receive.** Property that you have a legal right to receive but haven't gotten yet when you file for bankruptcy is included in your bankruptcy estate. Common examples include:
  - wages, royalties, or commissions you have earned but have not yet been paid
  - a tax refund legally due you
  - vacation or termination pay you've earned
  - property you've inherited but not yet received
  - proceeds of an insurance policy, if the death, injury, or other event that gives rise to payment has already occurred, and
  - money owed to you for goods or services you've provided (often called "accounts receivable").
- **Community property.** If you live in a community property state, all property and income either spouse acquires during the marriage is ordinarily considered "community property," owned

jointly by both spouses. (The community property states are Arizona, California, Idaho, Louisiana, Nevada, New Mexico, Texas, Washington, and Wisconsin, and—if you have a written community property agreement or trust—Alaska.) Gifts and inheritances to only one spouse are the most common exceptions; these are the separate property of the spouse who receives them. If you're married and file jointly for bankruptcy, all the community property you and your spouse own, as well as all of the separate property owned by each of you, is considered part of your bankruptcy estate. If your spouse doesn't file, then your bankruptcy estate consists of all of the community property and all of your separate property—your spouse's separate property isn't included.

- **Marital property in a common law property state.** If you are married and filing jointly, your bankruptcy estate includes all the property you and your spouse own, together and separately. If you are filing alone for bankruptcy in a common law property state (all states other than the community property states listed above), your bankruptcy estate includes:
  - your separate property (property that has only your name on a title certificate or that was purchased, received as a gift, or inherited by you alone), and

- half of the property that is jointly owned by you and your spouse, unless you own the property together, as tenants by the entirety. If you own property as tenants by the entirety, and both spouses file for bankruptcy, then the property is part of your bankruptcy estate. If only one spouse files, however, and the spouse that has not filed for bankruptcy is not obligated to pay any of the debts that are being discharged, it is possible that none of the property owned as tenants by the entireties becomes property of the bankruptcy estate. If there are joint debts, however, the entireties property may be included. The laws that determine this and whether or not property even qualifies for entireties ownership differ from state to state. Tenancy by the entireties ownership may depend on how you acquired the property, whether you were married when you acquired it, where you lived at the time, and the type of property it is. For example, some states only allow real estate to be owned as tenants by the entireties, while other states also allow personal property to be owned this way.

- **Certain property you receive within 180 days after filing for bankruptcy.** In Chapter 13, your income during the life of the plan is considered to be property of the bankruptcy estate but most other property you acquire during this time is not. There are a few exceptions for certain items you receive within the 180 days after you file. You must notify the trustee if, during this time frame, you receive or become entitled to receive money or property:

  - as the result of an inheritance (this can get tricky—while it can include money or property that you initially inherit during the 180 days, it can also include payments you receive during this time frame as a result of an inheritance that you became entitled to many years before the bankruptcy)
  - as the result of a divorce court order or property settlement agreement, and
  - as a beneficiary of a life insurance policy or a death benefit plan.

- **Property (revenue) generated by estate property.** This type of property typically consists of the proceeds of contracts—such as those providing for rent, royalties, and commissions—that were in effect at the time of the bankruptcy filing, but which produced earnings after that date. For example, if you are a composer or an author and receive royalties each year for a composition or a book that was written before you filed for bankruptcy, the trustee may collect those royalties as property of your estate. Proceeds from work you do after your filing date belong to you.

- **Property transferred within the previous two years**. If you transferred personal or real property to anyone within the last two years for less than it's worth, the trustee may decide to treat the property as part of your bankruptcy estate and file a lawsuit in the bankruptcy court to recover the property for the benefit of your creditors.

Property That's Not Part of Your Bankruptcy Estate

Property that is not in your bankruptcy estate is not subject to the bankruptcy court's jurisdiction, which means that you don't have to worry about whether or not it's exempt.

The most common examples of property that doesn't fall within your bankruptcy estate are:

- property you buy or receive after your filing date (with the few exceptions described above)
- pensions subject to the federal law known as ERISA (commonly, defined-benefit pensions, 401(k)s, and Keogh plans)
- property owned as tenants by the entirety when only one spouse files (if there are no joint debts)
- property pledged as collateral for a loan where a licensed lender (pawnbroker) retains possession of the collateral
- property in your possession that belongs to someone else (for instance, property you are storing for someone)

- wages that are withheld and employer contributions that are made for employee benefit and health insurance plans, and
- funds in a qualified tuition plan or Coverdell education savings account if you deposit the funds into the account at least one year before filing, and the beneficiary is your child, stepchild, grandchild, step-grandchild, or in some cases, foster child. There are monetary limits depending on how long the funds have been in the account.

Value Your Property

As you'll see below, many exemptions apply only up to a certain dollar value. This means that you need to know what your property is worth in order to figure out whether it's exempt. You must use the property's replacement value: what it would cost to buy that specific property from a retail merchant, considering its age and condition.

It's easy to enter a dollar amount for cash and most investments.

If you own a car, start with the middle *Kelley Blue Book* price. If the car needs repair, reduce the value by what it would cost you to fix the car. You can find the *Kelley Blue Book* at a public library or online at www.kbb.com. Or, use the NADA guide at www.nada.org.

Online, visit eBay (www.ebay.com) to get a fix on the going price for just about anything. Or you can visit local thrift shops and flea markets to see how used items in a similar condition are priced. As long as your valuations are based on the going retail price for similar used items, you should generally use the lowest value you can find. That means it is more likely to be exempt and not require payments to your nonpriority, unsecured creditors. On the other hand, low-ball valuations might provoke arguments with the trustee or your creditors about what the property is really worth. As long as the exemptions available to you cover the value you use, pricing your property more reasonably can help you avoid unnecessary hassles.

If you are filing separately and own something jointly with someone (other than a spouse with whom you would file for bankruptcy), reduce the value of the item to reflect only the portion you own. For example, you and your brother jointly bought a music synthesizer worth $10,000. If your ownership share is 40% and your brother's is 60%, the value of your portion is $4,000.

If you are married and filing separately in a community property state, include the total value of all the community property as well as the value of your separate property.

If you are married, you own the property with your spouse as tenants by the entirety, and you are filing separately, your ownership interest may not be 50% for purposes of computing your exemption. (Talk to your lawyer to find out what percentage of your tenancy by the entirety property you can claim as exempt.)

Applying Exemptions

Bankruptcy is intended to give debtors a fresh start—not to leave them utterly destitute. Exempt property can literally range from "the shirt on your back" to a million-dollar estate, depending on which state's exemptions you use.

State and Federal Exemption Systems

Every state has its own fairly lengthy list of exempt property. (You can find these lists in Appendix A.) In addition, some states and the District of Columbia offer bankruptcy filers an alternative choice of exemptions—a list of exempt property found in the federal Bankruptcy Code. States that offer this choice are: Alaska, Arkansas, Connecticut, Hawaii, Kentucky, Massachusetts, Michigan, Minnesota, New Hampshire, New Jersey, New Mexico, New York, Oregon, Pennsylvania, Rhode Island, Texas, Vermont, Washington, and Wisconsin. In these states, you must choose between the state exemption system and the federal exemption system; you can't mix and match.

California Note: Although California doesn't make the federal Bankruptcy Code exemptions available, it has two separate exemption systems—both created by state law. Debtors who use the California exemptions must choose between System 1 (the regular exemptions available to debtors in and out of bankruptcy) and System 2 (available only in bankruptcy and very similar to the federal exemptions).

How Exemptions Work

Under both the federal and state exemption systems, some types of property are exempt regardless of value. For example, in some states, home furnishings, wedding rings, or clothing are exempt without regard to value. In Florida and Texas, homes are exempt regardless of their value or the value of the bankruptcy filer's ownership (equity) in the home.

Other kinds of property are exempt up to a limited value. For instance, cars are often exempt up to a certain amount—typically $2,500 to $3,000. The home equity exemption ranges from thousands of dollars to hundreds of thousands, depending on the state. When there is a dollar limit on an exemption, any equity above the limit is considered nonexempt. (Your equity is the amount you would get to keep if you sold the property.)

Many states offer a "wildcard" exemption —a dollar amount that you can apply to any property, in order to make it (or more of it) exempt. This type of exemption typically runs from a few hundred to several thousand dollars (but more than $25,000 in California's System 2 exemptions).

> **EXAMPLE:** Fred and Susan are married and live in Virginia. They rent rather than own their home. Under the Virginia exemptions, equity in an automobile is limited to $6,000 ($12,000 for couples). Fred and Susan own $16,000 of equity in their cars. Fortunately for Fred and Susan, Virginia allows debtors to use the Virginia homestead exemption as a wildcard for their personal property, if they don't use it for a home. Because Fred and Susan rent, they can use this wildcard for their cars. The homestead exemption is $10,000 for couples. So, by adding $4,000 of the wildcard to their $12,000 car exemption, Fred and Susan can exempt all of their equity in their cars. They can apply the other $8,000 of the wildcard exemption to property that isn't otherwise protected by the Virginia exemptions.

Property Typically Not Exempt

The kinds of property listed below are typically not exempt unless you use a wildcard exemption:
- interests in real estate other than your home
- substantial equity in a newer-model motor vehicle
- expensive musical instruments unrelated to your job or business
- stamp, coin, and other collections
- cash, deposit accounts, stocks, bonds, and other investments
- business assets (except property that qualifies as tools of your trade, which you can typically exempt up to several thousand dollars)
- valuable artwork
- expensive clothing and jewelry, or
- antiques.

Domicile Requirements for Exemption Claims

You must meet certain domicile requirements before claiming a state's exemptions. Your domicile is where you live and plan to continue living for the indefinite future. For most people, their domicile is where they are living, period. But sometimes a person's domicile is in one state and his or her residence in another, such as a military family living on an army base in one state and maintaining a home in another, or a person living temporarily away from his or her home because of a job. Here are the domicile rules:

- If you have been living (been domiciled) in your current state for at least two years, you must use that state's exemptions (or the federal exemptions, if they are available).
- If you have been living (been domiciled) in your current state for less than two years, you must use the exemptions of the state where you were domiciled for the greater part of the 180-day period immediately prior to the two-year period preceding your filing—unless that state allows only current residents to use its exemptions. In that case, you can use the federal exemptions.
- If you have been domiciled in your current state for fewer than 91 days, you'll need to wait until you have lived there for 91 days to file in that state (and then use whatever exemptions are available to you according to the rules set out above).
- If the state you are filing in makes the federal exemptions available, you can use that exemption list regardless of how long you've been living in the state.
- If these rules deprive you of the right to use any state's exemptions, you can use the federal exemptions (even if your state doesn't make them available). For example, if you were living in another country during the 180-day period prior to the two years before you filed for bankruptcy, you can use the federal exemptions.

A longer domicile requirement applies to homestead exemptions: If you acquired a home in your current state less than 40 months before your filing date, your homestead exemption may be subject to a $160,375 cap regardless of which state's exemption system you use. This amount is effective as of April 1, 2016 and is adjusted every three years. People convicted of felonies and certain securities violations are also subject to this cap.

Using the Exemptions Appendix

You can find the exemptions for all 50 states in Appendix A. If you are considering filing for bankruptcy in one of the states listed below, you'll also want to look at the federal exemptions, which are listed in that appendix right after Wyoming.

States That Offer the Federal Exemptions	
Alaska	New Jersey
Arkansas	New Mexico
Connecticut	New York
District of Columbia	Oregon
Hawaii	Pennsylvania
Kentucky	Rhode Island
Massachusetts	Texas
Michigan	Vermont
Minnesota	Washington
New Hampshire	Wisconsin

Use Appendix A to find the applicable exemptions for your property, using the domicile rules set out above. Compare the type and value of your property, and the amount of equity you have in the property, with the exemptions.

Remember, if you are filing in a state that offers the federal bankruptcy exemptions, you should also check the federal exemption chart. Items that aren't exempt under the state exemptions available to you may be exempt under the federal system, and vice versa. However, you must pick one system or the other; you can't mix and match.

If you are married and filing jointly, you can double your exemptions unless the chart says that you can't. This will be indicated either at the top of the chart or next to a particular exemption.

If you have been domiciled in California for more than two years when you file, you may choose System 1 (the regular state exemptions) or System 2, a state list that is derived from the federal exemptions but differs in important particulars. If you file in California but haven't been domiciled there for two years, you can't use either California system—you'll have to use the domicile rules set out above to figure out which exemptions you can use.

Federal Nonbankruptcy Exemptions

If you are using the exemptions of a particular state rather than the federal exemptions, you may also exempt property listed in Appendix A under Federal Nonbankruptcy Exemptions. Don't confuse those with the federal bankruptcy exemptions, which may be used only if a state allows it and only as an alternative to the state exemptions.

Making the Decision

Now you have all of the information you need to decide whether you can—and should—file for Chapter 13 bankruptcy. To help you sort through this information, weigh the pros and cons, and reach a decision, this chapter provides a transcript of a consultation between a debtor and a lawyer.

As you'll see, the debtor, Georgia Cox, is trying to figure out whether to file for bankruptcy under Chapter 7 or Chapter 13. She has decided to consult with a bankruptcy lawyer to help her with her decision. The questions the lawyer asks will help remind you of factors you should consider as you evaluate your own situation.

Lawyer: Good morning. What's your name?

Debtor: Georgia Cox.

Lawyer: Hi, Georgia. How can I help you today?

Debtor: Well, I've run up quite a bit of debt, and I've decided to file for bankruptcy. I know there are different types of bankruptcy, but I think I need to learn more about them. I need some help figuring out what my options are.

Lawyer: Okay, I can help you with that. The two basic types of bankruptcy for individuals are Chapter 7 bankruptcy and Chapter 13 bankruptcy. There are a couple of major differences between them. In a Chapter 13 bankruptcy, you pay down some or all of your debts over a three- to five-year period and discharge (cancel) whatever is left at the completion of your plan. In a Chapter 7 bankruptcy, you don't pay down any of your debt, and the entire process takes between three and four months. But you may have to give up property you own so it can be sold and the proceeds distributed to your creditors.

In either type of bankruptcy, some debts will survive your bankruptcy, such as criminal fines and penalties. Some debts will survive a Chapter 7 bankruptcy but will be discharged at the end of a Chapter 13 bankruptcy, such as an obligation to an ex-spouse under a marital settlement agreement.

But we'll get to that later. Are you with me so far?

Debtor: Yes. I kind of already knew most of what you just told me by reading some articles on the Nolo website. Right now, I'm leaning toward Chapter 7 since it's over a lot sooner and seems like it's a lot simpler. But I wouldn't want to choose Chapter 7 if Chapter 13 would clearly be the better choice for me.

Lawyer: Okay. Well, let's start by figuring out whether you even have a choice. Some people aren't eligible to file for Chapter 7 bankruptcy. If both options are available to you, then we can talk about which one makes more sense.

Debtor: Okay.

Lawyer: What state do you live in?

Debtor: New Hampshire.

Lawyer: Who lives with you as part of your household? That includes not only relatives and dependents, but anyone else whose income and expenses are combined with yours to maintain your home.

Debtor: Just me and my two children. One is eight and the other just turned 12.

Lawyer: Okay. And do you operate a business?

Debtor: Actually, I do. What difference does that make?

Lawyer: Well, in some cases, your eligibility for Chapter 7 may turn on whether your debts are classified as business or consumer debts.

Debtor: Okay. I run my own business, repairing used electronic equipment.

Lawyer: Have you incorporated your business or is it a partnership?

Debtor: No, just me, a sole proprietor.

Lawyer: And do you have other work? In other words, do you have a regular job and operate your business on the side?

Debtor: No, just the business.

Lawyer: Is your income pretty steady?

Debtor: It was until recently. Near the end of 2017, my business tanked and I'll be lucky to bring in half of what I was earning not too long ago. Also, I receive alimony and child support, which helps stabilize my income, but my ex told me just last week that he's been laid off and can't find another job, so I expect that source of income to dry up as well.

Lawyer: So, to dig in a little deeper about the nature of your debt, I see from the worksheet you completed when you first contacted me that you have about $100,000 in mortgage debt and that you currently don't owe any back taxes. Is that right?

Debtor: Yep.

Lawyer: I gather from the worksheet that your overall debt, other than your mortgage, is far short of $100,000, is that right?

Debtor: Right again.

Lawyer: Well, since your home mortgage counts as a personal debt, that means that your personal debts are higher than your business debts. If your business debts comprised more than 50% of your debts you would qualify for Chapter 7 without having to deal with what's known as the means test, which we'll get to in a moment. But since that's not the case, we'll have to see if your income is low enough to qualify you for Chapter 7. First, let's look at your income over the previous six months. More specifically, what was your gross income from all sources, taxable or not, minus the expenses that were reasonable and necessary for operating the business?

Debtor: About $3,000 a month after expenses.

Lawyer: You mentioned you've been receiving child support and alimony. How much during that six-month period?

Debtor: About $1,000 a month in alimony and $800 a month for child support.

Lawyer: Any other income?

Debtor: No, that's it.

Lawyer: So, it looks like your average monthly earnings over the past six months are $3,000 from your business, $1,000 in alimony, and $800 for child support, for a total of $4,800. Does that sound right?

Debtor: Yes.

Lawyer: Under the bankruptcy law, if your income is less than the median annual income for a family of your size in your state, you are automatically eligible to file for Chapter 7 bankruptcy. You don't have to fill out a lengthy form comparing your income to your expenses and deductions for contractual obligations, such as a car note and mortgage. Does any of this sound familiar to you?

Debtor: Yes, I remember reading a few years ago that higher-income people won't be able to file for Chapter 7 anymore. Is that what you are talking about?

Lawyer: Yes, that's it. Also, if your income is less than the median for your state and you decide to file a Chapter 13 bankruptcy anyway, your repayment plan need only last for three years. On the other hand, if your income is more than the median, your plan would have to last for five years.

Debtor: I didn't know that.

Lawyer: So, let's see how these numbers work out. Your annual income based on your gross income for the last six months is $57,600. The New Hampshire median income for a household of three people is $90,338. So, you're under the median income and don't have to take the means test to prove your eligibility for Chapter 7 bankruptcy. And if you decide to use Chapter 13, you can repay your debts over three years, instead of five.

Debtor: I guess that's good news, but when it comes right down to it, I wish I earned more, even if that meant I had to take the means test and have a Chapter 13 case last longer. Of course, if I had more money, I guess I wouldn't be talking to you about filing for bankruptcy in the first place.

Lawyer: Even though you are eligible for Chapter 7 bankruptcy on the basis of your average income over the past six months, you may still be forced into a Chapter 13 bankruptcy (or optionally have your case dismissed) if it appears that your actual monthly net income going forward will be substantially more than your actual monthly expenses—which would make it feasible for you to pay off some of your debts under a repayment plan.

Debtor: I wish I did have some extra income, but I always fall short at the end of the month.

Lawyer: Well, as long as your basic living expenses are reasonable and more or less equal to your net income, and because your income is below the state median income, you have the option of filing for Chapter 7 bankruptcy.

Let's turn now to your residence. How long have you lived in New Hampshire?

Debtor: About three years.

Lawyer: Have you lived there continuously for the last three years, or did you live or maintain a residence somewhere else?

Debtor: I've lived here the whole time. I moved here from Vermont because of a job, but I didn't keep a home in Vermont. I vote and get my mail in New Hampshire.

Lawyer: Great. Because you've been living in New Hampshire for more than two years, we'll be able to use New Hampshire's property exemptions. These will determine what property you can keep if you file a Chapter 7, and the minimum amount you'll have to pay your unsecured creditors if you file a Chapter 13 bankruptcy.

Debtor: Why do the exemptions matter in a Chapter 13 bankruptcy? I thought I could keep all of my property if I use Chapter 13.

Lawyer: Yes, you're right about that. But the law doesn't want your creditors to be worse off if you use Chapter 13 rather than Chapter 7. A Chapter 13 repayment plan has to give your unsecured, nonpriority creditors at least as much as they would have received if you had filed for Chapter 7 bankruptcy. So, if you have any nonexempt property, your plan will need to pay your unsecured, nonpriority creditors at least the value of that property, less the trustee's commission and the costs of taking and selling the property.

Lawyer: Now, let's see if you have any nonexempt property. You own your own home, right?

Debtor: Yeah, although as you know, I owe $100,000 on my mortgage, which kind of means that the bank owns the home.

Lawyer: I know how you feel, but for bankruptcy purposes, if you are the owner on the title deed, you are considered the owner. Are you on the title deed?

Debtor: When I last looked.

Lawyer: Okay. How large are your mortgage payments?

Debtor: $1,200.

Lawyer: Are you current on your payments?

Debtor: Yes.

Lawyer: What's your home worth?

Debtor: $150,000. It used to be worth $200,000.

Lawyer: Okay. Under the New Hampshire homestead exemption, you are entitled to protect up to $120,000 of equity in your home. You have $50,000 of equity, so all of your equity is protected.

Debtor: What's a homestead exemption?

Lawyer: That's an exemption for equity you have in your home. You are entitled to keep equity in your home up to the amount of the exemption, even if you file for Chapter 7 bankruptcy. If your equity exceeded the exemption, you might lose the extra equity if you filed for Chapter 7. The trustee could sell your home, pay off the mortgage, pay you your exemption, and still have money left over to distribute among your creditors. But because your equity is protected by the exemption, there wouldn't be anything left for your creditors after you got your exemption amount and the mortgage was paid, so there is nothing for the trustee to take. That's how exemptions work.

We already discussed how exemptions work in Chapter 13. If you have equity in personal property or real estate that isn't protected by an exemption, your repayment plan has to pay unsecured creditors at least what they would have gotten from the sale of that property if you had filed Chapter 7.

Debtor: I remember reading that a new bankruptcy law made it harder for people to keep their homes. Will that affect me?

Lawyer: Nope. The law puts a cap of roughly $160,000 on the exemption amount for people who bought their home within the 40 months before they filed for bankruptcy. So it affects only people who bought a home more recently, and then only if their state would otherwise allow them to take a higher exemption. For example, even if

you bought your home in New Hampshire within the previous 40 months, the New Hampshire homestead is only $120,000, so the cap wouldn't make any difference.

Debtor: So, I don't have to worry about that.

Lawyer: Right. Oh, your homestead exemption might be affected if you used nonexempt property in the last ten years to buy your home in order to cheat your creditors. I guess I should ask how you got the money to pay for your home.

Debtor: I borrowed money from my parents.

Lawyer: Great. Your home equity is covered by New Hampshire's homestead exemption and you can keep it if you file for Chapter 7 bankruptcy.

Debtor: What happens to my home if I file for Chapter 13 bankruptcy?

Lawyer: As long as you keep making your mortgage payments and the other payments required by your Chapter 13 plan, there won't be a problem. However, if you fall behind on your payments, your lender can request permission from the court to proceed with a foreclosure, just as if you hadn't filed for bankruptcy.

Debtor: So I have to keep my mortgage payments current, no matter which type of bankruptcy I file?

Lawyer: That's right.

Debtor: While we're talking about mortgages, would you mind if I asked you about something my sister's going through?

Lawyer: Shoot.

Debtor: My sister owns a house that is now worth $100,000, but she owes $150,000 on her first mortgage and another $50,000 on her second mortgage. She's several months behind on her mortgage payments and her lender told her it's about to start foreclosure proceedings. She also lives in New Hampshire and she's been told that the lender can foreclose without having to go to court. Could bankruptcy help her keep her home?

Lawyer: The short answer is that Chapter 13 might help her keep her home. Chapter 7 would only delay the process for a few months. Even in Chapter 13, she might have to give up her home but unlike in Chapter 7, she could get more time to complete a modification with her lender. She could also get rid of the second mortgage lien on the property as part of her Chapter 13 plan, since the second mortgage lien is no longer secured by any equity in the home.

Debtor: That's really interesting

Lawyer: It is, isn't it? Anyway, moving on, what other debts do you owe?

Debtor: Mainly credit card debts, and one SBA bank loan for my business.

Lawyer: Is the SBA loan secured by any of your property? Often these loans are.

Debtor: No, it's just a bank loan.

Lawyer: How much are you paying on that loan?

Debtor: About $300 a month.

Lawyer: And how much credit card debt do you owe?

Debtor: About $20,000.

Lawyer: What were the credit card debts for?

Debtor: About $14,000 for personal expenses and $6,000 for paying off back taxes.

Lawyer: Oh yeah? What period did you owe the taxes for?

Debtor: The last couple of years.

Lawyer: That's interesting. I'll come back to this later. Bankruptcy law allows you to discharge credit card charges used to pay off taxes in a Chapter 13 bankruptcy but not in a Chapter 7 bankruptcy. So, if there is no other reason to choose one type of bankruptcy over the other, you would be wise to choose Chapter 13.

So, having paid those taxes, are you now current on your taxes for the past four years?

Debtor: Yes.

Lawyer: That's good. You can't file for Chapter 13 unless you have filed your state and federal taxes for the previous four years. How much was the bank loan for?

Debtor: $40,000.

Lawyer: Did anybody cosign on that loan?

Debtor: As matter of fact, my mother did.

Lawyer: Hmm. Even if you could get rid of that debt in bankruptcy, your mother would still be on the hook to repay it if you filed under Chapter 7. Even though you wouldn't be responsible for the debt anymore, she would be.

But if you file for Chapter 13 bankruptcy, your mother won't have to repay it while your plan is in place, as long as your plan provides for payment of some or all of that debt. So, assuming your plan lasts for three years, your mother won't be on the hook for that period. However, she will still be responsible for any amount you haven't paid when your plan ends. So, again, if there is no other reason to choose one type of bankruptcy instead of the other, it looks like Chapter 13 might be a good choice.

Do you have any other debts?

Debtor: Nothing significant, maybe a total of $2,000 in miscellaneous bills. And, oh, does child support count?

Lawyer: I thought you were receiving child support.

Debtor: I am, but I also owe child support, for a child from a previous marriage. I never paid because my ex never asked, but now he's seeking current support as well as $5,000 in back support.

Lawyer: How much will you owe?

Debtor: Under the court order, $300 a month.

Lawyer: Have you started paying the support?

Debtor: No. I have to start paying it next month.

Lawyer: If you decide to file for Chapter 13, you will have to remain current on your child support payments throughout the life of your plan. If you don't, your case will be dismissed or converted to a Chapter 7 bankruptcy.

Debtor: I understand.

Lawyer: Let's talk later about the back support you owe. When were you divorced?

Debtor: A couple of years ago.

Lawyer: Did you assume any of the debts in the course of your divorce?

Debtor: Yes, I assumed the credit card charges for personal expenses in exchange for my ex-husband's share of our home.

Lawyer: Okay. How much were these charges?

Debtor: About $3,000.

Lawyer: Hmmm, in a Chapter 7 bankruptcy, you can discharge this debt as to the creditor, but your ex can come after you for this debt if he is sued by the creditor. In Chapter 13 bankruptcy, the debt would be fully discharged, with respect to both the creditor and your ex, but only if it was not considered part of your support obligation in the divorce.

Debtor: It wasn't, so it sounds like I should probably file for Chapter 13.

Lawyer: Maybe, but we're not through yet. Let's talk about your other property. Other than your home, do you have any other property you would want to keep in your bankruptcy?

Debtor: Oh, yes. I have a concert piano and some copyright interests in several songs I wrote. Also, I have a car I want to hold on to and the tools I use in my business.

Lawyer: How much are the tools worth?

Debtor: About $3,000.

Lawyer: Great. New Hampshire allows you to keep up to $5,000 worth of tools for your occupation, so those are exempt. How much is the car worth?

Debtor: About $4,000 according to *Kelley Blue Book.*

Lawyer: Are you making payments on it?

Debtor: Yes.

Lawyer: How much is left on your note?

Debtor: About $8,000.

Lawyer: When did you buy it?

Debtor: Three years ago.

Lawyer: If you file for Chapter 13, you can pay off the value of the car rather than what you still owe on the note. This is called a cramdown, and it's another great reason for you to file for Chapter 13. And it's a good thing you didn't buy your car more recently: You couldn't use this cramdown procedure if you had bought the car within 2½ years of your bankruptcy filing date.

Now let's take a look at the New Hampshire exemptions, to see whether your other property is covered. Remember, exemptions like the homestead exemption and the tools of your occupation exemption are laws that determine what property you can keep in your bankruptcy. As I read them, the car is covered because you owe more than it's worth, so your creditors wouldn't get anything if it were sold. Because you don't have any equity in the car, you don't need to protect it with an exemption. As for the piano and your copyright interests, there are no state exemptions that specifically cover those items.

Debtor: Does that mean I'll lose my piano?

Lawyer: Not necessarily. Remember, if you file for Chapter 13, you don't lose any property—you just have to make sure you pay your creditors at least what they would have received in a Chapter 7 case. This would be a lot less than the value of the piano, because of the trustee's commission and the costs of taking the piano, storing it, and selling it at auction. And even though New Hampshire doesn't specifically exempt pianos, it has a $3,500 exemption for all your furniture. So depending on your piano's value, it might be covered by the furniture exemption.

Debtor: I think my piano would sell for about $12,000 and I guess my copyrights are pretty much worthless.

Lawyer: Why do you say your copyright interests are worthless?

Debtor: Well, they belong to three songs I wrote, but I've never had the songs published, so there is no one to sell them to.

Lawyer: Okay, let's forget about the songs. We're only talking about the piano. Looking at the New Hampshire exemptions, in addition to the portion of the piano's value arguably covered by the furniture exemption—$3,500—there are also some "wildcard" exemptions. This type of exemption can be used to protect any property you choose. New Hampshire's wildcard exemptions will provide an additional $8,000 that you can put toward the piano: That takes into account a $1,000 straight wildcard, plus a $7,000 wildcard that you can use if you don't fully take advantage of certain other exemptions. If you use these wildcards for your piano, only about $500 of its value is not exempt. Because of the trustee's commission and the costs of selling the piano, your creditors probably wouldn't get any of the proceeds if you use Chapter 7. So the nonexempt portion of your piano's value will add little or nothing to the cost of your Chapter 13 plan.

Debtor: Okay.

Lawyer: Here is a copy of the New Hampshire exemptions. Other than the piano, do you have any property that exceeds the exemption limit or that isn't listed in the exemption list?

Debtor: No, the piano is the only problem. But if I use the furniture exemption for my piano, my furniture won't be exempt. It's old furniture I bought at the Goodwill. I have nothing that would be of any value.

Lawyer: Well, that's up to the trustee. If you choose to use the entire furniture exemption for your piano, you might have to place some value on your furniture equal to what it would cost you to replace it.

Debtor: That would probably be about $1,000.

Lawyer: Okay, so you would have about $1,500 worth of nonexempt property, total. That's under the New Hampshire state exemptions. Some states allow a person to choose to use a different set of exemptions set out in the federal Bankruptcy Code termed the "federal exemptions." As it turns out, New Hampshire does allow use of the federal exemptions as an alternative to the New Hampshire state exemptions. You can choose from the federal exemption list or from the New Hampshire state list, but you can't mix or match.

Let's take a look and see if the federal exemptions would do you any good. The federal exemptions currently protect only $23,675 in your home equity. You have $50,000 equity to protect, so you wouldn't want to choose the federal exemptions.

So, we know you can file for Chapter 7 bankruptcy if you wish. You could keep your home and probably your piano, even though it isn't completely exempt. The cost of collecting and storing the piano, then selling it at auction, would probably be more than $500—the nonexempt portion—which means there wouldn't be anything left after selling it to pay to your unsecured creditors. If you had to use part of the furniture exemption for other pieces of furniture, however, $1,500 of the value of your piano would be nonexempt. If that were the case, the trustee might decide to take it and sell it, giving you the exempt amount and paying the rest to your unsecured creditors. Or, you could keep the piano if the trustee was willing to sell it to you for a negotiated price. Because the trustee would probably have to pay about $1,000 to sell it, you might be able to keep it by paying the trustee $500. But that's all in a Chapter 7 bankruptcy.

Debtor: It's still sounding to me like Chapter 13 is a good idea. But you said I have to make sure I'm eligible. What are the requirements?

Lawyer: Before we get to that, I have a couple more questions.

Debtor: Okay.

Lawyer: During the previous year, have you made payments on any loans you owe to relatives?

Debtor: Nope.

Lawyer: Good. If you had, the trustee might require the relative to return the money so it could be added to the amount your creditors would get.

Debtor: I wouldn't want that to happen.

Lawyer: Have you given away or sold any property to anyone within the past two years?

Debtor: No.

Lawyer: That also simplifies things. If you had given away some property, or you had sold some property for less than what it was worth, the difference in value might be considered nonexempt property. You'd have to add that to the amount you have to pay under your Chapter 13 plan. But you didn't sell any property, so this rule doesn't affect you.

Debtor: Wow, there's a lot to consider here. Are we done—isn't it clear that Chapter 13 is the right route for me?

Lawyer: Bear with me, just a few more issues to consider. Chapter 13 has some limitations on how much debt you can owe in order to be eligible. Let's see, you owe a total of $70,000 of unsecured debt—a $40,000 bank loan, $23,000 in credit card debts, $5,000 in child support arrearage, and $2,000 other debts. You owe a total of $108,000 secured debt (your home and car). This means you fall within the eligibility guidelines, which are currently $1,184,200 for secured debts and $394,725 for unsecured debts.

Debtor: That's good.

Lawyer: Now, let's see what debts you would have to pay in your Chapter 13 bankruptcy. Some debts have to be paid in full while others can be paid in part, depending on your income. Let's start with administrative expenses, which consist of part of my attorneys' fees and the trustee's fee. My total fees for a Chapter 13 bankruptcy are $4,000. I will need $1,500 up front and you can pay me the additional $2,500 through your plan. You'll also have to pay the trustee a fee, which is roughly 10% of whatever is paid out over the course of your plan. So, before we can know how much the trustee's fee will be, we'll need to figure out how much your plan will pay out.

Debtor: What happens to my credit card debts and my SBA loan?

Lawyer: That will depend on how much income you have left over after deducting your living expenses. If you'll have no income left over, you won't be able to file a Chapter 13 bankruptcy. If you'll have enough extra income to pay the debts that must be paid off in a Chapter 13 bankruptcy, but you won't have enough income to pay off any of your credit card debts or SBA loan, then those debts will be discharged at the end of your Chapter 13 without your paying a cent. This is what's known as a "zero percent" plan. Some judges refuse to confirm "zero percent" plans, so I can't tell you for sure what would happen in your particular case.

Debtor: So what are the mandatory debts that must be paid through the plan?

Lawyer: We start with the $5,000 child support arrears, which must be paid in full. Plus, you might have to pay a portion of the $1,500 nonexempt equity in your piano as well as my fee. Those items total $8,000. If that's all you'll have to pay under your plan, the trustee's fee would be $800, which means the total amount you'd have to pay through your plan would be $8,800. This amount might be a little less (depending on what you work out with the trustee about the piano) or perhaps a bit more if your bankruptcy judge makes you pay your car loan through the plan because you are cramming it down. And, of course, if your disposable income is high enough to repay some of your unsecured debt in addition to

the mandatory debts, then the total amount would be even higher.

Debtor: How can I tell whether I have enough income to meet the Chapter 13 requirements?

Lawyer: If you decide to file for Chapter 13 bankruptcy, you have to fill out some forms to determine your income and your expenses. These forms will basically show whether you can afford a Chapter 13 bankruptcy. If you don't have enough income to pay all necessary debts in three years, you can ask the judge to let you propose a five-year plan, so you can pay less each month.

Debtor: So, do you suggest that I file for Chapter 7? Or should I use Chapter 13?

Lawyer: As long as you have enough income left over in your budget to use Chapter 13, that would be an excellent choice for you because:

- It will protect your codebtor—your mother—for the life of the plan.
- It will allow you to keep your car and pay it off at market value rather than reaffirming the current note, which is twice what it's worth.
- Unlike Chapter 7, it fully discharges the credit card debts you assumed in your divorce.
- Unlike Chapter 7, it will allow you to discharge the credit card debts you incurred to pay off your taxes.
- It will allow you to pay off your child support arrearage—that is, the back

child support you owe—over the life of your plan, without worrying about wage garnishments and bank levies.

So, assuming you have enough income to propose a confirmable Chapter 13 plan and pay my fees, I recommend Chapter 13. If you can't propose a confirmable Chapter 13 plan, even over a five-year period, you might consider filing a Chapter 7 bankruptcy. It won't discharge your child support debt, and you can't cram down your car note. And you'll still owe the debt you assumed in your divorce, but you will be able to discharge all of your credit card debt and the SBA loan, as well as any other miscellaneous unsecured debts that you owe, and you'll be able to keep your home and your car as long as you remain current on your payments. If you hired me to represent you, my fees would be $1,800 up front, but that's all, plus the court filing fee of $335 and about $100 for prefiling and postfiling mandatory counseling sessions. And, if you wanted, you could probably represent yourself (and save yourself my $1,800 fee). Nolo publishes a great book called *How to File for Chapter 7 Bankruptcy*, which provides step-by-step instructions for filling out the official forms, which you can get on the Internet.

Filing for Chapter 13 Bankruptcy

Complete Your Bankruptcy Forms

In this chapter, we review the Chapter 13 bankruptcy petition as well as the schedules and other forms you will have to file for your Chapter 13 case (except for your repayment plan, which is covered in Ch. 8).

We discuss the purpose of each form, the type of information required, and legal issues to consider when completing the forms. Your bankruptcy attorney will prepare the forms for you, but it's important to know what information must be disclosed in a Chapter 13 bankruptcy, and why. This knowledge will help you:

- prepare for your first visit with your lawyer
- make decisions with your lawyer about how to proceed, and
- ensure that your petition is accurate and complete.

Required Forms, Fees, and Where to File

Here's a quick rundown of the official bankruptcy forms, fees to file your case, special local requirements, and where to file your petition.

Filing in the Right Bankruptcy Court

Because bankruptcy is a creature of federal, not state, law, you must file for bankruptcy in a special federal court. There are federal bankruptcy courts all over the country.

The federal court system divides the country into judicial districts. Every state has at least one judicial district; most have more. You can file in either:

- the district where you have been living for the greater part of the 180-day period before you file, or
- the district where you are domiciled— that is, where you maintain your home, even if you have been living elsewhere temporarily (such as on a military base).

Bankruptcy Filing Fees

The total fee to file for Chapter 13 bankruptcy is $310. Fees change, however. Your local bankruptcy attorney will have the up-to-date figures, or check with the court. This fee is due upon filing, unless you qualify for a waiver of fees or obtain court permission to pay in installments. Chapter 13 filers seldom qualify for either of these remedies, since the income level that is necessary to file a Chapter 13 is usually higher than the level of income required to qualify for a waiver or installment payments.

Required Bankruptcy Forms

Bankruptcy uses official forms prescribed by the federal office of the courts. These are the standard forms that must be filed in every Chapter 13 bankruptcy:

☐ Form 101—*Voluntary Petition for Individuals Filing for Bankruptcy*
  ☐ Form 101A—*Initial Statement About an Eviction Judgment Against You* (not everyone has to file this)
  ☐ Form 101B—*Statement About Payment of an Eviction Judgment Against You* (not everyone has to file this)
  ☐ Form 106Dec—*Declaration About an Individual Debtor's Schedules*
  ☐ Form 106Sum—*A Summary of Your Assets and Liabilities and Certain Statistical Information*
  ☐ Form 106A/B—*Schedule A/B: Property*
☐ Form 106C—*Schedule C: The Property You Claim as Exempt*
☐ Form 106D—*Schedule D: Creditors Who Hold Claims Secured by Property*
☐ Form 106E/F—*Schedule E/F: Creditors Who Have Unsecured Claims*
☐ Form 106G—*Schedule G: Executory Contracts and Unexpired Leases*
☐ Form 106H—*Schedule H: Your Codebtors*
☐ Form 106I—*Schedule I: Your Income*
☐ Form 106J—*Schedule J: Your Expenses*
  ☐ Form 106J-2—*Schedule J-2: Expenses for Separate Household of Debtor 2* (not everyone has to file this)
☐ Form 107—*Your Statement of Financial Affairs for Individuals Filing for Bankruptcy*
☐ Form 113—*Chapter 13 Plan* or local Chapter 13 plan form (covered in Ch. 8)

☐ Form 121—*Your Statement About Your Social Security Numbers*
☐ Form 122C-1—*Chapter 13 Statement of Your Current Monthly Income and Calculation of Commitment Period*
☐ Form 122C-2—*Chapter 13 Calculation of Your Disposable Income*
☐ Form 2030—*Attorney Fee Disclosure*
☐ Mailing Matrix and required local forms, if any.

With the exception of Forms 122C-1 and 122C-2, which require you to do some math, the forms addressed in this chapter are fairly straightforward.

All together, these forms usually are referred to as your "bankruptcy petition," although technically your petition is only Form 101. (In case you're wondering, Forms 102, 104, and 105 aren't used in voluntary Chapter 13 bankruptcy filings. Form 103 is an application to pay the filing fee in installments, which Chapter 13 filers generally won't file since they won't qualify.)

Where to Get the Official Forms

You can find copies of the official bankruptcy forms on the website of the United States Courts at www.uscourts.gov/forms/bankruptcy-forms. You may want to take a look at the forms as we describe each one in this chapter, or review them before you visit an attorney.

Your bankruptcy attorney will have software for completing all of the official forms.

Local Forms and Requirements

In addition to the official forms that every bankruptcy court uses, your local bankruptcy court may require you to file one or two additional forms that it has developed. It may also have special requirements or rules for filing your petition. Your bankruptcy attorney should have the correct forms and be familiar with what your local court requires. You can also get these forms and requirements from the bankruptcy court clerk.

RESOURCE

Finding your local bankruptcy court's website. Go to the court locator at www.uscourts.gov/court-locator. You can either choose the "Court Websites" link or choose your state on the map.

Things to Think About When Reviewing the Forms

Here are some things to keep in mind as you provide your attorney with the necessary information to complete the forms or review the forms completed by your attorney.

Be ridiculously thorough. Always err on the side of giving too much information to your attorney and the court, rather than too little. If you leave information out, the bankruptcy trustee may become suspicious of your motives. If you leave creditors off the forms, the debts you owe these creditors won't be discharged—hardly the result you would want. If you intentionally or carelessly fail to list all your property and debts, or fail to accurately describe your recent property transactions, the court, upon a request by the trustee, may rule that you acted with fraudulent intent. It may deny your bankruptcy discharge altogether.

Don't worry about repetition. Sometimes different forms—or different questions on the same form—may ask for the same or overlapping information. Be sure to provide the information completely each time it is requested. Your attorney will do the same—too much information is never a sin in bankruptcy. There's an exception to this general rule for Forms 122C-1 and 122C-2. When completing these forms, be careful not to list expenses twice.

Be scrupulously honest. As part of your official bankruptcy paperwork, you must complete declarations, under penalty of perjury, swearing that you've been truthful. It's important to realize that you could be prosecuted for perjury if it's evident that you deliberately lied. If your attorney leaves something out, you will be responsible for the error, so thoroughly review the paperwork completed by your attorney before you sign. And never sign forms that have not been filled out. A good attorney will not ask you to do this.

For Married Filers

If you are married, you and your spouse will have to decide whether one of you should file alone or whether you should file jointly.

To make this decision, you'll first have to make sure that you're married in the eyes of the federal law (a trickier issue than you might think), and then consider how filing together or separately will affect your debts and property.

Are You Married?

If you were married with a valid state license, you are married for purposes of filing a joint petition—and you can skip down to "Should You File Jointly?" below. However, if you were not married with a license and ceremony, or you are in a domestic partnership or civil union, read on.

Common Law Marriage

Some states allow couples to establish "common law" marriages, which the states will recognize as valid marriages even though the couples do not have a state marriage license or certificate. Contrary to popular belief, a common law marriage is not created when two people simply live together for a certain number of years. In order to have a valid common law marriage, the couple must do all of the following:

- live together for a significant period of time (not defined in any state)
- hold themselves out as a married couple—typically this means using the same last name, referring to the other as "my husband" or "my wife," and filing a joint tax return, and
- intend to be married.

Alabama, Colorado, the District of Columbia, Georgia, Idaho, Iowa, Kansas, Montana, New Hampshire (but only for inheritance purposes), Ohio, Oklahoma, Pennsylvania, Rhode Island, South Carolina, Texas, and Utah recognize some form of common law marriage, but the rules for what constitutes a marriage differ from state to state. Several of these states will only recognize common law marriages that were created before a certain date.

If you live in one of these states and you meet your state's requirements for a common law marriage, you have the option to file jointly, if you wish.

Domestic Partnerships and Civil Unions

Several states offer couples the option of entering into civil unions or domestic partnerships, which extend many of the rights and obligations of marriage. If you are in a domestic partnership or civil union, you cannot file a joint bankruptcy petition.

> **CAUTION**
>
> **Domestic partnerships may affect property rights.** In some situations your domestic partnership or civil union may affect what property is in your bankruptcy estate and how the exemption laws apply to you. Talk to your attorney.

Should You File Jointly?

Unfortunately, there is no simple formula that will tell you whether it's better to file alone or with your spouse. In the end, it will depend on which option allows you to discharge more of your debts and keep more of your property. Here are some of the factors you and your attorney should consider:

- If you are living in a community property state in which most of your debts were incurred, and your property was acquired during marriage, you should probably file jointly. Even if only one spouse files, all community property is considered part of the bankruptcy estate—and any of the property that is nonexempt will determine the amount that nonpriority unsecured creditors will be paid (see Ch. 5 for more information). The same is generally true for debts—all community debts must be listed and most will be dealt with in the repayment plan even though only one spouse files.

- If you have recently married, you haven't acquired any valuable assets as a married couple, and one of you has all the debts, it may make sense for that spouse to file for bankruptcy alone (especially if the nonfiling spouse has good credit to protect).

- You may want to file alone if you and your spouse own property as tenants by the entirety, all of the debts are in your own name, and you live in a state that excludes such property from the bankruptcy estate when one spouse files. This is a particularly important consideration if your home

would be nonexempt property if both spouses filed—that could push the level of payment to your nonpriority unsecured creditors past the point that you could afford to pay in your repayment plan. If most, but not all, of the debts are in your name, you should check with a local attorney before filing to find out what the effect may be. It varies by location.

- If the exemption system you are using allows married spouses to double their exemptions, filing jointly may reduce the amount you would have to pay to your nonpriority unsecured creditors.

- If you are still married but separated, you may have to file alone if your spouse won't cooperate. But even so, the bankruptcy filing will likely affect your spouse and it may affect property you own together. If you are in this situation, talk to an attorney. If your debts and property are joint rather than separate, a joint filing would probably be to your best advantage.

Form 101—*Voluntary Petition for Individuals Filing For Bankruptcy*

The voluntary petition (Official Form 101) provides the court with basic information about you, where you live, and your bankruptcy case. It also lets the court know if you have completed the required prebankruptcy credit counseling or if you qualify for an exception to the requirement.

Here are a few other tidbits you'll have to provide on the voluntary petition:

Prior bankruptcy cases. You are required to disclose all prior bankruptcy cases filed by you (or your spouse if you're filing jointly) within the last eight years. You must also disclose any pending cases filed by your spouse. (Ch. 3 discusses when previous bankruptcy discharges bar a current discharge.)

Information about a pending eviction. As explained in Ch. 2, certain evictions are allowed to proceed after you file for bankruptcy, despite the automatic stay. The petition asks a series of questions to figure out whether your landlord has already gotten a judgment for possession (eviction order) and whether you might be able to postpone the eviction.

Credit counseling. You will need to tell the court whether you've completed the pre-bankruptcy credit counseling requirement.

Forms 101A and 101B: Forms Relating to Eviction Judgments

If your landlord has obtained a judgment for eviction, unlawful detainer, or possession against you, you must complete one or both of these forms. If you do not fit into this category, you do not complete or file these forms with the court. You can learn more about these forms in Ch. 2.

Forms 106A–J—Schedules

Forms 106A to 106J are a series of schedules that provides the trustee and court with a picture of your current financial situation.

CAUTION

Get the correct addresses for your creditors. On many of these schedules, you must provide your creditors' addresses. The address that you provide must be sufficient to give your creditor notice of the bankruptcy filing. If you have multiple addresses for the creditor, you can list more than one on the schedules (these additional addresses are for noticing purposes and are not additional debts). If a collection agent or attorney has been contacting you, list addresses for *both* the creditor and the collection agent or attorney. You can use the payment address and the address listed by the creditor on the bill for correspondence. If there is ever a question about whether the creditor knew about the bankruptcy filing, you will want to be able to point to the schedules to show that the creditor was listed at all of its addresses, as it could affect whether or not the debt owed to the creditor is discharged in your bankruptcy.

Schedule A/B: Property

This is where you list everything you own.

Part 1. Real Property

Here your attorney will list all the real estate you own as of the date you'll file the petition.

The Definition of "Real Property"

Real property—land and things permanently attached to land—includes more than just a house. It can also include unimproved land, vacation cabins, condominiums, duplexes, rental property, business property, mobile home park spaces, agricultural land, airplane hangars, and any other buildings permanently attached to land.

You may own real estate even if you can't walk on it, live on it, or get income from it. This might be true, for example, if:

- You own real estate solely because you are married to a spouse who owns real estate and you live in a community property state.
- Someone else lives on property that you are entitled to receive in the future under a trust agreement.

Your attorney will list leases and time-shares on a different schedule (Schedule G).

What Is Your Legal Interest in the Property?
Your attorney will also have to provide the legal definition for the interest you (or you and your spouse) have in each piece of real estate. The most common type of interest—outright ownership—is called "fee simple." Even if you still owe money on your mortgage, as long as you have the right to sell the house, leave it to your heirs, and make alterations, your ownership is fee simple. A fee simple interest may be owned by one person or by several people jointly. Normally, when people are listed on a deed as the owners—even if they own the property as joint tenants, tenants in common, or tenants by the entirety—the ownership interest is in fee simple. Other types of real property interests include:

- **Life estate.** This is the right to possess and use property only during your lifetime. You can't sell the property, give it away, or leave it to someone when you die. Instead, when you die, the property passes to whomever was named in the instrument (trust, deed, or will) that created your life estate. This type of ownership is usually created when the sole owner of a piece of real estate wants a surviving spouse to live on the property for the rest of his or her life, but then have the property pass to the owner's children. In this situation, the surviving spouse has a life estate. Surviving spouses who are beneficiaries of AB, spousal, or marital bypass trusts have life estates.

- **Future interest.** This is your right to own property sometime in the future. A common future interest is owned by a person who—under the terms of a deed or an irrevocable trust—will inherit the property when its current possessor dies. Simply being named in a will or revocable living trust doesn't create a future interest, because the person who signed the deed or trust can amend the document to cut you out.

- **Contingent interest.** This ownership interest doesn't come into existence unless one or more conditions are fulfilled. Wills sometimes leave property to people under certain conditions. If the conditions aren't met, the property passes to someone else. For instance, Emma's will leaves her house to John, provided that he takes care of her until her death. If John doesn't care for Emma, the house passes to Emma's daughter Jane. Both John and Jane have contingent interests in Emma's home.

- **Lienholder.** If you are the holder of a mortgage, deed of trust, judgment lien, or mechanics' lien on real estate, you have an ownership interest in the real estate.

- **Easement holder.** If you are the holder of a right to travel on or otherwise use property owned by someone else, you have an easement.

- **Power of appointment.** If you have a legal right, given to you in a will or transfer of property, to sell a specified piece of someone's property, that's called a power of appointment and should be listed.

- **Beneficial ownership under a real estate contract.** This is the right to own property by virtue of having signed a binding real estate contract. Even though the buyer doesn't yet own the property, the buyer does have a "beneficial interest"—that is, the right to own the property once the formalities are completed. For example, property buyers have a beneficial ownership interest in property while the escrow is pending.

Valuing Your Real Property

You'll have to provide the court with the actual value of your real estate ownership interest. Your attorney will help you do this. But if your ownership is the usual "fee simple," and you want to get a head start, or a good estimate, you can compare it to similar real estate parcels in your neighborhood that have recently sold (comparables). You can also get information about the value of your real estate from websites such as www.realtor.com, www.trulia.com, and www.zillow.com.

If you own the property with someone else who is not joining you in your bankruptcy, your attorney will list only your ownership share. And if your ownership interest is one of the unusual types, like a life estate, the value of that interest will have to be set by a real estate appraiser.

Mobile Home Note

If you own a mobile home in a park, use the value of the mobile home in its current location. If the park is located in a desirable area, the park adds value to your mobile home even though you may not have any ownership interest in the park itself. A mobile home that may not be worth much on its own could be worth quite a bit if it's sitting in a great location. The opposite may also be true.

Mortgages, Liens, and Other Debts Secured by the Property

Your attorney will list all mortgages, deeds of trust, home equity loans, liens (judgment liens, mechanics' liens, materialman's liens, tax liens, or the like) that are claimed against the property.

If you don't know the payoff balance on your mortgage, deed of trust, or home equity loan, call the lender. Your attorney can help you find out the existence and values of liens recorded against your property. Or your attorney may order a title search, which will identify liens. If you are trying to get this information before visiting an attorney, you can visit the land records office in your county and look up the parcel in the records; the clerk can show you how.

> **TIP**
>
> **You might be able to get rid of liens.** If you have liens on your property that are no longer secured by your equity in the property, you may be able to strip them off and reduce the amount of your current mortgage expense. For example, if your property is worth $250,000, and you owe $250,000 or more on your first mortgage, any other liens listed here can be "stripped off" in your Chapter 13 bankruptcy and reclassified as unsecured debt. If your total mortgage payment is $2,500, and $1,750 of that is attributable to your first mortgage, you can reduce your mortgage payment by the remaining $750, which will make a Chapter 13 plan more feasible (although you'll likely have to pay some portion of this amount during the plan). Better yet, the junior mortgage will we wiped out completely after you complete your case. Keep in mind, however, that as home equity rises, it's less likely that this option will be available to you. (For more on lien stripping, see Ch. 1.)

Parts 2 through 7. Personal Property

Here your attorney will list and value all of your personal property, including property that is security for a debt and property that is exempt. The form requires you to list your personal property by category:

- Part 2—vehicles
- Part 3—personal and household items
- Part 4—financial assets
- Part 5—business property
- Part 6—farm and commercial fishing assets
- Part 7—everything else.

For each item, you must describe the property, identify its location, and assign it a value.

Be honest and thorough. Don't give in to the temptation to "forget" any of your assets. Bankruptcy law doesn't give you the right to decide that an asset isn't worth mentioning. Even if, for example, you've decided that your CD collection is worthless given the advent of the iPod, you still have to list it. You can explain on the form why you think it's worthless. If you omit something and get caught, your case can be dismissed—or your discharge revoked—leaving you with no bankruptcy relief for your current debts.

List property that may not be part of the bankruptcy. In your schedules, list everything you own. If you believe that something you own is exempt and will not be part of your bankruptcy estate, you still need to list it. If you don't list it, you can't claim it as exempt. And if the trustee finds out, you may be barred from later claiming the exemption or you could be surcharged to pay the fees and costs associated with identifying it and bringing it into the bankruptcy.

Use the property's replacement value. When estimating your property's worth, use the replacement value—what it would cost to purchase similar used property from a retail seller, given its age and condition.

Your attorney will probably ask you to fill out a detailed questionnaire with lots of categories for property. In addition to the usual suspects (personal goods, real estate, cars, and the like), here are some other things that count as property:

- **Cash on hand, money in financial accounts.** Be sure to explain the source of any money—for example, from wages, Social Security payments, or child support. This helps in figuring out whether any of this money qualifies as exempt property.
- **Education IRAs and qualified state tuition plans.** They may not be part of the bankruptcy estate, but tell your attorney about them anyway.
- **ERISA-qualified pension plans, IRAs, and 401(k)s.** Although probably not part of your bankruptcy estate, tell your attorney about them anyway.
- **Stock options.**
- **Accounts receivable.** If you are a sole proprietor or an independent contractor, you likely will be owed money by one or more of your customers. These debts belong to your bankruptcy estate as of your filing date, and may be used by the trustee to compute payments to your nonpriority, unsecured creditors under your plan unless you are able to claim them as exempt.
- **Child support or alimony arrears**—that is, money that should have been paid to you but hasn't been paid.
- **Debts owed you from a property settlement incurred in a divorce or dissolution.**
- **Money owed to you and not yet paid,** including judgments you've obtained.
- **"Equitable or future interests."** This is property owned by someone else that you will get sooner or later. For instance, if your parents' irrevocable trust gives you their home when they die, you have an "equitable interest" in the home while they're alive. This does not apply if you are named in a will that can still be changed.
- **Contingent interests in property.** For example, you are named the remainder beneficiary of an irrevocable trust (a trust that can't be undone by the person who created it). It's contingent because you may or may not get anything from the trust—it all depends on whether there's anything left by the time it gets to you. This includes wills or revocable living trusts that name you as a beneficiary. Even though you don't have an absolute right to inherit under these documents (they can be changed at any time prior to the person's death), the trustee wants to know this information. An inheritance becomes part of your bankruptcy estate if the person dies within the six-month

period following your bankruptcy filing date—and can result in your plan being modified to increase payments to your nonpriority unsecured creditors.

- **Claims that you have against others that might end up in a lawsuit.** For instance, if you were recently rear-ended in an automobile accident and are struggling with whiplash, you may have a cause of action against the other driver (and that driver's insurer). If you fail to list this type of claim, you might not be allowed to pursue it after bankruptcy.
- **Intellectual property,** such as patents, copyrights, and trademarks.
- **Licenses and franchises.**
- **Customer lists.**
- **Crops.**

Schedule C: The Property You Claim as Exempt

On this form, your attorney will list all your property that is legally exempt. In most bankruptcies filed by individuals, all—or virtually all—of the debtor's property is exempt. If, however, you have any property that is not exempt, you will have to pay your nonpriority, unsecured creditors at least what they would have received from the sale of this property if you had used Chapter 7 (see Ch. 5 for more information).

On the form you will state which exemption system you wish to use. If you live in the District of Columbia or one of the states that allows you to use the federal exemptions (below), you and your attorney will decide which system is better for you—the state exemptions or the federal exemptions. See Ch. 5 for information on residency requirements for using a state's exemptions and tips on how to choose between the federal and state exemption systems. As explained in Ch. 5, if you are living in a state that offers the federal exemption system, but you haven't been there long enough to meet the two-year residency requirement for the state exemptions, you can choose the federal system.

States That Allow Use of the Federal Exemptions	
Alaska	New Jersey
Arkansas	New Mexico
Connecticut	New York
District of Columbia	Oregon
Hawaii	Pennsylvania
Kentucky	Rhode Island
Massachusetts	Texas
Michigan	Vermont
Minnesota	Washington
New Hampshire	Wisconsin

Note that if you didn't acquire your home at least 1,215 days (approximately 40 months) before filing, and you didn't purchase it from the proceeds of selling a home in the same state, your homestead exemption may be capped at $160,375 regardless of the exemption available in the state where your home is located. (See Ch. 5 for detailed information on the homestead exemption cap.)

Bankruptcy law allows married couples to double all exemptions unless the state expressly prohibits it. That means that each of you can claim the entire amount of each exemption, if you are both filing and your state permits it.

Schedule D: Creditors Who Hold Claims Secured by Property

In this schedule, your attorney will list all creditors who hold claims secured by your property. These include:

- holders of a mortgage or deed of trust on your real estate
- creditors who have won lawsuits against you and recorded judgment liens against your property

---

When Credit Card Debt Is Secured

Most credit card debts, including a card issued by a bank, gasoline company, or department store, are unsecured and will be listed on *Schedule E/F*. Some stores, however, claim to retain a security interest in all durable goods, such as furniture, appliances, electronics equipment, and jewelry, bought using the store's credit card. Also, if you were issued a bank or store credit card as part of a plan to restore your credit, you may have had to post property or cash as collateral for debts incurred on the card. If either of these exceptions applies to you, you'll list the credit card debt on *Schedule D*.

- doctors or lawyers to whom you have granted a security interest in the outcome of a lawsuit, so that the collection of their fees would be postponed (the expected court judgment is the collateral)
- contractors who have filed mechanics' or materialmen's liens on your real estate
- taxing authorities, such as the IRS, that have obtained tax liens against your property
- creditors with either a purchase-money or nonpurchase-money security agreement (see "What Is the Nature of the Lien" below), and
- all parties who are trying to collect a secured debt, such as collection agencies and attorneys.

If you originally had a secured debt but the collateral was repossessed or foreclosed prior to your bankruptcy filing, the remaining debt is no longer secured and you should list it on *Schedule E/F* (see below).

What Is the Nature of the Lien?

You will also have to list the type of lien held by the creditor. Your attorney will help you figure this out, but here are the possible answers:

- **First mortgage.** You took out a loan to buy your house. (This is a specific kind of purchase-money security interest.)
- **Purchase-money security interest.** You took out a loan to purchase the property that secures the loan—for example,

a car loan. The creditor must have perfected the security interest under the applicable state law, by filing or recording it with the appropriate agency. Otherwise, the creditor has no lien and your attorney will list the debt on *Schedule E/F* (unsecured debt) instead.

- **Nonpossessory, nonpurchase-money security interest.** You borrowed money for a purpose other than buying the collateral. This includes refinanced home loans, home equity loans, or loans from finance companies.

- **Possessory, nonpurchase-money security interest.** This is when a lienholder, like a pawnbroker, holds the property that you pledged to secure repayment.

- **Judgment lien.** This means someone sued you, won a court judgment, and recorded a lien against your property.

- **Tax lien.** This means a federal, state, or local government agency recorded a lien against your property for unpaid taxes.

- **Child support lien.** This means that another parent or a government agency has recorded a lien against your property for unpaid child support.

- **Mechanics' or materialmen's lien.** This means someone performed work on your real property or personal property (for example, a car) but didn't get paid, and recorded a lien on that property. Such liens can be an unpleasant surprise if you paid for the work, but your contractor didn't pay a subcontractor

who got a lien against your property. Payment is a defense, so if this happens, the debt should be listed as disputed.

> **CAUTION**
> **Only "perfected" liens" count.**
> Every state has a law specifying the procedures that must be followed to make a mortgage or another secured agreement or lien valid (called perfecting the lien). If a lien is not properly recorded, or the document creating the lien is defective in some way, it won't count as a lien in bankruptcy. And liens that have not been perfected won't reduce your equity in your home. So, if you are counting on a lien to bring your equity within the exemption amount for your state, make sure the lien has been perfected through recording and proper documentation.

Is the Claim Contingent, Unliquidated, or Disputed?

You also have to note on *Schedules D* and *E/F* whether a particular claim is contingent, unliquidated, or disputed. Here's what each of these terms means:

- **Contingent.** The claim depends on some event that hasn't yet occurred and may never occur. For example, if you guaranteed a loan, you won't be liable unless the principal debtor defaults. Your liability as guarantor is contingent upon the default. List the entire amount of the debt, but mark it as contingent.

  This may be different if you cosigned an obligation with someone else. Under that circumstance, you are both obligated on the debt together. Although you may have an understanding with the codebtor that he or she is primarily responsible, the creditor is not bound by this agreement and can pursue payment from either or both of you. However, a cosigned debt *is* contingent if the creditor has agreed to pursue payment from your codebtor first.

- **Unliquidated.** This means that a debt may exist, but the exact amount hasn't been determined. For example, if you were at fault in a car accident that resulted in damage to the other vehicle, but the dollar amount of the damages has not yet been determined, the claim is unliquidated. If a claim is unliquidated, you do not have to list a particular amount as being owed. Instead, you can list the amount as unknown and mark it as unliquidated.

- **Disputed.** A claim is disputed if you and the creditor do not agree about the existence or amount of the debt. For instance, suppose the IRS says you owe $10,000 and you say you owe $500. List the full amount of the claim, not the amount you think you owe, and mark it as disputed.

TIP

You're not admitting you owe the debt by listing it in your petition. You may think you don't really owe a contingent, unliquidated, or disputed debt, or you may not want to "admit" that you owe the debt. By listing a debt on this schedule, however, you aren't admitting anything. Instead, you are making sure that, if you owe the debt after all, it will be discharged in your bankruptcy (if it is dischargeable).

Schedule E/F: Creditors Who Have Unsecured Claims

This is where you will list the majority of your debts.

Part 1. Priority Unsecured Claims

This section identifies certain creditors who —with the exception of child support claims assigned to a government agency—are entitled to be paid in full in your Chapter 13 case.

Here is a list of priority claims. Claims with dollar amounts are current as of April 1, 2016 and are adjusted every three years:

- **Domestic support obligations.**
- **Wages, salaries, and commissions owed by you (as an employer)** to a current or former employee and were earned within 180 days before you filed your petition or within 180 days of the date you ceased your business. In certain circumstances, this also includes money owed to an independent contractor who did work for you. Only the first $12,850 owed per employee or independent contractor is a priority debt.
- **Contributions to employee benefit plans if you are an employer.**
- **Money owed to a grain producer or U.S. fisherman for fish or fish products**

if you are a farmer or fisherman. Only the first $6,150 owed per person is a priority debt.

- **Deposits by individuals.** If you took money from people who planned to purchase, lease, or rent goods or services from you that you never delivered, you may owe a priority debt. For the debt to qualify as a priority, the goods or services had to have been planned for personal, family, or household use. Only the first $2,775 owed (per person) is a priority debt.

- **Taxes and certain other debts owed to governmental units,** such as unsecured back taxes or fines imposed for driving under the influence of drugs or alcohol. Not all tax debts are unsecured priority claims. For example, if the IRS has recorded a lien against your real property, and the equity in your property fully covers the amount of your tax debt, your debt is a secured debt and will be listed on *Schedule D*.

- **Claims** against you for death or personal injury resulting from your operation of a motor vehicle or vessel while intoxicated from using alcohol, a drug, or another substance. This priority doesn't apply to property damage— only to personal injury or death.

As in *Schedule D*, you'll have to note whether someone else can be legally forced to pay your debt to a priority creditor (this would be a codebtor).

Part 2. Nonpriority Unsecured Claims

In this section, your attorney will list all creditors you haven't listed in *Schedule D* or Part 1 of *Schedule E/F*. This will include debts that are or may be nondischargeable, such as student loans. Even if you believe that you don't owe the debt or you owe only a small amount and intend to pay it off, you must include it here. It's essential that you list every creditor to whom you owe, or possibly owe, money. The only way you can legitimately leave off a creditor is if your balance owed is $0.

Creditors That Are Often Overlooked

One debt may involve several different creditors. Remember to tell your lawyer about:

- your ex-spouse, if you are still obligated under a divorce decree or settlement agreement to pay joint debts, turn any property over to your ex, or make payments as part of your property division
- anyone who has cosigned a promissory note or loan application with you
- any holder of a loan or promissory note that you cosigned for someone else
- the original creditor, anybody to whom the debt has been assigned or sold, and any other person (such as a bill collector or attorney) trying to collect the debt, and
- anyone who might sue you in the future because of a car accident, business dispute, or the like.

Inadvertent errors or omissions on this schedule can come back to haunt you. If you don't list a debt you owe to a creditor, it won't be discharged in your Chapter 13 bankruptcy. Also, leaving a creditor off the schedule might raise suspicions that you deliberately concealed information, perhaps to give that creditor preferential treatment in violation of bankruptcy rules.

Part 3. Notification to Others About an Already Listed Debt

In this section, your attorney will list additional people or entities that should get notice of your bankruptcy. This might include collection agencies or attorneys who represent creditors of debts that you listed in Parts 1 and 2 of this schedule.

Schedule G: Executory Contracts and Unexpired Leases

In this form, you list every executory contract or unexpired lease to which you're a party. "Executory" means the contract is still in force—that is, both parties are still obligated to perform important acts under it. Similarly, "unexpired" means that the contract or lease period hasn't run out—that is, it is still in effect.

Common examples of executory contracts and unexpired leases are:

- car leases
- residential leases or rental agreements
- business leases or rental agreements

- service contracts
- business contracts
- time-share contracts or leases
- contracts of sale for real estate
- personal property leases, such as equipment used in a beauty salon
- copyright and patent license agreements
- leases of real estate (surface and underground) for the purpose of harvesting timber, minerals, or oil, and
- agreements for boat docking privileges.

> **CAUTION**
>
> **If you're behind in your payments.** If you are not current on payments that were due under a lease or an executory contract, the delinquency should also be listed as a debt on *Schedules D* or *E/F*.

Schedule H: Your Codebtors

In *Schedules D* and *E/F*, you will identify those debts for which you have codebtors. You will also list those codebtors here. In addition, you must list the name and address of any spouse or former spouse who lived with you in Puerto Rico or in a community property state during the eight-year period immediately preceding your bankruptcy filing.

The most common codebtors are:

- cosigners
- guarantors (people who guarantee payment of a loan)

What Happens to Executory Contracts and Unexpired Leases in Chapter 13 Bankruptcy?

The trustee has until the confirmation hearing on your plan (see Ch. 10) to decide whether an executory contract or unexpired lease should be assumed (continued in force) as property of the estate or terminated (rejected). As a general matter, most leases and contracts are liabilities and are rejected by the trustee.

If the trustee rejects the contract or lease, you can assume or reject the contract or lease in your Chapter 13 plan. If your plan rejects the lease or contract, you and the other parties to the agreement are cut loose from any obligations, and any money you owe the creditor will be treated as an unsecured debt in your plan, even if the debt arose after your filing date. For example, say you are leasing a car when you file for bankruptcy. You want out of the lease. The car dealer cannot repossess the car until the trustee rejects the lease, or you reject the lease in your plan. During this period, you may be required to make payments to adequately protect the creditor for any loss in its secured position due to the depreciation of the vehicle between the time you file your Chapter 13 case and the date your plan is confirmed. The amount of adequate protection payments has been the subject of much debate. Some courts

set the amount as a percentage of the value of the vehicle, per month. Others require a prime-plus-interest calculation (often prime plus one to three points, based on risk) to determine the proper adequate protection for the creditor. Some courts require payment to the creditor directly prior to confirmation. Other courts require payment of the adequate protection amounts to the trustee. Some courts require the trustee to immediately disburse adequate protection payments to the creditor, while others direct the trustee to hold the funds pending confirmation.

As a practical matter, if you are planning to keep the vehicle and are paying outside the plan, you will need to continue making your regular payments. If you are paying through the plan, you will need to begin making your plan payments to the trustee. The payment amount in the plan is usually more than sufficient to adequately protect the creditors.

Bankruptcy law has special rules for executory contracts related to intellectual property (copyrights, patents, trademarks, or trade secrets), real estate, and time-share leases. If you are involved in one of these situations, discuss it with your lawyer.

- ex-spouses with whom you jointly incurred debts before divorcing
- joint owners of real estate or other property
- coparties in a lawsuit
- nonfiling spouses in a community property state (most debts incurred in a community property state by a nonfiling spouse during marriage are considered community debts, making that spouse equally liable with the filing spouse for the debts), and
- nonfiling spouses in states other than community property states, for debts incurred by the filing spouse for basic living necessities such as food, shelter, clothing, and utilities.

In Chapter 13 bankruptcy, your codebtors will be responsible for whatever portion of the debts that are left after you complete your plan. For instance if the debt they cosigned on is $2,000, and you pay 50% of the debt in your Chapter 13 bankruptcy, they will be responsible for the remaining $1,000.

Schedule I: Your Income

In this schedule, you calculate your current income (not your average monthly income in the six months before you file, which you calculated in Form 122C-1 in Ch. 4).

You'll have to provide information about how many dependents you have, your current employment, and your income, including:

- estimated monthly gross income
- estimated monthly overtime pay
- payroll deductions
- income from the operation of a business or farm
- income from real property (real estate rentals, leases, or licenses, such as mineral exploration, oil, and the like)
- interest you receive from bank or security deposits and other investments, such as stocks
- payments from alimony, maintenance, and child support
- amounts you receive from Social Security, SSI, public assistance, disability payments, veterans' benefits, unemployment compensation, workers' compensation, or any other government benefit (although you don't have to report Social Security benefits on Form 122C-1, you do have to include them here—and some courts may consider them in determining how much you have to pay into your Chapter 13 plan every month)
- the value of any food stamps you receive
- pension or retirement income, and
- any other monthly income you receive on a regular basis (such as royalty payments or payments from a trust).

You will also be required to describe any increase or decrease in income reasonably anticipated to occur within the year following the filing of this schedule.

Three Different Income Figures

In your bankruptcy papers, you will report three different income figures.

- Your "current monthly income" in Form 122C-1 (this is your average gross income for the six months before you file).
- Your actual income in *Schedule I* (this is your net income going forward).
- Your annual income in your *Statement of Financial Affairs* (see below).

The figures on Forms 122C-1 and 122C-2 and *Schedule I* may be different. For example, if you lost your job a couple of months ago and now earn much less in your new job, your income on *Schedule I* will be less than it is on Form 122C-1.

RELATED TOPIC

How your income figures help determine your plan payment. See "If Your Actual Income Is Different From Your 'Current Monthly' Income: *Hamilton v. Lanning*" in Ch. 5 to learn how these various income figures help determine your Chapter 13 plan payment.

Schedule J: Your Expenses

Schedule J is discussed in Ch. 5. On it, you list your average monthly expenses and then describe any increases or decreases you anticipate might occur within the year after you file for bankruptcy.

Form 106Sum—A *Summary of Your Assets and Liabilities and Certain Statistical Information*

This form helps the bankruptcy trustee and judge get a quick look at your bankruptcy filing. It summarizes the figures you entered onto your schedules and then lists your total assets and total liabilities.

Form 106Dec—*Declaration About an Individual Debtor's Schedules*

In this form, you are required to make a statement under penalty of perjury that the information in your schedules is true and correct. Deliberate lying is a major offense in bankruptcy and could cost you your bankruptcy discharge, a fine of up to $250,000, up to 20 years in prison, or both.

Form 107—*Your Statement of Financial Affairs for Individuals Filing for Bankruptcy*

This provides detailed information about financial transactions made within certain time periods prior to your bankruptcy filing. You'll have to include information about things such as your employment and business income, payments to creditors, repossessions, foreclosures, lawsuits, wage attachments, garnishments, gifts, losses (for example from fire, theft, or gambling), property transfers, closed financial accounts, safe deposit boxes, and property you are holding for someone else. If you want to know the details, take a look at the form. Some of the items merit extra discussion, which you'll find below.

This information is required because under certain circumstances, the trustee may be entitled to take back property that you transferred to others prior to filing for bankruptcy and sell it for the benefit of all your unsecured creditors. This rarely happens in Chapter 13 cases. Instead, if there are any avoidable (recoverable) transfers, the trustee will not recommend confirmation of your plan unless you contribute additional money to your plan to cover the amount of the transfer. In some cases, where the transfer was involuntary, such as the seizure of your bank account to pay a judgment, you might want to assist the trustee in recovering the transfer rather than contributing additional funds to your plan.

> **CAUTION**
>
> **Be honest and complete.** Don't give in to the temptation to leave out a transfer or two, assuming that the trustee won't find or go after the property. You must sign this form under penalty of perjury. And, if the trustee or a creditor discovers that you left information out, your bankruptcy may be dismissed and you may be prosecuted.

Payments to creditors. When you list payments to creditors, you must distinguish between regular creditors and insiders.

An insider is essentially a relative or close business associate. All other creditors are regular creditors.

If your debts are primarily consumer debts, you'll have to list all payments made to a regular creditor that total more than $600 if those payments were made to repay a loan, an installment purchase, or another debt during the 90 days before you file your bankruptcy petition.

If your debts are primarily business debts, you'll have to list all payments or other transfers made to a creditor within 90 days of your bankruptcy filing if the payments involve property that is worth $6,425 or more.

Everyone (whether your debts are primarily consumer or business) will have to list all payments or other transfers made to an insider creditor within one year before filing the bankruptcy petition. This includes alimony and child support payments.

The purpose of these questions is to find out whether you have preferred any creditor over others. If you have paid a regular creditor during the 90 days before you file, or an insider during the year before you file, and the amount paid is not for goods or services you recently bought and exceeds any regular monthly payment due to the creditor, the payment may be avoidable (recoverable) by the trustee. Exceptions to this rule are payments you made toward a domestic support obligation (child support or alimony) or payments you made under an alternative repayment schedule arranged by an approved nonprofit budget and credit counseling agency.

Losses. If the loss was for an exempt item, most states also exempt the insurance proceeds, up to the exemption limit for the item. If the item was not exempt, the trustee is entitled to the insurance proceeds, if any. In either case, list any insurance proceeds you've received or expect to receive. If you experience a loss after you file, you should promptly amend your papers, as this question applies to losses both before you file and afterwards.

Payments related to debt counseling or bankruptcy. If you paid an improperly high fee to an attorney, a bankruptcy petition preparer, a debt consultant, or a debt consolidator, the trustee may try to get some of it back to distribute to your creditors.

Other transfers. You must list all real and personal property that you've sold or given to someone else during the two years before you file for bankruptcy. Examples include selling or abandoning (junking) a car, pledging your house as security (collateral) for a loan, granting an easement on real estate, or trading property. This doesn't include gifts or property you've parted with as a regular part of your business or financial affairs.

Transfers to irrevocable trusts. You must list all transfers of your own property you have made in the previous ten years to a self-settled trust—a trust that you created, put your assets in, and made yourself the beneficiary. Self-settled trusts are commonly used by wealthy people to shield their assets from creditors and by disabled people to preserve their right to receive government benefits. In bankruptcy, however, assets placed in a self-settled trust will be considered nonexempt, which means you will have to pay your unsecured creditors at least the value of those assets. There is an exception that applies to assets placed in certain special needs trusts. (*In re Schultz,* 368 B.R 832 (D. Minn. 2007).)

Setoffs. A setoff is when a creditor, often a bank, uses money in a customer's account to pay a debt owed to the creditor by that customer. You must include any setoffs your creditors have made during the last 90 days.

Form 121: *Your Statement About Your Social Security Numbers*

This form requires you to list your full Social Security number(s). It will be available to your creditors and the trustee but, to protect your privacy, will not be part of your regular bankruptcy case file.

Forms 122C-1 and 122C-2: *Chapter 13 Statement of Your Current Monthly Income and Calculation of Commitment Period* and *Chapter 13 Calculation of Your Disposable Income*

In these forms, you'll calculate your "disposable income," which will determine whether you have enough income to propose a confirmable plan and help determine what your monthly plan payments will be. By comparing your income to your state's median income, you also calculate whether your plan will last three or five years.

More details about these forms are found in Ch. 5.

Form 2030: Disclosure of Compensation of Attorney for Debtor

Rule 2016(b) of the Bankruptcy Code requires that your attorney file a form disclosing the fees he or she is charging in your case. You might want to check the form to make sure what you are paying matches the fees listed on the form.

Mailing Matrix

As part of your bankruptcy filing, your attorney will submit a list of all of your creditors and their addresses so the court can give them official notice of your bankruptcy. This is called the mailing matrix.

Income Deduction Order

Many courts have local rules that require you to draft and submit an income deduction order with the rest of your Chapter 13 bankruptcy papers. This is an order the bankruptcy court sends to your employer. It requires the employer to automatically deduct your monthly repayment plan amount from your wages and send it to the bankruptcy court. Some courts will waive the requirement if you file a motion requesting waiver and show good cause.

The Chapter 13 Plan

Your Chapter 13 plan is the most important document in your bankruptcy case and it will control your financial life while your bankruptcy is pending. The plan tells the court and your creditors how you intend to repay your debts, including the total amount you will pay each month, how much each creditor will receive under your plan, and how long your plan will last. With a few exceptions, you and your creditors will be bound by it once the court confirms (approves) the plan.

In this chapter, we review all of the elements of the plan. Keep in mind that putting your plan together can be quite complicated, which is why most attorneys use computer software. Even then, experienced Chapter 13 bankruptcy attorneys often find it necessary to amend a plan more than once before it is confirmed.

New National Chapter 13 Plan Form

Until recently, an official bankruptcy plan form didn't exist. Instead, local courts created their plan forms without any particular guidance. Most courts—and even some trustees—had specific formats and specific language that debtors had to use.

Of course, the fact that the format of your plan would depend on where you filed added even more complexity to an already complicated task. And, given all the variations, it was impossible to cover all of the plan formats in this book or to keep up with local changes.

The problems created by the lack of uniformity were well known and the solution—a standardized form—recently arrived. All debtors who file for Chapter 13 bankruptcy after December 1, 2017, will use either the new official *Chapter 13 Plan* (Form 113) or a new local form that meets national standards.

Now, instead of requiring a debtor to draft the plan without guidance, forms must provide a space for each of the different ways a debt can be handled in a plan. For instance, there's a dedicated space for listing property that you intend to surrender, as well as discrete sections for the following payment types:

- monthly secured claim payments and arrearages
- claims subject to cramdown, lien stripping, or judicial lien avoidance
- priority debt payments, and
- any remaining claims.

Organizing debts by debt treatment (as opposed to nondescriptive "class" labels that required knowledge of the legal coding system) will make creating a plan easier and more intuitive. The uniform approach also allows us to provide detailed instructions you can use in any bankruptcy jurisdiction. (More below under "Drafting Your Plan.")

New Bankruptcy Rules

Also, new law allows debtors to use the plan in a way that can save time, legal costs, and potentially, expert witness fees. Specifically, it's no longer necessary for a debtor to file a separate motion asking the court to determine the value of property when the debtor would like to reduce a secured claim balance (a necessary part of the cramdown and lien-stripping process). Instead, the debtor can make the request within the plan.

As part of the procedure, the debtor must follow new notice requirements so that the court doesn't reduce a creditor's claim without the creditor's knowledge. For instance, the debtor must follow more stringent service guidelines to ensure the creditor receives a copy of the plan. Also, the debtor must check a box at the top of the Chapter 13 form that warns all involved of the debtor's intent to reduce a secured claim (or include a nonstandard provision in the plan).

If the debtor follows the new procedures correctly, a creditor who opposes the valuation request must file an objection to the plan confirmation at least seven days before the confirmation hearing (different rules apply to governmental creditors). If the creditor doesn't object, the court can confirm the plan—including the lower claim valuation—without receiving evidence of the value of the collateral. (Rule 3015.)

If the creditor files a timely objection, the matter will proceed as if the debtor made the valuation request using the motion procedure (the motion procedure is still available, too). The debtor would need to prove the value of the property in question through the testimony of an appraiser or similar expert.

Chapter 13 Plan Requirements

Here we lay out the basics of a Chapter 13 plan, as well as the steps you'll need to take to complete the *Chapter 13 Plan* (Form 113).

What You Must Pay

To propose a plan that the judge will confirm, you must show that you will have sufficient income, after deducting allowed expenses, to pay certain debts in full over the life of your plan. Some of these debts must be paid through your Chapter 13 plan—that is, you must pay the trustee, who will then pay the creditor (after collecting a fee). You can pay other debts outside of your plan.

 RELATED TOPIC

If you have not read Chs. 1 through 5, do so now. To understand what goes into your plan, you need to know the basic rules for calculating your income and expenses, how to classify your debts, which debts you have to repay in Chapter 13, and how to determine how long your plan will last. All of this information is explained in detail in Chs. 1 through 5.

How Long Your Plan Will Last

If your income is more than the median for your state and household size, your plan must last for five years (with a few exceptions). If your income is less than the median, your plan may last for only three years. If you are a lower-income filer and you don't have enough income to pay all mandatory debts within the three-year period, you can ask the court to extend your repayment time to five years. If you don't have enough income to pay your mandatory debts within five years, you can't propose a feasible Chapter 13 plan. (See Ch. 4 for more on calculating your base income and finding your state's median income.)

Proposing a Three-Year Plan If You Have No Disposable Income

If your income is above the state median, but you don't have any disposable income left after deducting living expenses and repayment of secured and priority debts, some courts will confirm a 36-month plan. Other courts won't do this unless your plan pays creditors 100% of what they are owed. The Fourth, Sixth, Eighth, Ninth, and Eleventh Circuit Courts of Appeal have all ruled that above-median debtors must propose a 60-month plan, even if they have no disposable income, unless creditors are paid 100%. Check with your attorney for the common practice in your area.

Paying Off Your Plan Early

What happens if you come into extra money before completing your plan? Can you pay off the plan balance early and be done with the bankruptcy? If your plan doesn't pay off your creditors in full, it's likely that your creditors and the trustee will oppose the early payoff,

and in many cases, the court will side with the creditors, although it will depend on the particular facts of your situation.

Appellate courts that have considered the issue have ruled that in most cases, the plan cannot be paid off early—even if you are paying all of the money that was due under the plan. Bankruptcy law gives the benefit of any income increases during the plan period to your creditors by requiring all of your disposable income during that period (three or five years) to be contributed to your plan. If you have more income than you thought you would when you filed your plan, you may be required to pay the extra money to the Chapter 13 trustee and continue making your plan payments until your plan period ends or you have paid your creditors in full, whichever is first.

But in some situations, the court might allow an early payoff on an individual case basis—especially if the payment funds are coming from a third party (such as from a friend or relative) or from exempt assets (you sell property that you're entitled to keep and use it to pay off the plan balance). However, the court might also consider the length of time remaining under your plan, the percentage being paid to unsecured creditors, and the likelihood of your income increasing during the remaining time in the plan period. If your job prospects are on the upswing, the court will be less likely to grant your request. In that case, if you choose to stay in your plan, you could end up paying your creditors more than you originally anticipated.

What You Must Pay Through Your Plan

At a minimum, you must pay all of the following debts through your Chapter 13 plan:

- all priority debts (paid in full, other than child support owed to a government agency)
- all secured debts that are contractually due to end within the life of your plan, such as a home equity loan (if the debt is no longer secured when you file, you can strip off the lien and classify the debt as unsecured, then treat it just like your other unsecured debts)
- all other secured debts that aren't contractually due within the life of your plan (for example, a government tax lien on your property)
- any arrearage necessary to keep your home, car, or other secured property
- all administrative expenses, including lawyer fees and trustee fees (trustee fees are usually about 10% of your plan payment), and
- the portion of your remaining debts that you can pay with your "disposable" income.

Calculating your disposable income can be difficult. Essentially, you start with your income and subtract the following: living expenses, payments you'll make through the plan (listed above), and ongoing payments you'll make outside of the plan. There are lots of rules about what counts as income and what you can and cannot subtract for expenses.

Also, the amount the lowest tier of creditors is entitled to receive is subject to an additional rule: You must pay them an amount equal to what your unsecured, nonpriority creditors would have received if you had filed for Chapter 7 bankruptcy. You figured this out in Ch. 5 when you calculated the amount creditors would have received from the sale of your nonexempt property. All of this is discussed in detail in Ch. 5.

What You Must Pay Either Through or Outside of Your Plan

As discussed above, there are certain payments that you must make through your plan. If a payment type is not listed above, you might be able to make it outside of the plan (that is, you pay the creditor directly rather than the trustee). Common examples include ongoing mortgage payments, ongoing car payments, and current expenses.

If you are required to make these payments through your Chapter 13 plan, you will have to pay significantly more over the life of your plan to cover the trustee's fee. Trustee's fees vary, but usually, they get about 10% on all payments made through the plan and nothing on payments made outside of the plan. If your current monthly mortgage payment is $2,000, the trustee will get approximately 10% of your monthly payment, or $200 a month, if you paid through your plan. This amount is added to what you're already paying into the plan. Over the life of a five-year plan, paying your mortgage this way would require you to pay an extra $12,000. The lesson here is that it makes a huge difference whether you pay through or outside of the plan.

Obviously, you should try to pay outside of the plan if at all possible. Unfortunately, courts are split on whether mortgages must be paid through the plan. Some courts allow you to make all current payments on secured debt, such as mortgages and car loans, outside of the plan. Other courts require that all secured debt be paid through the plan. Still, others require that you pay secured debt through the plan until you are finished paying any arrearages, and the payments have been brought current.

In some courts, there are strings attached to paying outside the plan. For example, in the middle district of Florida, you can make current mortgage payments outside the plan, but the court lifts the stay for these creditors. If there is a dispute, the creditor can proceed as if the bankruptcy had not been filed. Ask your bankruptcy attorney about the policy in your local court. Current payments for rent, utilities, Internet services, telephone, child support, taxes, and the like can—and should—be made outside of the plan.

Repayment of Unsecured Debts: Allowed Claims

Payments of unsecured debts under your Chapter 13 plan are based on "allowed claims" filed by your creditors. After receiving notice of your bankruptcy,

unsecured creditors that want a share of the payments you make under your plan must file a *Proof of Claim*.

On December 1, 2017, the *Proof of Claim* filing deadline changed. Instead of being due 90 days after the meeting of creditors, creditors now have only 70 days after the case is filed to submit a claim (government creditors receive additional time). (Rule 3002.) The change helps minimize the chance that a creditor will file a claim after the confirmation hearing—the hearing where the judge either confirms (approves) your repayment plan or sends you back to the drawing board to make changes. If the problem does arise, most courts, but not all, will resolve this scheduling conflict by continuing your confirmation hearing to a date beyond the claims bar date if your plan is dependent upon the amount of the claim filed. If the claim filed will only affect the amount of the unsecured claims, and your plan proposes to pay unsecured creditors pro rata (each creditor gets a proportional share of a predetermined amount), the fact that the claims bar date is after your confirmation hearing should not be a problem.

Once the creditor files a *Proof of Claim*, you or the trustee can object to the claim. You can argue that you don't owe the claim or that you owe less than the creditor says, for example. (Objections to creditors' claims are covered briefly in Ch. 11.) The court will then decide which claims are allowed. Creditors with allowed claims are entitled to share in the money you pay into your plan.

Which Creditors Must File a *Proof of Claim*

All creditors that wish payment from bankruptcy funds must file a *Proof of Claim* —both secured and unsecured creditors alike. However, a secured creditor that fails to file a *Proof of Claim* won't lose its lien rights. A secured creditor that goes unpaid will still be able to reclaim the property serving as collateral, sell it, and use the proceeds to pay down the outstanding loan balance. (If the automatic stay is in place, the creditor will need to obtain permission from the court first.)

For instance, suppose that your mortgage company doesn't file a *Proof of Claim* form. If you want to keep the house, you'll either file the *Proof of Claim* on behalf of the mortgage company (you have 30 days to do so) so the lender gets paid through the plan or you'll pay the mortgage outside of the plan.

Dealing With Unfiled Claims

If a creditor doesn't file a *Proof of Claim* within the deadline and you want to pay the creditor in your plan, you'll have 30 days after the deadline to file a claim for the creditor. You might want to do this if, for example, the debt cannot be discharged in bankruptcy. By filing a *Proof of Claim*, you can make sure that at least part of the debt gets paid through your plan, so you won't owe as much when your bankruptcy case ends. (Ch. 11 covers filing a *Proof of Claim* on behalf of a creditor.)

Discharging Student Loans in Your Plan

Student loans cannot be discharged in bankruptcy unless you file a separate lawsuit in the bankruptcy court (called an adversary proceeding) and convince the judge that repayment would impose an undue hardship (typically, a difficult thing to prove). In the past, some bankruptcy courts have confirmed Chapter 13 plans that contained specific provisions which effectively discharged student loans after completion of payments provided under the plan, without a showing of undue hardship as long as the student loan creditor did not object to confirmation.

This practice was denounced in a recent U.S. Supreme Court decision. Although the court upheld the discharge of the student loan, the Court found that even if a student loan creditor does not object to the discharge of the student loan or fails to appear at the hearing on the issue, the bankruptcy court still has a duty to determine whether repayment would pose an undue hardship on the debtor prior to plan confirmation.

Most likely your attorney will assume that each of your creditors will file a *Proof of Claim* promptly and will include the following in your plan:

- payment of administrative expenses including your attorneys' fees and the trustee's fee

- payment in full to all secured creditors, except those with long-term debt, meaning that the prebankruptcy payment schedule lasts longer than your plan, such as a mortgage (these creditors are listed in *Schedule D*, as explained in Ch. 7)
- payment in full to all priority creditors, except child support owed to a government agency (the creditors are listed in Part I of *Schedule E/F*, as explained in Ch. 7), and
- if there is money left, full or partial payment to all unsecured, nonpriority creditors (these are the creditors listed in Part 2 of *Schedule E/F*, as explained in Ch. 7). The amounts these creditors receive will depend on your disposable income.

Your plan will also state whether you intend to object to any of the debts listed on *Schedules D* or *E/F*. If one or more of those creditors don't file timely *Proofs of Claim*, you can either file *Proofs of Claim* on the creditors' behalf (see Ch. 11) or amend your plan to take the failure to file a claim into account.

Drafting Your Plan

You'll use the following instructions when drafting a plan on the official *Chapter 13 Plan* (Form 113). Filers using a local form can use the same instructions; however, the numbering system might be different. You'll find a sample official *Chapter 13 Plan* (Form 113) at the end of the chapter.

Part One

Debtors have powerful tools in Chapter 13 bankruptcy. You're allowed to modify certain contracts between yourself and a creditor in ways that could result in the creditor receiving substantially less money than required by the original contract. Because of this, if you intend to cramdown a claim or strip off a lien, you must check the appropriate box in this section. You'll also check the appropriate box if your plan includes a nonstandard provision (a payment arrangement that isn't provided for on the plan form).

Part Two

Your plan will state how much you will pay each month, how long the repayment period will be, the manner in which you will make the payments, and how you'll handle tax refunds. This section is set up in a way that allows you to create a payment schedule using other than monthly intervals. For instance, if you are a seasonal worker, or if you receive a yearly bonus, you can draft a plan that calls for creditor payments that correspond with the particular manner in which you're paid.

TIP

Your first plan payment. You must make the first monthly plan payment to the trustee within 30 days after you file for bankruptcy. Failure to make this payment can result in dismissal of your Chapter 13 case. If you intend to draft a plan that calls for an alternative payment arrangement, be sure to discuss it with an attorney.

Part Three

In this section, you'll list how you will pay your secured creditors (those creditors with claims backed by collateral, such as your mortgage or car payment). There are five different ways that you can handle secured creditors, and each approach is dealt with in a separate section.

3.1 Here you'll include secured claims that you don't intend to reduce. Secured claims that will outlive your plan don't need to be listed if you're current—you can pay these on your own to keep the trustee's fee down. If you owe an arrearage on any secured debt, you'll list the total arrearage amount due, indicate how much you'll pay toward the arrearage each month (it must be paid entirely within the plan), and explain whether you or the trustee will make the payment by checking the appropriate box.

Also, be aware that you'll need to pay the following secured claims in full: tax liens, mechanics' liens, judicial liens that can't be avoided (see 3.4, below), and secured claims under a contract that expires during the plan period. For example, if you owe $20,000 on a claim for a secured debt under a contract that will expire in three years, and you are drafting a five-year plan, the claim must be paid in full.

3.2 If you intend to ask the court to reduce the amount of a secured claim to the actual value of the collateral, you'll list the claim here. In other words, this is where you list loans you intend to cram down or claims with liens attached that you intend to strip. As a general rule, you can't cram down your primary residential mortgage (commonly known as the "first"), but you might be able to strip off a wholly unsecured second or third residential mortgage or reduce the mortgage on a nonresidential property. (See Ch. 1 for more details.) You can also use this section to reduce the debt of any personal property other than a vehicle you purchased for your own use. Keep in mind that when you successfully cram down a claim, you'll have to pay the entire secured balance (the amount the court says the property is worth) within your plan. This rule often makes reducing nonresidential mortgages cost prohibitive. The amount declared unsecured gets paid with your other unsecured debt (which usually has no impact on your plan given you must pay all of your disposable income toward these claims anyway). (Read about how you might be able to avoid an evidentiary hearing in the "New Bankruptcy Rules" section above.)

3.3 You won't be able to use section 3.2 to reduce a vehicle loan that exceeds the value of the car you use for personal purposes because of special rules that apply. But you can cram down the loan if you owned it more than 910 days before filing. You'll list any vehicle that meets that criterion here. For example, suppose that you owe $10,000 on your car that is worth only $6,000. You can modify the claim so that the secured portion is reduced to the value of the property ($6,000 in this case). The rest of the claim ($4,000 in this example) is treated as an unsecured, nonpriority claim. (See Ch. 1 for more cramdown information.)

3.4 If a judicial lien (a property interest created by a court judgment) or another type of security interest interferes with your right to protect certain property with an exemption, you can ask the court to avoid the lien by listing the claim here. You'll have to serve the plan in the same manner that you'd serve a summons and complaint and check the appropriate warning box at the top of the plan.

3.5 You don't have to keep secured property. If you'd prefer to surrender it to the lender (and essentially not pay anything for it in your plan), list it here. For instance, you might need to surrender a house if you can't afford to catch up the arrearage payments in your plan. Also, it's a good idea to return a car you can't afford or don't want anymore. In most courts, any deficiency balance (the amount still due after the lender sells the property) must

be included with your other unsecured, nonpriority debt. This usually won't affect your budget or plan payment since you're required to devote 100% of your disposable income to your plan payments anyway.

Determining Interest Rates for Secured Debts in Chapter 13 Plans

In 2004, the U.S. Supreme Court announced a formula to be used in setting interest rates for secured claims other than mortgages in Chapter 13 cases. (*Till v. SCS Credit Corporation*, 541 U.S 465 (2004).) The Court said the rate should be the national prime rate, adjusted upward slightly for the additional risk of lending to a bankruptcy debtor. In that case, the risk was deemed to be 1.5% over prime. Lower courts have generally approved adjustments in the range of 1% to 3% over prime. The 2005 bankruptcy law did not address the *Till* case, so its holding still stands.

The bankruptcy court in your district may already have a rate stated on its standard Chapter 13 plan form. If your court has not set an interest rate, you and your creditor will have to negotiate a rate or ask the court to decide, using the formula announced by the Supreme Court.

Part Four

You'll list priority claims here. Usually, you don't pay interest on priority debts, but you must pay them in full over the course of the plan. Here's what you'll include in each section:

- 4.2 – trustee's fees
- 4.3 – attorneys' fees you still owe
- 4.4 – all priority claims other than attorneys' fees and domestic support obligations
- 4.5 – domestic support obligations.

You can propose to pay less than the full amount of a domestic support obligation owed a government entity, but not less than the creditor would have received in a Chapter 7 bankruptcy.

Part Five

All remaining claims—called "nonpriority unsecured claims"—go in this section.

The information you'll need to provide will include :

- the total amount you owe on these claims
- the plan amount for these claims (expressed in total dollars or as a percentage paid)
- whether you intend to continue paying a long-term installment amount (a long-term installment agreement is an unsecured debt with a payment period that extends beyond the plan period, such as a student loan or an unsecured personal loan with an extended payment term)
- whether you will cure any past-due balance, and

- the total amount your unsecured, nonpriority creditors would receive from the sale of your nonexempt property in a Chapter 7 case (see Ch. 4).

How much your nonpriority unsecured creditors get paid is determined by the amount of money you have left after your disposable income is used to pay administrative expenses, priority claims, and secured debts, including arrearages.

Space is available to list claims separately if needed. This is where you'd propose to pay a codebtor claim. (11 U.S.C. § 1322(b)(1).) Speak with an attorney about whether your court will allow you to pay a higher percentage for a codebtor claim (many filers prefer to pay such claims in full to protect the interests of a codebtor).

Part Six

You'll list any executory contracts or unexpired leases that you'd like to keep in this section. These are contracts that haven't been completed, such as a gym membership that you pay for monthly. If you fail to list it here, it will be deemed rejected.

Part Seven

When you file for bankruptcy, all of your property (with a few exceptions) will become part of the bankruptcy estate. Here, you'll indicate when ownership will revest with you—usually at the completion of the plan.

Part Eight

You'll include any nonstandard provisions here. To be valid, you'll need to check the appropriate warning box at the top of the plan.

Part Nine

Your attorney must sign certifying that the plan wording wasn't altered (with the exception of any nonstandard provisions.) You don't have to sign if you're represented by counsel. If you're filing without an attorney, you'll execute the certification.

Local Plan Language

In the past, most local plans have included standard language that reflects policies of the local district. As explained earlier, local plans must now contain the elements discussed above. Still, the local plan you'll be required to use might contain additional provisions. For instance, it might contain a requirement that you state whether you are seeking a mortgage modification (either outside the bankruptcy or as part of a loss mitigation program that exists in your court). Here are other issues that have been left to you and your local court to decide.

Adequate Protection Payments

The official *Chapter 13 Plan* doesn't address "adequate protection payments," leaving the decision of whether such payments need to be made to the local courts.

Creditors whose claims are secured by automobiles and personal property are entitled to "adequate protection payments" before your plan is confirmed and they start receiving payments under the plan. Adequate protection is intended to protect these creditors against any reduction in the value of their collateral, which often occurs as a result of depreciation. The payments must be applied to the debt. However, courts are not in agreement on how much these payments should be, how they should be calculated, or whether you must make the payment to the creditor directly or through the trustee.

Some courts require you to identify the portion of your plan payment that serves as adequate protection preconfirmation. Others require you to make adequate protection payments to the creditor directly and reduce the amount you pay to the trustee before the plan is confirmed. Many courts have local rules setting out the local requirements. You will need to follow the procedure in your area.

Order of Payment

The official *Chapter 13 Plan* also doesn't determine how the trustee will prioritize payments to creditors under your plan. Usually, the order of payment is as follows, although secured creditors may receive payments throughout the plan period:

- the trustee's fee
- domestic support orders
- administrative expenses (such as attorneys' fees) in an amount up to 10% of each payment until paid in full
- ongoing payments on secured debts that are made through your plan (as opposed to those you pay directly to the creditor), and
- all other claims.

The plan will not pay unsecured claims until all secured and priority claims are paid in full.

Where to Find Your Plan

If the bankruptcy court in your area has a particular form that must be used, it is likely available on the court's website. You can find your court's website by using the Federal Court Locator at www.uscourts. gov/court-locator. You can check your court's local rules and guidelines and also find the website of your local court's standing Chapter 13 trustee.

Even though the new form requirements are a welcome improvement, for most, drafting a confirmable Chapter 13 plan will remain complicated. Past statistics have shown that *pro se* filers (those without attorneys) are rarely successful, and it's likely that this trend will continue. To get the best possible outcome, and to use the sophisticated tools available to you in Chapter 13 to your advantage, it is almost always best to hire an attorney in your area who has experience in these matters. In most cases, you can pay a large part, or sometimes all, of your attorneys' fees through your Chapter 13 plan.

Sample Plan

Here is a sample Chapter 13 repayment plan using the official *Chapter 13 Plan* (Form 113). You'll complete your plan using your court's local form unless your court has opted to use the official *Chapter 13 Plan*.

The debtor is Carrie Ann Edwards, a divorced mother of two children who lives in Lakeport, California. Carrie was forced into Chapter 13 bankruptcy when faced with possible foreclosure on her mortgage because of an arrearage (which she can pay off over time through her Chapter 13 plan). She owns a car that she bought four years ago. It's currently valued at $8,000 although the balance on the car loan is $15,000. In Chapter 13, she can cram down the secured loan to $8,000. The remaining $7,000 becomes a nonpriority, unsecured debt. Finally, she will surrender her second car, a 2009 Mitsubishi Galant, to the lender.

Chapter 13 Plan

Debtor ___Edwards, Carrie Anne_____   Case number _____

3.2   Request for valuation of security, payment of fully secured claims, and modification of undersecured claims. *Check one.*

☒ **None.** *If "None" is checked, the rest of § 3.2 need not be completed or reproduced.*

The remainder of this paragraph will be effective only if the applicable box in Part 1 of this plan is checked.

☐ The debtor(s) request that the court determine the value of the secured claims listed below. For each non-governmental secured claim listed below, the debtor(s) state that the value of the secured claim should be as set out in the column headed *Amount of secured claim*. For secured claims of governmental units, unless otherwise ordered by the court, the value of a secured claim listed in a proof of claim filed in accordance with the Bankruptcy Rules controls over any contrary amount listed below. For each listed claim, the value of the secured claim will be paid in full with interest at the rate stated below.

The portion of any allowed claim that exceeds the amount of the secured claim will be treated as an unsecured claim under Part 5 of this plan. If the amount of a creditor's secured claim is listed below as having no value, the creditor's allowed claim will be treated in its entirety as an unsecured claim under Part 5 of this plan. Unless otherwise ordered by the court, the amount of the creditor's total claim listed on the proof of claim controls over any contrary amounts listed in this paragraph.

The holder of any claim listed below as having value in the column headed *Amount of secured claim* will retain the lien on the property interest of the debtor(s) or the estate(s) until the earlier of:

(a)   payment of the underlying debt determined under nonbankruptcy law, or

(b)   discharge of the underlying debt under 11 U.S.C. § 1328, at which time the lien will terminate and be released by the creditor.

Name of creditor	Estimated amount of creditor's total claim	Collateral	Value of collateral	Amount of claims senior to creditor's claim	Amount of secured claim	Interest rate	Monthly payment to creditor	Estimated total of monthly payments
_____	$_____	_____	$_____	$_____	$_____	___%	$_____	$_____
_____	$_____	_____	$_____	$_____	$_____	___%	$_____	$_____

Insert additional claims as needed.

3.3   Secured claims excluded from 11 U.S.C. § 506.

Check one.

☐ **None.** *If "None" is checked, the rest of § 3.3 need not be completed or reproduced.*

☒ The claims listed below were either:

(1)   incurred within 910 days before the petition date and secured by a purchase money security interest in a motor vehicle acquired for the personal use of the debtor(s), or

(2)   incurred within 1 year of the petition date and secured by a purchase money security interest in any other thing of value.

These claims will be paid in full under the plan with interest at the rate stated below. These payments will be disbursed either by the trustee or directly by the debtor(s), as specified below. Unless otherwise ordered by the court, the claim amount stated on a proof of claim filed before the filing deadline under Bankruptcy Rule 3002(c) controls over any contrary amount listed below. In the absence of a contrary timely filed proof of claim, the amounts stated below are controlling. The final column includes only payments disbursed by the trustee rather than by the debtor(s).

Name of creditor	Collateral	Amount of claim	Interest rate	Monthly plan payment	Estimated total payments by trustee
GMAC	vehicle	$ 8,000	7 %	$ 158.41 Disbursed by: ☒ Trustee ☐ Debtor(s)	$ 9,504.60
_____	_____	$_____	____ %	$_____ Disbursed by: ☐ Trustee ☐ Debtor(s)	$_____

Chapter 13 Plan (continued)

Debtor _____Edwards, Carrie Anne_____   Case number _____

2.2 Regular payments to the trustee will be made from future income in the following manner:

Check all that apply.

☒ Debtor(s) will make payments pursuant to a payroll deduction order.

☐ Debtor(s) will make payments directly to the trustee.

☐ Other (specify method of payment):_____.

2.3 Income tax refunds.

Check one.

☐ Debtor(s) will retain any income tax refunds received during the plan term.

☒ Debtor(s) will supply the trustee with a copy of each income tax return filed during the plan term within 14 days of filing the return and will turn over to the trustee all income tax refunds received during the plan term.

☐ Debtor(s) will treat income tax refunds as follows:

_____

_____

2.4 Additional payments.

Check one.

☒ **None.** *If "None" is checked, the rest of § 2.4 need not be completed or reproduced.*

☐ Debtor(s) will make additional payment(s) to the trustee from other sources, as specified below. Describe the source, estimated amount, and date of each anticipated payment.

_____

_____

2.5 The total amount of estimated payments to the trustee provided for in §§ 2.1 and 2.4 is $ _____.

Part 3:	Treatment of Secured Claims

3.1 Maintenance of payments and cure of default, if any.

Check one.

☐ **None.** *If "None" is checked, the rest of § 3.1 need not be completed or reproduced.*

☒ The debtor(s) will maintain the current contractual installment payments on the secured claims listed below, with any changes required by the applicable contract and noticed in conformity with any applicable rules. These payments will be disbursed either by the trustee or directly by the debtor(s), as specified below. Any existing arrearage on a listed claim will be paid in full through disbursements by the trustee, with interest, if any, at the rate stated. Unless otherwise ordered by the court, the amounts listed on a proof of claim filed before the filing deadline under Bankruptcy Rule 3002(c) control over any contrary amounts listed below as to the current installment payment and arrearage. In the absence of a contrary timely filed proof of claim, the amounts stated below are controlling. If relief from the automatic stay is ordered as to any item of collateral listed in this paragraph, then, unless otherwise ordered by the court, all payments under this paragraph as to that collateral will cease, and all secured claims based on that collateral will no longer be treated by the plan. The final column includes only payments disbursed by the trustee rather than by the debtor(s).

Name of creditor	Collateral	Current installment payment (including escrow)	Amount of arrearage (if any)	Interest rate on arrearage (if applicable)	Monthly plan payment on arrearage	Estimated total payments by trustee
Grand Junction Mortgage	residence___	$_____ Disbursed by: ☒ Trustee ☐ Debtor(s)	$ 6,000	7 %	$ 118.81	$ 7,128.37
_____	_____	$_____ Disbursed by: ☐ Trustee ☐ Debtor(s)	$_____	_____%	$_____	$_____

Insert additional claims as needed.

Chapter 13 Plan (continued)

Debtor   Edwards, Carrie Anne   Case number _____

3.2 **Request for valuation of security, payment of fully secured claims, and modification of undersecured claims.** *Check one.*

   ☒ **None.** *If "None" is checked, the rest of § 3.2 need not be completed or reproduced.*

    The remainder of this paragraph will be effective only if the applicable box in Part 1 of this plan is checked.

   ❑ The debtor(s) request that the court determine the value of the secured claims listed below. For each non-governmental secured claim listed below, the debtor(s) state that the value of the secured claim should be as set out in the column headed *Amount of secured claim*. For secured claims of governmental units, unless otherwise ordered by the court, the value of a secured claim listed in a proof of claim filed in accordance with the Bankruptcy Rules controls over any contrary amount listed below. For each listed claim, the value of the secured claim will be paid in full with interest at the rate stated below.

    The portion of any allowed claim that exceeds the amount of the secured claim will be treated as an unsecured claim under Part 5 of this plan. If the amount of a creditor's secured claim is listed below as having no value, the creditor's allowed claim will be treated in its entirety as an unsecured claim under Part 5 of this plan. Unless otherwise ordered by the court, the amount of the creditor's total claim listed on the proof of claim controls over any contrary amounts listed in this paragraph.

    The holder of any claim listed below as having value in the column headed *Amount of secured claim* will retain the lien on the property interest of the debtor(s) or the estate(s) until the earlier of:

    (a)   payment of the underlying debt determined under nonbankruptcy law, or

    (b)   discharge of the underlying debt under 11 U.S.C. § 1328, at which time the lien will terminate and be released by the creditor.

Name of creditor	Estimated amount of creditor's total claim	Collateral	Value of collateral	Amount of claims senior to creditor's claim	Amount of secured claim	Interest rate	Monthly payment to creditor	Estimated total of monthly payments
_____	$_____	_____	$____	$_____	$____	__%	$____	$_____
_____	$_____	_____	$____	$_____	$____	__%	$____	$_____

    Insert additional claims as needed.

3.3 **Secured claims excluded from 11 U.S.C. § 506.**

  Check one.

   ❑ **None.** *If "None" is checked, the rest of § 3.3 need not be completed or reproduced.*

   ☒ The claims listed below were either:

    (1)   incurred within 910 days before the petition date and secured by a purchase money security interest in a motor vehicle acquired for the personal use of the debtor(s), or

    (2)   incurred within 1 year of the petition date and secured by a purchase money security interest in any other thing of value.

    These claims will be paid in full under the plan with interest at the rate stated below. These payments will be disbursed either by the trustee or directly by the debtor(s), as specified below. Unless otherwise ordered by the court, the claim amount stated on a proof of claim filed before the filing deadline under Bankruptcy Rule 3002(c) controls over any contrary amount listed below. In the absence of a contrary timely filed proof of claim, the amounts stated below are controlling. The final column includes only payments disbursed by the trustee rather than by the debtor(s).

Name of creditor	Collateral	Amount of claim	Interest rate	Monthly plan payment	Estimated total payments by trustee
GMAC	vehicle	$ 8,000	7 %	$ 158.41 Disbursed by: ☒ Trustee ❑ Debtor(s)	$ 9,504.60
_____	_____	$_____	____%	$_____ Disbursed by: ❑ Trustee ❑ Debtor(s)	$_____

    Insert additional claims as needed.

Chapter 13 Plan (continued)

Debtor ___Edwards, Carrie Anne_____   Case number _____

3.4 Lien avoidance.

Check one.

☒ **None.** *If "None" is checked, the rest of § 3.4 need not be completed or reproduced.*

The remainder of this paragraph will be effective only if the applicable box in Part 1 of this plan is checked.

☐ The judicial liens or nonpossessory, nonpurchase money security interests securing the claims listed below impair exemptions to which the debtor(s) would have been entitled under 11 U.S.C. § 522(b). Unless otherwise ordered by the court, a judicial lien or security interest securing a claim listed below will be avoided to the extent that it impairs such exemptions upon entry of the order confirming the plan. The amount of the judicial lien or security interest that is avoided will be treated as an unsecured claim in Part 5 to the extent allowed. The amount, if any, of the judicial lien or security interest that is not avoided will be paid in full as a secured claim under the plan. See 11 U.S.C. § 522(f) and Bankruptcy Rule 4003(d). *If more than one lien is to be avoided, provide the information separately for each lien.*

Information regarding judicial lien or security interest	Calculation of lien avoidance		Treatment of remaining secured claim
Name of creditor _____	a. Amount of lien	$_____	**Amount of secured claim after avoidance** (line a minus line f) $_____
	b. Amount of all other liens	$_____	
Collateral _____	c. Value of claimed exemptions	+ $_____	**Interest rate** (if applicable)
	d. Total of adding lines a, b, and c	$_____	_____ %
Lien identification (such as judgment date, date of lien recording, book and page number) _____ _____	e. Value of debtor(s)' interest in property	– $_____	**Monthly payment on secured claim** $_____
	f. Subtract line e from line d.	$_____	**Estimated total payments on secured claim** $_____
	Extent of exemption impairment *(Check applicable box)*: ☐ **Line f is equal to or greater than line a.** The entire lien is avoided. *(Do not complete the next column.)* ☐ **Line f is less than line a.** A portion of the lien is avoided. *(Complete the next column.)*		

Insert additional claims as needed.

3.5 Surrender of collateral.

Check one.

☐ **None.** *If "None" is checked, the rest of § 3.5 need not be completed or reproduced.*

☒ The debtor(s) elect to surrender to each creditor listed below the collateral that secures the creditor's claim. The debtor(s) request that upon confirmation of this plan the stay under 11 U.S.C. § 362(a) be terminated as to the collateral only and that the stay under § 1301 be terminated in all respects. Any allowed unsecured claim resulting from the disposition of the collateral will be treated in Part 5 below.

Name of creditor	Collateral
ZYX Auto Financing	2009 Mitsubishi Galant

Insert additional claims as needed.

Chapter 13 Plan (continued)

Debtor Edwards, Carrie Anne _____   Case number _____

4.1 General

Trustee's fees and all allowed priority claims, including domestic support obligations other than those treated in § 4.5, will be paid in full without postpetition interest.

4.2 Trustee's fees

Trustee's fees are governed by statute and may change during the course of the case but are estimated to be ___10___% of plan payments; and during the plan term, they are estimated to total $__2,970____.

4.3 Attorney's fees

The balance of the fees owed to the attorney for the debtor(s) is estimated to be $_____.

4.4 Priority claims other than attorney's fees and those treated in § 4.5.

Check one.

❑ **None.** *If "None" is checked, the rest of § 4.4 need not be completed or reproduced.*

☒ The debtor(s) estimate the total amount of other priority claims to be _$7,470_____.

4.5 Domestic support obligations assigned or owed to a governmental unit and paid less than full amount.

Check one.

☒ **None**. *If "None" is checked, the rest of § 4.5 need not be completed or reproduced.*

❑ The allowed priority claims listed below are based on a domestic support obligation that has been assigned to or is owed to a governmental unit and will be paid less than the full amount of the claim under 11 U.S.C. § 1322(a)(4). *This plan provision requires that payments in § 2.1 be for a term of 60 months; see 11 U.S.C. § 1322(a)(4).*

Name of creditor	Amount of claim to be paid
_____	$_____
_____	$_____

Insert additional claims as needed.

5.1 Nonpriority unsecured claims not separately classified.

Allowed nonpriority unsecured claims that are not separately classified will be paid, pro rata. If more than one option is checked, the option providing the largest payment will be effective. *Check all that apply.*

☒ The sum of $ _5,597.03__.

❑ _____% of the total amount of these claims, an estimated payment of $_____.

❑ The funds remaining after disbursements have been made to all other creditors provided for in this plan.

If the estate of the debtor(s) were liquidated under chapter 7, nonpriority unsecured claims would be paid approximately $___0_____. Regardless of the options checked above, payments on allowed nonpriority unsecured claims will be made in at least this amount.

Chapter 13 Plan (continued)

Debtor **Edwards, Carrie Anne** _____   Case number _____

5.2 Maintenance of payments and cure of any default on nonpriority unsecured claims. *Check one.*

☒ **None.** *If "None" is checked, the rest of § 5.2 need not be completed or reproduced.*

☐ The debtor(s) will maintain the contractual installment payments and cure any default in payments on the unsecured claims listed below on which the last payment is due after the final plan payment. These payments will be disbursed either by the trustee or directly by the debtor(s), as specified below. The claim for the arrearage amount will be paid in full as specified below and disbursed by the trustee. The final column includes only payments disbursed by the trustee rather than by the debtor(s).

Name of creditor	Current installment payment	Amount of arrearage to be paid	Estimated total payments by trustee
_____	$ _____ Disbursed by: ☐ Trustee ☐ Debtor(s)	$ _____	$ _____
_____	$ _____ Disbursed by: ☐ Trustee ☐ Debtor(s)	$ _____	$ _____

Insert additional claims as needed.

5.3 Other separately classified nonpriority unsecured claims. *Check one.*

☒ **None.** *If "None" is checked, the rest of § 5.3 need not be completed or reproduced.*

☐ The nonpriority unsecured allowed claims listed below are separately classified and will be treated as follows.

Name of creditor	Basis for separate classification and treatment	Amount to be paid on the claim	Interest rate (if applicable)	Estimated total amount of payments
_____	_____	$ _____	_____ %	$ _____
_____	_____	$ _____	_____ %	$ _____

Insert additional claims as needed.

Part 6:   Executory Contracts and Unexpired Leases

6.1 The executory contracts and unexpired leases listed below are assumed and will be treated as specified. All other executory contracts and unexpired leases are rejected. *Check one.*

☒ **None.** *If "None" is checked, the rest of § 6.1 need not be completed or reproduced.*

☐ **Assumed items.** Current installment payments will be disbursed either by the trustee or directly by the debtor(s), as specified below, subject to any contrary court order or rule. Arrearage payments will be disbursed by the trustee. The final column includes only payments disbursed by the trustee rather than by the debtor(s).

Chapter 13 Plan (continued)

Debtor ___Edwards, Carrie Anne_____   Case number _____

Name of creditor	Description of leased property or executory contract	Current installment payment	Amount of arrearage to be paid	Treatment of arrearage (Refer to other plan section if applicable)	Estimated total payments by trustee
_____	_____	$_____ Disbursed by: ☐ Trustee ☐ Debtor(s)	$_____	_____ _____	$_____
_____	_____	$_____ Disbursed by: ☐ Trustee ☐ Debtor(s)	$_____	_____ _____	$_____

Insert additional contracts or leases as needed.

Part 7:   Vesting of Property of the Estate

7.1 Property of the estate will vest in the debtor(s) upon

Check the applicable box:

☐ plan confirmation.

☒ entry of discharge.

☐ other: _____.

Part 8:   Nonstandard Plan Provisions

8.1 Check "None" or List Nonstandard Plan Provisions

☒ **None.** *If "None" is checked, the rest of Part 8 need not be completed or reproduced.*

Under Bankruptcy Rule 3015(c), nonstandard provisions must be set forth below. A nonstandard provision is a provision not otherwise included in the Official Form or deviating from it. Nonstandard provisions set out elsewhere in this plan are ineffective.

The following plan provisions will be effective only if there is a check in the box "Included" in § 1.3.

_____
_____
_____
_____
_____
_____

Chapter 13 Plan (continued)

Debtor ___Edwards, Carrie Anne_____   Case number _____

Part 9:   **Signature(s):**

9.1 Signatures of Debtor(s) and Debtor(s)' Attorney

If the Debtor(s) do not have an attorney, the Debtor(s) must sign below; otherwise the Debtor(s) signatures are optional. The attorney for the Debtor(s), if any, must sign below.

✗ *Carrie Anne Edwards*   ✗ _____
Signature of Debtor 1   Signature of Debtor 2

Executed on ___01/01/2018____   Executed on _____
　　　　　　　MM / DD / YYYY　　　　　　　　　　　　　　　　　　MM / DD / YYYY

✗ _____   Date _____
Signature of Attorney for Debtor(s)   MM / DD / YYYY

By filing this document, the Debtor(s), if not represented by an attorney, or the Attorney for Debtor(s) also certify(ies) that the wording and order of the provisions in this Chapter 13 plan are identical to those contained in Official Form 113, other than any nonstandard provisions included in Part 8.

Chapter 13 Plan—Exhibit

Exhibit: Total Amount of Estimated Trustee Payments

The following are the estimated payments that the plan requires the trustee to disburse. If there is any difference between the amounts set out below and the actual plan terms, the plan terms control.

a. **Maintenance and cure payments on secured claims** (*Part 3, Section 3.1 total*) $ 7,128.37

b. **Modified secured claims** (*Part 3, Section 3.2 total*) $_____

c. **Secured claims excluded from 11 U.S.C. § 506** (*Part 3, Section 3.3 total*) $ 9,504.60

d. **Judicial liens or security interests partially avoided** (*Part 3, Section 3.4 total*) $_____

e. **Fees and priority claims** (*Part 4 total*) $ 7,470.00

f. **Nonpriority unsecured claims** (*Part 5, Section 5.1, highest stated amount*) $ 5,597.03

g. **Maintenance and cure payments on unsecured claims** (*Part 5, Section 5.2 total*) $_____

h. **Separately classified unsecured claims** (*Part 5, Section 5.3 total*) $_____

i. **Trustee payments on executory contracts and unexpired leases** (*Part 6, Section 6.1 total*) $_____

j. **Nonstandard payments** (*Part 8, total*) + $_____

Total of lines a through j $ 29,700.00

Filing the Bankruptcy Case

After preparing the necessary forms and drafting your repayment plan, your attorney will file your bankruptcy case. Here's a rundown of the documents you'll have to gather, whether you can pay the filing fee in installments, what's required to file an emergency bankruptcy petition, and what happens to your property immediately after you file.

File Documents in Addition to the Bankruptcy Forms

In addition to a sizable stack of official bankruptcy forms and your repayment plan, you must also submit a number of other papers. These are:

- your credit counseling certificate
- any repayment plan that was developed during your credit counseling session
- your most recent tax return or a transcript of the return
- proof that you've filed your tax returns for the last four years with the IRS, and
- your pay stubs or pay advices for the last 60 days, if you were working, and
- other documents required by the facts of your case (and the trustee), such as bank and financial statements, proof of insurance, or a marital settlement agreement.

Credit Counseling

As explained in Ch. 1, almost everyone who files a consumer bankruptcy must first attend credit counseling. This credit counseling must be provided by an agency approved by the United States Trustee's Office within the 180-day period before you file for bankruptcy. The counseling can be done by phone, on the Internet, or in person. You can obtain a list of approved counselors by visiting the website of the U.S. Trustee at www.justice.gov/ust (click on "Credit Counseling & Debtor Education"). The agencies are listed by jurisdiction. Scroll down until you find your court. Most likely your attorney will recommend a particular counseling agency that he or she has worked with before.

Repayment Plans

The purpose of the credit counseling is to analyze your financial situation, identify possible alternatives to bankruptcy, and help to determine what is best for you, whether it be bankruptcy or an available alternative. Some credit counseling agencies also provide debt repayment plan services. These plans may or may not assist with your financial problems. When considering them, keep in mind that credit counseling agencies do not have any special power to alter or reduce your debt obligation. They can only negotiate with your creditors. And unless a creditor agrees in writing to accept a lower payment, lower or suspend interest on your account, or accept a compromise amount in satisfaction of your debt, you will still owe the entire amount and the creditor can move forward to sue you if you fall behind, or to foreclose or repossess your property.

Counseling Fees

Most of these credit counseling agencies charge a modest sum ($15 to $30 is common) for the counseling and the certificate of completion that you'll need to file with your other bankruptcy papers.

Agencies are legally required to offer their services without regard to your ability to pay. If an agency wants to charge more than you can afford (which is rare in the case of Chapter 13 filers), you can request that it lower or waive its fee based on your income.

Exceptions to the Counseling Requirement

You don't have to get counseling if the U.S. Trustee certifies that there is no appropriate agency available to you in the district where you will be filing. However, counseling can be provided by telephone or online, so it is unlikely that approved debt counseling will ever be "unavailable."

You can also avoid the requirement if you move the court to grant an exception and prove to the court's satisfaction that "exigent circumstances" prevented you from meeting the counseling requirement. To prove exigent circumstances, you must show that:

- You had to file for bankruptcy immediately.
- You were unable to obtain counseling within five days after requesting it.

Many of the agencies on the U.S. Trustee's list will counsel you the same day you ask for it, so it will be tough to show that you couldn't get counseling when you requested it. In other words, once you decide to file for Chapter 13 bankruptcy, you should immediately seek credit counseling and don't rely on the exigent circumstances exception.

> **CAUTION**
>
> **A foreclosure may not be "exigent" enough.** Some courts look with disfavor on debtors who wait until the last minute to get their credit counseling. For example, courts found that no exigent circumstances exist when a debtor files for bankruptcy on the day of a scheduled foreclosure sale.

If you can prove that you didn't receive counseling due to exigent circumstances, your attorney must file a certification with the court explaining your situation, and you must complete the counseling within 30 days after you file (you can ask the court to extend this deadline by 15 days).

You may also escape the credit counseling requirement if, after notice and hearing, the bankruptcy court determines that you couldn't participate because of:

- a physical disability that prevents you from attending counseling (this exception probably won't apply if the counseling is available on the Internet or over the phone)
- mental incapacity (you are unable to understand and benefit from the counseling), or
- your active duty in a military combat zone.

> **CAUTION**
> **"Same-day" counseling might not count.** Some courts have ruled that getting credit counseling on the same day you file for bankruptcy does not satisfy the requirement that the counseling take place "within 180 days prior to your filing date." Other courts have allowed same-day counseling. Your local bankruptcy attorney will know what your bankruptcy court requires. To be safe, get your counseling no later than the day before you file.

Your Tax Return or Transcript

You must give the trustee your most recent IRS tax return no later than seven days before the meeting of creditors. (11 U.S.C. § 521(e)(2).) You also have to provide the return to any creditor who asks for it. To protect your privacy, you can redact (black out) your date of birth and Social Security number and those of your dependents. If you don't provide your tax return on time, your case will likely be dismissed.

If you can't find a copy of your most recent tax return, you can ask the IRS to give you a transcript of the basic information in your return—and you can use the transcript as a substitute for your return. You might be able to get these transcripts online through the IRS website. If not, contact the IRS directly. Because it can take some time to receive the transcript (the IRS says two weeks), you should make your request as soon as you can.

> **CAUTION**
> **Your taxes must be current for the last four years.** Before you file for Chapter 13 bankruptcy, you must be able to show that you have filed tax returns for the previous four years. If you are behind on your tax filings, contact an accountant, an enrolled tax agent, or a tax preparation service right away.

Wage Stubs or Pay Advices

If you are employed, you receive a pay stub or pay advice when you are paid. You are required to produce these for the 60-day period before you file. If you don't have them, you have three options: Ask your employer for copies; wait 60 days (and keep the new ones) before filing; or go ahead and file, hand over what you have, and explain why you don't have 60 days' worth. It's likely the court will require you to get copies to avoid dismissal of your case.

If you do not have an employer—for instance you are self-employed or operate a business as a sole proprietor—this won't apply to you. However, most courts have a local form requiring you to declare the reason you aren't submitting pay advices.

Paying the Filing Fee in Installments

In theory, you can pay the $310 filing fee in up to four installments over 120 days. In practice, however, this is almost never done because Chapter 13 is for people with regular income. If you want to try to pay in installments, discuss it with your attorney.

Electronic Filing

Virtually all bankruptcy courts require attorneys to file bankruptcy petitions electronically. The attorney is required to have what's called a "wet copy" in his or her files, meaning a print copy of your papers that you have actually signed with pen and ink. At any point in a bankruptcy case, the trustee can demand that your attorney produce the wet copy, although this is rarely

done. The advantage of electronic filing is that papers can be filed around the clock, holidays and weekends included. So, if you are faced with an emergency and have to get your bankruptcy filed right away in order to stop a foreclosure or repossession, the calendar should not present a barrier to getting that done.

Emergency Filing

If you want to file for bankruptcy in a hurry—typically, to get the protection of the automatic stay (described in Ch. 2)— you can accomplish that (in most places) by filing your bankruptcy *Petition,* mailing matrix and cover sheet (if required by local rules), Form 121 (*Your Statement About Your Social Security Numbers*), and your credit counseling certificate. Some courts also require you to file a cover sheet and an order dismissing your Chapter 13 case, which will be processed if you don't file the rest of your required papers within 14 days.

If you don't follow up by filing the additional documents within 14 days, your bankruptcy case will be dismissed. You can file again, if necessary. However, if your case was dismissed when you opposed a creditor's request to lift the stay, you'll have to wait 180 days to refile. And even if you don't have to wait to file, you'll have to ask the court to keep the automatic stay in effect once 30 days have passed after you file. (See Ch. 2.)

After You File

Filing a bankruptcy petition has a dramatic effect on your creditors and your property.

The Automatic Stay

The instant you file for Chapter 13 bankruptcy, your creditors are subject to the automatic stay, as described in detail in Ch. 2.

Property Ownership

When you file your bankruptcy papers, the trustee becomes the owner of all the property in your bankruptcy estate as of that date. However, the trustee won't actually take physical control of the property and the property will revest (revert to your legal possession) after your plan is confirmed.

Despite the fact that ownership of your property will revest in you at confirmation, if you decide to sell any assets during your Chapter 13 case, other than in the ordinary course of your business operations, you may need to obtain court approval. It may not be a problem if you claimed the property as exempt. If, however, you sell nonexempt property during your Chapter 13 case, you may have to give the sale proceeds to the trustee who will then use it to pay your creditors. Talk to your attorney before you commit to selling any assets while your Chapter 13 case is pending. Also talk to your attorney before settling any pending lawsuits or claims. You may need court approval for this as well, and the proceeds may go to your creditors.

Handling Routine Matters After You File

Once you have filed all of your Chapter 13 bankruptcy papers, including your repayment plan, the bankruptcy trustee and the court take over. They will examine your papers and schedule court hearings. Your creditors also get into the act; it's time for them to file their claims, so they can get paid by the trustee once you start making plan payments. They may also object to your plan if they think they are getting shortchanged.

This chapter tells you how to move your bankruptcy case along once you file. Your attorney will probably have to make two or three court appearances and do some negotiating with creditors.

> **CAUTION**
>
> **Emergency filing reminder.** If you have not filed all your bankruptcy papers, you must do so within 15 days of when you filed your petition. (Bankruptcy Rules 1007(c), 3015(b).) If you do not, the bankruptcy court will dismiss your case.

The Automatic Stay

When you file your bankruptcy papers, the automatic stay will go into effect. (See Ch. 2 for detailed information on how the automatic stay works.) Creditors won't know about your case until they receive notice of your bankruptcy filing from the court, however. It might take several days for this notice to reach your creditors. If you want quicker results (particularly if you are facing aggressive collection efforts), you can notify the creditors yourself by providing them with your case number, the date of filing, the court that your case was filed in, and the name of your case (your name, your spouse's name if filing jointly, and the name of your business if it is included). If you are involved in a court action, such as a foreclosure proceeding or collection lawsuit, you can notify the parties and the court by filing with the court where the lawsuit is pending something called a Suggestion of Bankruptcy.

The court almost always lifts (removes) the stay at the end of the confirmation hearing, because your creditors are now bound by your plan. This means they cannot sue you or take other action to get paid. Their only means of being paid is through the terms of the confirmed plan.

Dealing With the Trustee

Within a few days after you file your bankruptcy petition, the bankruptcy court assigns a Chapter 13 trustee to oversee your case. You will receive a *Notice of Appointment of Trustee* from the court, giving the name, address, and phone number of the trustee. It may also include a list of any financial documents the trustee wants copies of, such as bank statements, canceled checks, and tax returns, and the date by which the trustee wants them.

Within a few days after the trustee is appointed, the court will send you and your creditors a *Notice of Chapter 13 Bankruptcy Case*. This notice usually contains:

- a summary of your Chapter 13 plan (if you filed it with your petition)
- an explanation of the automatic stay
- the date, time, and place of the meeting of creditors (see below)
- the date, time, and place of the confirmation hearing (see below), and
- the date by which creditors must file their claims (see below).

You and your attorney may also receive a letter of introduction from the trustee explaining how this trustee runs a Chapter 13 case. For example, the letter may inform you that the trustee only accepts payments by cashier's check or money order.

Many Chapter 13 trustees play a fairly active role in the cases they administer. This is especially true in small suburban or rural judicial districts or districts with a lot of Chapter 13 bankruptcy cases. For example, a trustee may:

- give you financial advice and assistance, such as helping you create a realistic budget (the trustee cannot, however, give you legal advice)
- actively participate in modifying your plan at the meeting of the creditors, and
- participate at any hearing on the value of an item of secured property, possibly even hiring an appraiser.

For more information on the role of the Chapter 13 trustee, see Ch. 1.

Hold on to Property You Owned Before Filing

Once you file your bankruptcy papers, the property you owned before filing is under the supervision of the bankruptcy court. Don't throw out, give away, sell, or otherwise dispose of any property unless and until the bankruptcy trustee says otherwise.

Report Certain Property You Receive After Filing

Despite the trustee's great interest in your finances, your financial relationship with the trustee is not as stifling as it may sound. In general, you still have complete control over money and property you acquire after filing—as long as you make the payments called for under your repayment plan and you make all regular payments on your secured debts. If you don't make those payments, your creditors may object at the confirmation hearing or even file a motion to dismiss your case.

You can use income you earn after filing that's not going toward your plan payments to purchase everyday items such as groceries, personal effects, and clothing. If you have any questions about using your postfiling income, ask your attorney.

If you receive certain kinds of property (or become entitled to receive it) within 180 days after filing for bankruptcy, you must report it to the bankruptcy trustee. Here's the list:

- property you inherit or become entitled to inherit
- property from a marital settlement agreement or divorce decree, or
- death benefits or life insurance policy proceeds.

If any of this property is nonexempt, you might have to modify your plan to make sure your unsecured creditors are still getting paid at least as much as they would have gotten if you had filed under Chapter 7. (Ch. 5 explains how to calculate how much your unsecured creditors are entitled to receive.)

Provide the Trustee With Proof of Insurance

If you are behind on payments on a secured debt, such as a car loan, and you plan to make up the payments and get back on track during your Chapter 13 case, you may have to give the trustee proof that you have adequate insurance on the collateral. This requirement is meant to protect the creditor if the collateral is destroyed or damaged.

Make Adequate Protection Payments

Within 30 days after you file for bankruptcy, you will have to start making payments (called adequate assurance payments or adequate protection payments) to creditors whose claims are secured by personal property to cover the period between the date you file and the date your plan is confirmed.

Courts are not in agreement as to how or when you make these payments or how to calculate the amount of the payments. As a general rule, if you are paying the creditor outside of your plan, you will need to continue to make regular payments to the creditor. If you are paying the creditor through the plan, your plan should allocate a portion of each plan payment to the secured creditor. Since you must make your first plan payment to the trustee within 30 days of the bankruptcy filing, in most cases the amount allocated to the secured creditor will be sufficient to cover the adequate protection requirement. If your case is dismissed or converted to Chapter 7 before your Chapter 13 plan is confirmed, any adequate protection payments collected by the trustee and paid to the creditor will not be refunded to you.

Make Your First Payment

Within 30 days after you file your petition, you must make the first payment proposed in your Chapter 13 repayment plan. This deadline usually comes up before the meeting of creditors, and always before your confirmation hearing. The reason you must make the payment so early is to show that you are filing in good faith and that you can, in fact, make the payments.

It's crucial to meet this first deadline. So that you don't forget, count out 30 days from the date you filed your petition and mark the deadline on a calendar. It might be better, though, to make the payment a little earlier—for example, the day after you get paid, so you'll be sure to have the funds. If your wages are currently subject to wage attachments, garnishments, or voluntary payroll deductions, your attorney will get those removed so that you have the money to make your Chapter 13 payments.

If you do not make your first payment on time, the bankruptcy court can convert your case to a Chapter 7 bankruptcy, dismiss your case, or deny confirmation of your plan. A few courts consider the failure to make the first payment evidence that the plan was not submitted in good faith and is an abuse of the Chapter 13 bankruptcy system. In that case, the court would lift the automatic stay and allow your creditors to continue their collection efforts. If the court felt you were egregiously abusing the system—for example, this is the fourth Chapter 13 bankruptcy case you've filed without making payments in any of them—the court would likely dismiss your case and possibly fine you and bar you from ever filing for Chapter 13 bankruptcy again.

If You Operate a Business

If you operate a business, by all means keep running it after you file your Chapter 13 papers. If your business has employees, don't forget to make all required payroll tax and withholding deposits with the IRS and your state taxing authority.

The trustee can require the following from you:

- an inventory of your business property, and
- a report on the recent operation of the business, including a statement of receipts and disbursements, if you didn't include one in your bankruptcy papers (you may already have attached one to *Schedule I: Your Income* or Form 107— *Your Statement of Financial Affairs for Individuals Filing for Bankruptcy*). (11 U.S.C. § 1304; Bankruptcy Rule 2015(c).)

As in a regular Chapter 13 case, you must file an income and expense statement every year through the life of your plan. If your net business income increases while the plan is in effect, the trustee may require you to amend the plan to reflect your higher income.

The trustee may also direct you to send notice of your bankruptcy case to all entities who hold money or property that belongs to you. This includes financial institutions where you have accounts, landlords and utility companies who hold security deposits, and insurance companies where you have business insurance with a cash surrender value. If the balance of the money or value of the property is significant and your plan provides little or no payment to your unsecured creditors, the trustee might try to take this money or property for them.

The Meeting of Creditors

Your first court appearance is a fairly informal one; the bankruptcy judge isn't even present. The purpose of the creditors'

How a Typical Chapter 13 Bankruptcy Proceeds	
Step	**When It Happens**
1. You file for Chapter 13 bankruptcy.	
2. The automatic stay takes effect. It bars your creditors, once they learn of your filing, from taking any actions to collect what you owe.	When you file the bankruptcy petition
3. The court appoints a trustee to oversee your case. You will receive a *Notice of Appointment of Trustee* from the court.	Within a few days after you file the bankruptcy petition
4. The court sends you and your creditors a *Notice of Chapter 13 Case*, which usually contains: • general information about Chapter 13 bankruptcy • a summary of your Chapter 13 plan • the date of the meeting of creditors • the date of the confirmation hearing, and • the deadline by which creditors must file their claims.	Within a few days after you file your Chapter 13 plan
5. Creditors file written objections to your plan, if they wish.	At least 25 days before the confirmation hearing
6. You provide your most recent tax return to the trustee. You may black out certain personal information, such as your Social Security number.	At least seven days before the scheduled date of the first meeting of creditors
7. You begin making payments under your repayment plan. (If your plan is never approved, the trustee will return your money, less administrative costs.)	Within 30 days after you file the bankruptcy petition
8. You attend the meeting of the creditors, where the trustee and any creditors who show up can ask you about information in your papers. A creditor may raise objections to your plan with the hope of getting you to modify it before the confirmation hearing. You must bring any documents the trustee requests and proof that you've filed tax returns for the last four years.	Within 40 days after you file the bankruptcy petition

How a Typical Chapter 13 Bankruptcy Proceeds (continued)	
Step	**When It Happens**
9. You file a modified plan, if you wish.	Anytime before the confirmation hearing. You must send a copy of the modified plan to all creditors, who are entitled to 20 days' notice before the confirmation hearing. If you don't give 20 days' notice, you will have to schedule a new hearing date.
10. You or your attorney attend the confirmation hearing, where the court addresses any objections raised by creditors or the trustee and approves your repayment plan.	The hearing must be held between 20 and 45 days after the creditors' meeting, unless the court wants to hold it earlier and there is no objection to the earlier date.
11. Creditors file their *Proofs of Claim*, specifying how much they are owed. You may also have to file *Proofs of Claim* for creditors who don't file their own proofs.	Within 70 days after the petition filing date (180 days for creditors that are government agencies). If you have to file *Proofs of Claim* on behalf of creditors, you must do so within 30 days after the 90-day or 180-day limit.
12. You or the trustee files written objections to creditors' claims, if you have a reason to object.	As soon as possible after the creditors file their claims. You must notify your creditors at least 30 days in advance of the hearing on your objections.
13. The trustee sends you periodic statements showing: • who has filed claims and for how much • how much money has been paid to each creditor, and • the balance due each creditor.	Commonly, twice a year
14. You give the trustee annual income and expense statements.	Every year while your Chapter 13 plan is in effect, if requested by the court, trustee, U.S. Trustee, or a creditor
15. You file a *Certificate About a Financial Management Course* (Form 423) showing that you completed a course in personal financial management.	Before you make your last plan payment
16. The court grants your discharge. The court may schedule a brief final court appearance called a "discharge hearing." If there's no discharge hearing, you'll be mailed formal notice of your discharge.	36 to 60 months after you file if you complete your plan payments; sooner if you seek and obtain a hardship discharge

meeting is to allow the trustee and your creditors to ask you about the information in your bankruptcy papers, including your repayment plan. The trustee will want to be sure that you can make the payments you've proposed in your plan.

You (and your spouse, if you are filing jointly) must attend. If you don't, you may be fined $100 or so by the judge. Even worse, your case may be dismissed. If you know in advance that you can't attend the creditors' meeting, your attorney should try to reschedule it.

Prepare for the Meeting

Some courts require you to bring to the meeting or provide to the trustee in advance, the following documents:

- file-stamped copies of all the papers you've filed with the bankruptcy court
- copies of all documents that describe your debts and property, such as bills, deeds, contracts, and licenses, and
- financial records, such as recent tax returns, checkbooks, and bank statements.

Bring proof of your state and federal tax filings for the previous four years to the creditors' meeting. Also, some trustees ask you to hand over all of your major credit cards. (Not all trustees require this.) You should be able to hold on to your debit cards that have the Visa or MasterCard logo

on them. This will give you a card to use for your online accounts and rental cars.

If you lack the necessary documents at the creditors' meeting, the trustee will postpone the meeting to a later date when you can produce them. Often, if you get the documents to the trustee before the rescheduled meeting, you won't have to appear again; the trustee will simply review your documents, then close the meeting.

If you are feeling anxious about the meeting of creditors, find out when and where the next scheduled meeting will occur. Then, attend the meeting. That way, you can observe the proceedings and get comfortable with the process before you have to attend your own meeting.

The night before the creditors' meeting, thoroughly review the papers you filed with the bankruptcy court. If you discover mistakes, make careful note of them. You may have to correct your papers after the meeting, an easy process that your attorney can handle.

If your papers are internally consistent and there are no problem areas, the trustee is likely to ask you very few questions, perhaps nothing more than whether you have provided complete and accurate information. But sometimes the trustee may delve into a particular subject in more detail. For instance, the trustee may be interested in how you put a value on property such as real estate or a business.

Or, if you recently sold some property, the trustee may want to know the details of the transaction and what you did with the proceeds. Or, if one part of your bankruptcy papers shows that you owe a debt but that debt hasn't been identified on the appropriate schedule, the trustee will want to know why. And finally, the trustee may want a better understanding of how your plan proposes to pay your creditors.

Clearly, there are an infinite number of situations where the trustee may want to go deeper into the facts. So how can you prepare for this? The single best way is to do a complete and accurate job of providing your attorney with information in the first place. Then, as mentioned, carefully review your papers before the meeting to make sure you understand all the information they contain and how you arrived at particular estimates and appraisals. Even if your attorney prepared your papers, you and you alone are responsible for what goes in them.

Getting to the Meeting

Most creditors' meetings take place in a room in or near the bankruptcy courthouse or federal courthouse. The date and time of the meeting are commonly stated on the notice of filing sent out by the court; if they are not, ask your attorney. Give yourself at least an extra hour to find the right place, park, find the right building, go through security, and find the right room.

> **CAUTION**
>
> **You'll have to prove your identity.** To show that you are really who you say you are, you'll need to produce a picture ID and official proof of your Social Security number. Your Social Security card, or a letter from Social Security with your number on it, is the best proof. If you don't have either of these, contact the trustee's office prior to the meeting to find out if there is anything else it will accept. Failure to produce such documents will result in your meeting being reset for a later date. Also, you'll need your picture ID to gain entrance to the federal building where the meeting is being held.

Tight Court Security

On your way to any court hearing, you will probably spend some time getting through security. Like airports, federal buildings have metal detectors, but set to an even higher sensitivity. If you set the detector off, you'll have to empty your pockets, take off any offending articles, such as a jacket or belt, and go through again. If you set it off again, the security guard may scan your body with a handheld metal detector. In addition, items you're carrying—such as a purse, briefcase, or knapsack—must go through an X-ray scanner. The security guard may confiscate objects such as pocket knives or cell phones. The guard might not be willing to hold these items for you, so check before you go.

When you get to the right room, look for your attorney. You may have to sign in. Then just sit down and wait your turn.

What Happens at the Meeting

Most bankruptcy trustees set aside one or two days a month to hold Chapter 13 bankruptcy creditors' meetings. This means that when you show up for your creditors' meeting, many other people who have filed for bankruptcy will be there, too. And commonly, many cases are set for the same time. That means that 25 to 30 cases may all be scheduled for 9:00 a.m. In the alternative, the cases may be set at short intervals. Sometimes one case takes longer than expected, causing the trustee to get behind schedule. Plan to spend some time waiting just in case.

To get a rough idea of when your name will be called, check the posted schedule. If your name is near the top of the list, you may not have too long to wait. If you're toward the bottom, you may be sitting there for quite some time.

In many courts, creditors' meetings are held in the same room where you wait. If this is the case in your district, you should stay and observe a few meetings before it is your turn. You can see what the meetings are like, what types of questions the trustee asks, and where you should sit or stand. If you are nervous, watching other cases may calm you down—you'll quickly see that many people have the same financial issues as you.

Your creditors' meeting, if it's typical, will last less than 15 minutes. When your name is called, you'll be asked to sit at a table near the front of the room. Your attorney will sit next to you. The trustee will swear you in and ask your name, address, and other identifying information. The trustee will also ask to see your photo ID and proof of Social Security number.

Your Attorney's Role at the Creditors' Meeting

Even though you are represented by an attorney, it will be your job to answer directly any questions put to you by a creditor or the bankruptcy trustee. With rare exceptions, your attorney will sit quietly and not object to the questions or intervene with answers he or she thinks would be best. Only if a question is inappropriate or the attorney has reason to believe your answer might incriminate you will he or she pipe up. Of course if the question is about a legal matter that only the attorney would know about, you can refer the question to the attorney for an answer.

The Trustee's Questions

The trustee will briefly go over your forms with you, probably asking at least a few questions. Your answers should be both truthful and consistent with your bankruptcy papers. The trustee is likely to be most interested in the fairness of your plan (that is, that it treats all similarly situated creditors the same) and your ability to make the payments you have proposed.

If you have valued some of your property at or near the exemption limit, the trustee may question you more closely on how you came up with your valuation figures. For example, if you estimate that your home is worth $100,000, and your state's homestead exemption protects $100,000 worth of equity, the trustee may dig a little to see whether your property might be worth more. Depending on home price trends in your area when you file, the trustee might even initiate an independent appraisal in the hopes that the value of your property exceeds the homestead protection enough to add significantly to your nonexempt property—and, therefore, require an increase in plan payments to your unsecured creditors. Asking about these types of things is part of the financial investigation that is the trustee's job. In addition, the commission structure (whereby the more you pay into your plan, the more the trustee collects as a fee) serves as a motivator.

Questions From Your Creditors

Often, not a single creditor attends the meeting. Sometimes, however, a secured creditor will show up to find out what you plan to do with your secured property. Or a student loan creditor will come to remind you that your debt will not be discharged. Unsecured creditors rarely appear. Although sometimes an unsecured creditor comes because it thinks its appearance is required in order to file a claim—which it's not.

A creditor might also attend if it believes you have hidden property or transferred property out of the reach of creditors and not disclosed it to the trustee. An ex-spouse might attend to find out whether he or she will continue to receive support or property settlements. Anyone that does appear has the right to ask you questions under oath.

Creditors who disagree with your plan may attend for the sole purpose of speaking with you after the meeting in order to negotiate a resolution. You don't need to stay for this. But it may be in your best interest to listen and try to work out your problems, so it is a good idea to be prepared for this. If you reach an agreement that requires a change to your plan, you will need to file an amended plan.

Changing Your Plan Before the Confirmation Hearing

You have an absolute right to file an amended plan with the bankruptcy court any time before the confirmation hearing. Most Chapter 13 debtors amend their plan at least once. Your attorney will file the new plan with the bankruptcy court clerk and send notice of the new plan to all of your creditors. The new plan replaces the old one.

Here are some common reasons to amend a plan:

- to correct errors—such as to add overlooked creditors or debts
- to reflect financial changes—such as a new job, a raise, an inheritance or

insurance settlement, reduction in income, or destruction of property secured by a debt

- to reduce your proposed payments— for example, if you just lost your job or had your income reduced
- to respond to creditors' objections (for instance, that you undervalued property) or include terms you negotiated with a creditor at the end of the meeting of the creditors, or
- to add debts you incurred after filing. In general, you should not incur debts after you file, other than day-to-day expenses. (In fact, the trustee will probably make you hand over your credit cards.) You can modify your plan, however, to add any debts that are necessary for you to keep following your plan (such as a medical bill) or unanticipated debts (such as a tax bill). (This is covered in Ch. 12.)

At a minimum, the notice of your plan amendment must:

- identify the debtor (you)
- identify each creditor whose claim is affected by your modification
- describe your proposed modification with particularity (for instance, if you're proposing to reduce your payment to a creditor, your notice has to make that clear), and
- if secured property is involved, state (or restate) whether you plan to keep making payments or surrender the collateral.

(See *In re Friday*, 304 B.R. 537 (N.D. Ga. 2003).)

Most courts require you to send a copy of the amended plan to, at a minimum, the affected creditors.

The Confirmation Hearing

A judge must approve your Chapter 13 plan for it to take effect. This is done at a confirmation hearing, where the judge addresses any objections raised by creditors or the trustee. Typically, a Chapter 13 debtor doesn't attend the confirmation hearing; it is handled by the attorney. In a few courts, a confirmation hearing is held only if a creditor or the trustee has filed a formal motion objecting to the plan. If no hearing is scheduled, it means your plan is approved as filed.

The confirmation hearing must be held no sooner than 20 or later than 45 days after the creditors' meeting, unless the court wants to hold it earlier and no one objects. However, the deadline for filing *Proofs of Claims*—which creditors must file to get paid through your plan—is 70 days after the petition filing date. Assuming that the creditors' meeting is actually held on the scheduled date (it usually is), creditors might not have to file their *Proofs of Claim* until 45 to 70 days after the confirmation hearing. This means that plans up for confirmation often have to estimate which debts will be paid, and in what amounts. If creditors file claims after the court approves your plan, you may need to pay more into the plan than you expected. Later, we explain how to handle claims that are filed late and when you should file a claim on a creditor's behalf.

Dealing With Disputed Debts

If you want to dispute whether you actually owe a particular debt, you'll need to file your objection with the court and provide a copy to the creditor. The creditor will get time to respond. If you can't resolve the issue, the court will hold a hearing and issue a ruling on whether you owe the debt.

Ideally, you want the court to rule on your objection before your plan is confirmed. Otherwise you'll have to modify your plan if the court ultimately agrees with your objection. And until you get the court's ruling, you'll also have to start paying off the debt if these payments come due under your Chapter 13 plan. Unfortunately, many courts hold confirmation hearings early in the case—even as early as the creditors' meeting—so it may be difficult if not impossible to get a ruling prior to confirmation. If this happens in your case, you may want to ask the court to order the trustee to hold any distributions to that particular creditor until a hearing is held.

What Happens at the Confirmation Hearing

As mentioned, your attorney can represent you at the confirmation hearing. However, if you plan to attend, here's what to expect.

Unlike a creditors' meeting, the confirmation hearing usually is run by a bankruptcy judge. Judges like to get easy cases in and out of their courtrooms as quickly as possible. This means that all uncontested matters will be heard first. Next will be cases where the outcome is fairly obvious—often motions to dismiss in cases where the plans were approved but the debtors have missed several payments. If the trustee or a creditor has filed an objection in your case, your confirmation hearing will probably be toward the end. Bring a big book with you (but not an eReader—you might not get it through security).

The judge is most interested in your ability to make the payments under your plan and will question your attorney about that or about plan provisions that are unclear.

After these questions, the judge will ask whether objections raised by the trustee or creditors have been resolved. If they haven't, the judge may ask the trustee or creditors to elaborate on their objections, ask your attorney for any response, and then make a ruling. If the trustee doesn't think your plan is feasible, the trustee will raise that issue now. If the judge still has a lot of cases to get through, the judge may reschedule the rest of the hearing to a less busy day.

If the judge agrees with an objection, you will probably be allowed to submit a modified plan. (See "Changing Your Plan After a Failed Confirmation Hearing," below.) But if it's obvious that Chapter 13 bankruptcy just isn't realistic for you—for example, you earn very little money to pay into a plan—the judge will order that your case be dismissed or give you the option of converting it to a Chapter 7 bankruptcy.

TIP

If you were already forced out of Chapter 7. If you had to file for Chapter 13 because you couldn't pass the means test (see Ch. 4), you may also be unable to propose a confirmable Chapter 13 repayment plan. If your income has declined since the six-month period before you filed, however, you may now find yourself eligible to use Chapter 7. (Remember, the means test is based on your average monthly income in the six months before you file.)

If you convert to Chapter 7 from a Chapter 13 case, you may avoid the means test altogether. Some courts have ruled that the means test doesn't apply to Chapter 7 cases that have been converted from Chapter 13. (See, e.g., *In re Guarin*, 2009 WL 4500476 (Bankr. D. Mass. 2009); *In re Willis*, 408 B.R. 803 (Bankr. W.D. Missouri 2009); *In re Dudley*, 405 B.R. 790 (Bankr. W.D. Va. 2009).) Other courts have gone the opposite way, ruling that if you convert to Chapter 7 from Chapter 13, you must still pass the means test in order to be eligible for Chapter 7 relief. (See, e.g., *In re Chapman*, 447 B.R. 250 (B.A.P. 8th Cir. 2011); *In re Lassiter*, 2011 WL 2039363 (Bankr. E.D. Va. 2011); *In re Phillips*, 417 B.R. 30 (Bankr. S.D. Ohio 2009).) Still other courts have not yet addressed the issue.

Income Deduction Orders

If you have a regular job with regular income, the bankruptcy judge may order, at the confirmation hearing, that your monthly plan payments be automatically deducted from your wages and sent to the bankruptcy court. (11 U.S.C. § 1325(c).) This is called an income deduction order. Income deduction orders work if you are regularly paid a salary or wages. They are almost impossible to use, however, if you are:

- self-employed
- funding your plan with public benefits, such as Social Security (the Social Security Act prohibits the Social Security Administration from complying with an income deduction order), or
- funding your plan with pension benefits—many pension plans prohibit the administrator from paying proceeds to anyone other than the beneficiary (you), which means that the administrator will ignore the income deduction order.

In many districts, the bankruptcy court automatically issues an income deduction order at the confirmation hearing—and possibly even earlier. In some districts, the bankruptcy court leaves it up to the debtor whether or not to issue an order. And in a few districts, the court doesn't issue the order unless you miss a payment in your plan.

You may not like the idea of the order, but the court is likely to deny your plan for lack of feasibility if you refuse to comply with it. And you should realize that the order will probably make it easier for you to complete your plan. The success rate of Chapter 13 cases is higher for debtors with income deduction orders than for debtors who pay the trustees themselves.

One benefit of an income deduction order is that it usually forbids your employer from making other deductions from your paycheck. This means that all wage attachments, garnishments, and voluntary payroll deductions will end (if they haven't already) when the order takes effect.

If the court does issue an income deduction order, you might inform the payroll department at your job that you've filed for Chapter 13 bankruptcy and to expect an income deduction order from the bankruptcy court.

Once the income deduction order takes effect, your attorney will need to tell the trustee if you change jobs.

The Judge's Order Confirming Your Plan

A court order granting confirmation of your repayment plan is binding on your creditors; they must accept the payments the trustee will make to them under the terms of your plan. This includes creditors who do not file claims by the deadline and creditors who unsuccessfully objected to your plan. (11 U.S.C. § 1327(a).)

Your Employer Can't Fire You for Filing for Bankruptcy

Bankruptcy law prohibits employers from firing or discriminating against an employee solely because the employee filed for bankruptcy. But some people are concerned that a bankruptcy filing will still adversely affect their employment in some way other than termination or obvious discrimination. If you are filing in a court that requires income deduction orders and you have reason to believe that it may have an adverse effect on your employment, you can ask the court to waive the requirement. Some courts will waive it on this basis and others won't. Your attorney should know what the standard practice is in your district.

As a practical matter, many employers have had or currently have employees who have filed for Chapter 13 bankruptcy; they rarely care. If an employer does punish you for filing for bankruptcy, tell your attorney so he or she can take the appropriate action. (See Ch. 14 for more on the laws against this type of discrimination.)

When the court approves your plan, the *Order Confirming Chapter 13 Plan* will be filed with the bankruptcy court clerk and notice that your plan was confirmed will be sent to all your creditors.

Changing Your Plan After a Failed Confirmation Hearing

If your plan isn't confirmed at the hearing, the court will usually give you a certain amount of time in which to try again. If you don't submit an amended plan by the deadline (or if the court found that you acted in bad faith or that Chapter 13 is not a feasible option for you), the court will dismiss your case or convert it to a Chapter 7 bankruptcy case. In that situation, the trustee must return your payments to you, less administrative expenses.

In most cases, you'll need to do one or more of the following to get your amended plan confirmed:

- extend your plan (if it's for less than five years)
- arrange to pay off your secured debt arrears faster
- change an interest rate on secured debt arrears
- increase the secured portion of a debt that is partially secured and partially unsecured
- create or eliminate a class of unsecured creditors, or
- increase the amount a particular class of creditors receives.

When your attorney files the amended plan, he or she will also schedule a new confirmation hearing. The hearing must be at least 25 days after the modified plan is filed. This gives your creditors an opportunity to object.

Amending Your Bankruptcy Forms

You have a right to amend the bankruptcy forms you have filed at any time before your final discharge. (You can also modify your plan after it's confirmed if the judge consents.) This means that if you made a mistake on your schedules, you can correct it easily. Also, you must amend your papers if you receive certain property within 180 days after filing. (These are described in "Dealing With the Trustee," above.)

If your mistake means that notice of your bankruptcy filing must be sent to additional creditors (for instance, if you inadvertently left off a creditor who must be notified), you'll have to pay a fee to file the amendment. If your mistake doesn't require new notice (for example, you just add information about property you owned when you filed), you may not have to pay an additional filing fee. If you amend your schedules to add creditors before the meeting of creditors, you'll usually be required to provide the newly listed creditors with notice of the meeting as well as notice of your amendment.

If you become aware of debts or property that you should have included in your papers, amending your papers will help you avoid any suspicion that you're trying to conceal things from the trustee. If you fail to amend your papers in this situation and someone else discovers your error, the judge may dismiss your bankruptcy case or rule that one or more of your debts is nondischargeable.

Filing a Change of Address

If you move while your bankruptcy case is still open, you must give the court, the trustee, and your creditors your new address.

Filing Tax Returns

The court, a creditor, the trustee, or the U.S. Trustee may request that you file copies of your federal tax returns (or transcripts) with the bankruptcy court when you file those returns with the IRS, while your case is pending. This rule applies to returns for current years and for the three years before you file your bankruptcy petition. If you don't comply with a request to file your returns, your case will be dismissed.

Before you provide your returns to the court or a creditor, you can redact (black out) information that identifies you personally. The following information may be redacted:

- **Social Security number.** You may redact all but the last four digits of any Social Security number that appears in the documents.
- **Names of minor children.** You may redact the names and use only initials.
- **Dates of birth.** You may redact the day and month of birth and use only the year.
- **Financial account numbers.** If any account numbers are included, you may redact all but the last four digits.

Filing Annual Income and Expense Statements

The court, a creditor, the trustee, or the U.S. Trustee may request that you file an annual income and expense statement. This statement must include your income and expenditures during the most recently concluded tax year, and it must show how you calculated your income (both monthly and annually) and your expenses.

If required in your district, by your trustee, or by your confirmation order, you must file the first statement 90 days after the end of the last tax year or one year after the date you filed your case (whichever is later), if your plan has not yet been confirmed by the later date. Once your plan is confirmed, you must file an annual statement at least 45 days before the anniversary of the date your plan is confirmed. It's hard to imagine that anyone will be paying close attention to these dates, as long as you are proceeding in good faith. Still, you should mark these dates on your calendar, just in case someone makes the request.

The income and expense statement must identify the amount and sources of your income, any person who contributed money to your household, and the amount that person contributed. Unless the trustee tells you otherwise or your court provides its own form, the best way to prepare this statement is to use blank copies of *Schedules I* and *J* to compute your annual and monthly income and your expenses. You can find these forms at www.uscourts.gov. (For more information, see "Getting the Official Bankruptcy Forms," in Ch. 4.)

Personal Financial Management Counseling

Before your last plan payment is due, you must complete a two-hour course in financial management and file a certificate of completion with the court. If you don't complete the course and file the certificate, the court can close your case without granting you a discharge. Although it isn't terribly difficult to reopen your case and file the certificate, it's better to avoid that extra step. Along with the certificate, your attorney will also file Form 423.

You must use an agency that's been approved by the U.S. Trustee's office. You can find a list of approved providers at the U.S. Trustee's website, www.justice.gov/ust. If you were satisfied with the agency that provided you with credit counseling before you filed your case, you can probably use it again—typically, the same agencies are approved to provide both types of counseling.

You might think that requiring you to complete this course is overkill. After all, to complete your repayment plan, you have had to live on a pretty strict budget for three to five years. Nevertheless, the law requires the court to get proof that you've completed this counseling before a discharge can be granted.

Form 2830—Domestic Support and Homestead Exemption

Before you get your discharge, your attorney must also file a form certifying that you have paid any required domestic support obligations (child support and alimony). On the same form, you must provide information on your use of a homestead exemption, if applicable. This information is used to determine whether your homestead exemption should be limited because you were convicted of a felony or securities violation. While this form must be filed before a discharge is entered, the trustee usually requires it at the beginning of the case.

Making Your Plan Work

Common Legal Issues

Hopefully, your bankruptcy case will go smoothly, without any challenges or unexpected complications. In some situations, however, your attorney might have to make an extra court appearance or two. This might happen if you need to ask the court to rule in your favor on an issue—for example, to eliminate a lien from your property. You might also have to defend against a creditor's objection to your plan or object to a creditor's claim for repayment. This chapter explains these types of contingencies in more detail.

Filing Motions

While your bankruptcy case is pending, you may learn that you need the judge to rule on a particular point. For example, you may have to modify your repayment plan (see Ch. 10) or have your debts discharged on the basis of hardship because you can't complete your plan (see Ch. 13). Requests for the court to intervene in your case—to make a decision or take some action, for example—are called motions.

In this section, we briefly review the general requirements that apply to all motions brought in bankruptcy court.

There are two basic types of motions:

- ex parte motions, which are typically decided by the judge on the application of one party, without a hearing, and
- noticed motions, which give the other side enough time to come into court and oppose your request.

Ex Parte Motions

Ex parte motions are typically used when you are clearly entitled to the action you are asking the court to take. For example, let's say you want to file a noticed motion to modify your repayment plan, but you can only give the creditor 20 days' notice, rather than the 25 days generally required for a noticed motion. In this situation, your attorney could file an ex parte motion seeking an "order shortening time." With the motion, the attorney includes an order for the judge to sign and a declaration—a statement signed under penalty of perjury—that the attorney contacted or tried to contact the other side about the motion and certifying that the requested order will not have an adverse effect on any creditor.

Ex parte motions can also be used to dismiss your Chapter 13 bankruptcy case, because you have an absolute right to do so.

Noticed Motions

Noticed motions are much more common. Your attorney will prepare the motion, which explains what you want the court to do and why, along with other required documents, such as declarations (signed statements of fact) and a memorandum of law (this part sets out the law and explains why the court should grant the motion). In addition to filing the motion and accompanying documents and serving a copy on your creditors, your attorney must send notice to the affected parties.

There are two types of notice:

- Notice of the date and time of the hearing. In this situation, your attorney will schedule a hearing. The opposing side will have an opportunity to respond in writing.

- Notice that the other side must schedule a hearing if it wants to contest the motion. In this situation, if the opposing party doesn't respond within the 25-day notice period, your attorney can ask the court for a default (which means you automatically win the motion).

At the hearing on the motion, your attorney and the opposing side will have an opportunity to argue their points.

Then, the judge will either announce a decision or take the matter under advisement or submission (think about it for a while). The judge may or may not include a written memorandum in the order. The judge may also ask the party that won the motion to prepare a formal order.

Dealing With Creditors' Motions

In most Chapter 13 cases, you'll be able to work out any minor glitches as they arise. On rare occasions, however, a creditor throws a monkey wrench into the works by filing a motion that, if successful, could mean a major disruption or even a dismissal of your case.

If you are faced with a creditor motion, take heart: Even when creditors file motions to challenge your right to file for Chapter 13 bankruptcy or discharge a particular debt, few Chapter 13 trustees want to deal with them. Most trustees handle thousands of cases a year. They do not want to get involved in drawn-out court battles unless the result is likely to have an impact on many other debtors in your district. In most cases, the trustee will encourage you and the creditor to work things out without a hearing. Some trustees even discourage creditors from filing a lot of controversial motions (and a creditor needs to stay on the trustee's good side).

If you receive a motion from a creditor, your attorney will have a period of time to file a written response or appear at a hearing to oppose the motion. Procedures vary.

Here are a few common types of motions a creditor might file.

Objections to Your Eligibility to Use Chapter 13

A creditor (or the trustee) might file a motion claiming that your debts exceed the Chapter 13 bankruptcy limits; as explained in Ch. 3, these limits are $394,725 for unsecured debts and $1,184,200 for secured debts. A creditor may raise this kind of objection if your liability for a debt is relatively certain (even though it hasn't yet been determined), and the creditor is afraid you'll wipe it out in bankruptcy.

EXAMPLE: A few years ago, you and a partner started a business. It failed, you both lost a lot of money, and your former partner blames you for the whole mess, with some justification. He has been threatening to sue you for the money he claims you are responsible for causing him to lose. During your business's lean times, you missed several house payments, didn't pay your personal income taxes, and charged up your credit cards. You have filed for Chapter 13 bankruptcy, and your plan proposes to pay only 10% of your unsecured debts. Your ex-partner objects, claiming that you owe him at least $400,000, which puts you over the limit for unsecured debts.

Motion for Adequate Protection

Your secured creditors will probably insist that you agree to protect the property securing their debts against loss, damage, or general depreciation. This is called providing adequate protection. (See Ch. 10 for more information.) The protection you provide could take the form of money, additional liens, or proof of insurance. If you refuse to provide adequate protection, the creditor may file a motion asking the court to order you to do so or to grant the creditor relief from the stay.

Motion for Relief From the Automatic Stay

When you file for bankruptcy, the automatic stay prohibits most creditors from taking any action to collect the debts you owe them, unless and until the court says otherwise. If you have had two or more dismissals entered in bankruptcy cases within the past year, you are not protected by the automatic stay and will need a court order to protect you against actions by a specific creditor. If you have one dismissal entered in the past year, the automatic stay only lasts for 30 days, absent a court order. (For more on the automatic stay, see Ch. 2.)

In a Chapter 13 bankruptcy, the automatic stay bars creditors from going after the property and wages you acquire after you file your petition and before your confirmation hearing. If the confirmation hearing is delayed, however, your creditors may file a motion asking the judge to lift the stay early. The court is likely to grant such a motion if any of the following are true:

- You refuse to provide adequate protection to a secured creditor. (See "Motion for Adequate Protection," above.)
- Your filing is obviously in bad faith, or your plan is completely unfeasible.
- You have no equity in an item of secured property, and the creditor (who wants to repossess it) claims that you don't need the item to carry out your Chapter 13 plan. You may be able to get around a motion that makes this argument if:
  - Your plan includes payments on the secured item.
  - You can show that you need the property to generate income. For

example, you could argue that you need to keep a car because you have to drive to work and have no adequate alternative means of transportation.

- The property is your family home. Many courts rule that the family home is always necessary. Some courts rule otherwise, however, if the creditor can show that comparable housing is available to you for less money. You would have to emphasize your children's ties to their school and neighborhood, your proximity to work, and/or the cost of finding new housing and moving.

Motions to Lift the Stay and Proceed With Foreclosure

If your mortgage lender or servicer initiated foreclosure proceedings before you filed for bankruptcy, the lender will likely ask the court to lift the automatic stay so it can proceed with the foreclosure. To obtain this type of relief, the lender's motion must be accompanied with paperwork demonstrating that it has an ownership interest in the property. The foreclosing party can do this by way of a promissory note listing the lender (or other party bringing the foreclosure action) as the note's owner, by showing that the promissory note was properly assigned to the party by an earlier owner, or by demonstrating legal authority to proceed on the mortgage holder's behalf.

If the court grants the motion and lifts the automatic stay, you still might be able to challenge the legality of the foreclosure or the mortgage by opposing the lender's *Proof of Claim*. (See "Objecting to a Creditor's Claim," below.) However, in most instances you will have to defend against the foreclosure in state court.

Motions to Lift the Stay and Proceed With an Eviction

The same basic rules apply to evictions: The bankruptcy court is likely to lift the automatic stay and allow the landlord to proceed with an eviction. And, in some cases, that might not even be necessary. If the landlord already has a judgment of possession when you file for bankruptcy, or the landlord wants to evict you for endangering the property or illegally using controlled substances on the premises, the automatic stay generally won't apply to stop the eviction, except in the limited circumstances described in Ch. 2.

Motions to Dismiss by the Trustee and Others

Creditors and trustees can file a variety of motions to dismiss your case. Typically, these motions argue that you failed to comply with procedural bankruptcy rules. For example, you might face:

- a motion by the trustee to dismiss your case because you failed to provide your most recent tax return at least seven days before the creditors' meeting

- a motion by the trustee to dismiss or convert your case (to Chapter 7) if you fail to prove that you filed your tax returns for the previous four years
- a motion by the trustee, the U.S. Trustee, or a creditor to dismiss your case because you failed to provide them, on their request, with the income tax returns you filed while your case was pending
- a motion by the trustee to dismiss your case because you didn't stay current on your income tax filings, or
- a motion by an ex-spouse or the trustee to dismiss your case because you didn't stay current on your child support or alimony payments while your case was pending.

If the person bringing this type of motion is right—that is, you really didn't file your tax returns or stay current on your child support payments—your only defense is that the failure was beyond your control. If you can show, for example, that a natural disaster prevented you from filing your tax return on time, you might have a shot at success.

If an Unsecured Creditor Objects to Your Plan

It might seem odd to you that an unsecured creditor would object to your Chapter 13 plan. After all, in a Chapter 13 case, the creditor might get some money. By contrast, if you ignored the creditor or filed for Chapter 7 bankruptcy, the creditor probably wouldn't get anything.

A creditor who objects to your plan isn't trying to derail your bankruptcy, however: Instead, the creditor wants you to modify your plan to ensure that you will be able to make the payments it requires. Because so many Chapter 13 filers eventually dismiss their cases or convert to Chapter 7, your creditors have good reason to doubt that you'll be able to follow through. A creditor objects to a plan precisely because the creditor wants it to succeed.

A creditor who objects to your plan will probably attend the creditors' meeting and try to convince you to modify your plan before the confirmation hearing, which typically takes place from 20 to 40 days after the creditors' meeting.

> **CAUTION**
>
> **If a creditor requests a deposition.** It's rare, but a creditor who thinks you are hiding assets and could pay more into your plan might try to gather evidence about your finances through a formal legal process called "discovery." The discovery technique the creditor is most likely to use is a specific type of deposition called a "Rule 2004" examination—a proceeding in which you answer questions posed by the creditor's attorney orally, under oath, before a court reporter. If a creditor sends you a discovery request, the court may postpone the confirmation hearing to give the creditor time to gather evidence.

Bankruptcy Rule 2004 permits the creditor to make a very broad examination into your financial circumstances, including looking for a new basis for an objection to the confirmation of your plan. If the creditor has already filed an objection to the confirmation of your plan, the creditor can't use a 2004 examination and must take an ordinary deposition that limits the inquiry to the specific objection filed.

This section describes the four most common objections creditors raise to Chapter 13 plans.

The Plan Is Not Submitted in Good Faith

Probably the most common objection creditors raise is that a Chapter 13 plan was not proposed in good faith. The bankruptcy rules don't define good faith, but bankruptcy courts will take this type of objection seriously if you have proposed a plan that appears to be impossible for you to carry through. However, if you filed your papers with the honest intention of getting back on your feet and making all payments required in a Chapter 13 case by the Bankruptcy Code (11 U.S.C. §§ 1322 and 1325), you should be able to overcome this objection.

Occasionally, creditors make a good-faith objection as a negotiating ploy. They want you to change your plan to satisfy them rather than argue the issue to the judge. If you think this is going on, your lawyer will help you figure out whether you have anything to worry about—that is, whether there are any valid, good-faith objections to your plan.

When a creditor makes a good-faith objection, most bankruptcy courts look at these factors:

- **How often you have filed for bankruptcy.** Filing multiple bankruptcies in and of itself does not show bad faith. If, however, you've filed and dismissed two or more other bankruptcy cases within a year, the court may find that you lack good faith if your papers are inconsistent or you can't show that your circumstances have changed since the previous dismissal. Changed circumstances sufficient to support a refiling might include:
  - an increase in your income
  - a reduction of your debt
  - a new job that will permit use of an income deduction order
  - your spouse's decision to file jointly with you, or
  - the end of a condition that required your previous dismissal, such as illness or unemployment.

  The court might also find a lack of good faith if you file for Chapter 13 bankruptcy within four years after filing a case in which you received a Chapter 7 discharge, and you propose to pay your unsecured creditors substantially less than what you owe them. In this situation, the court may well find that you are using Chapter 13 to circumvent Chapter 7's prohibition on filing a second Chapter 7 case within eight years of receiving a prior discharge.

- **The accuracy of your bankruptcy papers and statements.** The court is likely to find a lack of good faith if you misrepresent your income, debts, expenses, or assets or you lie at the creditors' meeting or a deposition. Creditors will look for discrepancies by comparing your written and oral statements with credit applications and financial data you submitted to them—such as tax returns and bank statements. Even if your mistakes were purely accidental, the appearance of sloppiness (such as failing to mention property or minor debts, providing the wrong Social Security number, listing insufficient or incorrect information about creditors, or incorrectly valuing your property) will lead some courts to dismiss your case on the ground that you failed to meet your obligations as a debtor. If you discover any inaccuracy in your papers after you file them, be sure to point it out to the trustee at the creditors' meeting and promptly make the appropriate amendments.

- **Your motive for filing for Chapter 13 bankruptcy.** If you want to cure your mortgage default and get back on track with your house payments, pay off a tax debt, or get some breathing room to pay off your creditors, you have nothing to worry about. If the court finds that you have either of the following motives, however, it might also find a lack of good faith:

  - You filed for bankruptcy solely to reject a lease or contract, such as a time-share or car lease.

  - You filed for bankruptcy to handle only one debt, other than mortgage arrears or back taxes. The court is particularly likely to find lack of good faith if you file only to restructure payment on a nondischargeable debt, such as a student loan or criminal fine.

- **Your efforts to repay your debts.** If you will pay your nonpriority, unsecured creditors less than the full amount you owe, you will have to show the court that you are stretching your budget as much as you can. The court will want to see that the expenses you deduct from your income when calculating your disposable income are reasonably necessary to support yourself and your dependents. You'll have few problems if you can show that you've eliminated payments on luxury items, depleted your investments, canceled your country club membership, brought down your living expenses, and/or increased your hours at work.

- **The cause of your financial trouble.** Bankruptcy courts are reluctant to find bad faith if your financial problems are due to events beyond your control, such as exceptional medical expenses or an accident, job loss, or death in the family.

The Plan Is Not Feasible

The second most likely objection is that your plan is not feasible—that is, that you won't be able to make required payments or comply with the other terms of the plan.

There are two arguments a creditor might make:

- Your Forms 122C-1 and 122C-2 (along with *Schedules I* and *J*) do not show that you have enough income to pay all required debts. For instance, if you owe $35,000 in priority taxes (which must be paid in full) but your current monthly income won't allow you to pay $583 a month ($34,980) for the next five years, you can't propose a feasible plan.

- Your income as shown in *Schedule I* (your actual current income) does not exceed your expenses as listed in *Schedule J* by enough to pay all required debts. If, on the other hand, your *Schedule I* income, when compared to your *Schedule J* expenses, is sufficient to pay all your mandatory debts, you may be able to propose a feasible plan even if you have nothing left over to pay your unsecured creditors. This will depend on whether or not your bankruptcy court lets you use your *Schedules I* and *J* to propose a feasible plan or whether you are forced to use the figures listed on Forms 122C-1 and 122C-2. (For more information, see "If Your Actual Income Is Different From Your 'Current Monthly Income': *Hamilton v. Lanning,*" in Ch. 5.)

Your creditors might also question your job stability, the likelihood that you'll incur extraordinary expenses, and whether you have any outside sources of money. The court will likely find that your plan is not feasible—and refuse to confirm it—if any of the following is true:

- Your business has been failing, but you have predicted a rebound (on a wing and a prayer) and intend to use the proceeds to make your plan payments.
- You propose making plan payments from the proceeds of the sale of certain property, but a sale isn't imminent. For example, if your house has been on the market for a long time and you haven't received any offers, the court probably won't confirm a plan that depends on your house selling.
- Your plan includes a balloon payment, but you haven't identified a source of money you'll use to make the payment.
- You owe back child support or alimony and have been held in contempt of court for failing to pay.
- You've been convicted of a crime and face a likely jail sentence.

The Plan Is Not in the Best Interests of the Creditors

When you file for Chapter 13 bankruptcy, you must pay your unsecured creditors at least as much as they would have received if you had filed for Chapter 7 bankruptcy—in other words, you must pay them at least the value of your nonexempt property less the trustee's fee and costs of sale. (See Ch. 5 for more information on this requirement.) This is called the "best interests of the creditors" test.

If a creditor raises this objection, your attorney will prepare a written "liquidation analysis" that provides the value of the property (including how you came up with that value), the exemption you are claiming, the trustee's statutory commission, and the costs of sale, if any. The final result—the value of the property, less your exempt amount, the trustee's commission, and the costs of sale—is the proper value to use when determining whether your plan satisfies the best interests of the creditors. You may be called on to negotiate one or more numbers in your liquidation analysis, but the burden will be on the creditor to prove why your numbers are wrong.

If you lose on this point, you'll need to raise the amount of your monthly payments to your nonpriority, unsecured creditors or extend the life of your plan (if it doesn't already last for five years).

The Plan Unfairly Discriminates

In your plan, you must specify which unsecured creditors will be paid in full and which, if any, will get less. To do that, you can create classes of unsecured creditors, specifying how much (or what percentage of your payments) each class will receive, as long as you do not unfairly discriminate against any particular creditor. (Classes of creditors are explained in Ch. 8.)

Handling Creditor Claims

After you file for bankruptcy, the trustee sends a notice of your bankruptcy filing to all the creditors you listed in your papers. In general, creditors who want to be paid must file a claim within 70 days after the bankruptcy filing date (the period is longer for government creditors).

Sometimes, a creditor you want to pay through your Chapter 13 plan forgets to file a claim. If this happens, you may have to file a *Proof of Claim* on behalf of the creditor. For example, if you want the trustee to pay the creditor under your plan and the trustee won't make the payment without a *Proof of Claim*, you will have to file one for the creditor. The time limit for filing a *Proof of Claim* on a creditor's behalf is short—you have only 30 days after the deadline the creditor missed to file your papers. (Bankruptcy Rule 3004.)

Secured creditors. The Bankruptcy Code requires secured creditors to file claims in order to be paid, like any other creditor But, if a secured creditor doesn't file a claim, it doesn't mean you won't have to pay the debt to keep the property. The creditor's lien stays on the property so if you fail to pay the debt—either through the plan or outside of the plan—the creditor will be able to enforce the lien rights, sell the property, and use the proceeds to pay down the debt balance.

CAUTION

To pay arrearages on a secured debt, you must file a *Proof of Claim*. If you want to make up missed payments on a secured debt in your Chapter 13 case and the secured creditor doesn't file a claim, you will have to file it on the creditor's behalf. For example, if you have missed three house payments, but the lender doesn't file a claim, the trustee won't pay your arrears through your plan unless you file the claim yourself. If you don't, the lender would probably ask the court for permission to proceed with a foreclosure.

Priority creditors. Priority creditors must file a claim to be paid. Most priority creditors must file the claim within 70 days after the filing of the petition. Government agencies must file a *Proof of Claim* within 180 days after the date you filed your case. The government can get an extension if it formally requests one before the 180 days expire. (Bankruptcy Rule 3002(c) (1).) The IRS is notoriously late in filing claims, but it is usually granted extensions.

Nonpriority, unsecured creditors. Nonpriority, unsecured creditors must file a claim to be paid. If a nonpriority, unsecured creditor does not, that creditor's debt will be discharged when you complete your plan, unless the debt is nondischargeable.

If you want to pay a nondischargeable unsecured debt through your Chapter 13 plan (to avoid having the debt remain after your case ends) and the creditor doesn't file a claim, you will have to file it on the creditor's behalf.

Objecting to a Creditor's Claim

Unless you file a written objection to a creditor's claim, the trustee will pay the claim. (In bankruptcy legalese, claims the trustee pays are called "allowed" claims.) You can file an objection at any time, but the sooner the better. You'll have to give notice and schedule a court hearing, at which the creditor must prove you owe the claim. This is where you get to contest the validity of a disputed debt, such as a mortgage or tax debt.

Possible reasons for objecting to a creditor's claim include:

- You owe less than the creditor claims you do.
- A secured creditor has overstated the value of the collateral.
- The creditor has characterized the debt as secured (meaning you'll have to pay it in full), and you think it's unsecured.
- The claim was filed late. Most courts disallow late claims. Some, however, allow late claims if the creditor shows "excusable neglect" or another good reason for the failure to file on time.
- The creditor hasn't provided a paper trail proving that it owns the lien—for example, the creditor can't come up with a copy of your original promissory note and security agreement or can't produce assignments linking itself to those original documents. (This ground for objecting to a claim is increasingly common in cases involving foreclosures.)

Asking the Court to Eliminate Liens

During your Chapter 13 case, you may be able to get the court to reduce or eliminate liens on your property. If you succeed, you'll still owe the debt, but it will be unsecured. The creditor then shares in what you are paying your other unsecured creditors and you keep the property, free of the lien. (See *In re Lane*, 280 F.3d 663 (6th Cir. 2002).)

Which Liens Can Be Avoided

Lien avoidance is a procedure by which you ask the bankruptcy court to allow you to "avoid" (eliminate or reduce) certain liens. If your Chapter 13 repayment plan proposes to pay nothing or very little on your unsecured debts, lien avoidance makes a lot of sense. As long as there's a lien, you have to pay it in full to keep your secured property.

Lien avoidance is available only in very limited circumstances, and only for certain types of liens.

Security Interest Liens

A security interest is a secured debt you take on voluntarily, by pledging property as collateral for the debt. The creditor's interest in the collateral is secured by a lien. Common security interests include mortgages, home equity loans, car loans, store charges that contain a security agreement, and bank loans for which you pledge collateral.

You can avoid a security interest lien only if it meets these criteria:

1. **You obtained the loan by pledging property you already own (not property you purchased with the loan).** This is called a nonpossessory, nonpurchase-money security interest. It sounds complicated, but it's easier to understand when you break it down:

   - Nonpossessory means the creditor does not physically keep the property you pledge as collateral—you do. (In contrast, if you leave you property at a pawnshop to get a loan, that would be a possessory security interest, for which lien avoidance is not available.)
   - Nonpurchase money means you didn't use the money from the loan to buy the collateral.
   - Security interest means the lien was created by agreement between you and the creditor.

2. **You are able to claim the pledged property as exempt.** Exemptions are explained in Ch. 5.

3. **The collateral you pledged and claimed as exempt fits into certain categories of property.** These categories are:

   - household furnishings, household goods, clothing, appliances, books, musical instruments, or jewelry that is primarily for your personal, family, or household use
   - health aids professionally prescribed for you or a dependent

Objecting to a *Proof of Claim* for a Credit Card Debt

The court will presume that a *Proof of Claim* submitted on a credit card debt (most likely by your credit card company) is valid if it is accompanied by a statement that includes the following information:

- if the entity filing the *Proof of Claim* is not the original lender or card issuer (for example, if the claim holder is a collection agency or the original issuer sold your account to someone else), the name of the entity that the claim holder purchased the account from
- the name of the entity to whom the debt was owed when you made your last transaction on the account
- the date of your last transaction on the account
- the date of your last payment on the account, and
- if the account was charged off, the date on which this was done.

The claim holder must also state the amount of the debt prior to your bankruptcy filing and break down any additional charges, such as interest, late fees, and attorneys' fees.

If the *Proof of Claim* includes this information, then you have the burden of refuting the claim as part of your objection. If the *Proof of Claim* doesn't include this information, the creditor must prove the claim. Finally, if the holder of the claim is not the original creditor, the creditor must provide documentation that ownership of the claim has been transferred, in addition to providing the other information. (See *In re Armstrong*, 320 B.R. 97 (N.D. Tex. 2005).)

If you are proposing to pay a very small percentage of your nonpriority, unsecured debt, it may not be worth your time to object to a credit card claim. Even if you win, that just means you will have to pay your other nonpriority, unsecured creditors a little more. Remember, the amount you have to pay to these creditors is based on your disposable income. You shouldn't spend time worrying about which creditors get what. Or, as the old saying goes, "Don't sweat the small stuff."

- animals or crops held primarily for your personal, family, or household use, or
- implements, professional books, or tools used in a trade (yours or a dependent's).

These rules prevent you from eliminating liens on real estate or on motor vehicles, unless the vehicle is a tool of your trade.

Generally, a vehicle is not considered a tool of the trade unless it is an integral part of your business—for example, you are a door-to-door salesperson or make deliveries. If you just use your vehicle to get to and from work, it isn't considered a tool of the trade, even if you have no other way to commute.

TIP
You can strip certain liens from your home. Although you cannot avoid liens like the first mortgage on your residence, you may be able to get rid of second mortgages and home loans through a process known as lien stripping. Depending on your state's law, you may also be able to strip homeowners' association or condominium association liens. See Ch. 1 for details.

You Cannot Avoid Liens That Attach to Later-Acquired Property

In California and many other states, a creditor who has sued you in court and obtained a money judgment can record that judgment as a lien even if you don't own any property in the county. If you later acquire real estate in the county where the judgment is recorded, a lien will attach to that real estate. (If you have recorded a homestead declaration, however, that might prevent the lien from attaching to a later-acquired home.)

The U.S. Supreme Court has ruled that you cannot avoid liens in bankruptcy if the lien attached to later-acquired property. (*Farrey v. Sanderfoot*, 500 U.S. 291 (1991).) Also see *In re Bailey*, 2011 WL 1576958 (Bankr. D. Idaho 2011).

Nonconsensual Liens

A nonconsensual lien—a secured debt that you didn't agree to—can be avoided only if:
- It's a judicial lien.
- You can claim the collateral as exempt.
- The lien, if honored, would deprive you of your full exemption.

You can remove judicial liens from any exempt property, including real estate and cars.

Tax Liens

If your federal tax debt is secured, you may have a basis for challenging the lien. Quite often, the IRS makes mistakes when it records a Notice of Federal Tax Lien.

Here are some possible grounds for asking the court to remove a tax lien:
- The Notice of Federal Tax Lien was never recorded, though the IRS claims it was.
- The Notice of Federal Tax Lien was recorded after the automatic stay took effect.

Even if the Notice of Federal Tax Lien was recorded correctly, you still may have a basis to fight it if:
- The lien expired (liens last only ten years).
- The lien is based on an invalid tax assessment by the IRS.

Carrying Out Your Plan

Once the court has approved your repayment plan, you should be in for smooth sailing as long as you make your monthly payments. If an unforeseen problem arises, and you think you're going to have trouble making a payment, notify your attorney right away. Your attorney will notify the trustee and help you work something out.

The trustee is interested in your successful completion of your Chapter 13 plan. Remember, the trustee gets a cut of everything paid to creditors under your plan. If you have to convert to Chapter 7 or your case is dismissed, the trustee's income from your case will be cut off.

This chapter covers issues that might arise after your plan is confirmed as well as what happens once you complete your plan.

Your Income Increases

There are a couple of ways for the trustee to keep track of your income as your case proceeds. You may be asked to submit an annual income and expense statement to the trustee (and to any creditor who requests one). In addition, you must remain current on your tax returns throughout your case and might have to provide a copy of your tax return to the trustee (and to any creditor who makes a request). (For more information on these requirements, see Ch. 10.) From these documents, the trustee can determine whether your income has increased.

If your financial condition improves sufficiently to allow you to pay more to your unsecured creditors (assuming your plan doesn't provide for them to be paid in full), the trustee or an unsecured creditor may file a motion with the bankruptcy court to amend your plan. The motion will request that the court order you to increase each payment, pay a lump sum amount (especially if you've inherited valuable property or won the lottery), or extend your plan (unless it already lasts for five years). The bankruptcy court will most likely grant the motion.

What If Your Income Increases Because You Pay Off a 401(k) Loan?

If, during the course of your Chapter 13 plan, you pay off a loan you took out from your 401(k) plan, your income will effectively increase (since you'll no longer be making those loan payments). Do you have to modify your plan to pay more into it?

One court has ruled that in this situation your plan payments can remain the same. The idea being that you can contribute the amount formerly dedicated to repaying the loan to your 401(k) plan. (*In re Egan*, 458 B.R. 836 (Bankr. E.D. Pa. 2011).)

However, other courts have ruled the opposite: That you must modify your plan so that unsecured creditors get paid more. (See, for example, *In re Seafort*, 669 F.3d 662 (6th Cir. 2012) and *In re Brann*, 457 B.R. 738 (Bankr. C.D. Ill. 2011).)

If You Get a Windfall

If you win the lottery, get a substantial raise, or receive an inheritance, or if your house goes way up in value, you may be able to dismiss your case and pay off your debts outside of bankruptcy. But keep in mind that the interest (and sometimes the penalties) on your debts that stopped accruing while you were in bankruptcy can be added back when you dismiss your case. And, don't assume you can use the equity in your home to apply for and obtain a loan. Don't dismiss your case and then apply for the loan. If you are rejected, you'll just have to refile for bankruptcy.

Selling Property

While you are in a Chapter 13, if you want to sell any of your property and the sale is not in the ordinary course of the operation of a business, you will need to file a motion with the court and obtain court permission. You must send notice of the motion to authorize the sale of property to all creditors and the trustee so that all parties have an opportunity to object. It is possible that any money you realize from the sale, after all of the liens are paid, will have to be paid into the plan if you have not claimed the property as exempt.

Modifying Your Plan When Problems Come Up

Chapter 13 bankruptcy isn't easy. You must live under a strict budget for three to five years. Problems are bound to arise. Fortunately, the Chapter 13 bankruptcy system has built-in procedures designed to handle the disruptions. Any time after your plan is confirmed, you, the trustee, or an unsecured creditor who filed a claim can file a motion with the court, asking permission to modify the plan. Keep in mind that your modified plan cannot last more than five years after the date your plan originally began.

This section discusses five common situations in which you might need to modify your plan.

You Miss a Payment

If the trustee doesn't receive a plan payment, that's a problem. Sometimes, the problem will be easy to solve—the payment got lost in the mail, your employer forgot to send it (if there is an income deduction order), or you changed jobs and forgot to change the income deduction order.

If you missed the payment because you are struggling to make ends meet, resolving the problem may be more complicated. But don't lose heart. If the problem looks temporary, and you are several months or years into your plan, the trustee may suggest that you modify your plan to do any of the following:

- skip a few payments altogether, meaning your unsecured creditors would receive less than you originally proposed
- skip a few payments now and extend your plan to make them up, assuming your plan is not already scheduled to last five years
- make a lump sum payment to make up the payments you've missed, or
- increase several payments to cover the payments you missed.

If the problem looks likely to continue, or it happens very early in your Chapter 13 case, the trustee is less likely to support a modification of your plan. Instead, the trustee (or a creditor) is likely to file a motion to have your case dismissed or require you to convert to Chapter 7.

If you file a motion to modify your plan because you've missed some payments, a creditor may ask that the modified plan contain what is called a drop-dead clause. Such a clause provides that if you miss another payment, your case will automatically convert to Chapter 7 bankruptcy or be dismissed by the court. Many courts include drop-dead clauses in modified plans.

Your plan payment isn't the only payment you might miss. If the court approved your request to make direct payments to certain creditors (such as a mortgage lender) and you miss a payment, the creditor will take action. If the stay was already lifted for the creditor, it will be able to proceed without getting court permission. If the stay is in place, the creditor will likely file a motion to lift the stay so that it can proceed to foreclose or repossess its collateral.

If it's early in your plan and you haven't missed any other payments, ask the court for permission to modify your plan to pay the new arrears immediately. If the stay has already been lifted, this may not be possible.

Your Disposable Income Decreases

You wouldn't have filed for Chapter 13 bankruptcy if you hadn't had debt problems in your past—perhaps because of job losses or reduced work hours. Filing for bankruptcy doesn't make those kinds of problems go away.

If your income goes down, you or your spouse suffers a serious illness or goes on maternity leave, or you incur an extraordinary expense, call the trustee. The trustee is likely to suggest that you suspend payments for a month or two. You can make up the difference by modifying your plan to:

- make a lump sum payment when your income goes back up
- extend your plan, if it is scheduled to last less than five years, or
- decrease the amount or percentage that a certain class of creditor receives—for example, you might have originally proposed to pay your general unsecured creditors 75% of what you owe but will now file a modified plan that calls for them to get only 45%.

Creditors rarely object to a short suspension in payments, and bankruptcy courts routinely grant those modifications. If you propose a longer-term suspension, however, your secured creditors may object, especially if collateral is involved that is decreasing in value. You may have to continue your payments on secured debts and suspend only the unsecured portion for a while.

You Need to Replace Your Car

A lot can go wrong with a car during the three to five years you're paying into your Chapter 13 plan—especially if you bought a used car before you filed to minimize your expenses. Chapter 13 trustees often hear from debtors whose cars have died or are on their last legs. This situation raises several issues in a Chapter 13 bankruptcy case.

Taking out a new loan. Let's say your car dies, you need another one, and you want to take out a loan to pay for it. You file a motion to modify your plan to include payments for the new loan. Will the court confirm the new plan? The court is likely to say "yes" if you *must* have the car to complete your plan—for example, you're a salesperson. If, however, the car is just a convenience, the payments will significantly increase your monthly expenses, and you've had trouble making your plan payments, the court will probably turn you down.

For most people, the need for a car isn't all or nothing. In that case, the court will probably allow you to take out the loan if the effect is to lower your bills (for example, you were still making payments on your previous car and the loan will reduce your payments) or to increase your income (for instance, it would take two hours each way to get to work by public transit and only 30 minutes by car, so with a car you can get paid for three more hours' work a day).

Giving back a wrecked car. Now let's assume that after your plan is confirmed, your car is wrecked or won't run. You want to give the car back to the lender and modify your plan to treat the balance due (called a deficiency) as an unsecured claim. Several courts have allowed this. Other courts have ruled that a secured creditor cannot be reclassified as an unsecured creditor after a plan has been confirmed and that the debtor still must pay the full balance owed the lender.

A court might look at how you got into the situation. If your negligence or recklessness caused the problem, the court may be more inclined to deny modification of your plan.

What happens to insurance proceeds. If your car loan is paid off and your car is damaged in an accident, you may get some insurance money. The court will probably want you to use that money to get the new car you need. If your car wasn't paid off, the insurance money will go to pay off your lender. If the insurance proceeds exceed what you owe the lender under your plan, you may be able to use the difference. Remember, once the court determines the amount a secured creditor is entitled to get under the plan, that's all the creditor gets.

You Incur New Debt

If you incur new debt after your plan is confirmed, such as unexpected medical bills, you can amend your plan so the creditor is paid through your plan. You may have anticipated this by creating a class of postpetition creditors in your plan. If so, your plan should specify that these creditors receive 100% of what they are owed, plus interest. If you didn't create such a class, you'll have to handle postpetition debts as they arise.

No matter what your plan provides, your postpetition creditors will need to file a claim with the trustee in order to get paid through your plan.

If Your Plan Includes a Class of Postpetition Creditors

If your plan includes 100% payment of your postpetition debts, your postpetition creditors are unlikely to object to being paid through the trustee.

If your plan pays less than 100% of these debts and the creditor disagrees with the terms of your plan or you miss a plan payment, the creditor might object. If this happens, you will have to modify your plan to handle the creditor's objection. If the creditor is still not satisfied, the creditor might be allowed to pursue collection outside of the bankruptcy court.

> **EXAMPLE:** For the first year and a half of your plan, you will be paying your priority tax debt and your mortgage arrears. Not until Month 19 will the trustee pay your unsecured creditors, including a class of postpetition creditors. Three months into your plan, the court lets you incur a medical debt. The doctor objects to being paid through the plan because the first payment won't come for at least 16 months. You will probably have to amend your plan to add the medical debt to the other debts that will be paid off early in the plan.

If Your Plan Does Not Include a Class of Postpetition Creditors

If your plan does not include a class of postpetition creditors, and you want to pay a new creditor through your plan, you will have to modify your plan. Sometimes, a postpetition creditor files a motion to be included in a modified Chapter 13 plan. The motion is likely to be granted.

If you don't modify your plan to include postpetition creditors to whom you default, the creditor may be able to take collection efforts outside of the bankruptcy court.

You Buy Health Insurance

Chapter 13 debtors can reduce what they pay into their repayment plans by the actual amount they spend to buy health insurance for themselves and their families. This is intended to help reduce the number of people who go without health insurance.

To take advantage of this rule, you have to demonstrate a number of facts, including:

- The insurance is necessary.
- The cost of the insurance is reasonable.
- The cost is not significantly more than the cost of your previous policy or the cost necessary to maintain the lapsed policy (if you were previously insured).
- You have not already claimed the cost as an expense for purposes of determining your disposable income (on Forms 122C-1 and 122C-2 or *Schedule J*).
- You actually purchased the policy.

Attempts to Revoke Your Confirmation

If a creditor or the trustee thinks you obtained your confirmation fraudulently—for example, because you used a false name, address, or Social Security number—one of them may file something called an adversary proceeding asking the court to revoke your confirmation. This is extremely rare. An adversary proceeding to revoke a confirmation must be filed within 180 days of the confirmation.

An adversary proceeding is much more formal than a motion. It creates an entirely new lawsuit, separate from your bankruptcy case, and proceeds like any other lawsuit. You will need a lawyer to help you.

The bankruptcy court won't revoke your confirmation because of fraud unless it finds that:

- You made a materially (significant) false statement in your papers, in a deposition, or in court.
- You either knew the statement was false or made the statement with reckless disregard to its truth.
- You intended to induce the court into relying on the statement.
- The court did rely on the statement.

When You Complete Your Plan

It's quite an accomplishment—and something to be proud of—to stick with a Chapter 13 plan to the end. After you have made all of your payments under your plan, filed a certificate showing that you have completed your financial management counseling, and certified that you are current on your domestic support obligations (if any), the court grants a "full payment" discharge. In most courts, the trustee simply files the discharge order on behalf of the court after determining that all payments have been made. In other courts, you must ask the trustee to file the discharge order.

TIP

File Form 423 right away. You must complete a financial management counseling course—and file a certification, Form 423, stating that you have done so—before you make your last plan payment. If you don't file Form 423 on time, the court will close your case without granting you a discharge. To get your discharge, you will have to reopen the case and pay fees. To avoid this fate, file Form 423 as soon as you complete your counseling, even if you haven't yet reached your final plan payment.

Debts Covered by the Discharge

Your Chapter 13 discharge wipes out the balance owed on all of your debts, as long as the debt is included in your plan and does not fall into one of these categories:

- long-term obligations for which the last payment is still due—that is, it will be paid after you've made the final payment on your plan
- nondischargeable debts, as described in Ch. 1, or
- debts you incurred after filing your Chapter 13 case, if the creditor was not paid or was only partially paid through the plan.

The Discharge Hearing

After struggling for years to repay your debts, the long-awaited end of your bankruptcy case may be a little anticlimactic. The court may hold a brief hearing, called a discharge hearing, and require you to attend. At the hearing, the judge explains the effects of discharging your debts in bankruptcy and may lecture you about staying clear of debt.

Few courts, however, schedule a discharge hearing in Chapter 13 cases. Whether or not you must attend a discharge hearing, you'll receive a copy of your discharge order from the court within about four weeks after you complete your payments. If you don't, contact the trustee. Make several photocopies of the order and keep them in a safe place. If it's necessary, send copies to creditors who attempt to collect their debt after your case is over or to credit bureaus that continue to report that you owe a discharged debt.

Ending the Income Deduction Order

The trustee will probably remember to stop your income deduction order after you've made your last payment. If the trustee forgets, however, you may need to contact the trustee.

Debtor Rehabilitation Program

A few Chapter 13 bankruptcy courts have created debtor rehabilitation/credit reestablishment programs. The purpose is to reward people who choose Chapter 13 bankruptcy instead of Chapter 7 bankruptcy and who succeed in completing their Chapter 13 cases.

If you have paid off a high percentage of your unsecured debts (often 75% or more), you may apply for credit from certain creditors.

In the typical program, the court staff includes a "credit liaison." This person will help you:

- acquire, review, and correct your credit file—in particular, to get your credit file to show that you completed a Chapter 13 bankruptcy in which you paid back a high percentage of your debts
- set up a budget

- analyze your ability to repay new debts
- understand the different types of credit
- identify possible sources of credit and credit limits
- fill out credit applications
- obtain information to support your application, such as your Chapter 13 payment history and completed plan
- prepare for any in-person interview with a creditor (for a car loan, for example), and
- understand how creditors make their decisions about extending credit.

Ask the trustee whether your court has a rehabilitation program. If it doesn't, find out from the trustee if a nearby bankruptcy court has one in which you might participate. If there's nothing nearby, you'll have to take your own steps to rebuild your credit. (See Ch. 14.)

If You Cannot Complete Your Plan

Despite your best efforts to keep a handle on your finances and make your regular plan payments, you may be unable to complete your plan. If this happens to you, take solace in the fact that you aren't alone—a significant percentage of Chapter 13 debtors eventually find themselves in this position.

If you can't complete your plan, you have three options: Dismiss your case, convert it to a Chapter 7 bankruptcy, or ask the court to grant you a hardship discharge.

Dismiss Your Case

You have the absolute right to dismiss your Chapter 13 bankruptcy case at any time, as long as:

- The court doesn't believe that you filed your bankruptcy case in bad faith (see Ch. 11).
- You didn't start in another type of bankruptcy (typically, Chapter 7) and then convert to Chapter 13 bankruptcy.

If you converted to Chapter 13 from a different type of bankruptcy, you have to file a noticed motion asking the court for permission to dismiss your case. (See Ch. 11 for information on noticed motions.) The court may deny your request—and order you to convert to Chapter 7 bankruptcy—if it feels that you are abusing the bankruptcy system. Or, it may grant your request, but

attach conditions, such as issuing a sanction barring you from filing for bankruptcy again for a certain period of time.

If your case is dismissed, there are several important consequences:

- All liens that you had removed from your property in your Chapter 13 case are reinstated.
- All money you have paid the trustee that has not yet been disbursed to your creditors will be returned to you, less the trustee's expenses.
- The automatic stay ends, which means that your creditors are free to go after you and your assets for payment.
- Interest (and in some cases penalties) that stopped accruing during your bankruptcy will be added on to your debts.
- You cannot refile for bankruptcy—Chapter 13, Chapter 7, or any other kind—within 180 days if you dismissed your case after a creditor filed a motion asking the bankruptcy court to lift the automatic stay.

If you change your mind and decide that you want your case to proceed, you can file a motion with the bankruptcy court within ten days of the dismissal asking that your case be reinstated. Unless you have a history of filing and dismissing, or you've had serious problems making the payments under this plan, the court will probably grant your motion.

Convert Your Case to Chapter 7 Bankruptcy

You have an absolute right to convert your Chapter 13 bankruptcy case to a Chapter 7 bankruptcy case at any time, as long as you haven't received a Chapter 7 discharge in a case filed within the previous eight years.

When you convert to Chapter 7, the bankruptcy forms you filed for your Chapter 13 case will usually become a part of your new case. A few bankruptcy courts require you to file an entirely new set of schedules, even if nothing has changed. Within 30 days after you convert, you must file an additional bankruptcy form called the *Statement of Intention for Individuals Filing Under Chapter 7*. It tells the court what you plan to do with your secured debts. You will also have to attend a new meeting of creditors.

Because any debts you incurred after filing your Chapter 13 case can be discharged in your Chapter 7 case (if they are otherwise dischargeable), you must file a report under Bankruptcy Rule 1019(5) listing all of the unpaid debts that you incurred after you filed for Chapter 13. You must then amend the appropriate bankruptcy forms to list these new debts.

If, in your Chapter 13 case, the court established a value for certain items of property or determined the amount of a secured claim, those values and amounts will not necessarily apply in the converted case. (11 U.S.C. § 348(f)(1)(B).)

When you convert to Chapter 7, property you have acquired during your Chapter 13 is not property of the Chapter 13 bankruptcy estate. But, if the court determines that your conversion to Chapter 7 bankruptcy is in bad faith, the court can order that the property acquired during Chapter 13 be included in your Chapter 7 bankruptcy estate. (11 U.S.C. § 348(f)(2).)

Most courts take the position that the conversion to Chapter 7 does not restart the time for the trustee and creditors to object to your exemptions if that time period expired in the Chapter 13. There are a few courts, however, that do allow an additional 30-day period for objection to exemptions after the conversion.

If your creditors have filed *Proofs of Claim*, those claims carry over to your Chapter 7 case. However, if you dismiss your Chapter 13 case and refile a Chapter 7 case, your creditors will have to file new claims, assuming you have assets to be distributed.

CAUTION

You may have to pass the means test when you convert to Chapter 7. Just because you have a right to convert your Chapter 13 case to Chapter 7 doesn't mean you will necessarily qualify for Chapter 7 relief. In particular, if you cannot pass the means test because of your income, you may run into trouble in some districts. Some bankruptcy courts (and one Bankruptcy Appellate Panel) have ruled that if you convert to Chapter 7 from a Chapter 13 case, you must still pass the means test in order to be eligible for Chapter 7 relief. (See, e.g., *In re Chapman*, 447 B.R. 250 (B.A.P. 8th Cir. 2011); *In re Lassiter*, 2011 WL 2039363 (Bankr. E.D. Va. 2011); *In re Phillips*, 417 B.R. 30 (Bankr. S.D. Ohio 2009).) Other courts, however, have ruled that the means test doesn't apply to Chapter 7 cases that have been converted from Chapter 13. (See, e.g., *In re Guarin*, 2009 WL 4500476 (Bankr. D. Mass. 2009); *In re Willis*, 408 B.R. 803 (Bankr. W.D. Missouri 2009); *In re Dudley*, 405 B.R. 790 (Bankr. W.D. Va. 2009).) Some courts have not yet addressed the issue.

RESOURCE

Resource for Chapter 7 bankruptcy. *How to File for Chapter 7 Bankruptcy*, by Cara O'Neill (Nolo), contains detailed information on Chapter 7 bankruptcy.

Seek a Hardship Discharge

If you cannot complete your Chapter 13 repayment plan, you can file a motion with the bankruptcy court asking for a hardship discharge. (11 U.S.C. § 1328(b).) The court will grant your request only if three conditions are met:

- You failed to complete your plan payments due to circumstances "for which you should not justly be held accountable." Your burden is to show the maximum possible misery and the worst of awfuls—that is, more than just a temporary job loss or temporary physical disability. Proving that your condition is permanent is usually key; you may need to bring medical evidence to court.

- Based on what you have already paid into the plan, your unsecured creditors have received at least what they would have received if you had filed for Chapter 7. (This is typically a hard condition to meet unless you have little or no nonexempt property.)

- Modification of your plan is not practical. To meet this requirement, you do not have to file a motion for modification and lose it; you just have to show the bankruptcy court that you wouldn't be able to make payments even under a modified plan.

Debts That Are Not Discharged

If the court grants your motion for a hardship discharge, only unsecured, nonpriority, dischargeable debts are discharged. The following debts typically are not wiped out in a hardship discharge:

- priority debts
- secured debts
- arrears on secured debts
- debts you didn't list in your bankruptcy papers
- student loans
- most federal, state, and local taxes, as well as any amounts you borrowed or charged on a credit card to pay those taxes
- child support, alimony, and debts resulting from a divorce or separation decree

- fines or restitution imposed in a criminal-type proceeding
- debts for death or personal injury resulting from your intoxicated driving
- debts for dues or special assessments you owe to a condominium or cooperative association
- debts you couldn't discharge in a previous bankruptcy that was dismissed due to fraud or misfeasance, and
- debts you owe to a pension, profit-sharing, stock bonus, or other plan established under various sections of the Internal Revenue Code.

Debts That Are Not Discharged If the Creditor Successfully Objects

Some debts will be discharged in a hardship discharge unless the creditor files a successful objection to the discharge in court. These debts include:

- debts incurred through your fraudulent acts, including using a credit card when you knew you would be unable to pay the bill
- debts from willful and malicious injury you caused to another person or property, and
- debts from embezzlement, larceny, or breach of trust (fiduciary duty).

If you have a debt that falls into one of these categories, your best strategy is to do nothing and hope the creditor does the same. If the creditor objects, the court will examine the circumstances in which you incurred the debt to determine whether or not it can be legally eliminated. If you want the debt to be discharged, you should respond to the creditor's objection.

Life After Bankruptcy

Congratulations! After you receive your final discharge and your case is closed, you can get on with your life and enjoy the fresh start that bankruptcy offers. This chapter explains how you can start to rebuild your credit and how to deal with any problems that come up.

Rebuilding Your Credit

A bankruptcy filing can legally remain on your credit record for ten years after you filed your papers, although most credit bureaus remove a Chapter 13 bankruptcy filing after seven years.

What effect a Chapter 13 bankruptcy will have on your credit score depends on several factors, including the status of your credit before filing and how many accounts were included in the bankruptcy. According to Fair Isaac (the largest credit scoring company in the nation), if you have good credit prior to bankruptcy, your score will likely plummet (at least initially) when you file. However, if you have lots of negative marks on your credit report and a low credit score, filing for bankruptcy will probably have only a modest impact on your credit. Fair Isaac also warns that the more accounts included in your bankruptcy, the more the bankruptcy will negatively affect your score.

Many people believe that filing for Chapter 7 bankruptcy is worse for your credit than filing for Chapter 13. Fair Isaac, however, says both types of bankruptcy have an equally negative impact on your score.

Ironically, in many cases, filing for bankruptcy will help you start building good credit sooner than if you don't file. If you are struggling with more debt than you can pay, the late and missed payments will mount up, and you'll max out your available credit (both big negatives for your credit rating).

Postbankruptcy, your strategy for rebuilding credit is simple: Stick to a budget, always pay your bills on time, and gradually take on credit that you can afford to pay off each month.

 RESOURCE

Resource for rebuilding credit. For more information on rebuilding your credit—including obtaining a copy of your credit file, requesting that a credit reporting agency correct mistakes, contacting creditors directly, and getting positive information into your credit file—see *Credit Repair*, by Amy Loftsgordon and Cara O'Neill (Nolo).

Create a Budget

The first step in rebuilding your credit is to create a budget. Making a budget will help you control impulses to overspend and help you start saving money.

Fortunately, the bankruptcy law requires you to participate in budget counseling prior to getting a discharge. You will be able to apply what you learn in your budget counseling class to our suggestions in this chapter.

Don't Take on Too Much Debt Too Soon

Habitual overspending can be just as hard to overcome as excessive gambling or drinking. If you think you may be a compulsive spender, avoid getting new credit. Instead, get a handle on your spending habits.

Debtors Anonymous, a 12-step support program similar to Alcoholics Anonymous, has programs nationwide. If a Debtors Anonymous group or a therapist recommends that you stay out of the credit system for a while, follow that advice. Even if you don't feel you're a compulsive spender, paying as you spend may still be the way to go.

To find a Debtors Anonymous meeting close by, go to www.debtorsanonymous.org or call 781-453-2743 or 800-421-2383.

Before you try to limit how much you spend, take some time to find out exactly how much money you spend now. Tally up all of your regular expenses, like your mortgage or rent, car payments, insurance, health care costs, food, dry cleaning, and the like. It's often helpful to track your spending for a month by writing down everything you spend each day. This helps you figure out how much you spend on things like entertainment and gifts. Don't forget to add in yearly or quarterly expenses, like homeowners' insurance or car insurance.

When you review your expenses and spending log, look for problem areas. Do you buy things on impulse? Are you spending more than you thought in a certain category? Also think about changes you can make so that you can save money at the end of each week, even if it's just a small amount. Then set a weekly or monthly savings goal.

Once you understand your spending habits and identify the changes you need to make, you're ready to make a budget. At the top of a sheet of paper, write down your monthly net income—that is, the amount you bring home after taxes and other mandatory deductions. At the left, list everything you spend money on in a month, any investments you plan to make (including into a savings or money market account), and any nondischargeable or other debts you make payments on. To the right of each item, write down the amount of money you spend, deposit, or pay each month. Finally, total up the amount. If it exceeds your monthly income, make some changes—eliminate or reduce expenditures for nonnecessities—and start over. Once your budget is final, stick to it.

Keep Your Credit Report Accurate

When you apply for credit, the creditor will contact a credit reporting agency and request a copy of your credit report or it will get your credit score from a credit scoring company, such as Fair Isaac. Your credit score is based on information in your report. Creditors use your report and score to decide whether to grant or deny your credit requests. In addition, some insurance companies, landlords, and employers obtain credit reports when evaluating potential insurance policyholders, tenants, or employees.

To make sure that creditors and others who use your credit report see you in the best light, review your report regularly and take steps to remove inaccurate and old information and add current positive information.

Start by obtaining a copy of your report from each of the "big three" reporting agencies (Equifax, Experian, and TransUnion). You are entitled to a free copy of your report from each agency every 12 months. You can get your free report at www.annual creditreport.com.

If you need your report more than once within 12 months, don't request reports from all three reporting agencies at once. Instead, stagger your requests over the course of the year, as needed. Also, you can get another

---

Avoiding Financial Problems

These nine rules, suggested by people who have been through bankruptcy, will help you stay out of financial hot water.

1. Create a realistic budget and stick to it.

2. Don't buy on impulse. When you see something you hadn't planned to purchase, go home and think it over. It's unlikely you'll return to the store and buy it.

3. Avoid sales unless you are looking for something you absolutely need. Buying a $500 item on sale for $400 isn't a $100 savings if you didn't need the item in the first place—it's spending $400 unnecessarily.

4. Get medical insurance. You can't avoid medical emergencies, so living without medical insurance is an invitation to financial ruin.

5. Charge items only if you can pay for them now. Don't charge based on future income; sometimes that income doesn't materialize.

6. Avoid large house payments. Obligate yourself only for what you can now afford and increase your mortgage payments only as your income increases. Again, don't obligate yourself based on future income that you might not have.

7. Think long and hard before agreeing to cosign or guarantee a loan for someone. Your signature obligates you as if you were the primary borrower. You can't be sure that the other person will pay.

8. If possible, avoid joint obligations with people who have questionable spending habits. If you incur a joint debt, you're probably liable for it all if the other person defaults.

9. Avoid high-risk investments, such as speculative real estate, penny stocks, and junk bonds. Invest conservatively in things such as certificates of deposit, money market funds, and government bonds. And never invest more than you can afford to lose.

free report in certain circumstances, or you can purchase one for a small fee. To learn more, get *Credit Repair*, by Amy Loftsgordon and Cara O'Neill (Nolo).

In addition to your credit history, your credit report will contain the sources of the information and the names of people or businesses who have requested your report within the last year, or within the last two years if those people sought your report for employment reasons.

Most types of negative credit information can remain on your report for seven years. Bankruptcies can remain on your report for up to ten years, although they often drop off after seven years. Some adverse information about student loans can remain on your report even longer.

Review your report for errors, inaccuracies, and incomplete or old information. You have the right to dispute all incomplete, inaccurate or outdated information. You can do this online or by mail. The credit reporting agency has three business days to remove the information, or between 30 and 45 days to investigate, and then an additional five days to remove the information or notify you of its decision.

If the credit reporting agency does not remove the information, you can submit a brief statement giving your side of the story that will be included in your report. Be aware, however, that your statement will remain on your report for seven years, which may be longer than the negative item you write about. Most creditors don't read

sample statements, but it usually doesn't hurt to include one (unless you don't want it in your report for seven years).

You also want to keep new negative information out of your report. To do this, remain current on your bills. What you owe, as well as how long it takes you to pay, will go in your report.

Avoid Credit Repair Agencies

You've probably seen ads for companies that claim they can fix your credit, qualify you for a loan, and get you a credit card. Stay clear of these companies. Their practices are almost always deceptive and sometimes illegal. Some steal the credit reports or Social Security numbers of people who have died or live in places like Guam or the U.S. Virgin Islands and replace your report with these other reports. Others create new identities for debtors by applying to the IRS for taxpayer ID numbers and telling debtors to use them in place of their Social Security numbers (which is illegal).

Even the legitimate companies can't do anything for you that you can't do yourself. If items in your credit report are correct, these companies cannot get them removed. About the only difference between using a legitimate credit repair agency and doing it yourself is the money you save by doing it yourself.

In addition to information about credit accounts, credit reports also contain information from public records, including criminal records. After receiving your bankruptcy discharge, be sure to modify public records to reflect what occurred in the bankruptcy, so wrong information won't appear in your credit report. For example, if a court case was pending against you at the time you filed for bankruptcy, and, as part of the bankruptcy, the potential judgment against you was discharged, be sure the court case is formally dismissed. You may need the help of an attorney. (See Ch. 15 for information on finding one.)

Negotiate With Current Creditors

If you owe any debts that show up as past due on your credit report (perhaps the debt wasn't discharged in your bankruptcy or was incurred after you filed), you can take steps to make them current. Contact the creditor and ask that the item be removed in exchange for full or partial payment. On a revolving account (with a department store, for example), ask the creditor to "re-age" the account so that it is shown as current. For help in negotiating with your creditors, consider contacting a local consumer credit counseling agency.

CAUTION
Think carefully before re-aging an account. There is a downside to asking a creditor to re-age an account. It resets the clock on the seven-year period that the creditor can report the delinquent account to credit reporting agencies. If you think you might have trouble paying the account down the line, think twice before asking the creditor to re-age it.

TIP
Choosing a credit counseling agency. Unscrupulous debt relief service agencies abound. They take your money and do little or nothing to help you. Your best bet, when looking for a legitimate credit counseling agency, is to choose one affiliated with the Consumer Credit Counseling Service (CCCS). You can find one at www.nfcc.org or call 800-388-2227. Or use an agency approved by the Office of the U.S. Trustee (the same agencies that you must use to get your prebankruptcy credit counseling).

Stabilize Your Income and Employment

Your credit history and score are not the only thing lenders will consider in deciding whether to give you credit. They also look carefully at the stability of your income and employment. Plus, if you start getting new credit before you're back on your feet financially, you'll end up in the same mess that led you to file for bankruptcy in the first place.

Get Credit and Use It Responsibly

Once you've gotten your finances under control, created a budget, and saved some money, it's time to start adding positive information into your credit report. One of the best ways to do this is to pay your bills on time. Payment history is weighted heavily by creditors and credit scoring agencies. But you can also improve your credit by getting and using small amounts of credit responsibly. Here are a few ways to do that.

Use an Existing Credit Card or Get a New Credit Card

If you have a credit card already, you can charge small amounts and pay the entire balance off each month. This will show creditors that you can use credit responsibly. But be honest with yourself: if you aren't going to pay the balance in full each month, don't use the card.

Getting a new credit card may not be as hard as you think. Many people who have filed for bankruptcy report getting credit card offers shortly after receiving a bankruptcy discharge. Keep in mind, though, that these cards will likely have high interest rates, annual fees, and other charges. Again, use the card to make small charges that you pay off every month.

Get a Secured Credit Card

If you can't get a regular credit card, you may be able to get a secured credit card. This option is good for people who need a credit card to book air travel or hotels. You deposit a sum of money into a bank or credit union savings account and are given a credit card with a credit limit that is a percentage of the amount you deposit (often between 50% and 120% of the amount you deposit).

Secured credit cards often come with extremely high interest rates. So use them carefully. Also, many banks and credit unions don't report payments on secured cards to the credit reporting agencies. If this is the case, using one responsibly will do nothing to improve your credit. Before you get a secured card, find out if the issuer will report payments to the credit reporting agencies. Or look for a secured card that will let you convert it to a regular credit card down the line. Finally, never get a secured credit card that is secured by your home.

Borrow From a Bank

Bank loans provide an excellent way to rebuild credit. A few banks offer something called a passbook savings loan, which is a lot like a secured credit card. You deposit a sum of money into a savings account, and in exchange the bank makes you a loan. You have no access to your savings account while your loan is outstanding. If you don't repay it, the bank will use the money in your savings account. The amount you can borrow depends on how much the bank requires you to deposit.

In most cases, though, you'll have to apply for a standard bank loan. You probably won't qualify unless you bring in a cosigner, offer some property as collateral, or agree to a very high rate of interest.

Banks that offer passbook loans typically give you one to three years to repay the loan. But don't pay the loan back too soon—give it about six to nine months to appear on your credit report. Standard bank loans are paid back on a monthly schedule, usually for a year or two.

Before you take out any loan, be sure you understand the terms:

- **Interest rate.** The interest rate on the loan is usually between two and six percentage points more than what the bank charges its customers with the best credit.

- **Prepayment penalties.** Usually, you can pay the loan back as soon as you want without incurring any prepayment penalties—fees that banks sometimes charge if you pay back a loan early and the bank doesn't collect as much interest from you as it had expected. The penalty is usually a small percentage of the loan amount.

- **Whether the bank reports the loan to a credit bureau.** This is key; the whole reason you take out the loan is to rebuild your credit. You may have to make several calls to find a bank that reports the loan.

Using a Debit Card Instead of a Credit Card

If you can't get a regular credit card, and you need one to book things like rental cars and hotels or to buy things over the Internet, you can probably get a debit card from your bank that doubles as a Visa or MasterCard.

Like secured credit cards, however, debit cards are not an ideal solution. You must use them very carefully to avoid trouble. Some of the downsides:

- No grace period (the money is taken directly from your account).
- Unlike credit cards, there's no protection for defective purchases.
- There's less protection than regular credit cards if your card is lost or stolen or someone makes an unauthorized transfer.
- Debit cards are not subject to fee limits and banks may change terms with little or no notice.
- Debit cards are more susceptible to theft than are credit cards.
- Overdraft fees can be extremely expensive. It's easy to incur overdraft fees if you don't keep careful track of your purchases. Fees can be as high as $35 per charge (which means you can incur hundreds of dollars on one day if you make several small charges that are in excess of your account limit). Do not opt into the bank's overdraft protection plan. If you have a debit card, call your bank and make sure you don't have overdraft protection. It's better to have the card declined than to incur overdraft fees.
- Using a debit card provides no benefit to your credit history.

Work With a Local Merchant

Another step to consider in rebuilding your credit is to approach a local merchant, such as a jewelry or furniture store, about purchasing an item on credit. Many local stores will work with you in setting up a payment schedule, but be prepared to put down a deposit of up to 30%, pay a high rate of interest, or find someone to cosign the loan. This isn't an ideal way to rebuild your credit, but if all other lenders turn you down, it may be your only option. Again, ask if the merchant will report your payments to the credit reporting agencies.

Attempts to Collect Clearly Discharged Debts

If a debt was discharged in bankruptcy, the law prohibits the creditor from filing a lawsuit, sending you collection letters, calling you, withholding credit, or threatening to file or actually filing a criminal complaint against you. (11 U.S.C. § 524.) If a creditor tries to collect a debt that clearly was discharged in your bankruptcy, you should respond at once with a letter like the one shown below.

The court doesn't give you a list of debts that were discharged. But you can assume a debt was discharged if you listed it in your bankruptcy papers, the creditor didn't successfully object to its discharge, and it isn't in one of the nondischargeable categories listed in Ch. 1. Also, if you live in a community property state and your spouse filed alone, you can assume that your share of the community debts was also discharged.

Letter to Creditor

1905 Fifth Road
N. Miami Beach, FL 35466

March 18, 20xx

Bank of Miami
2700 Finances Highway
Miami, FL 36678

To Whom It May Concern:

I've been contacted once by letter and once by phone by Rodney Moore of your bank. Mr. Moore claims that I owe $4,812 on Visa account Number 1234 567 890 123.

As you're well aware, this debt was discharged in bankruptcy (Case number 111-999 in the Western District of Tennessee) on February 1, 20xx. Thus, your collection efforts violate federal law, 11 U.S.C. § 524. If they continue, I won't hesitate to pursue my legal rights, including bringing a lawsuit against you for harassment.

Sincerely,

Dawn Schaffer

Dawn Schaffer

If the collection efforts don't immediately stop, you may want to hire a lawyer to write the creditor again—sometimes, a lawyer's letterhead gets results. If that doesn't work, you can sue the creditor for harassment. You can bring a lawsuit in state court or in the bankruptcy court. The bankruptcy court should be more familiar with the prohibitions against collection and more sympathetic to you.

Anticipating Postbankruptcy Debt Collections

Sometimes you can anticipate that a particular creditor will consider a debt to be nondischargeable and go after you for it after your bankruptcy case is closed. In that event, your attorney can file an action in the bankruptcy court while your case is still open to obtain a determination of whether the debt is dischargeable. If the court rules in your favor, the creditor will be prevented from pursuing the debt in state court.

If the creditor sues you over the debt, you'll want to raise the discharge as a defense and sue the creditor yourself to stop the illegal collection efforts. The court has the power to hold the creditor in contempt of court. The court may also fine the creditor for the humiliation, inconvenience, and anguish caused you and order the creditor to pay your attorneys' fees. For example, a bankruptcy court in

North Carolina fined a creditor $900 for attempting to collect a discharged debt. (*In re Barbour*, 77 B.R. 530 (E.D. N.C. 1987).)

If the creditor sues you (almost certainly in state court), you or your attorney can file papers requesting that the case be transferred ("removed") to the bankruptcy court.

Postbankruptcy Discrimination

Although filing for bankruptcy has serious consequences, it might not be as bad as you think. There are laws that will protect you from postbankruptcy discrimination by the government and by private employers.

Governmental Discrimination

All federal, state, and local governmental units are prohibited from discriminating against you solely because you filed for bankruptcy. (11 U.S.C. § 525(a).) This includes denying, revoking, suspending, or refusing to renew a license, permit, charter, franchise, or other similar grant. This part of the Bankruptcy Code provides important protections, but it does not insulate debtors from all adverse consequences of filing for bankruptcy. Lenders, for example, can consider a debtor's bankruptcy filing when reviewing an application for a government loan or an extension of credit. (See, for example, *Watts v. Pennsylvania Housing Finance Co.*, 876 F.2d 1090 (3d Cir. 1989), and *Toth v. Michigan State Housing*

Development Authority, 136 F.3d 477 (6th Cir. 1998).) Still, under this provision of the Bankruptcy Code, the government cannot:

- deny you a job or fire you
- deny you or terminate your public benefits
- evict you from public housing (although if you have a Section 8 voucher, you may not be protected)
- deny you or refuse to renew your state liquor license
- withhold your college transcript
- deny you a driver's license, or
- deny you a contract, such as one for a construction project.

In addition, lenders can't exclude you from participating in a government-guaranteed student loan program. (11 U.S.C. § 525(c).)

In general, once any government-related debt has been discharged, all acts against you that arise out of that debt also must end. If, for example, you lost your driver's license because you didn't pay a court judgment that resulted from a car accident, once the debt is discharged, you must be granted a license. If, however, the judgment wasn't discharged, you can still be denied your license until you pay up.

Keep in mind that only denials based solely on your bankruptcy are prohibited. You may be denied a loan, a job, or an apartment for reasons unrelated to the bankruptcy or for reasons related to your future creditworthiness—for example, because the government concludes you won't be able to repay a Small Business Administration loan.

Nongovernmental Discrimination

Private employers may not fire you or otherwise discriminate against you solely because you filed for bankruptcy. (11 U.S.C. § 525(b).) While the Bankruptcy Code expressly prohibits employers from firing you, most courts have found that it does not prohibit employers from refusing to hire someone because of a prior bankruptcy.

Other forms of discrimination in the private sector aren't illegal. If you seek to rent an apartment and the landlord does a credit check, sees your bankruptcy, and refuses to rent to you, there's not much you can do other than try to show that you'll pay your rent and be a responsible tenant. Paying several months' rent in advance can work wonders in these situations.

If you suffer illegal discrimination because of your bankruptcy, you can sue in state court or in the bankruptcy court. You'll probably need the assistance of an attorney.

Attempts to Revoke Your Discharge

In extremely rare instances, the trustee or a creditor can ask the bankruptcy court to revoke your discharge. The trustee or creditor must file a lawsuit within one year of your discharge.

Your discharge can be revoked only if the creditor or trustee proves that you obtained the discharge through fraud, which was discovered after your discharge. If your discharge is revoked, you'll owe your creditors as if you had not filed for bankruptcy. Any payment your creditors received from the trustee, however, will be credited against what you owe.

SEE AN EXPERT

Help from a lawyer. If someone asks the bankruptcy court to revoke your discharge, consult a bankruptcy attorney right away.

Help Beyond the Book

Hiring and Working With a Lawyer

As we've mentioned several times throughout this book, it's very difficult to represent yourself in a Chapter 13 bankruptcy case. The vast majority of filers will benefit from hiring a bankruptcy lawyer. But just because you're going to hire a lawyer doesn't mean you can hide your head in the sand. In order to get the best representation possible, you must hire the right lawyer and then maintain a good working relationship with him or her.

Our advice: Stay informed and actively participate in your case. Finding a lawyer who will let you do this is the first step, and then working with your lawyer effectively is the second step.

What Does Legal Representation Mean?

By agreeing to represent you, your lawyer becomes responsible for making sure that all of your paperwork is filed on time, the information in your paperwork is accurate, and you propose a repayment plan the judge will confirm. These duties require the lawyer to review various documents—for instance, your credit report, tax returns, and home value appraisal—both to ensure the accuracy of your paperwork and that you are filing for bankruptcy under the appropriate chapter.

Unbundled Legal Services and Chapter 13 Bankruptcy

Since the 1990s, lawyers have been increasingly willing to offer their services on a piecemeal basis, such as reviewing paperwork for a self-represented client or handling a hearing on the dischargeability of a debt. When lawyers do specific jobs at a client's request but don't contract for full-service representation in the underlying case, they are said to be providing unbundled services. They often do so for an hourly fee.

Unfortunately, because filing a Chapter 13 bankruptcy got more complicated with the 2005 bankruptcy law changes, few people can represent themselves effectively in Chapter 13, and even fewer attorneys are willing to handle just a piece of the case. Essentially, unbundled services are not an option for the vast majority of Chapter 13 filers.

If you decide to file for Chapter 7 bankruptcy, however, unbundled services may be a possibility. If you are representing yourself in a Chapter 7 case, you may be able to find an attorney who, for example, is willing to handle a court hearing for an hourly fee, review your paperwork before you file, or give you legal advice before and during your bankruptcy. However, in some states, attorneys are not allowed to provide unbundled services.

Your lawyer will also be responsible for appearing with you at the meeting of creditors and on your behalf at the plan confirmation hearing. Your lawyer will also represent your interests if a creditor objects to your plan or opposes the discharge of a debt, or if you need to eliminate liens that the bankruptcy laws allow to be stripped from your property.

How to Find a Bankruptcy Lawyer

Bankruptcy lawyers are regular lawyers who specialize in handling bankruptcy cases. When seeking legal representation in a Chapter 13 bankruptcy, look for an experienced bankruptcy lawyer, not a general practitioner.

There are several ways to find the best bankruptcy lawyer for your job:

- **Personal referrals.** This is your best approach. If you know someone who was pleased with the services of a bankruptcy lawyer, call that lawyer first.
- **Referrals from other lawyers.** If you, a family member, or a friend used a lawyer in a nonbankruptcy matter, ask that lawyer if they know of any good bankruptcy attorneys.
- **Group legal plans.** If you're a member of a plan that provides free or low-cost legal assistance and the plan covers bankruptcies, make that your first stop in looking for a lawyer.

- **Lawyer-referral panels.** Most county bar associations will give you the names of bankruptcy attorneys who practice in your area. Keep in mind that most bar associations do not screen the lawyers. It's up to you to check out the credentials and experience of the person to whom you're referred.
- **Internet directories.** Both bar associations and private companies provide lists of bankruptcy lawyers on the Internet. A good directory will provide lots of information about the lawyers, such as the types of cases they handle, their philosophy on representing clients, and typical fees. One good place to start is Nolo's lawyer directory, at www.nolo.com/lawyers. Also, check out www.nacba.org, a site that provides contact information for members of the National Association of Consumer Bankruptcy Attorneys. Or visit www.legalconsumer.com, a site that provides a variety of free services and information, including bankruptcy lawyer listings by zip code.
- **Legal Aid.** Legal Aid offices are partially funded by the federal Legal Services Corporation and offer legal assistance in many areas. A few offices may do bankruptcies, although most do not. To qualify for Legal Aid, you must have a very low income, so few Chapter 13 bankruptcy filers will qualify.

- **Legal clinics.** Many law schools sponsor legal clinics and provide free legal advice to consumers. Some legal clinics have the same income requirements as Legal Aid; others offer free services to low- and moderate-income people.

Bankruptcy Petition Preparers

Bankruptcy petition preparers (BPPs) are nonlawyers who assist people with filling out and filing bankruptcy forms. BPPs are not allowed to provide legal advice—their services are restricted to entering data on forms, printing the forms, and organizing the forms for filing. If you are filing for Chapter 7 bankruptcy without a lawyer and want someone to input your information onto the forms, you might consider using a BPP. For purposes of Chapter 13 bankruptcy, however, BPPs are really not an option. They cannot help you draft a repayment plan, nor can they provide legal advice. As we've said already, most Chapter 13 filers do best by getting a lawyer.

What to Look for in a Lawyer

A big part of finding the right lawyer to represent you is knowing what to look for. Get some basic information before you make an appointment. Then schedule an initial consultation so you can find out more about the lawyer before you decide whom to hire.

Before You Make an Appointment

Whether you are browsing Internet directories, calling lawyers referred to you by friends, or getting names from a bar association referral service, here are some things to look for in a lawyer:

Experience. Look for an experienced bankruptcy attorney. Years of practice are not always the best indication of this. Ask how many bankruptcy cases the attorney has handled and what types. If a lawyer has handled tons of Chapter 7 cases, but not many Chapter 13s, he or she might not be for you. On the other hand, if the lawyer only handles Chapter 13 bankruptcies, that might be a red flag. You don't want to be represented by someone who pushes clients in the direction of Chapter 13 when a Chapter 7 might be better. (Lawyers often make a better profit from Chapter 13 bankruptcies.)

Competence. This is a tricky one to figure out. A lawyer may have practiced bankruptcy law for 20 years, but done a bad job of it. On the flip side, if a lawyer who recently graduated from law school is smart, hardworking, and mentored by an experienced bankruptcy attorney, he or she might be a good choice. Ask for referrals from former clients, and, if possible, speak directly to those clients.

Reasonable fees. Before you make an appointment, find out what the lawyer typically charges for a Chapter 13 case. Cheaper isn't always better—you don't want someone cutting corners nor do you necessarily want your case handled by a "bankruptcy mill" that cranks out bankruptcy paperwork without giving clients individual attention. On the other hand, high fees don't always correlate to the best representation. Shop around to find out what most bankruptcy lawyers charge in your area.

What to Look for in the First Meeting

Many lawyers will provide an initial consultation for free. But even if a lawyer charges for a consultation, it might be worth the money to pay for a few consults to find the right lawyer. Here are some things to assess in the first meeting:

How available is the lawyer? When making an appointment, ask to talk directly to the lawyer. If you can't, this may give you a hint as to how accessible he or she is. Of course, if you're told that a paralegal will be handling the routine aspects of your case under the supervision of a lawyer, you may be satisfied with that arrangement. Ask how long it will take for your phone calls to get returned or how hard it is to schedule appointments.

How does the lawyer communicate? Ask specific questions. Do you get clear, concise answers?

Does the lawyer listen to you? Often people want to "tell their story" to the bankruptcy attorney and get miffed if the attorney isn't interested. Customer service considerations usually dictate that the attorney will let you talk for fifteen minutes or so just to get things off your chest. However, the fact is that most of what Chapter 13 clients are concerned about has little or nothing to do with what must be included in your bankruptcy petition or how your bankruptcy will proceed. As a general rule, most Chapter 13 bankruptcies are routine and after a brief introductory conversation the attorney will probably have you complete an online questionnaire that asks about your debts, assets, and financial affairs over the past couple of years. The attorney (or a member of the attorney's staff) will review the questionnaire and ask a few questions (often by email) about the information you provide or leave out. When the lawyer (or assistant) has everything needed for your bankruptcy, the attorney will contact you about what will happen next. Of course there are exceptions and if you feel you need a full interview with the lawyer, by all means go for it, as long as you realize that bankruptcy lawyers tend to be task-oriented and generally make poor confidants.

How does your lawyer feel about your legal knowledge? If you've read this book, you're already better informed than most clients (and many lawyers). How does the lawyer respond to this? Some lawyers are threatened by clients who have done their homework. Others welcome clients that are well-informed and willing to participate fully in their case.

Does the lawyer carry malpractice insurance? If the answer is no, consider finding a lawyer who does. But keep in mind that malpractice insurance is far more protective of the lawyer than the client, and the fact that a lawyer is insured may make it more, rather than less, difficult to recover damages from the lawyer if he or she is professionally negligent.

Do the lawyer's recommendations seem sound? One of your goals at the initial conference is to find out what the lawyer recommends in your particular case. Go home and think about the lawyer's suggestions. If they don't make sense or you have other reservations, call someone else.

What are the lawyer's fees? Now that you've given the lawyer a brief overview of your situation, and the lawyer has made a preliminary recommendation, find out what the lawyer's services will cost.

Personality. No matter how experienced or competent the lawyer is, if you don't feel comfortable with him or her during the first meeting, you may want to keep looking.

Paying Your Lawyer

Because lawyer duties for even a simple Chapter 13 bankruptcy case have drastically increased under the 2005 bankruptcy law, typical lawyer fees have gone way up.

For a routine Chapter 13 bankruptcy, a lawyer will likely charge you somewhere between $2,500 and $3,500 (plus the $310 filing fee and the fees you'll have to pay for credit counseling and personal debt management counseling, about $25 each).

Attorneys' fees in bankruptcy cases are somewhat unusual in that they must be disclosed to and approved by the court. The reasoning behind this rule is twofold. First, since every penny you pay to a bankruptcy lawyer is a penny not available to your creditors (at least in theory), the trustee and court have an interest in making sure the fees are reasonable. Second, because many bankruptcy clients are financially vulnerable and even desperate when they seek legal assistance, they are susceptible to fee gouging. Prior to the fee disclosure rule, the bankruptcy bar was known for overcharging clients. (Of course, many bankruptcy lawyers did not engage in this abuse.) Court oversight of attorneys' fees was instituted in an attempt to curb this problem.

However, even though the court oversees attorneys' fees, the trustee rarely challenges the rates charged in a particular case. (The U.S. Trustee and the court itself may also challenge fees.) This is because attorneys know the range of fees generally allowed by local bankruptcy judges and set their fees accordingly. Even if challenged, attorneys are given the opportunity to justify a fee that seems unusually large.

Bankruptcy Lawyer Fees Are Not Fixed

Some people think that bankruptcy lawyer fees are fixed. This is not the case. Although some courts do establish presumptive fee maximums, these are not set in stone. An attorney can overcome the maximum by providing reasons why a higher fee is reasonable. Essentially, individual lawyers are free to decide what to charge, based on what services you want and how complicated your case is likely to be.

Standard Fees and Extra Fees

The scope and range of services that the attorney promises you in return for your initial fee will be listed in what's called a Rule 2016 Attorney Fee Disclosure Form. This form is filed as part of your bankruptcy papers. In the typical Chapter 13 case, the attorney's fee will include the routine tasks associated with a bankruptcy filing: counseling, preparing bankruptcy forms, drafting your repayment plan, and attending the creditors' meeting and confirmation hearing. Any task not included in the Rule 2016 disclosure form is subject to a separate fee.

If your case will likely require more attorney time, you may—and probably will—be charged extra, according to the attorney's hourly fee or other criteria he or she uses. A typical consumer bankruptcy attorney charges between $250 and $350

an hour (rural and urban). Many charge a minimum of roughly $400 to $600 for a court appearance.

How those extra fees are covered varies. Some attorneys will add these fees to their standard fee and require you to pay it all in advance. For example, say the attorney's standard fee is $3,000, but the attorney believes she will have to perform work in addition to the usual aspects of representation. The attorney may charge $4,000 or $4,500 up front, in anticipation of the additional hours.

Other attorneys will charge you their standard fee up front and wait until after you file to charge you for the extra work. Because these fees are earned after your bankruptcy filing, they won't be discharged in your bankruptcy and the attorney need not collect them up front; they will be added to your plan payments. Whatever method the attorney uses to charge you, you have some protection against fee gouging. An attorney must file a supplemental Rule 2016 form to obtain the court's permission for any postfiling fees.

How and When Fees Are Paid

Some (but not many) lawyers allow you to pay their full fee through your repayment plan, without paying anything up front. Most lawyers require an initial payment—for example, $2,000—and let you pay the rest through your plan. Sometimes a lawyer's choice as to timing of payment depends on how likely it is that your plan will be confirmed, and whether the lawyer thinks you'll complete it. For example, if you have plenty of income to cover your mandatory debts and you are filing for Chapter 13 to save your home, the lawyer might charge only a minimal initial fee, because you are likely to complete your plan and finish paying the fee that way. On the other hand, if you barely have enough income to propose a confirmable plan and you don't own a home, the lawyer might be skeptical of your ability to complete the plan—and might demand the entire fee up front.

Fee Agreements

When you decide on a lawyer, it's important to get an agreement for services and payment in writing. Your contract should include:

- a description of the services your attorney will provide
- the type and amount of fees, how they will be paid, and whether extra work is included in the fee or will be charged separately
- an outline of likely costs and how they will be paid. These would include, at a minimum, filing fees and fees for debt counseling, but might also include

costs for property appraisals and expert witnesses.
- your obligations; sometimes fee agreements include your duties as a client. For example it might state that you agree to be truthful with your lawyer and to provide information when requested.

Working With Your Lawyer

A good working relationship between you and your lawyer will help the case go more smoothly, reduce your frustration, and ensure the best results possible. Here are some tips:

- **Stay informed.** Insist that your lawyer update you on what's going on with your case.
- **Provide your lawyer with documents and information.** Provide your lawyer with all information that might pertain to your case. More information is better than less. If your lawyer asks for documents, provide them as quickly as possible.
- **If you don't understand something, ask.** You can't make informed decisions about your case if you don't fully understand what's going on.

Legal Research

While your bankruptcy lawyer will be a good resource for finding out what the law is, especially in your district, there are times when you might want to do some sleuthing yourself. In particular, if you are still in the initial stages of considering bankruptcy, you may want to learn more about a particular issue before you plunk down the money to see a lawyer.

Even if you plan to get a lawyer or already have one, knowing how to find the law if you need it is still valuable. Being informed about the law will allow you to ask the right questions of your lawyer and better equip you to make decisions about your case. Reading the book is an excellent way to get informed, and in most cases will more than suffice. But in the event you are facing an issue that isn't covered in this book (because, for example, it only affects a tiny percentage of filers) or you want to know how a cutting edge issue is being treated in your district, you can also do some legal research on your own.

Legal research can vary from the very simple to the hopelessly complex. In this chapter, we stay on the simple side. If you would like to learn more about legal research or if you find that our suggestions come up a bit short in your particular case, we recommend that you obtain a copy of *Legal Research: How to Find & Understand the Law*, by Stephen Elias and the Editors of Nolo (Nolo), which provides a plain-English tutorial on legal research in the law library and on the Internet.

Sources of Bankruptcy Law

Bankruptcy law comes from a variety of sources:

- federal bankruptcy statutes passed by Congress
- federal rules about bankruptcy procedure issued by a federal judicial agency
- local rules issued by individual bankruptcy courts
- federal and bankruptcy court cases applying bankruptcy laws to specific disputes
- laws (statutes) passed by state legislatures that define the property you can keep in bankruptcy, and
- state court cases interpreting state exemption statutes.

Not so long ago, you would have had to visit a law library to find these resources. Now you can find most of them on the Internet. However, if you are able to visit a decent-sized law library, your research will be the better for it. Reading relevant cases with court interpretations of the underlying statutes and rules is crucial to getting a clear picture of what the laws and rules really mean.

There is another important reason to visit the law library. Many have computer terminals that offer access to one or both of the major online legal research libraries: Westlaw and LexisNexis. With proper training, you can find just about anything in these online libraries that you could find in the law library itself. In fact, some libraries have started replacing hard copy books with online materials, to save money and space. When visiting your local library, ask the librarian whether it has access to Westlaw or Lexis and, if so, for some tips on using the bankruptcy materials the online library carries. For example, Westlaw offers a set of bankruptcy materials with forms, cases, articles, and treatises, all searchable by keywords. Learning how to use these materials will be an enormous timesaver in your research.

Below, we show you how to get to the resources you'll most likely be using, whether you are doing your research on the Internet or in the law library.

Bankruptcy Background Materials: Overviews, Encyclopedias, and Treatises

Before digging into the primary law sources (statutes, rules, cases, and so on) that we discuss below, you may want to do some background reading to get a firm grasp of your issue or question.

The Internet

A number of Internet sites contain large collections of articles written by experts about various aspects of bankruptcy. Good starting places are Nolo's website, at www. nolo.com, and www.legalconsumer.com, which offer lots of information and resources.

How to Use Law Libraries

Law libraries that are open to the public are most often found in and around courthouses. Law schools also frequently admit the public at least some of the time (typically not during exam time, over the summer, or during other breaks in the academic year).

Almost without exception, law libraries come with law librarians. The law librarians will be helpful as long as you ask them the right questions. For example, the law librarians will help you find specific library resources (for instance, where you can find the federal bankruptcy statutes or rules), but they normally won't teach you the ins and outs of legal research. Nor will they give an opinion about what a law means, how you should deal with the court, or how your particular question should be answered. For instance, if you want to find a state case interpreting a particular exemption, the law librarian will show you where your state code is located on the shelves and may even point out the volumes that contain the exemptions. The librarian won't, however, help you interpret the exemption, apply the exemption to your specific facts, or tell you how to raise the exemption in your bankruptcy case. Nor is the librarian likely to tell you what additional research steps you can or should take. When it comes to legal research in the law library, self-help is the order of the day.

Westlaw is likely where you'll want to start, but it can be expensive. You'll likely be able to use it at no cost at your local library.

Another approach to searching for bankruptcy-related materials is Google. Both the basic Google search and Google Scholar (http://scholar.google.com) are amazingly responsive to plain-language queries. For example, if you want to know more about discharging student loans, you would use Google Scholar, click the "Articles" radio button and enter "discharging student loans in bankruptcy" in the search box and pull up a bevy of links to related articles. Similarly, if you want to read court opinions about discharging student loans in bankruptcy you would do the same search but use the "Case Laws" button.

The Law Library

Providing you with a good treatise or encyclopedia discussion of bankruptcy is where the law library shines. You can find these materials in hard copy or on the Westlaw or Lexis online research libraries.

Collier on Bankruptcy

It's a good idea to get an overview of your subject before trying to find a precise answer to a precise question. The best way to do this is to find a general commentary on your subject by a bankruptcy expert. For example, if you want to find out whether a particular debt is nondischargeable, you should start by reading a general discussion about the type of debt you're dealing with. Or, if you don't know whether you're entitled to claim certain property as exempt, a good overview of your state's exemptions would get you started on the right track.

The most complete source of this type of background information is a set of books known as *Collier on Bankruptcy*, by Lawrence P. King, et al. (Matthew Bender). It's available in virtually all law libraries. *Collier* is both incredibly thorough and meticulously up to date; semiannual supplements, with all the latest developments, are in the front of each volume. In addition to comments on every aspect of bankruptcy law, *Collier* contains the bankruptcy statutes, rules, and exemption lists for every state.

Collier is organized according to the bankruptcy statutes. This means that the quickest way to find information in it is to know what statute you're looking for. (See the Bankruptcy Code sections set out below.) If you still can't figure out the governing statute, start with the *Collier* subject matter index. Be warned, however, that the index can be difficult to use because it contains a lot of bankruptcy jargon you may be unfamiliar with. A legal dictionary will be available in the library.

Bankruptcy (National Edition) Published by The Rutter Group

This is a four-volume set of looseleaf binders that covers every aspect of bankruptcy.

Bankruptcy Code Sections (11 U.S.C.)	
§ 101 Definitions	§ 501 Filing of Creditors' Claims
§ 109 Who May File for Which Type of Bankruptcy; Credit Counseling Requirements	§ 506 Allowed Secured Claims and Lien Avoidance
§ 110 Rules for Bankruptcy Petition Preparers	§ 507 Priority Claims
§ 111 Budget and Credit Counseling Agencies	§ 521 Paperwork Requirements and Deadlines
§ 302 Who Can File Joint Cases	§ 522 Exemptions; Residency Requirements for Homestead Exemption; Stripping Liens From Property
§ 326 How Trustees Are Compensated	
§ 332 Consumer Privacy Ombudsmen	§ 523 Nondischargeable Debts
§ 341 Meeting of Creditors	§ 524 Effect of Discharge and Reaffirmation of Debts
§ 342 Notice of Creditors' Meeting; Informational Notice to Debtors; Requirements for Notice by Debtors	§ 525 Prohibited Postbankruptcy Discrimination
	§ 526 Restrictions on Debt Relief Agencies
	§ 527 Required Disclosures by Debt Relief Agencies
§ 343 Examination of Debtor at Creditors' Meeting	§ 528 Requirements for Debt Relief Agencies
§ 348 Converting From One Type of Bankruptcy to Another	§ 541 What Property Is Part of the Bankruptcy Estate
	§ 547 Preferences
§ 349 Dismissing a Case	§ 548 Fraudulent Transfers
§ 350 Closing and Reopening a Case	§ 554 Trustee's Abandonment of Property in the Bankruptcy Estate
§ 362 The Automatic Stay	
§ 365 How Leases and Executory Contracts Are Treated in Bankruptcy	§ 707 The Means Test
	§ 1301 Stay of Action Against Codebtor
§ 366 Continuing or Reconnecting Utility Service	§ 1305 Proof of Claims

Although these books are written for lawyers, they aren't too difficult to understand and use. You'll find information on exemptions, Chapter 13 plans, lien stripping, filing and opposing motions, and much more.

Other Background Resources

For general discussions of bankruptcy issues, there are several other good places to start. An excellent all-around resource is called *Consumer Bankruptcy Law and Practice*. This volume, published by the National Consumer Law Center, is updated every year. It contains a complete discussion of Chapter 13 bankruptcy procedures, the official bankruptcy forms, and a marvelous bibliography.

Another good treatise is a legal encyclopedia called *American Jurisprudence*,

2nd Series. Almost all law libraries carry it. The article on bankruptcy has an extensive table of contents, and the entire encyclopedia has an index. Between these two tools, you should be able to zero in on helpful material.

Finding Federal Bankruptcy Statutes

Title 11 of the United States Code contains all the statutes that govern your bankruptcy.

The Internet

If you are using the Internet, go to the Legal Information Institute of Cornell University Law School site (www.law.cornell.edu), which lets you browse laws by subject matter and also offers a keyword search. To find the Bankruptcy Code, go to www.law. cornell.edu, select "U.S. Code" from the menu available under the "Constitutions and Codes" tab, then select Title 11. Use the table above to find the code sections you need.

The Law Library

Virtually every law library has at least one complete set of the annotated United States Code ("annotated" means that each statute is followed by citations and summaries of cases interpreting that provision). If you already have a citation to the statute you are seeking, you can use the citation to find the statute. However, if you have no citation—which is frequently the case—you can use either the index to Title 11 (the part of the Code that applies to bankruptcy) or the table we set out above, which matches various issues that are likely to interest you with specific sections of Title 11.

Once you have found and read the statute, you can browse the one-paragraph summaries of written opinions issued by courts that have interpreted that particular statute. You will be looking to see whether a court has addressed your particular issue. If so, you can find and read the entire case in the law library. Reading what a judge has had to say about the statute regarding facts similar to yours is an invaluable guide to understanding how a judge is likely to handle the issue in your case, although when and where the case was decided may be important.

Finding the Federal Rules of Bankruptcy Procedure (FRBP)

The Federal Rules of Bankruptcy Procedure govern what happens if an issue is contested in the bankruptcy court. They also apply to certain routine bankruptcy procedures, such as deadlines for filing paperwork. Any law library will have these rules. Your bankruptcy court's website will have a link to the rules, as does www.law.cornell.edu.

Finding Local Court Rules

Every bankruptcy court operates under a set of local rules that governs how it does business and what is expected of the parties who use it. Each court also has its own forms that debtors must use, and these forms vary from court to court.

Your bankruptcy court clerk's office will have the local rules available for you. Most courts also post their local rules and forms on their own websites. To find the website for your court, take these steps:

Step 1: Go to www.uscourts.gov/court-locator.

Step 2: Select "Bankruptcy" court from the pulldown menu and enter your location information.

Step 3: Browse the list until you find your court and click on it.

Step 4: Click on the local rules and forms link (each website is set up differently so call the court clerk if you need help).

These court websites usually contain other helpful information as well, including case information, official bankruptcy forms, court guidelines (in addition to the local rules), information for lawyers, information about the court and its judges, and the court calendar.

At the law library, the *Collier Bankruptcy Practice Manual* has the local rules for most (if not all) of the nation's bankruptcy courts.

Finding Federal Court Bankruptcy Cases

Court opinions are vital to understanding how a particular law might apply to your individual case. The following levels of federal courts issue bankruptcy-related opinions:

- the U.S. Supreme Court
- the U.S. Courts of Appeals
- the Bankruptcy Appellate Panels
- the U.S. District Courts, and
- the bankruptcy courts.

Most bankruptcy-related opinions are, not surprisingly, issued by the bankruptcy courts. By comparison, very few bankruptcy opinions come out of the U.S. Supreme Court. The other courts are somewhere in the middle.

The Internet

Depending on the date the case was decided, U.S. Supreme Court decisions and U.S. Court of Appeals decisions are available for free on the Internet. For a reasonable monthly fee you can also subscribe to VersusLaw (at www. versuslaw.com), which provides U.S. Court of Appeals cases for an earlier period than you can get for free—often back to 1950. VersusLaw doesn't require you to sign a long-term contract. VersusLaw also publishes many U.S. District Court cases on its website. Westlaw and Lexis are generally too costly to use from home, unless you do a lot of research. However, you will be able to find either or both of these at your local law library.

U.S. Supreme Court. To find a Supreme Court case, go to https://www.supreme court.gov.

U.S. Court of Appeals. You can find a U.S Circuit Court of Appeals case back to roughly 1996. Follow these steps:

Step 1: Go to www.law.cornell.edu.

Step 2: Click "Federal law," then "Federal Court of Appeals Decisions."

Step 3: Click on "Search All Circuit Court Opinions on the Internet."

Again, if you are looking for a case decided prior to 1996, your best bet is to sign up for VersusLaw, described above.

U.S. District Court and Bankruptcy Court. You can often find these cases on Google Scholar (http://scholar.google.com), but if you are looking for rulings from the bankruptcy court you will be filing in, it might be best to start with your local bankruptcy court's website. Many courts now post representative decisions that, if you're lucky, may be indexed by topic or by the section of the bankruptcy law that they discuss. If you can't find what you are looking for in these places, you may need to make a trip to the law library to do some book research or else access the cases through an online database such as Lexis or Westlaw.

The Law Library

U.S. Supreme Court cases are published in three different book series:

- *Supreme Court Reports*
- *Supreme Court Reporter*, and
- *Supreme Court Lawyer's Edition.*

Some law libraries carry all three of these publications; others have only one.

The cases are the same, but each series has different editorial enhancements.

U.S. Court of Appeals cases are published in the *Federal Reporter* (abbreviated simply as "F."). Most law libraries, large and small, carry this series.

Many U.S. District Court cases are published in the *Federal Supplement* (F.Supp.), a series available in most law libraries.

Written opinions of bankruptcy judges, and related appeals, are published in the *Bankruptcy Reporter* (B.R.), available in most mid- to large-sized libraries. To accurately understand how your bankruptcy court is likely to interpret the laws in your particular case, sooner or later you will need access to the *Bankruptcy Reporter.*

State Statutes

The secret to understanding what property you can keep frequently lies in the exemptions that your state allows you to claim. These exemptions are found in your state's statutes.

The Internet

Every state has its statutes online, including its exemption statutes. This means that you can read your state's exemption statutes for yourself. Start by checking your state's legislative website.

The Law Library

Your law library will have your state's statutes in book form, usually referred to as your state's code, annotated statutes, or compiled laws. Use Appendix A in this book to find a reference to the exemption statute you want to read, then use that reference to locate the exemption statute in the code. Once you find and read the statute, you can browse the summaries of court opinions interpreting the statute and, if you wish, read the cases in their entirety.

Alternatively, if your library has a copy of *Collier on Bankruptcy* (see above), you can find the exemptions for your state, accompanied by annotations summarizing state court interpretations.

State Court Cases

State courts are sometimes called on to interpret exemption statutes. If a court has interpreted the statute in which you are interested, you'll definitely want to chase down the relevant case and read it for yourself.

The Internet

All states make their more recent cases available free on the Internet—usually back to about 1996. To find these cases for your state:

Step 1: Go to www.law.cornell.edu/opinions. html#state.

Step 2: Click on your state.

Step 3: Locate the link to the court opinions for your state. This may be one link, or there may be separate links for your state's supreme court and your state's courts of appeal (the lower trial courts seldom publish their opinions, so you probably won't be able to find them).

If you want to go back to an earlier case, consider subscribing to VersusLaw at www.versuslaw.com. As mentioned earlier, you don't have to sign a long-term contract.

The Law Library

Your law library will have a collection of books that contain opinions issued by your state's courts. If you have a citation, you can go right to the case. If you don't have a citation, you'll need to use a digest to find relevant bankruptcy cases. Finding cases by subject matter is a little too advanced for this brief summary. See *Legal Research: How to Find & Understand the Law*, by Stephen Elias and the Editors of Nolo (Nolo), for more help.

Other Helpful Resources

Probably the most helpful bankruptcy website is maintained by the Office of the United States Trustee, at www.justice.gov/ust. This site provides lists of approved credit and financial management counseling agencies, median income figures for every state, and the IRS national, regional, and local expenses you will need to complete the means test.

You can download official bankruptcy forms from the U.S. Courts website at www.uscourts.gov/forms/bankruptcy-forms. However, this site doesn't include required local forms; for those, you'll have to visit your court or its website.

As part of the bankruptcy process, you are required to give the replacement (retail) value for all of the property you list in Schedule A/B. These figures are also the key to figuring out which of your property is exempt. Here are some tips on finding these values:

- **Cars:** Use the *Kelley Blue Book*, at www.kbb.com, or the website of the National Auto Dealers Association, www.nada.com.
- **Other personal property:** Check prices on eBay, www.ebay.com.
- **Homes:** To value your property, compare it to similar real estate parcels in your neighborhood that have recently sold (comparables). You can get free information (purchase price, sales date, and address) from sites such as www.realtor.com, www.zillow.com, and www.trulia.com.
- For the most up-to-date and detailed information, talk to a local real estate agent.

Our Websites

Nolo's website, www.nolo.com, offers lots of free information on bankruptcy, credit repair, student loans, and much more. You can also view information on the Nolo products mentioned in this book, including links to legal updates highlighting important developments that occurred after this book went to press.

Nolo author Albin Renauer also maintains a website that provides a free means test calculator, helpful information about Chapter 7 and Chapter 13 bankruptcies, and a means test law browser that provides summaries and references to developing case law, at www.legalconsumer.com.

Glossary

341 hearing. See "meeting of creditors."

341 notice. A notice sent to the debtor and the debtor's creditors announcing the date, time, and place for the first meeting of creditors. The 341 notice is sent along with the notice of bankruptcy filing and information about important deadlines by which creditors have to take certain actions, such as filing objections.

342 notice. A notice that the court clerk is required to give to debtors pursuant to Section 342 of the Bankruptcy Code, to inform them of their obligations as bankruptcy debtors and the consequences of not being completely honest in their bankruptcy cases.

707(b) action. An action taken by the U.S. Trustee, the regular trustee, or any creditor, under authority of Section 707(b) of the Bankruptcy Code, to dismiss a debtor's Chapter 7 filing on the ground of abuse.

Abuse. Misuse of the Chapter 7 bankruptcy remedy. This term is typically applied to a Chapter 7 bankruptcy filing that should have been filed under Chapter 13 because the debtor appears to have enough disposable income to fund a Chapter 13 repayment plan.

Accounts receivable. Money or other property that one person or business owes to another for goods or services. Accounts receivable most often refer to the debts owed to a business by its customers.

Adequate protection payment. A payment or designated portion of a payment, made before a Chapter 13 plan is confirmed, that goes toward a claim secured by personal property. An adequate protection payment is intended to protect the creditor from losses due to depreciation in the value of its collateral, and is not refundable in the event the case is dismissed or converted to Chapter 7 bankruptcy.

Administrative expenses. The trustee's fee, the debtor's attorneys' fee, and other costs of bringing a bankruptcy case that a debtor must pay in full in a Chapter 13 repayment plan. Administrative costs are typically 10% of the debtor's total payments under the plan.

Administrative Office of the United States Courts. The federal government agency that issues court rules and forms to be used by the federal courts, including bankruptcy courts.

Adversary action. Any lawsuit that begins with the filing of a formal complaint and formal service of process on the parties being sued. In a bankruptcy case, adversary actions are often brought to determine the dischargeability of a debt or to recover property transferred by the debtor shortly before filing for bankruptcy.

Affidavit. A written statement of facts, signed under oath in front of a notary public.

Allowed secured claim. A debt that is secured by collateral or a lien against the debtor's property, for which the creditor has filed a *Proof of Claim* with the bankruptcy court. The claim is secured only to the extent of the value of the property—for example, if a debtor owes $5,000 on a note for a car that is worth only $3,000, the remaining $2,000 is an unsecured claim.

Amendment. A document filed by the debtor that changes one or more documents previously filed with the court. A debtor often files an amendment because the trustee requires changes to the debtor's paperwork based on the testimony at the meeting of creditors.

Animals. An exemption category in many states. Some states specifically exempt pets or livestock and poultry. If your state simply allows you to exempt "animals," you may include livestock, poultry, or pets. Some states exempt only domestic animals, which are usually considered to be all animals except pets.

Annuity. A type of insurance policy that pays out during the life of the insured, unlike life insurance, which pays out at the insured's death. Once the insured reaches the age specified in the policy, he or she receives monthly payments until death.

Appliance. A household apparatus or machine, usually operated by electricity,

gas, or propane. Examples include refrigerators, stoves, washing machines, dishwashers, vacuum cleaners, air conditioners, and toasters.

Arms and accoutrements. Arms are weapons (such as pistols, rifles, and swords); accoutrements are the furnishings of a soldier's outfit, such as a belt or pack, but not clothes or weapons.

Arms-length creditor. A creditor with whom the debtor deals in the normal course of business, as opposed to an insider (a friend, relative, or business partner).

Articles of adornment. See "jewelry."

Assessment benefits. See "stipulated insurance."

Assisted person. Any person contemplating or filing for bankruptcy who receives bankruptcy assistance, whose debts are primarily consumer debts, and whose nonexempt property is valued at less than $150,000. A person or an entity that offers help to an assisted person is called a "debt relief agency."

Automatic stay. An injunction automatically issued by the bankruptcy court when a debtor files for bankruptcy. The automatic stay prohibits most creditor collection activities, such as filing or continuing lawsuits, making written requests for payment, or notifying credit reporting bureaus of an unpaid debt.

Avails. Any amount available to the owner of an insurance policy other than the actual proceeds of the policy. Avails include dividend payments, interest, cash or surrender value (the money you'd get if you sold your policy back to the insurance company), and loan value (the amount of cash you can borrow against the policy).

Bankruptcy Abuse Prevention and Consumer Protection Act of 2005. The formal name of the bankruptcy law that took effect on October 17, 2005.

Bankruptcy administrator. The official responsible for supervising the administration of bankruptcy cases, estates, and trustees in Alabama and North Carolina, where there is no U.S. Trustee.

Bankruptcy Appellate Panel. A specialized court that hears appeals of bankruptcy court decisions (available only in some regions).

Bankruptcy assistance. Goods or services provided to an "assisted person" for the purpose of providing information, advice, counsel, document preparation or filing, or attendance at a creditors' meeting; appearing in a case or proceeding on behalf of another person; or providing legal representation.

Bankruptcy Code. The federal law that governs the creation and operation of the bankruptcy courts and establishes bankruptcy procedures. (You can find the Bankruptcy Code in Title 11 of the United States Code.)

Bankruptcy estate. All of the property you own when you file for bankruptcy, except for most pensions and educational trusts. The trustee technically takes control of your bankruptcy estate for the duration of your case.

Bankruptcy lawyer. A lawyer who specializes in bankruptcy and is licensed to practice law in the federal courts.

Bankruptcy petition preparer. Any nonlawyer who helps someone with his or her bankruptcy. Bankruptcy petition preparers (BPPs) are a special type of debt relief agency, regulated by the U.S. Trustee. Because they are not lawyers, BPPs can't represent anyone in bankruptcy court or provide legal advice.

Bankruptcy Petition Preparer's Notice, Declaration and Signature. A written notice that bankruptcy petition preparers must provide to debtors who use their services. The notice explains that bankruptcy petition preparers aren't attorneys and that they are permitted to perform only certain acts, such as entering information in the bankruptcy petition and schedules under the direction of their clients.

Benefit or benevolent society benefits. See "fraternal benefit society benefits."

Building materials. Items, such as lumber, brick, stone, iron, paint, and varnish, that are used to build or improve a structure.

Burial plot. A cemetery plot.

Business bankruptcy. A bankruptcy in which the debts arise primarily from the operation of a business, including bankruptcies filed by corporations, limited liability companies, and partnerships.

Certification. The act of signing a document under penalty of perjury. (The document that is signed is also called a certification.)

Chapter 7 bankruptcy. A liquidation bankruptcy, in which the trustee sells the debtor's nonexempt property and distributes the proceeds to the debtor's creditors. At the end of the case, the debtor receives a discharge of all remaining debts, except those that cannot legally be discharged.

Chapter 9 bankruptcy. A type of bankruptcy restricted to governmental units.

Chapter 11 bankruptcy. A type of bankruptcy intended to help businesses reorganize their debt load in order to remain in business. A Chapter 11 bankruptcy is typically much more expensive than a Chapter 7 or 13 bankruptcy because all of the lawyers must be paid out of the bankruptcy estate.

Chapter 12 bankruptcy. A type of bankruptcy designed to help small farmers reorganize their debts.

Chapter 13 bankruptcy. A type of consumer bankruptcy designed to help individuals reorganize their debts and pay all or a portion of them over three to five years.

Chapter 13 plan. A document filed in a Chapter 13 bankruptcy in which the debtor shows how all of his or her projected disposable income will be used over a three- to five-year period to pay all mandatory debts—for example, back child support, taxes, and mortgage arrearages—as well as some or all unsecured, nonpriority debts, such as medical and credit card bills.

Chapter 13 *Calculation of Your Disposable Income*. The official bankruptcy form used in conjunction with the *Chapter 13 Statement of Your Current Monthly Income and Calculation of Commitment Period* in order to calculate a Chapter 13 debtor's projected disposable income. This figure determines how much the debtor must pay to unsecured creditors.

Chapter 13 *Statement of Your Current Monthly Income and Calculation of Commitment Period*. The official bankruptcy form used to calculate a Chapter 13 debtor's current monthly income and to determine how long the Chapter 13 plan must last. Used in conjunction with the *Chapter 13 Calculation of Your Disposable Income*.

Claim. A creditor's assertion that the bankruptcy filer owes it a debt or obligation.

Clothing. As an exemption category, the everyday clothes you and your family need for work, school, household use, and protection from the elements. In many states, luxury items and furs are not included in the clothing exemption category.

Codebtor. A person who assumes an equal responsibility, along with the debtor, to repay a debt or loan.

Collateral. Property pledged by a borrower as security for a loan.

Common law property states. States that don't use a community property system to classify marital property.

Community property. Certain property owned by married couples in Arizona, California,

Idaho, Louisiana, Nevada, New Mexico, Texas, Washington, Wisconsin, and, if both spouses agree, Alaska. Very generally, all property acquired during the marriage is considered community property, belonging equally to both spouses, except for gifts and inheritances by one spouse. Similarly, all debts incurred during the marriage are considered community debts, owed equally by both spouses, with limited exceptions.

Complaint. A formal document that initiates a lawsuit.

Complaint to determine dischargeablity. A complaint initiating an adversary action in bankruptcy court that asks the court to decide whether a particular debt should be discharged at the end of the debtor's bankruptcy case.

Condominium. A building or complex in which separate units, such as townhouses or apartments, are owned by individuals, and the common areas (lobby, hallways, stairways, and so on) are jointly owned by the unit owners.

Confirmation. The bankruptcy judge's ruling approving a Chapter 13 plan.

Confirmation hearing. A court hearing conducted by a bankruptcy judge in which the judge decides whether a debtor's proposed Chapter 13 plan appears to be feasible and meets all applicable legal requirements.

Consumer bankruptcy. A bankruptcy in which most of the debt was incurred for personal, family, or household purposes.

Consumer debt. A debt incurred by an individual for personal, family, or household purposes.

Contingent debts. Debts that may be owed if certain events happen or conditions are satisfied.

Contingent interests in the estate of a decedent. The right to inherit property if one or more conditions to the inheritance are satisfied. For example, a debtor who will inherit property only if he survives his brother has a contingent interest.

Conversion. When a debtor who has filed one type of bankruptcy switches to another type—as when a Chapter 7 debtor converts to a Chapter 13 bankruptcy, or vice versa.

Cooperative housing. A building or another residential structure that is owned by a corporation formed by the residents. In exchange for purchasing stock in the corporation, the residents have the right to live in particular units.

Cooperative insurance. Compulsory employment benefits provided by a state or federal government, such as old age, survivors', disability, and health insurance, to assure a minimum standard of living for lower- and middle-income people. Also called social insurance.

Court clerk. The court employee who is responsible for accepting filings and other documents and generally maintaining an accurate and efficient flow of paper and information in the court.

Cramdown. In a Chapter 13 bankruptcy, the act of reducing a secured debt to the replacement value of the collateral securing the debt.

Credit and debt counseling. Counseling that explores the possibility of repaying debts outside of bankruptcy and educates the debtor about credit, budgeting, and financial management. Under the new bankruptcy law, a debtor must undergo credit counseling with an approved provider before filing for bankruptcy.

Credit insurance. An insurance policy that covers a borrower for an outstanding loan. If the borrower dies or becomes disabled before paying off the loan, the policy will pay off the balance due.

Creditor. A person or an institution to whom money is owed.

Creditor committee. In a Chapter 11 bankruptcy, a committee that represents the unsecured debtors in reorganization proceedings.

Creditor matrix. A specially formatted list of creditors that a debtor must file with the bankruptcy petition. The matrix helps the court notify creditors of the bankruptcy filing and the date and time set for the first meeting of creditors.

Creditors' meeting. See "meeting of creditors."

Crops. Products of the soil or earth that are grown and raised annually and gathered in a single season. Thus, oranges (on the tree or harvested) are crops; an orange tree isn't.

Current market value. What property could be sold for. Prior to 2005, this is how a debtor's property was valued for purposes of determining whether the property is

protected by an applicable exemption. Now property must be valued at its "replacement cost."

Current monthly income. As defined by bankruptcy law, a bankruptcy filer's total gross income (whether taxable or not), averaged over the six-month period immediately preceding the month in which the bankruptcy is filed. The current monthly income is used to determine whether the debtor can file for Chapter 7 bankruptcy, among other things.

Debt. An obligation of any type, including a loan, credit, or promise to perform a contract or lease.

Debt relief agency. An umbrella term for any person or agency—including lawyers and bankruptcy petition preparers, but excluding banks, nonprofit and government agencies, and employees of debt relief agencies—that provides "bankruptcy assistance" to an "assisted person."

Debtor. Someone who owes money to another person or business. Also, the generic term used to refer to anyone who files for bankruptcy.

Declaration. A written statement that is made under oath but not witnessed by a notary public.

Declaration of homestead. A form filed with the county recorder's office to put on record your right to a homestead exemption. In most states, the homestead exemption is automatic—that is, you are not required to record a homestead declaration in order to claim the homestead exemption. A few states do require such a recording, however.

Deed in lieu of foreclosure. The document created when a homeowner dissolves his or her responsibility for a mortgage by deeding the property over to the mortgage owner. The homeowner's credit report will be negatively affected just as if the home were lost through foreclosure.

Disability benefits. Payments made under a disability insurance or retirement plan when the insured is unable to work (or retires early) because of disability, accident, or sickness.

Discharge. A court order, issued at the conclusion of a Chapter 7 or Chapter 13 bankruptcy case, that legally relieves the debtor of personal liability for debts that can be discharged in that type of bankruptcy.

Discharge exceptions. Debts that are not discharged in a bankruptcy case. The debtor continues to owe these debts even after the bankruptcy is concluded.

Discharge hearing. A hearing conducted by a bankruptcy court to explain the discharge, urge the debtor to stay out of debt, and review reaffirmation agreements to make sure they are feasible and fair.

Dischargeability action. An adversary action brought by a party who asks the court to determine whether a particular debt qualifies for discharge.

Dischargeable debt. A debt that is wiped out at the conclusion of a bankruptcy case,

unless the judge decides that it should not be.

Disclosure of Compensation of Bankruptcy Petition Preparer. An official form bankruptcy petition preparers must file with the bankruptcy court to disclose their fees.

Dismissal. When the court orders a case to be closed without providing the relief available under the bankruptcy laws. For example, a Chapter 13 case might be dismissed because the debtor fails to propose a feasible plan; a Chapter 7 case might be dismissed for abuse.

Disposable income. The difference between a debtor's "current monthly income" and allowable expenses. This is the amount that the bankruptcy law deems available to pay into a Chapter 13 plan.

Domestic animals. See "animals."

Domestic support obligation. An obligation to pay alimony or child support to a spouse, child, or government entity pursuant to an order by a court or other governmental unit.

Doubling. The ability of married couples to double the amount of certain property exemptions when filing for bankruptcy together. The federal bankruptcy exemptions allow doubling. State laws vary— some permit doubling and some do not.

Education individual retirement account. A type of account to which a person can contribute a certain amount of tax-deferred funds every year for the educational benefit of the debtor or certain relatives. Such an account is not part of the debtor's bankruptcy estate.

Emergency bankruptcy filing. An initial bankruptcy filing that includes only the petition and the creditor matrix, filed right away because the debtor needs the protection of the automatic stay to prevent a creditor from taking certain action, such as a foreclosure. An emergency filing case will be dismissed if the other required documents and forms are not filed in a timely manner.

Endowment insurance. An insurance policy that gives an insured who lives for a specified time (the endowment period) the right to receive the face value of the policy (the amount paid at death). If the insured dies sooner, the beneficiary named in the policy receives the proceeds.

Equity. The amount you get to keep if you sell property—typically the property's market value, less the costs of sale and the value of any liens on the property.

ERISA-qualified benefits. Pensions that meet the requirements of the Employee Retirement Income Security Act (ERISA), a federal law that sets minimum standards for such plans and requires beneficiaries to receive certain notices.

Executory contract. A contract in which one or both parties still have a duty to carry out one or more of the contract's terms.

Exempt property. Property described by state and federal laws (exemptions) that a debtor is entitled to keep in a Chapter 7 bankruptcy. Exempt property cannot be taken and sold by the trustee for the benefit of the debtor's unsecured creditors.

Exemptions. State and federal laws specifying the types of property creditors are not entitled to take to satisfy a debt, and the bankruptcy trustee is not entitled to take and sell for the benefit of the debtor's unsecured creditors.

Farm tools. Tools used by a person whose primary occupation is farming. Some states limit farm tools of the trade to items that can be held in the hand, such as hoes, axes, pitchforks, shovels, scythes, and the like. In other states, farm tools also include plows, harnesses, mowers, reapers, and so on.

Federal exemptions. A list of exemptions contained in the federal Bankruptcy Code. Some states give debtors the option of using the federal exemptions rather than state exemptions.

Federal Rules of Bankruptcy Procedure. A set of rules issued by the Administrative Office of the United States Courts that governs bankruptcy court procedures.

Filing date. The date a bankruptcy petition in a particular case is filed. With few exceptions, debts incurred after the filing date are not discharged. Similarly, property owned before the filing date is part of the bankruptcy estate, while property acquired after the filing date is not.

Fines, penalties, and restitution. Debts owed to a court or a victim as a result of a sentence in a criminal matter. These debts are generally not dischargeable in bankruptcy.

Foreclosure. The process by which a creditor with a lien on real estate forces a sale of the property in order to collect on the lien. Foreclosure typically occurs when a homeowner defaults on a mortgage.

Fraternal benefit society benefits. Benefits, often group life insurance, paid for by fraternal societies, such as the Elks, Masons, Knights of Columbus, or the Knights of Maccabees, for their members. Also called benefit society, benevolent society, or mutual aid association benefits.

Fraud. Generally, an act that is intended to mislead another for the purpose of financial gain. In a bankruptcy case, fraud is any writing or representation intended to mislead creditors for the purpose of obtaining a loan or credit, or any act intended to mislead the bankruptcy court or the trustee.

Fraudulent transfer. In a bankruptcy case, a transfer of property to another for less than the property's value for the purpose of hiding the property from the bankruptcy trustee—for instance, when a debtor signs a car over to a relative to keep it out of the bankruptcy estate. Fraudulently transferred property can be recovered and sold by the trustee for the benefit of the creditors.

Fraudulently concealed assets. Property that a bankruptcy debtor deliberately fails to disclose as required by the bankruptcy rules.

Furnishings. An exemption category recognized in many states, that includes furniture, fixtures in your home (such as a heating unit, furnace, or built-in lighting), and other items with which a home is furnished, such as carpets and drapes.

Good faith. In a Chapter 13 case, when a debtor files for bankruptcy with the sincere purpose of paying off debts over the period of time required by law rather than for manipulative purposes—such as to prevent a foreclosure that by all rights should be allowed to proceed.

Goods and chattels. See "personal property."

Group life or group health insurance. A single insurance policy covering individuals in a group (for example, employees) and their dependents.

Head of household. A person who supports and maintains, in one household, one or more people who are closely related to the person by blood, marriage, or adoption. Also referred to as "head of family."

Health aids. Items needed to maintain their owner's health, such as a wheelchair, crutches, prosthesis, or a hearing aid. Many states require that health aids be prescribed by a physician.

Health benefits. Benefits paid under health insurance plans, such as Blue Cross or Blue Shield, to cover the costs of health care.

Heirloom. An item with special monetary or sentimental value, that is passed down from generation to generation.

Home equity loan. A loan made to a homeowner on the basis of the equity in the home—and secured by the home in the same manner as a mortgage.

Homestead. A state or federal exemption applicable to property where the debtor lives when he or she files bankruptcy—usually including boats and mobile homes.

Homestead declaration. See "declaration of homestead."

Household good. As an exemption category, an item of permanent nature (as opposed to items consumed, like food or cosmetics) used in or about the house. This includes linens, dinnerware, utensils, pots and pans, and small electronic equipment like radios. Many state laws specifically list the types of household goods that fall within this exemption, as do the federal bankruptcy laws.

Householder. A person who supports and maintains a household, with or without other people. Also called a "housekeeper."

Impairs an exemption. When a lien, in combination with any other liens on the property and the amount the debtor is entitled to claim as exempt, exceeds the value of the property the debtor could claim in the absence of any liens. For example, if property is worth $15,000, there are $5,000 worth of liens on the property, and the debtor is entitled to a $5,000 exemption in the property, another lien that exceeded $5,000 would impair the debtor's exemption. Certain types of liens that impair an exemption may be removed (avoided) by the debtor if the court so orders.

Implement. As an exemption category, an instrument, tool, or utensil used by a person to accomplish his or her job.

In lieu of homestead (or burial) exemption. Designates an exemption that is available only if you don't claim the homestead (or burial) exemption.

Individual Debtor's Statement of Intention. An official bankruptcy form that debtors with secured debts must file to indicate what they want to do with the property that secures the debt. For instance, a debtor with a car note must indicate whether he or she wants to keep the car and continue the debt (reaffirmation), pay off the car note at a reduced price (redemption), or give the car back to the creditor and cancel the debt.

Injunction. A court order prohibiting a person or an entity from taking specified actions—for example, the automatic stay (in reality an automatic injunction), that prevents most creditors from trying to collect their debts.

Insider creditor. A creditor with whom the debtor has a personal relationship, such as a relative, friend, or business partner.

Intangible property. Property that cannot be physically touched, such as an ownership share in a corporation or a copyright. Documents—such as a stock certificate—may provide evidence of intangible property.

Involuntary dismissal. When a bankruptcy judge dismisses a case because the debtor fails to carry out his or her duties—such as filing papers in a timely manner and cooperating with the trustee—or because the debtor files the bankruptcy in bad faith or engages in abuse by wrongfully filing for Chapter 7 when he or she should have filed for Chapter 13.

Involuntary lien. A lien that is placed on the debtor's property without the debtor's consent—for instance, when the IRS places a lien on property for back taxes.

IRS expenses. A table of national and regional expense estimates published by the IRS. Debtors whose "current monthly income" is more than their state's "median family income" must use the IRS expenses to calculate their average net income in a Chapter 7 case or their disposable income in a Chapter 13 case.

Jewelry. Items created for personal adornment; usually includes watches. Also called "articles of adornment."

Joint debtors. Married people who file for bankruptcy together and pay a single filing fee.

Judgment proof. A description of a person whose income and property are such that a creditor can't (or won't) seize them to enforce a money judgment—for example, a dwelling protected by a homestead exemption or a bank account containing only a few dollars.

Judicial foreclosure. A foreclosure that occurs through a court proceeding, usually when the party seeking the foreclosure files a complaint in court seeking a court order authorizing it.

Judicial lien. A lien created by the recording of a court money judgment against the debtor's property, usually real estate.

Lease. A contract that governs the relationship between an owner of property (such as a car or real estate) and a person who wishes to use the property for a specific period of time.

Lien. A legal claim against property that must be paid before title to the property can be transferred. Liens can also often be collected through repossession (personal property) or foreclosure (real estate), depending on the type of lien.

Lien avoidance. A bankruptcy procedure in which certain types of liens can be removed from certain types of property. Liens that are not avoided survive the bankruptcy even though the underlying debt may be canceled. For instance, a lien remains on a car even if the debt evidenced by the car note is discharged in the bankruptcy.

Lien stripping. A method by which a wholly unsecured lien is removed from property. It is used mainly in Chapter 13 bankruptcies.

Life estate. The right to live in, but not own, a specific home until your death.

Life insurance. A policy that provides for the payment of money to an individual (called the beneficiary) in the event of the death of another (called the insured). The policy matures (becomes payable) only when the insured dies.

Lifting the stay. When a bankruptcy court allows a creditor to continue with debt collection or other activities that are otherwise banned by the automatic stay. For instance, the court might allow a landlord to proceed with an eviction or a lender to repossess a car because the debtor has defaulted on the note.

Liquid assets. Cash or items that are easily convertible into cash, such as a money market account, stock, U.S. Treasury bill, or bank deposit.

Liquidated debt. An existing debt for a specified amount arising out of a contract or court judgment. In contrast, an unliquidated debt is a claim for an as-yet uncertain amount, such as for injuries suffered in a car accident before the case goes to court.

Lost future earnings. The portion of a lawsuit judgment intended to compensate an injured person for the money he or she won't be able to earn in the future because of the injury. Also called lost earnings payments or recoveries.

Luxuries. In bankruptcy, goods or services purchased by the debtor that a court decides were not appropriate in light of the debtor's insolvency. This might include vacations, jewelry, costly cars, or frequent meals at expensive restaurants.

Mailing matrix. See "creditor matrix."

Marital adjustment deduction. A deduction used in connection with Chapter 13 bankruptcy to determine a debtor's current monthly income when only one spouse is filing for bankruptcy. A debtor may take this deduction for the amount of the non-filing spouse's income that is used to pay the nonfiling spouse's expenses only, and not used for household expenses.

Marital debts. Debts owed jointly by a married couple.

Marital property. Property owned jointly by a married couple.

Marital settlement agreement. An agreement between a divorcing couple that sets out who gets what percentage (or what specific items) of the marital property, who pays what marital debts, and who gets custody and pays child support if there are children of the marriage.

Materialmen's and mechanics' liens. Liens imposed by statute on real estate when suppliers of materials, labor, and contracting services used to improve the real estate are not properly compensated.

Matured life insurance benefits. Insurance benefits that are currently payable because the insured person has died.

Means test. A formula that uses predefined income and expense categories to determine whether a debtor whose income is more than the median family income for his or her state should be allowed to file a Chapter 7 bankruptcy.

Median family income. An annual income figure for which there are as many families with incomes below that level as there are above that level. The U.S. Census Bureau publishes median family income figures for each state and for different family sizes. In bankruptcy, the median family income is used as a basis for determining whether a debtor must pass the means test to file Chapter 7 bankruptcy, and whether a debtor filing a Chapter 13 bankruptcy must commit all of his or her projected disposable income to a five-year repayment plan.

Meeting of creditors. A meeting that the debtor is required to attend in a bankruptcy case, at which the trustee and creditors may ask the debtor questions about his or her property, information in the documents and forms he or she filed, and his or her debts.

Mortgage. A contract in which a loan to purchase real estate is secured by the real estate as collateral. If the borrower defaults on loan payments, the lender can foreclose on the property.

Motion. A formal legal procedure in which the bankruptcy judge is asked to rule on a dispute in the bankruptcy case. To bring a motion, a party must file a document explaining what relief is requested, the facts of the dispute, and the legal reasons why the court should grant the relief. The party bringing the motion must mail these documents to all affected parties and let them know when the court will hear argument on the motion.

Motion to avoid judicial lien on real estate. A motion brought by a bankruptcy debtor that asks the bankruptcy court to remove a judicial lien on real estate because the lien impairs the debtor's homestead exemption.

Motion to lift stay. A motion in which a creditor asks the court for permission to continue a court action or collection activities in spite of the automatic stay.

Motor vehicle. A self-propelled vehicle suitable for use on a street or road. This includes a car, truck, motorcycle, van, and moped. See also "tools of the trade."

Musical instrument. An instrument having the capacity, when properly operated, to produce a musical sound. Pianos, guitars, drums, drum machines, synthesizers, and harmonicas are all musical instruments.

Mutual aid association benefits. See "fraternal benefit society benefits."

Mutual assessment or mutual life. See "stipulated insurance."

Necessities. Articles needed to sustain life, such as food, clothing, medical care, and shelter.

Newly discovered creditors. Creditors whom the debtor discovers after the bankruptcy is filed. If the case is still open, the debtor can amend the list to include the creditor; if the case is closed, it usually can be reopened to accommodate the amendment.

Nonbankruptcy federal exemptions. Federal laws that allow a debtor who has not filed for bankruptcy to keep creditors away from certain property. The debtor can also use these exemptions in bankruptcy if the debtor is using a state exemption system.

Nondischargeable debt. Debt that survives bankruptcy, such as back child support and most student loans.

Nonexempt property. Property in the bankruptcy estate that is unprotected by the exemption system available to the debtor (this is typically—but not always—the exemption system in the state where the debtor files bankruptcy). In a Chapter 7 bankruptcy, the trustee may sell it for the benefit of the debtor's unsecured creditors. In a Chapter 13 bankruptcy, debtors must propose a plan that pays their unsecured creditors at least the value of their unsecured property.

Nonjudicial foreclosure. A foreclosure that occurs outside of court, usually when a trustee of a deed of trust first records a notice of default and then a notice of sale in an auction, typically held on the courthouse steps.

Nonpossessory, nonpurchase-money lien. A lien placed on property that is already owned by the debtor and is used as collateral for the loan without being possessed by the lender. In contrast, a nonpurchase-money, possessory lien exists on collateral that is held by a pawnshop.

Nonpriority debt. A type of debt that is not entitled to be paid first in bankruptcy, as priority debts are. Nonpriority debts do not have to be paid in full in a Chapter 13 case.

Nonpriority, unsecured claim. A claim that is not for a priority debt (such as child support) and is not secured by collateral or other property. Typical examples include credit card debt, medical bills, and student loans. In a Chapter 13 repayment plan, nonpriority, unsecured claims are paid only after all other debts are paid.

Notice of appeal. A form that must be filed with a court when a party wishes to appeal a judgment or an order issued by the court. Often, the notice of appeal must be filed within ten days of the date the order or judgment is entered in the court's records.

Objection. A document one party files to oppose a proposed action by another party—for instance, when a creditor or trustee files an objection to a bankruptcy debtor's claim of exemption.

Order for relief. The court's automatic injunction against certain collection and other activities that might negatively affect the bankruptcy estate. Another name for the "automatic stay."

Oversecured debt. A debt that is secured by collateral that is worth more than the amount of the debt.

PACER. An online, fee-based database containing bankruptcy court dockets (records of proceedings in bankruptcy cases) and federal court documents, such as court rules and recent appellate court decisions.

Pain and suffering damages. The portion of a court judgment intended to compensate for past, present, and future mental and physical pain, suffering, impairment of ability to work, and mental distress caused by an injury.

Partially secured debt. A debt secured by collateral that is worth less than the debt itself—for instance, when a person owes $15,000 on a car that is worth only $10,000.

Party in interest. Any person or entity that has a financial interest in the outcome of a bankruptcy case, including the trustee, the debtor, and all creditors.

Pension. A fund into which payments are made to provide an employee income after retirement. Typically, the beneficiary can't access the account without incurring a significant penalty, usually a tax. There are many types of pensions, including defined benefit pensions provided by many large corporations and individual pensions (such as 401(k) and IRA accounts). In bankruptcy, most pensions are not considered part of the bankruptcy estate and are therefore not affected by a bankruptcy filing.

Personal financial management counseling. Under the new bankruptcy law, a two-hour class intended to teach budget skills. Every consumer bankruptcy filer must attend such a class in order to obtain a discharge in Chapter 7, Chapter 12, or Chapter 13 bankruptcy.

Personal injury cause of action. The right to seek compensation for physical and mental suffering, including injury to body, reputation, or both. For example, someone who is hit and injured by a car might have a personal injury cause of action against the driver.

Personal injury recovery. The portion of a lawsuit judgment or insurance settlement that is intended to compensate someone for physical and mental suffering, including physical injury, injury to reputation, or both. Bankruptcy exemptions usually do not apply to compensation for pain or suffering or punitive damages—in other words, that part of the recovery can be taken by the trustee in a Chapter 7 case.

Personal property. All property not classified as real property, including tangible items, such as cars and jewelry, and intangible property, such as stocks and pensions.

Petition. The document a debtor files to officially begin a bankruptcy case and ask for relief. Other documents and schedules must be filed to support the petition at the time it is filed, or shortly afterwards.

Pets. See "animals."

Preference. A payment made by a debtor to a creditor within a defined period prior to filing for bankruptcy—within three months for arms-length creditors (regular commercial creditors) and one year for insider creditors (friends, family, business associates). Because a preference gives that debtor an edge over other debtors in the bankruptcy case, the trustee can recover the preference and distribute it among all of the creditors.

Prepetition. Any time prior to the moment the bankruptcy petition is filed.

Prepetition counseling. Debt or credit counseling that occurs before the bankruptcy petition is filed—as opposed to personal financial management counseling, which occurs after the petition is filed.

Presumed abuse. In a Chapter 7 bankruptcy, when the debtor has a current monthly income in excess of the family median income for the state where the debtor lives, and has sufficient income to propose a Chapter 13 plan under the "means test." If abuse is presumed, the debtor has to prove that his or her Chapter 7 filing is not abusive in order to proceed further.

Primarily business debts. When the majority of debt owed by a bankruptcy debtor—in dollar terms—arises from debts incurred to operate a business.

Primarily consumer debts. When the majority of debt owed by a bankruptcy debtor—in dollar terms—arises from debts incurred for personal or family purposes.

Priority claim. See "priority debt."

Priority creditor. A creditor who has filed a "*Proof of Claim*" showing that the debtor owes it a priority debt.

Priority debt. A type of debt that is paid first if there are distributions to be made from the bankruptcy estate. Priority debts include alimony and child support, fees owed to the trustee and attorneys in the case, and wages owed to employees. With one exception (back child support obligations assigned to government entities), priority claims must be paid in full in a Chapter 13 bankruptcy.

Proceeds for damaged exempt property. Money received through insurance coverage, arbitration, mediation, settlement, or a lawsuit to pay for exempt property that has been damaged or destroyed. For example, if a debtor had the right to use a $30,000 homestead exemption, but his or her home was destroyed by fire, the debtor can instead exempt $30,000 of the insurance proceeds.

Projected disposable income. The amount of income a debtor will have left over each month, after deducting allowable expenses, payments on mandatory debts, and administrative expenses from his or her current monthly income. This is the amount the debtor must pay toward his or her unsecured nonpriority debts in a Chapter 13 plan.

Proof of Claim. A formal document filed by bankruptcy creditors in a bankruptcy case to assert their right to payments from the bankruptcy estate, if any payments are made.

Proof of Service. A document signed under penalty of perjury by the person serving a document showing how the service was made, who made it, and when.

Property of the estate. See "bankruptcy estate."

Purchase-money loans. Loans that are made to purchase specific property items and that use the property as collateral to assure repayment, such as car loans and mortgages.

Purchase-money security interest. A claim on property owned by the holder of a loan that was used to purchase the property and that is secured by the property (as collateral).

Reaffirmation. An agreement entered into after a bankruptcy filing (postpetition) between the debtor and a creditor in which the debtor agrees to repay all or part of a prepetition debt after the bankruptcy is over. For instance, a debtor makes an agreement with the holder of a car note that the debtor can keep the car and must continue to pay the debt after bankruptcy.

Real property. Real estate (land and buildings on the land, usually including mobile homes attached to a foundation).

Reasonable investigation. Bankruptcy attorneys' obligation, under bankruptcy law, to look into the information provided to them by their clients.

Redemption. In a Chapter 7 bankruptcy, when the debtor obtains legal title to collateral for a secured debt by paying the secured creditor the replacement value of the collateral in a lump sum. For example, a debtor may redeem a car note by paying the lender the replacement value of the car (what a retail vendor would charge for the car, considering its age and condition).

Reopen a case. To open a closed bankruptcy case, usually for the purpose of adding an overlooked creditor or filing a motion to avoid an overlooked lien. A debtor must request that the court reopen the case.

Repayment plan. An informal plan to repay creditors most or all of what they are owed outside of bankruptcy. Also refers to the plan proposed by a debtor in a Chapter 13 case.

Replacement cost. What it would cost to replace a particular item by buying it from a retail vendor, considering its age and condition—for instance, when buying a car from a used car dealer, furniture from a used furniture shop, or electronic equipment on eBay.

Repossession. When a secured creditor takes property used as collateral because the debtor has defaulted on the loan secured by the collateral.

Request to lift the stay. A written request filed in bankruptcy court by a creditor, that seeks permission to engage in debt collection activity otherwise prohibited by the automatic stay.

Schedule A/B. The official bankruptcy form a debtor must file to describe all of his or her property.

Schedule C. The official bankruptcy form a debtor must file to describe the property the debtor is claiming as exempt and the legal basis for the claims of exemption.

Schedule D. The official bankruptcy form a debtor must file to describe all secured debts owed by the debtor, such as car notes and mortgages.

Schedule E/F. The official bankruptcy form a debtor must file to describe all debts owed by the debtor.

Schedule G. The official bankruptcy form a debtor must file to describe any leases and executory contracts (contracts under which one or both parties still have obligations) to which the debtor is a party.

Schedule H. The official bankruptcy form a debtor must file to describe all codebtors that might be affected by the bankruptcy.

Schedule I. The official bankruptcy form a debtor must file to describe the debtor's income.

Schedule J. The official bankruptcy form a debtor must file to describe the debtor's actual monthly expenses.

Schedules. Official bankruptcy forms a debtor must file, detailing the debtor's property, debts, income, and expenses.

Second deed of trust. A loan against real estate made after the original mortgage (or first deed of trust). Most home equity loans are second deeds of trust.

Secured claim. A debt secured by collateral under a written agreement (for instance, a mortgage or car note) or by operation of law—such as a tax lien.

Secured creditor. The owner of a secured claim.

Secured debt. A debt secured by collateral.

Secured interest. A claim to property used as collateral. For instance, a lender on a car note retains legal title to the car until the loan is paid off.

Secured property. Property that is collateral for a secured debt.

Serial bankruptcy filing. A practice used by some debtors to file and dismiss one bankruptcy after another to obtain the protection of the automatic stay, even though the bankruptcies themselves offer no debt relief—for instance, when a debtor files successive Chapter 13 cases

to prevent foreclosure of his or her home even though there are no debts to repay.

Short sale. When a homeowner sells his or her home for less than is owed on the mortgage and turns the proceeds over to the mortgage owner. The homeowner's credit report will be negatively affected just as if the home were lost through foreclosure.

Sickness benefits. See "disability benefits."

State exemptions. State laws that specify the types of property creditors are not entitled to take to satisfy a debt, and the bankruptcy trustee is not entitled to take and sell for the benefit of the debtor's unsecured creditors.

Statement of Intention for Individuals Filing Under Chapter 7. The official bankruptcy form a debtor must file in a Chapter 7 case to tell the court and secured creditors how the debtor plans to treat his or her secured debts—that is, reaffirm the debt, redeem the debt, or surrender the property and discharge the debt.

Statutory lien. A lien imposed on property by law, such as tax liens and mechanics' liens, as opposed to voluntary liens (such as mortgages) and liens arising from court judgments (judicial liens).

Stay. See "automatic stay."

Stipulated insurance. An insurance policy that allows the insurance company to assess an amount on the insured, above the standard premium payments, if the company experiences losses worse than had been calculated into the standard premium. Also called assessment, mutual assessment, or mutual life insurance.

Stock options. A contract between a corporation and an employee that gives the employee the right to purchase corporate stock at a specific price mentioned in the contract (the strike price).

Strip down of lien. In a Chapter 13 bankruptcy, when the amount of a lien on collateral is reduced to the collateral's replacement value. See "cramdown."

Student loan. A type of loan made for educational purposes by nonprofit or commercial lenders with repayment and interest terms dictated by federal law. Student loans are not dischargeable in bankruptcy unless the debtor can show that repaying the loan would impose an "undue hardship."

Substantial abuse. Under pre-2005 bankruptcy law, filing a Chapter 7 bankruptcy when a Chapter 13 bankruptcy was feasible.

Suggestion of bankruptcy. A notice, usually filed by a bankruptcy debtor, in non-bankruptcy litigation to inform the court and the other parties that a bankruptcy has been filed and the litigation may be stayed.

Suits, executions, garnishments, and attachments. Activities engaged in by creditors to enforce money judgments, typically involving the seizure of wages and bank accounts.

Summary of Your Assets and Liabilities and Certain Statistical Information. The official bankruptcy form a debtor must file to summarize the property and debt information contained in a debtor's schedules.

Surrender value. See "avails."

Surrendering collateral. In Chapter 7 bankruptcy, the act of returning collateral to a secured lender in order to discharge the underlying debt—for example, returning a car to discharge the car note.

Tangible personal property. See "tangible property" and "personal property."

Tangible property. Property that may be physically touched. Examples include money, furniture, cars, jewelry, artwork, and houses. Compare "intangible property."

Tax lien. A statutory lien imposed on property to secure payment of back taxes—typically income and property taxes.

Tenancy by the entirety. A way that married couples can hold title to property in about half of the states. When one spouse dies, the surviving spouse automatically owns 100% of the property. In most cases, this type of property is not part of the bankruptcy estate if only one spouse files.

To ____ acres. A limitation on the size of a homestead that may be exempted.

Tools of the trade. Items needed to perform a line of work that you are currently doing and relying on for support. For a mechanic, plumber, or carpenter, for example, tools of trade are the implements used to repair, build, and install. Traditionally, tools of the trade were limited to items that could be held in the hand. Most states, however, now embrace a broader definition, and a debtor may be able to fit many items under a tools of trade exemption.

Transcript of tax return. A summary of a debtor's tax return provided by the IRS upon the debtor's request, usually acceptable as a substitute for the return in the instances when a return must be filed under bankruptcy law.

Trustee. An official appointed by the bankruptcy court to carry out the administrative tasks associated with a bankruptcy and to seize and sell nonexempt property in the bankruptcy estate for the benefit of the debtor's unsecured creditors.

Undersecured debt. A debt secured by collateral that is worth less than the debt.

Undue hardship. The conditions under which a debtor may discharge a student loan—for example, when the debtor has no income and little chance of earning enough to repay the loan in the future.

Unexpired lease. A lease that is still in effect.

Unmatured life insurance. A policy that is not yet payable because the insured is still alive.

Unscheduled debt. A debt that is not included in the schedules accompanying a bankruptcy filing, perhaps because it was overlooked or intentionally left out.

Unsecured creditor. A creditor whose debt is not secured by collateral, and who therefore has no right to seize a particular item of the debtor's property if the debtor defaults on the debt.

Unsecured priority claims. Priority claims that aren't secured by collateral, such as back child support or taxes for which no lien has been placed on the debtor's property.

U.S. Trustee. An official employed by the Office of the U.S. Trustee (a division of the U.S. Department of Justice) who is responsible for overseeing the bankruptcy trustees, regulating credit and personal financial management counselors, regulating bankruptcy petition preparers, auditing bankruptcy cases, ferreting out fraud, and generally making sure that the bankruptcy laws are obeyed.

Valuation of property. The act of determining the replacement value of property for the purpose of describing it in the bankruptcy schedules, determining whether it is protected by an applicable exemption, redeeming secured property, or cramming down a lien in Chapter 13 bankruptcy.

Voluntary dismissal. When a bankruptcy debtor dismisses his or her Chapter 7 or Chapter 13 case on his or her own, without coercion by the court.

Voluntary lien. A lien agreed to by the debtor, as when the debtor signs a mortgage, car note, or second deed of trust.

Weekly net earnings. The earnings a debtor has left after mandatory deductions, such as income tax, mandatory union dues, and Social Security contributions, have been subtracted from his or her gross income.

Wholly unsecured lien. A lien that is not secured by any equity in the collateral because more senior liens that must be paid first equal or exceed the value of the collateral.

Wildcard exemption. A dollar value that the debtor can apply to any type of property to make it—or more of it—exempt. In some states, filers may use the unused portion of a homestead exemption as a wildcard exemption.

Willful and malicious act. An act done with the intent to cause harm. In a Chapter 7 bankruptcy, a debt arising from the debtor's willful and malicious act is not discharged if the victim proves to the bankruptcy court's satisfaction that the act occurred.

Willful or malicious act resulting in a civil judgment. A bad act that was careless or reckless, but was not necessarily intended to cause harm. In a Chapter 13 case, a debt arising from the debtor's act that was either willful or malicious is not discharged if it is part of a civil judgment.

Wrongful death cause of action. The right to seek compensation for having to live without a deceased person. Usually only the spouse and children of the deceased have a wrongful death cause of action.

Wrongful death recoveries. The portion of a lawsuit judgment intended to compensate a plaintiff for having to live without a deceased person. The compensation is intended to cover the earnings and the emotional comfort and support the deceased would have provided.

Your Statement of Financial Affairs for Individuals Filing for Bankruptcy. The official bankruptcy form a debtor must file to describe the debtor's legal, economic, and business transactions for the several years prior to filing, including gifts, preferences, income, closing of deposit accounts, lawsuits, and other information that the trustee needs to assess the legitimacy of the bankruptcy and the true extent of the bankruptcy estate.

Your Statement of Your Social Security Numbers. The official bankruptcy form a debtor must file to disclose the debtor's complete Social Security number.

Federal and State Exemption Tables

The charts in this appendix are divided into categories of property, such as insurance, personal property, and wages. Following each exemption, we provide the numerical citation to the state statute that includes the exemption.

The states are listed alphabetically, followed by the federal exemptions. We also note which states allow you to choose between the federal and state bankruptcy exemptions.

 RELATED TOPIC

Need help understanding a term?
Many of the categories, types of property, and other terms used in these charts are defined in the Glossary, which you'll find right before this appendix.

Doubling

When a married couple files for bankruptcy jointly, federal law and the laws of some states allow them each to claim the full amount of an exemption. (11 U.S.C. § 522.) Because a couple gets to claim twice the amount available to those who file alone, this practice is informally known as "doubling."

Not all states allow doubling, however. And some states allow married filers to double only certain exemptions (for example, they might be allowed to double personal property exemptions but not the homestead exemption). In the charts that follow, we indicate exemptions that cannot be doubled and states that don't allow doubling at all. Unless you see a note stating that you cannot double, assume that you can.

Wage Garnishment Laws and Exemptions in Bankruptcy

Almost all states have a wage garnishment law that applies to judgment creditors, limiting how much they can take from your paycheck. In most states, you can use the wage garnishment law as an exemption in bankruptcy. Some states, however, don't allow this. If your state doesn't let bankruptcy filers use the wage garnishment law as an exemption, we indicate that on the chart. Some states have a specific statute that exempts a certain portion of wages in bankruptcy— obviously, you can use this in bankruptcy.

The federal bankruptcy exemptions do not have a separate exemption for wages. If you use the federal exemptions (assuming your state gives you the choice), the only way you can protect wages is by using the wildcard exemption.

What Income Is Exempt?

In most states, you can use the wage garnishment law to protect income that was already earned but not yet received on the day you filed for bankruptcy—called "earned but unpaid wages."

In some states, the wage garnishment exemption also protects wages you received before you filed for bankruptcy (it's easiest to claim the exemption if these wages are not mixed with other funds). In other states, the wage garnishment exemption does not protect wages that you received prior to filing for bankruptcy.

Some state exemptions protect all kinds of "earnings," regardless of type, while others protect only wages for the "performance of services," and exclude other kinds of income.

Checking the Law in Your State

Before relying on a wage garnishment statute to protect your wages, make sure that the judge in your jurisdiction agrees that the garnishment statute creates an exemption that can be used in bankruptcy. Often, the best way to do this is to ask a local bankruptcy attorney. (Many provide free initial consultations.)

You can also find information about this issue on www.legalconsumer.com. It tracks a dozen or so collected cases on wage garnishment and bankruptcy (search for "Do wage garnishment laws create an exemption in bankruptcy?").

Retirement Accounts

Virtually all types of tax-exempt retirement accounts are exempt in bankruptcy, whether you use the state or federal exemptions. You can exempt 401(k)s, 403(b)s, profit-sharing and money purchase plans, IRAs (including Roth, SEP, and SIMPLE IRAs), and defined-benefit plans.

These exemptions are unlimited—that is, the entire account is exempt, regardless of how much money is in it—except in the case of traditional and Roth IRAs. For these types of IRAs only, the exemption is limited to a total value of $1,283,025 per person

(this figure will be adjusted every three years for inflation). If you have more than one traditional or Roth IRA, you don't get to exempt $1,283,025 per account: Your total exemption, no matter how many accounts you have, is $1,283,025.

If you are using the federal bankruptcy exemptions, you can find this new retirement account provision at 11 U.S.C. § 522(d)(12). If you are using state exemptions, cite 11 U.S.C. § 522(b)(3)(C) as the applicable exemption when you complete your bankruptcy papers.

Confirm the Exemptions Before Relying on Them

The exemptions in the following charts were current when this book went to press, but your state may have changed the law since then. In addition, states often carve out exceptions to the exemptions, which are far too detailed to list here. For instance, even if an item is listed as exempt in one of these charts, you might have to give it up to pay child support or a tax debt.

Before relying on any particular exemption, consider:

- reading the exemption statute yourself, using the research information in Ch. 11, and
- cross-checking the chart's information against the exemptions for your state listed on www.legalconsumer.com.

Last, but certainly not least, consult with a bankruptcy lawyer.

CAUTION

These charts provide general information only. There are exceptions to state exemption laws that are much too detailed to include here. Consider doing further legal research or consulting an attorney about the exemptions you plan to claim, particularly if you anticipate—or are facing—a challenge to your exemption claims.

Alabama

Federal bankruptcy exemptions not available. All law references are to Alabama Code unless otherwise noted.

ASSET	EXEMPTION	LAW
homestead	Real property or mobile home to $15,000; property cannot exceed 160 acres	6-10-2
	Must record homestead declaration before attempted sale of home	6-10-20
insurance	Annuity proceeds or avails to $250 per month	27-14-32
	Disability proceeds or avails to an average of $250 per month	27-14-31
	Fraternal benefit society benefits	27-34-27
	Life insurance proceeds or avails	6-10-8; 27-14-29
	Life insurance proceeds or avails if clause prohibits proceeds from being used to pay beneficiary's creditors	27-15-26
	Mutual aid association benefits	27-30-25
pensions	Tax-exempt retirement accounts, including 401(k)s, 403(b)s, profit-sharing and money purchase plans, SEP and SIMPLE IRAs, and defined-benefit plans	11 U.S.C. § 522(b)(3)(C)
	Traditional and Roth IRAs to $1,283,025 per person	11 U.S.C. § 522(b)(3)(C); (n)
	IRAs, Roth IRAs & other retirement accounts	19-3B-508
	Judges (only payments being received)	12-18-10(a),(b)
	Law enforcement officers	36-21-77
	Spendthrift trusts (with exceptions)	19-3B-501 to 503
	State employees	36-27-28
	Teachers	16-25-23
personal property	Books of debtor & family	6-10-6
	Burial place for self & family	6-10-5
	Church pew for self & family	6-10-5
	Clothing of debtor & family	6-10-6
	Family portraits or pictures	6-10-6
public benefits	Aid to blind, aged, disabled & other public assistance, including earned income tax credit(*In re James*, 406 F. 3d 1340 (11th Cir 2005))	38-4-8; 38-5-5
	Crime victims' compensation	15-23-15(e)
	Southeast Asian War POWs' benefits	31-7-1; 31-7-2
	Unemployment compensation	25-4-140
	Workers' compensation	25-5-86
tools of trade	Arms, uniforms, equipment that state military personnel are required to keep	31-2-78
wages	With respect to consumer loans, consumer credit sales & consumer leases, 75% of weekly net earnings or 30 times the federal minimum hourly wage; all other cases, 75% of earned but unpaid wages; bankruptcy judge may authorize more for low-income debtors	5-19-15; 6-10-7
wildcard	$7,500 of any personal property, except wages	6-10-6; 6-10-126

Alaska

Alaska exemption amounts are adjusted regularly by administrative order. Current amounts are found at 8 Alaska Admin. Code tit. 8, § 95.030. Amounts reflect adjustment as of 10/1/2012.

ASSET	EXEMPTION	LAW
homestead	$72,900 (joint owners may each claim a portion, but total can't exceed $72,900)	09.38.010(a)
insurance	Disability benefits	09.38.015(b); 09.38.030(e)(1),(5)
	Fraternal benefit society benefits	21.84.240
	Life insurance or annuity contracts, total avails to $500,000	09.38.025
	Medical, surgical, or hospital benefits	09.38.015(a)(3)
miscellaneous	Alimony, to extent wages exempt	09.38.030(e)(2)
	Child support payments made by collection agency	09.38.015(b)
	Liquor licenses	09.38.015(a)(7)
	Property of business partnership	09.38.100(b)
pensions	Tax-exempt retirement accounts, including 401(k)s, 403(b)s, profit-sharing and money purchase plans, SEP and SIMPLE IRAs, and defined-benefit plans	11 U.S.C. § 522(b)(3)(C)
	Traditional and Roth IRAs to $1,283,025 per person	11 U.S.C. § 522(b)(3)(C); (n)
	Elected public officers (only benefits building up)	09.38.015(b)
	ERISA-qualified benefits deposited more than 120 days before filing bankruptcy	09.38.017
	Judicial employees (only benefits building up)	09.38.015(b)
	Public employees (only benefits building up)	09.38.015(b); 39.35.505
	Roth & traditional IRAs, medical savings accounts	09.38.017(e)(3)
	Teachers (only benefits building up)	09.38.015(b)
	Other pensions, to extent wages exempt (only payments being received)	09.38.030(e)(5)
personal property	Books, musical instruments, clothing, family portraits, household goods & heirlooms to $4,050 total	09.38.020(a)
	Building materials	34.35.105
	Burial plot	09.38.015(a)(1)
	Cash or other liquid assets to $1,890; for sole wage earner in household, $2,970 (restrictions apply—see wages)	09.38.030(b)
	Deposit in apartment or condo owners' association	09.38.010(e)
	Health aids needed	09.38.015(a)(2)
	Jewelry to $1,350	09.38.020(b)
	Money held in mortgage escrow accounts after July 1, 2008	09.38.015(e)
	Motor vehicle to $4,050; vehicle's market value can't exceed $27,000	09.38.020(e)
	Personal injury recoveries, to extent wages exempt	09.38.030(e)(3)
	Pets to $1,350	09.38.020(d)
	Proceeds for lost, damaged, or destroyed exempt property	09.38.060
	Tuition credits under an advance college tuition payment contract	09.38.015(a)(8)
	Wrongful death recoveries, to extent wages exempt	09.38.030(e)(3)

public benefits	Adult assistance to elderly, blind, disabled	47.25.550
	Alaska benefits for low-income seniors	09.38.015(a)(11)
	Alaska longevity bonus	09.38.015(a)(5)
	Crime victims' compensation	09.38.015(a)(4)
	Federally exempt public benefits paid or due	09.38.015(a)(6)
	General relief assistance	47.25.210
	Senior care (prescription drug) benefits	09.38.015(a)(10)
	20% of permanent fund dividends	43.23.065
	Unemployment compensation	09.38.015(b); 23.20.405
	Workers' compensation	23.30.160
tools of trade	Implements, books & tools of trade to $3,780	09.38.020(c)
wages	Weekly net earnings to $473; for sole wage earner in a household, $743; if you don't receive weekly or semimonthly pay, you can claim $1,890 in cash or liquid assets paid any month; for sole wage earner in household, $2,970	9.38.030(a),(b); 9.38.050(b)
wildcard	None	

Arizona

Federal bankruptcy exemptions not available. All law references are to Arizona Revised Statutes unless otherwise noted.

ASSET	EXEMPTION	LAW
homestead	Real property, an apartment, or mobile home you occupy to $150,000; sale proceeds exempt 18 months after sale or until new home purchased, whichever occurs first (spouses may not double)	33-1101(A)
	May record homestead declaration to clarify which one of multiple eligible parcels is being claimed as homestead	33-1102
insurance	Fraternal benefit society benefits	20-877
	Group life insurance policy or proceeds	20-1132
	Health, accident, or disability benefits	33-1126(A)(4)
	Life insurance cash value or proceeds, or annuity contract if owned at least two years and beneficiary is dependent family member	33-1126(A)(6); 20-1131(D)
	Life insurance proceeds to $20,000 if beneficiary is spouse or child	33-1126(A)(1)
miscellaneous	Alimony, child support needed for support	33-1126(A)(3)
	Minor child's earnings, unless debt is for child	33-1126(A)(2)
pensions *see also wages*	Tax-exempt retirement accounts, including 401(k)s, 403(b)s, profit-sharing and money purchase plans, SEP and SIMPLE IRAs, and defined-benefit plans	11 U.S.C. § 522(b)(3)(C)
	Traditional and Roth IRAs to $1,283,025 per person	11 U.S.C. § 522(b)(3)(C); (n)
	Board of regents members, faculty, & administrative officers under board's jurisdiction	15-1628(I)
	District employees	48-227
	ERISA-qualified benefits deposited over 120 days before filing	33-1126(B)
	IRAs & Roth IRAs (*In re Herrscher*, 121 B.R. 29 (D. Ariz. 1989))	33-1126(B)
	Firefighters	9-968
	Police officers	9-931
	Public Safety Personnel Retirement System	38-850(c)
	Rangers	41-955
	State employees' retirement & disability	38-792; 38-797.11

personal property *spouses may double all personal property*	Household furniture & appliances not covered by other exemptions to $6,000 total	33-1123
	Bank deposit to $300 in one account	33-1126(A)(9)
	Bible; bicycle; sewing machine; typewriter; computer; burial plot; rifle, pistol, or shotgun to $1,000 total	33-1125
	Books to $250; clothing to $500; wedding & engagement rings to $2,000; watch to $150; pets, horses, milk cows & poultry to $800; musical instruments to $400	33-1125
	Food & fuel to last 6 months	33-1124
	Funeral deposits to $5,000	32-1391.05(4)
	Health aids	33-1125(9)
	Motor vehicle to $6,000 ($12,000, if debtor is physically disabled)	33-1125(8)
	Prepaid rent or security deposit to $2,000 or 1½ times your rent, whichever is less, in lieu of homestead	33-1126(C)
	Proceeds for sold or damaged exempt property	33-1126(A)(5),(8)
	Wrongful death awards	12-592
public benefits	Unemployment compensation	23-783(A)
	Welfare benefits	46-208
	Workers' compensation	23-1068(B)
tools of trade *husband & wife may double*	Arms, uniforms, & accoutrements of profession or office required by law	33-1130(3)
	Farm machinery, utensils, seed, instruments of husbandry, feed, grain, & animals to $5,000 total	33-1130(2)
	Library & teaching aids of teacher	33-1127
	Tools, equipment, instruments, & books to $2,500	33-1130(1)
wages	75% of earned but unpaid weekly net earnings or 30 times the federal minimum hourly wage; 50% of wages for support orders; bankruptcy judge may authorize more for low-income debtors	33-1131
wildcard	None	

Arkansas

Federal bankruptcy exemptions available. All law references are to Arkansas Code Annotated unless otherwise noted.

Note: In 1990, the 8th Circuit Court of Appeals declared Arkansas' bankruptcy exemption statute (found at Ark. Code Ann. § 16-66-218) unconstitutional for bankruptcy purposes as it relates to personal property. (*In re Holt*, 894 F.2d 1005 (8th Cir. 1990).) The court said that the Arkansas Constitution's provision of a $200 exemption for any personal property ($500 if married) acted as a cap and overrode the more generous exemption amounts in the statute. The personal property exemptions may be used in a nonbankruptcy context, however.

ASSET	EXEMPTION	LAW
homestead *choose Option 1 or 2*	1. For married person or head of family: unlimited exemption on real or personal property used as residence to ¼ acre in city, town, or village, or 80 acres elsewhere; if property is between ¼ and 1 acre in city, town, or village, or 80 to 160 acres elsewhere, additional limit is $2,500; homestead may not exceed 1 acre in city, town, or village, or 160 acres elsewhere (spouses may not double)	Constitution 9-3; 9-4, 9-5; 16-66-210; 16-66-218(b)(3), (4); *In re Stevens*, 829 F.2d 693 (8th Cir. 1987)
	2. Real or personal property used as residence to $800 if single; $1,250 if married	16-66-218(a)(1)

insurance	Annuity contract	23-79-134
	Disability benefits	23-79-133
	Fraternal benefit society benefits	23-74-403
	Group life insurance	23-79-132
	Life, health, accident, or disability cash value or proceeds paid or due to $500	16-66-209; Constitution 9-1, 9-2; *In re Holt*, 894 F.2d 1005 (8th Cir. 1990)
	Life insurance proceeds if clause prohibits proceeds from being used to pay beneficiary's creditors	23-79-131
	Life insurance proceeds or avails if beneficiary isn't the insured	23-79-131
	Mutual assessment life or disability benefits to $1,000	23-72-114
	Stipulated insurance premiums	23-71-112
pensions	Tax-exempt retirement accounts, including 401(k)s, 403(b)s, profit-sharing and money purchase plans, SEP and SIMPLE IRAs, and defined-benefit plans	11 U.S.C. § 522(b)(3)(C)
	Traditional and Roth IRAs to $1,283,025 per person	11 U.S.C. § 522(b)(3)(C); (n)
	Disabled firefighters	24-11-814
	Disabled police officers	24-11-417
	Firefighters	24-10-616
	IRA deposits to $20,000 if deposited over 1 year before filing for bankruptcy	16-66-218(b)(16)
	Police officers	24-10-616
	School employees	24-7-715
	State police officers	24-6-205; 24-6-223
personal property	Burial plot to 5 acres, if choosing federal homestead exemption (Option 2)	16-66-207; 16-66-218(a)(1)
	Clothing	Constitution 9-1, 9-2
	Prepaid funeral trusts	23-40-117
public benefits	Crime victims' compensation	16-90-716(e)
	Unemployment compensation	11-10-109
	Workers' compensation	11-9-110
tools of trade	Implements, books & tools of trade to $750	16-66-218(a)(4)
wages	Earned but unpaid wages due for 60 days; in no event less than $25 per week	16-66-208; 16-66-218(b)(6)
wildcard	$500 of any personal property if married or head of family; $200 if not married	Constitution 9-1, 9-2

California—System 1

Federal bankruptcy exemptions not available. California has two systems; you must select one or the other. All law references are to California Code of Civil Procedure unless otherwise noted. Many exemptions do not apply to claims for child support.

Note: California's exemption amounts are no longer updated in the statutes themselves. California Code of Civil Procedure Section 740.150 deputized the California Judicial Council to update the exemption amounts every three years. (The next revision will be in 2016.) As a result, the amounts listed in this chart will not match the amounts that appear in the cited statutes. The current exemption amounts can be found on the California Judicial Council website, www.courts.ca.gov/forms.htm.

ASSET	EXEMPTION	LAW
homestead	Real or personal property you occupy including mobile home, boat, stock cooperative, community apartment, planned development, or condo to $75,000 if single & not disabled; $100,000 for families if no other member has a homestead (if only one spouse files, may exempt one-half of amount if home held as community property & all of amount if home held as tenants in common); $175,000 if 65 or older, or physically or mentally disabled; $175,000 if 55 or older, single & earn gross annual income under $25,000 or married & earn gross annual income under $35,000 & creditors seek to force the sale of your home; forced sale proceeds received exempt for 6 months after (spouses may not double); separated married debtor may claim homestead in community property homestead occupied by other spouse	704.710; 704.720; 704.730; *In re McFall*, 112 B.R. 336 (9th Cir. B.A.P. 1990)
	May file homestead declaration to protect exemption amount from attachment of judicial liens and to protect proceeds of voluntary sale for 6 months	704.920
insurance	Disability or health benefits	704.130
	Fidelity bonds	Labor 404
	Fraternal benefit society benefits	704.170
	Fraternal unemployment benefits	704.120
	Homeowners' insurance proceeds for 6 months after received, to homestead exemption amount	704.720(b)
	Life insurance proceeds if clause prohibits proceeds from being used to pay beneficiary's creditors	Ins. 10132; Ins. 10170; Ins. 10171
	Matured life insurance benefits needed for support	704.100(c)
	Unmatured life insurance policy cash surrender value completely exempt; loan value exempt to $12,800	704.100(b)
miscellaneous	Business or professional licenses	695.060
	Inmates' trust funds to $1,600 (spouses may not double)	704.090
	Property of business partnership	Corp. 16501-04
pensions	Tax-exempt retirement accounts, including 401(k)s, 403(b)s, profit-sharing and money purchase plans, SEP and SIMPLE IRAs, and defined-benefit plans	11 U.S.C. § 522(b)(3)(C)
	Traditional and Roth IRAs to $1,283,025 per person	11 U.S.C. § 522(b)(3)(C); (n)
	County employees	Gov't 31452
	County firefighters	Gov't 32210
	County peace officers	Gov't 31913
	Private retirement benefits, including IRAs & Keoghs	704.115
	Public employees	Gov't 21255
	Public retirement benefits	704.110

personal property	Appliances, furnishings, clothing, & food	704.020
	Bank deposits from Social Security Administration to $3,200 ($4,800 for husband & wife); unlimited if SS funds are not commingled with other funds Bank deposits of other public benefits to $1,600 ($2,375 for husband & wife)	704.080
	Building materials to repair or improve home to $3,200 (spouses may not double)	704.030
	Burial plot	704.200
	Funds held in escrow	Fin. 17410
	Health aids	704.050
	Jewelry, heirlooms, & art to $8,000 total (spouses may not double)	704.040
	Motor vehicles to $3,050, or $3,050 in auto insurance for loss or damages (spouses may not double)	704.010
	Personal injury & wrongful death causes of action	704.140(a); 704.150(a)
	Personal injury & wrongful death recoveries needed for support; if receiving installments, at least 75%	704.140(b), (c), (d); 704.150(b), (c)
public benefits	Aid to blind, aged, disabled; public assistance	704.170
	Financial aid to students	704.190
	Relocation benefits	704.180
	Unemployment benefits	704.120
	Union benefits due to labor dispute	704.120(b)(5)
	Workers' compensation	704.160
tools of trade	Tools, implements, materials, instruments, uniforms, one commercial vehicle, books, furnishings, & equipment to $8,000 total ($15,975 total if used by both spouses in same occupation)	704.060
	Commercial vehicle (Vehicle Code § 260) to $4,850 ($9,700 total if used by both spouses in same occupation) (this counts toward total tools of trade exemption)	704.060
wages	Minimum 75% of wages paid within 30 days prior to filing	704.070
	Public employees' vacation credits; if receiving installments, at least 75%	704.113
wildcard	None	

California—System 2

Refer to the notes for California—System 1, above.

Note: Married couples may not double any exemptions. (*In re Talmadge*, 832 F.2d 1120 (9th Cir. 1987); *In re Baldwin*, 70 B.R. 612 (9th Cir. B.A.P 1987).)

ASSET	EXEMPTION	LAW
homestead	Real or personal property, including co-op, used as residence to $26,800; unused portion of homestead may be applied to any property	703.140(b)(1)
insurance	Disability benefits	703.140(b)(10)(C)
	Life insurance proceeds needed for support of family	703.140(b)(11)(C)
	Unmatured life insurance contract accrued avails to $14,325	703.140(b)(8)
	Unmatured life insurance policy other than credit	703.140(b)(7)
miscellaneous	Alimony, child support needed for support	703.140(b)(10)(D)

pensions	Tax-exempt retirement accounts, including 401(k)s, 403(b)s, profit-sharing and money purchase plans, SEP and SIMPLE IRAs, and defined-benefit plans	11 U.S.C. § 522(b)(3)(C)
	Traditional and Roth IRAs to $1,283,025 per person	11 U.S.C. § 522(b)(3)(C); (n)
	ERISA-qualified benefits needed for support	703.140(b)(10)(E)
personal property	Animals, crops, appliances, furnishings, household goods, books, musical instruments, & clothing to $675 per item	703.140(b)(3)
	Burial plot to $26,800, in lieu of homestead	703.140(b)(1)
	Health aids	703.140(b)(9)
	Jewelry to $1,600	703.140(b)(4)
	Motor vehicles to $5,350	703.140(b)(2)
	Personal injury recoveries to $26,800	703.140(b)(11)(D), (E)
	Wrongful death recoveries needed for support	703.140(b)(11)(B)
public benefits	Crime victims' compensation	703.140(b)(11)(A)
	Public assistance	703.140(b)(10)(A)
	Social Security	703.140(b)(10)(A)
	Unemployment compensation	703.140(b)(10)(A)
	Veterans benefits	703.140(b)(10)(B)
tools of trade	Implements, books & tools of trade to $8,000	703.140(b)(6)
wages	None	
wildcard	$1,425 of any property	703.140(b)(5)
	Unused portion of homestead or burial exemption of any property	703.140(b)(5)

Colorado

Federal bankruptcy exemptions not available. All law references are to Colorado Revised Statutes unless otherwise noted.

ASSET	EXEMPTION	LAW
homestead	Real property, mobile home, manufactured home, or house trailer you occupy to $75,000; $105,000 if owner, spouse, or dependent is disabled or at least 60 years old; sale proceeds exempt 2 years after received	38-41-201; 38-41-201.6; 38-41-203; 38-41-207; *In re Pastrana*, 216 B.R. 948 (D. Colo., 1998)
	Spouse or child of deceased owner may claim homestead exemption	38-41-204
insurance	Disability benefits to $200 per month; if lump sum, entire amount exempt	10-16-212
	Fraternal benefit society benefits	10-14-403
	Group life insurance policy or proceeds	10-7-205
	Homeowners' insurance proceeds for 1 year after received, to homestead exemption amount	38-41-209
	Life insurance cash surrender value to $100,000, except contributions to policy within past 48 months	13-54-102(1)(l)
	Life insurance proceeds if clause prohibits proceeds from being used to pay beneficiary's creditors	10-7-106
miscellaneous	Child support or domestic support obligation	13-54-102(u); 13-54-102.5
	Property of business partnership	7-60-125

pensions *see also wages*	Tax-exempt retirement accounts, including 401(k)s, 403(b)s, profit-sharing and money purchase plans, SEP and SIMPLE IRAs, and defined-benefit plans	11 U.S.C. § 522(b)(3)(C)
	Traditional and Roth IRAs to $1,283,025 per person	11 U.S.C. § 522(b)(3)(C); (n)
	ERISA-qualified benefits, including IRAs & Roth IRAs	13-54-102(1)(s)
	Firefighters & police officers	31-30.5-208; 31-31-203
	Public employees' pensions, deferred compensation & defined contribution plans	24-51-212
	Veterans pension for veteran, spouse, or dependents if veteran served in war or armed conflict	13-54-102(1)(h); 13-54-104
personal property	1 burial plot per family member	13-54-102(1)(d)
	Clothing to $2,000	13-54-102(1)(a)
	Food & fuel to $600	13-54-102(1)(f)
	Health aids	13-54-102(1)(p)
	Household goods to $3,000	13-54-102(1)(e)
	Jewelry & articles of adornment to $2,500	13-54-102(1)(b)
	Motor vehicles or bicycles used for work to $7,500; $12,500 if used by a debtor or by a dependent who is disabled or 60 or over	13-54-102(j)(I), (II)
	Personal injury recoveries	13-54-102(1)(n)
	Family pictures & books to $2,000	13-54-102(1)(c)
	Proceeds for damaged exempt property	13-54-102(1)(m)
	Security deposits	13-54-102(1)(r)
public benefits	Aid to blind, aged, disabled; public assistance	26-2-131
	Crime victims' compensation	13-54-102(1)(q); 24-4.1-114
	Disability benefits to $3,000	13-54-102(v)
	Earned income tax credit or refund	13-54-102(1)(o)
	Unemployment compensation	8-80-103
	Veterans benefits for veteran, spouse, or child if veteran served in war or armed conflict	13-54-102(1)(h)
	Workers' compensation	8-42-124
tools of trade	Livestock or other animals, machinery, tools, equipment, & seed of person engaged in agriculture, to $50,000 total	13-54-102(1)(g)
	Professional's library to $3,000 (if not claimed under other tools of trade exemption)	13-54-102(1)(k)
	Stock in trade, supplies, fixtures, tools, machines, electronics, equipment, books & other business materials, to $30,000 total	13-54-102(1)(i)
	Military equipment personally owned by members of the National Guard	13-54-102(1)(h.5)
wages	Minimum 75% of weekly net earnings or 30 times the federal or state minimum wage, whichever is greater, including pension & insurance payments. *In re Nye*, 210 B.R. 857 (D. Colo. 1997); *In re Kobemusz*, 160 B.R. 844 (D. Colo. 1993)	13-54-104
wildcard	None	

Connecticut

Federal bankruptcy exemptions available. All law references are to Connecticut General Statutes Annotated unless otherwise noted.

ASSET	EXEMPTION	LAW
homestead	Owner-occupied real property, including co-op or mobile manufactured home, to $75,000; applies only to claims arising after 1993, but to $125,000 in the case of a money judgment arising out of services provided at a hospital	52-352a(e); 52-352b(t)
insurance	Disability benefits paid by association for its members	52-352b(p)
	Fraternal benefit society benefits	38a-637
	Health or disability benefits	52-352b(e)
	Life insurance proceeds if clause prohibits proceeds from being used to pay beneficiary's creditors	38a-454
	Life insurance proceeds or avails	38a-453
	Unmatured life insurance policy avails to $4,000 if beneficiary is dependent	52-352b(s)
miscellaneous	Alimony, to extent wages exempt	52-352b(n)
	Child support	52-352b(h)
	Farm partnership animals & livestock feed reasonably required to run farm where at least 50% of partners are members of same family	52-352d
pensions	Tax-exempt retirement accounts, including 401(k)s, 403(b)s, profit-sharing and money purchase plans, SEP and SIMPLE IRAs, and defined-benefit plans	11 U.S.C. § 522(b)(3)(C)
	Traditional and Roth IRAs to $1,283,025 per person	11 U.S.C. § 522(b)(3)(C); (n)
	ERISA-qualified benefits, including IRAs, Roth IRAs & Keoghs, to extent wages exempt	52-321a; 52-352b(m)
	Medical savings account	52-321a
	Municipal employees	7-446
	State employees	5-171; 5-192w
	Teachers	10-183q
personal property	Appliances, food, clothing, furniture, bedding	52-352b(a)
	Burial plot	52-352b(c)
	Health aids needed	52-352b(f)
	Motor vehicle to $3,500	52-352b(j)
	Proceeds for damaged exempt property	52-352b(q)
	Residential utility & security deposits for 1 residence	52-352b(l)
	Spendthrift trust funds required for support of debtor & family	52-321(d)
	Transfers to a licensed debt adjuster	52-352b(u)
	Tuition savings accounts	52-321a(E)
	Wedding & engagement rings	52-352b(k)
public benefits	Crime victims' compensation	52-352b(o); 54-213
	Public assistance	52-352b(d)
	Social Security	52-352b(g)
	Unemployment compensation	31-272(c); 52-352b(g)
	Veterans benefits	52-352b(g)
	Workers' compensation	52-352b(g)
tools of trade	Arms, military equipment, uniforms, musical instruments of military personnel	52-352b(i)
	Tools, books, instruments, & farm animals needed	52-352b(b)
wages	Minimum 75% of earned but unpaid weekly disposable earnings, or 40 times the state or federal hourly minimum wage, whichever is greater	52-361a(f)
wildcard	$1,000 of any property	52-352b(r)

Delaware

Federal bankruptcy exemptions not available. All law references are to Delaware Code Annotated (in the form "title number-section number") unless otherwise noted.

Note: A single person may exempt no more than $25,000 total in all exemptions (not including retirement plans and principal residence); a husband and wife may exempt no more than $50,000 total (10-4914).

ASSET	EXEMPTION	LAW
homestead	Real property or manufactured home used as principal residence to $125,000 in 2012; $125,000 for working or married persons where one spouse is 65 or older (spouses may not double)	10-4914(c)
	Property held as tenancy by the entirety may be exempt against debts owed by only one spouse	*In re Kelley*, 289 B.R. 38 (Bankr. D. Del. 2003)
insurance	Annuity contract proceeds to $350 per month	18-2728
	Fraternal benefit society benefits	18-6218
	Group life insurance policy or proceeds	18-2727
	Health or disability benefits	18-2726
	Life insurance proceeds if clause prohibits proceeds from being used to pay beneficiary's creditors	18-2729
	Life insurance proceeds or avails	18-2725
pensions	Tax-exempt retirement accounts, including 401(k)s, 403(b)s, profit-sharing and money purchase plans, SEP and SIMPLE IRAs, and defined-benefit plans	11 U.S.C. § 522(b)(3)(C)
	Traditional and Roth IRAs to $1,283,025 per person	11 U.S.C. § 522(b)(3)(C); (n)
	IRAs, Roth IRAs & any other retirement plans	10-4915
	Kent County employees	9-4316
	Police officers	11-8803
	State employees	29-5503
	Volunteer firefighters	16-6653
personal property	Bible, books, & family pictures	10-4902(a)
	Burial plot	10-4902(a)
	Church pew or any seat in public place of worship	10-4902(a)
	Clothing, includes jewelry	10-4902(a)
	College investment plan account (limit for year before filing is $5,000 or average of past two years' contribution, whichever is more)	10-4916
	Principal and income from spendthrift trusts	12-3536
	Pianos & leased organs	10-4902(d)
	Sewing machines	10-4902(c)
public benefits	Aid to blind	31-2309
	Aid to aged, disabled; general assistance	31-513
	Crime victims' compensation	11-9011
	Unemployment compensation	19-3374
	Workers' compensation	19-2355
tools of trade	Tools of trade and/or vehicle necessary for employment to $15,000 each	10-4914(c)
	Tools, implements & fixtures to $75 in New Castle & Sussex Counties; to $50 in Kent County	10-4902(b)
wages	85% of earned but unpaid wages	10-4913
wildcard	$500 of any personal property, except tools of trade, if head of family	10-4903

District of Columbia

Federal bankruptcy exemptions available. All law references are to District of Columbia Code unless otherwise noted.

ASSET	EXEMPTION	LAW
homestead	Any property used as a residence or co-op that debtor or debtor's dependent uses as a residence	15-501(a)(14)
	Property held as tenancy by the entirety may be exempt against debts owed by only one spouse	*Estate of Wall*, 440 F.2d 215 (D.C. Cir. 1971)
insurance	Disability benefits	15-501(a)(7); 31-4716.01
	Fraternal benefit society benefits	31-5315
	Group life insurance policy or proceeds	31-4717
	Life insurance payments	15-501(a)(11)
	Life insurance proceeds if clause prohibits proceeds from being used to pay beneficiary's creditors	31-4719
	Life insurance proceeds or avails	31-4716
	Other insurance proceeds to $200 per month, maximum 2 months, for head of family; else $60 per month	15-503
	Unmatured life insurance contract other than credit life insurance	15-501(a)(5)
miscellaneous	Alimony or child support	15-501(a)(7)
pensions *see also wages*	Tax-exempt retirement accounts, including 401(k)s, 403(b)s, profit-sharing and money purchase plans, SEP and SIMPLE IRAs, and defined-benefit plans	11 U.S.C. § 522(b)(3)(C)
	Traditional and Roth IRAs to $1,283,025 per person	11 U.S.C. § 522(b)(3)(C); (n)
	ERISA-qualified benefits, IRAs, Keoghs, etc. to maximum deductible contribution	15-501(b)(9)
	Any stock bonus, annuity, pension, or profit-sharing plan	15-501(a)(7)
	Judges	11-1570(f)
	Public school teachers	38-2001.17; 38-2021.17
personal property	Appliances, books, clothing, household furnishings, goods, musical instruments, pets to $425 per item or $8,625 total	15-501(a)(2)
	Cemetery & burial funds	43-111
	Cooperative association holdings to $500	29-928
	Food for 3 months	15-501(a)(12)
	Health aids	15-501(a)(6)
	Higher education tuition savings account	47-4510
	Residential condominium deposit	42-1904.09
	All family pictures; all the family library to $400	15-501(a)(8)
	Motor vehicle to $2,575	15-501(a)(1)
	Payment, including pain & suffering, for loss of debtor or person depended on	15-501(a)(11)
	Uninsured motorist benefits	31-2408.01(h)
	Wrongful death damages	15-501(a)(11); 16-2703

public benefits	Aid to blind, aged, disabled; general assistance	4-215.01
	Crime victims' compensation	4-507(e); 15-501(a)(11)
	Social Security	15-501(a)(7)
	Unemployment compensation	51-118
	Veterans benefits	15-501(a)(7)
	Workers' compensation	32-1517
tools of trade	Library, furniture, tools of professional or artist to $300	15-501(a)(13)
	Tools of trade or business to $1,625	15-501(a)(5)
	Mechanic's tools to $200	15-503(b)
	Seal & documents of notary public	1-1206
wages	Minimum 75% of earned but unpaid wages, pension payments; bankruptcy judge may authorize more for low-income debtors	16-572
	Nonwage (including pension & retirement) earnings to $200 per month for head of family; else $60 per month for a maximum of two months	15-503
	Payment for loss of future earnings	15-501(e)(11)
wildcard	Up to $850 in any property, plus up to $8,075 if you don't use the homestead exemption	15-501(a)(3)

Florida

Federal bankruptcy exemptions not available. All law references are to Florida Statutes Annotated unless otherwise noted.

ASSET	EXEMPTION	LAW
homestead	Real or personal property including mobile or modular home to unlimited value; cannot exceed half acre in municipality or 160 acres elsewhere; spouse or child of deceased owner may claim homestead exemption	222.01; 222.02; 222.03; 222.05; Constitution 10-4; *In re Colwell*, 196 F.3d 1225 (11th Cir. 1999)
	May file homestead declaration	222.01
	Property held as tenancy by the entirety may be exempt against debts owed by only one spouse	*Havoco of America, Ltd. v. Hill*, 197 F.3d 1135 (11th Cir. 1999)
insurance	Annuity contract proceeds; does not include lottery winnings	222.14; *In re Pizzi*, 153 B.R. 357 (S.D. Fla. 1993)
	Death benefits payable to a specific beneficiary, not the deceased's estate	222.13
	Disability or illness benefits	222.18
	Fraternal benefit society benefits	632.619
	Life insurance cash surrender value	222.14
miscellaneous	Alimony, child support needed for support	222.201
	Damages to employees for injuries in hazardous occupations	769.05
pensions *see also wages*	Tax-exempt retirement accounts, including 401(k)s, 403(b)s, profit-sharing and money purchase plans, SEP and SIMPLE IRAs, and defined-benefit plans	11 U.S.C. § 522(b)(3)(C)
	Traditional and Roth IRAs to $1,283,025 per person	11 U.S.C. § 522(b)(3)(C); (n)
	County officers, employees	122.15
	ERISA-qualified benefits, including IRAs & Roth IRAs	222.21(2)
	Firefighters	175.241
	Police officers	185.25
	State officers, employees	121.131
	Teachers	238.15

personal property	Any personal property to $1,000 (husband & wife may double); to $4,000 if no homestead claimed	222.25(4) Const. Art. X. § 4(a)(2)
	Health aids	222.25(2)
	Motor vehicle to $1,000	222.25(1)
	Preneed funeral contract deposits	497.56(8)
	Prepaid college education trust deposits	222.22(1)
	Prepaid hurricane savings accounts	222.22(4)
	Prepaid medical savings account & health savings account deposits	222.22(2)
public benefits	Crime victims' compensation, unless seeking to discharge debt for treatment of injury incurred during the crime	960.14
	Earned income tax credit	222.25(3)
	Public assistance	222.201
	Social Security	222.201
	Reemployment assistance	222.201; 443.051(2), (3)
	Veterans benefits	222.201; 744.626
	Workers' compensation	440.22
tools of trade	None	
wages	100% of wages for heads of family up to $750 per week either unpaid or paid & deposited into bank account for up to 6 months	222.11
	Federal government employees' pension payments needed for support & received 3 months prior	222.21
wildcard	See personal property	

Georgia

Federal bankruptcy exemptions not available. All law references are to the Official Code of Georgia Annotated unless otherwise noted.

ASSET	EXEMPTION	LAW
homestead	Real or personal property, including co-op, used as residence to $21,500 (to $43,000 if married and debtor spouse is sole owner); up to $5,000 of unused portion of homestead may be applied to any property	44-13-100(a)(1); 44-13-100(a) (6); *In re Burnett*, 303 B.R. 684 (M.D. Ga. 2003)
insurance	Annuity & endowment contract benefits	33-28-7
	Disability or health benefits to $250 per month	33-29-15
	Fraternal benefit society benefits	33-15-62
	Group insurance	33-30-10
	Proceeds & avails of life insurance	33-26-5; 33-25-11
	Life insurance proceeds if policy owned by someone you depended on, needed for support	44-13-100(a)(11)(C)
	Unmatured life insurance contract	44-13-100(a)(8)
	Unmatured life insurance dividends, interest, loan value, or cash value to $2,000 if beneficiary is you or someone you depend on	44-13-100(a)(9)
miscellaneous	Alimony, child support needed for support	44-13-100(a)(2)(D)

pensions	Tax-exempt retirement accounts, including 401(k)s, 403(b)s, profit-sharing and money purchase plans, SEP and SIMPLE IRAs, and defined-benefit plans	11 U.S.C. § 522(b)(3)(C)
	Traditional and Roth IRAs to $1,283,025 per person	11 U.S.C. § 522(b)(3)(C); (n)
	Employees of nonprofit corporations	44-13-100(a)(2.1)(B)
	ERISA-qualified benefits & IRAs	18-4-22
	Public employees	44-13-100(a)(2.1)(A); 47-2-332
	Payments from IRA necessary for support	44-13-100(a)(2)(F)
	Other pensions needed for support	18-4-22; 44-13-100(a)(2)(E); 44-13-100(a)(2.1)(C)
personal property	Animals, crops, clothing, appliances, books, furnishings, household goods, musical instruments to $300 per item, $5,000 total	44-13-100(a)(4)
	Burial plot, in lieu of homestead	44-13-100(a)(1)
	Compensation for lost future earnings needed for support to $7,500	44-13-100(a)(11)(E)
	Health aids	44-13-100(a)(10)
	Jewelry to $500	44-13-100(a)(5)
	Motor vehicles to $5,000	44-13-100(a)(3)
	Personal injury recoveries to $10,000	44-13-100(a)(11)(D)
	Wrongful death recoveries needed for support	44-13-100(a)(11)(B)
public benefits	Aid to blind	49-4-58
	Aid to disabled	49-4-84
	Crime victims' compensation	44-13-100(a)(11)(A)
	Local public assistance	44-13-100(a)(2)(A)
	Old age assistance	49-4-35
	Social Security	44-13-100(a)(2)(A)
	Unemployment compensation	44-13-100(a)(2)(A)
	Veterans benefits	44-13-100(a)(2)(B)
	Workers' compensation	34-9-84
tools of trade	Implements, books & tools of trade to $1,500	44-13-100(a)(7)
wages	Minimum 75% of earned but unpaid weekly disposable earnings, or 30 times the state or federal hourly minimum wage, whichever is greater, for private & federal workers; bankruptcy judge may authorize more for low-income debtors	18-4-20; 18-4-21
wildcard	$600 of any property	44-13-100(a)(6)
	Unused portion of homestead exemption to $5,000	44-13-100(a)(6)

Hawaii

Federal bankruptcy exemptions available. All law references are to Hawaii Revised Statutes unless otherwise noted.

ASSET	EXEMPTION	LAW
homestead	Head of family or over 65 to $30,000; all others to $20,000; property cannot exceed 1 acre; sale proceeds exempt for 6 months after sale (spouses may not double)	651-91; 651-92; 651-96
	Property held as tenancy by the entirety may be exempt against debts owed by only one spouse or reciprocal beneficiary	509-2; *Security Pacific Bank v. Chang*, 818 F.Supp. 1343 (D. Haw. 1993)

insurance	Annuity contract or endowment policy proceeds if beneficiary is insured's spouse, child, or parent	431:10-232(b)
	Accident, health, or sickness benefits	431:10-231
	Fraternal benefit society benefits	432:2-403
	Group life insurance policy or proceeds	431:10-233
	Life insurance proceeds if clause prohibits proceeds from being used to pay beneficiary's creditors	431:10D-112
	Life or health insurance policy for spouse or child	431:10-234
miscellaneous	Property of business partnership	425-125
pensions	Tax-exempt retirement accounts, including 401(k)s, 403(b)s, profit-sharing and money purchase plans, SEP and SIMPLE IRAs, and defined-benefit plans	11 U.S.C. § 522(b)(3)(C)
	Traditional and Roth IRAs to $1,283,025 per person	11 U.S.C. § 522(b)(3)(C); (n)
	IRAs, Roth IRAs, and ERISA-qualified benefits deposited over 3 years before filing bankruptcy	651-124
	Firefighters	88-169
	Police officers	88-169
	Public officers & employees	88-91; 653-3
personal property	Appliances & furnishings	651-121(1)
	Books	651-121(1)
	Burial plot to 250 sq. ft. plus tombstones, monuments, & fencing	651-121(4)
	Clothing	651-121(1)
	Jewelry, watches, & articles of adornment to $1,000	651-121(1)
	Motor vehicle to wholesale value of $2,575	651-121(2)
	Proceeds for sold or damaged exempt property; sale proceeds exempt for 6 months after sale	651-121(5)
public benefits	Crime victims' compensation & special accounts created to limit commercial exploitation of crimes	351-66; 351-86
	Public assistance paid by Department of Health Services for work done in home or workshop	346-33
	Temporary disability benefits	392-29
	Unemployment compensation	383-163
	Unemployment work relief funds to $60 per month	653-4
	Workers' compensation	386-57
tools of trade	Tools, implements, books, instruments, uniforms, furnishings, fishing boat, nets, motor vehicle, & other property needed for livelihood	651-121(3)
wages	Prisoner's wages held by Department of Public Safety (except for restitution, child support, & other claims)	353-22.5
	Unpaid wages due for services of past 31 days	651-121(6)
wildcard	None	

Idaho

Federal bankruptcy exemptions not available. All law references are to Idaho Code unless otherwise noted.

ASSET	EXEMPTION	LAW
homestead	Real property or mobile home to $100,000; sale proceeds exempt for 6 months (spouses may not double)	55-1003; 55-1113
	Must record homestead exemption for property that is not yet occupied	55-1004
insurance	Annuity contract proceeds to $1,250 per month; if not yet receiving payments from the annuity, cash surrender value to amount of premiums paid during 6 months before bankruptcy petition	41-1836
	Death or disability benefits	11-604(1)(a); 41-1834
	Fraternal benefit society benefits	41-3218
	Group life insurance benefits	41-1835
	Homeowners' insurance proceeds to amount of homestead exemption	55-1008
	Life insurance proceeds if clause prohibits proceeds from being used to pay beneficiary's creditors	41-1930
	Life insurance proceeds or avails for beneficiary other than the insured	11-604(d); 41-1833
	Medical, surgical, or hospital care benefits & amount in medical savings account	11-603(5)
	Unmatured life insurance contract, other than credit life insurance, owned by debtor	11-605(9)
	Unmatured life insurance contract interest or dividends to $5,000 owned by debtor or person debtor depends on	11-605(10)
miscellaneous	Alimony, child support	11-604(1)(b)
	Liquor licenses	23-514
pension *see also wages*	Tax-exempt retirement accounts, including 401(k)s, 403(b)s, profit-sharing and money purchase plans, SEP and SIMPLE IRAs, and defined-benefit plans	11 U.S.C. § 522(b)(3)(C)
	Traditional and Roth IRAs to $1,283,025 per person	11 U.S.C. § 522(b)(3)(C); (n)
	ERISA-qualified benefits	55-1011
	Firefighters	72-1422
	Government & private pensions, retirement plans, IRAs, Roth IRAs, Keoghs, etc.	11-604A
	Police officers	50-1517
	Public employees	59-1317
personal property	Appliances, furnishings, books, clothing, pets, musical instruments, family portraits, & sentimental heirlooms to $750 per item, $7,500 total	11-605(1)
	Building materials	45-514
	Burial plot	11-603(1)
	College savings program account	11-604A(4)(b)
	Crops cultivated on maximum of 50 acres, to $1,000; water rights to 160 inches	11-605(6) and (7)
	Firearm (1) to $750	11-605(8)
	Health aids	11-603(2)
	Jewelry to $1,000	11-605(2)
	Motor vehicle to $7,000	11-605(3)
	Personal injury recoveries	11-604(1)(c)
	Proceeds for damaged exempt property for 3 months after proceeds received	11-606
	Provisions (food, water, and storage equipment) sufficient for up to 12 months	11-605(4)
	Wrongful death recoveries	11-604(1)(c)

public benefits	Aid to blind, aged, disabled	56-223
	Federal, state & local public assistance, including earned income tax credit (but not child or education tax credit) (*In re Jones*, 107 B.R. 751 (Bankr. D. Idaho 1989; *In re Steinmetz*, 261 B.R. 32 (Bankr. D. Idaho 2001); *In re Crampton*, 249 B.R. 215 (Bankr.D. Idaho 2000))	11-603(4)
	General assistance	56-223
	Social Security	11-603(3)
	Unemployment compensation	11-603(6)
	Veterans benefits	11-603(3)
	Workers' compensation	72-802
tools of trade	Arms, uniforms & accoutrements that peace officer, National Guard, or military personnel is required to keep	11-605(6)
	Implements, books & tools of trade to $2,500	11-605(3)
wages	Minimum 75% of earned but unpaid weekly disposable earnings, or 30 times the federal hourly minimum wage, whichever is greater but not more than $1,500 in a calendar year; pension payments; bankruptcy judge may authorize more for low-income debtors	11-207; 11-605-12; 11-206
wildcard	$800 in any tangible personal property	11-605(11)

Illinois

Federal bankruptcy exemptions not available. All law references are to Illinois Compiled Statutes Annotated unless otherwise noted.

Note: Although one court has held that the Illinois Wage Deduction Act creates a bankruptcy exemption, *In re Mayer*, 288 B.R. 869 (Bankr. N.D. Ill. 2008) (Wedoff, J.), most other Illinois courts addressing the issue have found that it does not. (*In re Radzilowsky*, 448 B.R. 767 (Bankr. N.D. Ill. May 6, 2011); *In re Kapusta*, 2011 WL 2173675 (C.D. Ill. June 2, 2011); *In re Koeneman*, 410 B.R. 820 (C.D. Ill. 2009); *In re Thum*, 329 B.R. 848 (Bankr. C.D. Ill. 2005).)

ASSET	EXEMPTION	LAW
homestead	Real or personal property including a farm, lot & buildings, condo, co-op, or mobile home to $15,000; sale proceeds exempt for 1 year	735-5/12-901; 735-5/12-906
	Spouse or child of deceased owner may claim homestead exemption	735-5/12-902
	Illinois recognizes tenancy by the entirety, with limitations	750-65/22; 765-1005/1c; *In re Gillissie*, 215 B.R. 370 (Bankr. N.D. Ill. 1998); *Great Southern Co. v. Allard*, 202 B.R. 938 (N.D. Ill. 1996)
insurance	Fraternal benefit society benefits	215-5/299.1a
	Health or disability benefits	735-5/12-1001 (g)(3)
	Homeowners' proceeds if home destroyed, to $15,000	735-5/12-907
	Life insurance, annuity proceeds, or cash value if beneficiary is insured's child, parent, spouse, or other dependent	215-5/238; 735-5/12-1001(f)
	Life insurance proceeds to a spouse or dependent of debtor to extent needed for support	735-5/12-1001(f), (g)(3)
miscellaneous	Alimony, child support	735-5/12-1001 (g)(4)
	Property of business partnership	805-205/25

pensions	Tax-exempt retirement accounts, including 401(k)s, 403(b)s, profit-sharing and money purchase plans, SEP and SIMPLE IRAs, and defined-benefit plans	11 U.S.C. § 522(b)(3)(C)
	Traditional and Roth IRAs to $1,283,025 per person	11 U.S.C. § 522 (b)(3)(C); (n)
	Civil service employees	40-5/11-223
	County employees	40-5/9-228
	Disabled firefighters; widows & children of firefighters	40-5/22-230
	IRAs and ERISA-qualified benefits	735-5/12-1006
	Firefighters	40-5/4-135; 40-5/6-213
	General Assembly members	40-5/2-154
	House of correction employees	40-5/19-117
	Judges	40-5/18-161
	Municipal employees	40-5/7-217(a); 40-5/8-244
	Park employees	40-5/12-190
	Police officers	40-5/3-144.1; 40-5/5-218
	Public employees	735-5/12-1006
	Public library employees	40-5/19-218
	Sanitation district employees	40-5/13-805
	State employees	40-5/14-147
	State university employees	40-5/15-185
	Teachers	40-5/16-190; 40-5/17-151
personal property	Bible, family pictures, schoolbooks & clothing	735-5/12-1001(a)
	Health aids	735-5/12-1001(e)
	Illinois College Savings Pool accounts invested more than 1 year before filing if below federal gift tax limit, or 2 years before filing if above	735-5/12-1001(j)
	Motor vehicle to $2,400	735-5/12-1001(c)
	Personal injury recoveries to $15,000	735-5/12-1001 (h)(4)
	Preneed cemetery sales funds, care funds & trust funds	235-5/6-1; 760-100/4; 815-390/16
	Prepaid tuition trust fund	110-979/45(g)
	Proceeds of sold exempt property	735-5/12-1001
	Wrongful death recoveries	735-5/12-1001 (h)(2)
public benefits	Aid to aged, blind, disabled; public assistance, including earned income tax credit and child tax credit (applies to future payments but not funds already received) (*In re Fish*, 224 B.R. 82 (Bankr. S.D. Ill 1998); *In re Vazquez*, No. 13-32174 (Bankr. N.D. Ill 2014); *In re Frueh*, No. 14-B-81029 (Bankr. W.D. Ill 2014))	305-5/11-3; 735-5/12-1001 (g)(1)
	Crime victims' compensation	735-5/12-1001 (h)(1)
	Restitution payments on account of WWII relocation of Aleuts & Japanese Americans	735-5/12-1001 (12)(h)(5)
	Social Security	735-5/12-1001 (g)(1)
	Unemployment compensation	735-5/12-1001 (g)(1), (3)
	Veterans benefits	735-5/12-1001 (g)(2)
	Workers' compensation	820-305/21
	Workers' occupational disease compensation	820-310/21
tools of trade	Implements, books, & tools of trade to $1,500	735-5/12-1001(d)
wages	Minimum 85% of earned but unpaid weekly wages or 45 times the federal minimum hourly wage (or state minimum hourly wage, if higher); bankruptcy judge may authorize more for low-income debtors (some judges may not allow this exemption). See note at beginning of Illinois chart.	735-5/12-803
wildcard	$4,000 of any personal property (does not include wages)	735-5/12-1001(b)

Indiana

Federal bankruptcy exemptions not available. All law references are to Indiana Statutes Annotated unless otherwise noted.

ASSET	EXEMPTION	LAW
homestead see also wildcard	Real or personal property used as residence to $19,300	34-55-10-2(c)(1)
	Property held as tenancy by the entirety may be exempt against debts incurred by only one spouse	34-55-10-2(c)(5); 32-17-3-1
insurance	Employer's life insurance policy on employee	27-1-12-17.1
	Fraternal benefit society benefits	27-11-6-3
	Group life insurance policy	27-1-12-29
	Life insurance policy, proceeds, cash value, or avails if beneficiary is insured's spouse or dependent	27-1-12-14
	Life insurance proceeds if clause prohibits proceeds to be used to pay beneficiary's creditors	27-2-5-1
	Mutual life or accident proceeds needed for support	27-8-3-23; In re Stinnet, 321 B.R. 477 (S.D. Ind. 2005)
miscellaneous	Property of business partnership	23-4-1-25
pensions	Tax-exempt retirement accounts, including 401(k)s, 403(b)s, profit-sharing and money purchase plans, SEP and SIMPLE IRAs, and defined-benefit plans	11 U.S.C. § 522(b)(3)(C)
	Traditional and Roth IRAs to $1,283,025 per person	11 U.S.C. § 522(b)(3)(C); (n)
	Firefighters	36-8-7-22; 36-8-8-17
	Police officers	36-8-8-17; 10-12-2-10
	Public employees	5-10.3-8-9
	Public or private retirement benefits & contributions	34-55-10-2(c)(6)
	Sheriffs	36-8-10-19
	State teachers	5-10.4-5-14
personal property	Education savings account (529 and Coverdell) contributions made more than 2 years prior to filing; contributions made more than 1 but less than 2 years prior to filing to $5,000; no exemption for contributions made less than 1 year prior to filing	34-55-10-2(c)(9), (10)
	Health aids	34-55-10-2(c)(4)
	Money in medical care savings account or health savings account	34-55-10-2(c)(7), (8)
	Spendthrift trusts	30-4-3-2
	$400 of any intangible personal property, except money owed to you	34-55-10-2(c)(3)
public benefits	Crime victims' compensation, unless seeking to discharge the debts for which the victim was compensated	5-2-6.1-38
	Earned income tax credit (but not child tax credit) (In re King, 508 B.R. 71 (Bankr. N.D. Ind. 2014); In re Jackson, No. 12–9635–RLM–7A (Bankr. S.D. In. 2013))	34-55-10-2(c)(11)
	Supplemental state fair relief fund	34-13-8; 34-55-102(c)(13)
	Unemployment compensation	22-4-33-3
	Veterans disability benefits	34-55-10-2(c)(12)
	Workers' compensation	22-3-2-17
tools of trade	National Guard uniforms, arms & equipment	10-16-10-3
wages	Minimum 75% of earned but unpaid weekly disposable earnings, or 30 times the federal hourly minimum wage; bankruptcy judge may authorize more for low-income debtors. (In re Haraughty, 403 B.R. 607 (Bankr. S.D. Indiana 2009).)	24-4.5-5-105
wildcard	$10,250 of any real estate or tangible personal property	34-55-10-2(c)(2)

Iowa

Federal bankruptcy exemptions not available. All law references are to Iowa Code Annotated unless otherwise noted.

ASSET	EXEMPTION	LAW
homestead	May record homestead declaration	561.4
	Real property or an apartment to an unlimited value; property cannot exceed ½ acre in town or city, 40 acres elsewhere (spouses may not double)	499A.18; 561.2; 561.16
insurance	Accident, disability, health, illness, or life proceeds or avails	627.6(6)
	Disability or illness benefit	627.6(8)(c)
	Employee group insurance policy or proceeds	509.12
	Fraternal benefit society benefits	512B.18
	Life insurance proceeds if clause prohibits proceeds from being used to pay beneficiary's creditors	508.32
	Life insurance proceeds paid to spouse, child, or other dependent (limited to $10,000 if acquired within 2 years of filing for bankruptcy)	627.6(6)
	Upon death of insured, up to $15,000 total proceeds from all matured life, accident, health, or disability policies exempt from beneficiary's debts contracted before insured's death	627.6(6)(c)
miscellaneous	Alimony, child support needed for support	627.6(8)(d)
	Liquor licenses	123.38
pensions *see also wages*	Tax-exempt retirement accounts, including 401(k)s, 403(b)s, profit-sharing and money purchase plans, SEP and SIMPLE IRAs, and defined-benefit plans	11 U.S.C. § 522(b)(3)(C)
	Traditional and Roth IRAs to $1,283,025 per person	11 U.S.C. § 522(b)(3)(C); (n)
	Disabled firefighters, police officers (only payments being received)	410.11
	Federal government pension	627.8
	Firefighters	411.13
	Other pensions, annuities & contracts fully exempt; however, contributions made within 1 year prior to filing for bankruptcy not exempt to the extent they exceed normal & customary amounts	627.6(8)(e)
	Peace officers	97A.12
	Police officers	411.13
	Public employees	97B.39
	Retirement plans, Keoghs, IRAs, Roth IRAs, ERISA-qualified benefits	627.6(8)(f)
personal property	Bibles, books, portraits, pictures & paintings to $1,000 total	627.6(3)
	Burial plot to 1 acre	627.6(4)
	Clothing & its storage containers, household furnishings, appliances, musical instruments, and other personal property to $7,000	627.6(5)
	Health aids	627.6(7)
	Jewelry to $2,000	627.6(1)(6)
	Residential security or utility deposit, or advance rent, to $500	627.6(14)
	Rifle or musket; shotgun	627.6(2)
	One motor vehicle to $7,000	627.6(9)
	Wedding or engagement rings, limited to $7,000 (minus any amounts used under the jewelry exemption) if purchased after marriage and within last two years	627.6(1)(a)
	Wrongful death proceeds and awards needed for support of debtor and dependents	627.6(15)

public benefits	Adopted child assistance	627.19
	Aid to dependent children	239B.6
	Any public assistance benefit, including earned income tax credit and child tax credit (*In re Hatch*, 13-03342-als7 (Bankr. N.D. Iowa 2014); *In re Longstreet*, 246 B.R. 611 (Bankr. S.D. Iowa 2000))	627.6(8)(a)
	Social Security	627.6(8)(a)
	Unemployment compensation	627.6(8)(a)
	Veterans benefits	627.6(8)(b)
	Workers' compensation	627.13
tools of trade	Farming equipment; includes livestock, feed to $10,000	627.6(11)
	National Guard articles of equipment	29A.41
	Nonfarming equipment to $10,000	627.6(10)
wages	Expected annual earnings Amount NOT exempt per year	642.21

Expected annual earnings	Amount NOT exempt per year
$0 to $11,999	$250
$12,000 to $15,999	$400
$16,000 to $23,999	$800
$24,000 to $34,999	$1,000
$35,000 to $49,999	$2,000
More than $50,000	10%

	In re Irish, 311 B.R. 63 (8th Cir. B.A.P. 2004) Not exempt from spousal or child support	
	Wages or salary of a prisoner	356.29
wildcard	$1,000 of any personal property, including cash	627.6(14)

Kansas

Federal bankruptcy exemptions not available. Although Kansas has opted out of the federal exemptions, it does allow debtors to use exemptions in 11 U.S.C.A. § 522(d)(10). See K.S.A. 60-2312(b). All law references are to Kansas Statutes Annotated unless otherwise noted.

ASSET	EXEMPTION	LAW
homestead	Real property or mobile home you occupy or intend to occupy to unlimited value; property cannot exceed 1 acre in town or city, 160 acres on farm	60-2301; Constitution 15-9
insurance	Cash value of life insurance; not exempt if obtained within 1 year prior to bankruptcy with fraudulent intent	60-2313(a)(7); 40-414(b)
	Disability & illness benefits	60-2313(a)(1)
	Fraternal life insurance benefits	60-2313(a)(8)
	Life insurance proceeds	40-414(a)
miscellaneous	Alimony, maintenance & support	60-2312(b)
	Liquor licenses	60-2313(a)(6); 41-326
pensions	Tax-exempt retirement accounts, including 401(k)s, 403(b)s, profit-sharing and money purchase plans, SEP and SIMPLE IRAs, and defined-benefit plans	11 U.S.C. § 522(b)(3)(C)
	Traditional and Roth IRAs to $1,283,025 per person	11 U.S.C. § 522(b)(3)(C); (n)
	Elected & appointed officials in cities with populations between 120,000 & 200,000	13-14a10
	ERISA-qualified benefits	60-2308(b)
	Federal government pension needed for support & paid within 3 months of filing for bankruptcy (only payments being received)	60-2308(a)

pensions (continued)	Firefighters	12-5005(e); 14-10a10
	Judges	20-2618
	Police officers	12-5005(e); 13-14a10
	Public employees	74-4923; 74-49,105
	State highway patrol officers	74-4978g
	State school employees	72-5526
	Payment under a stock bonus, pension, profit-sharing, annuity, or similar plan or contract on account of illness, disability, death, age, or length of service, to the extent reasonably necessary for support	60-2312(b)
personal property	Burial plot or crypt	60-2304(d)
	Clothing to last 1 year	60-2304(a)
	Earned income tax credit	60-2315
	Food & fuel to last 1 year	60-2304(a)
	Funeral plan prepayments	60-2313(a)(10); 16-310(d)
	Furnishings & household equipment	60-2304(a)
	Jewelry & articles of adornment to $1,000	60-2304(b)
	Motor vehicle to $20,000; if designed or equipped for disabled person, no limit	60-2304(c)
public benefits	Crime victims' compensation	60-2313(a)(7); 74-7313(d)
	Earned income tax credit	60-2315
	General assistance	39-717(c)
	Social Security	60-2312(b)
	Unemployment compensation	60-2313(a)(4); 44-718(c)
	Veterans benefits	60-2312(b)
	Workers' compensation	60-2313(a)(3); 44-514
tools of trade	Books, documents, furniture, instruments, equipment, breeding stock, seed, grain & stock to $7,500 total	60-2304(e)
	National Guard uniforms, arms & equipment	48-245
wages	Minimum 75% of disposable weekly wages or 30 times the federal minimum hourly wage per week, whichever is greater; bankruptcy judge may authorize more for low-income debtors; *In re Urban* 262 B.R. 865 (Bankr. D. Kan. 2001)	60-2310
wildcard	None	

Kentucky

Federal bankruptcy exemptions available. All law references are to Kentucky Revised Statutes unless otherwise noted.

ASSET	EXEMPTION	LAW
homestead	Real or personal property used as residence to $5,000; sale proceeds exempt	427.060; 427.090
insurance	Annuity contract proceeds to $350 per month	304.14-330
	Cooperative life or casualty insurance benefits	427.110(1)
	Fraternal benefit society benefits	427.110(2)
	Group life insurance proceeds	304.14-320
	Health or disability benefits	304.14-310
	Life insurance policy if beneficiary is a married woman	304.14-340
	Life insurance proceeds if clause prohibits proceeds from being used to pay beneficiary's creditors	304.14-350
	Life insurance proceeds or cash value if beneficiary is someone other than insured	304.14-300
miscellaneous	Alimony, child support needed for support	427.150(1)

pensions	Tax-exempt retirement accounts, including 401(k)s, 403(b)s, profit-sharing and money purchase plans, SEP and SIMPLE IRAs, and defined-benefit plans	11 U.S.C. § 522(b)(3)(C)
	Traditional and Roth IRAs to $1,283,025 per person	11 U.S.C. § 522(b)(3)(C); (n)
	ERISA-qualified benefits, including IRAs, SEPs & Keoghs deposited more than 120 days before filing	427.150
	Firefighters	67A.620; 95.878
	Police officers	427.120; 427.125
	State employees	61.690
	Teachers	161.700
	Urban county government employees	67A.350
personal property	Burial plot to $5,000, in lieu of homestead	427.060
	Clothing, jewelry, articles of adornment & furnishings to $3,000 total	427.010(1)
	Health aids	427.010(1)
	Lost earnings payments needed for support	427.150(2)(d)
	Medical expenses paid & reparation benefits received under motor vehicle reparation law	304.39-260
	Motor vehicle to $2,500	427.010(1)
	Personal injury recoveries to $7,500 (not to include pain & suffering or pecuniary loss)	427.150(2)(c)
	Prepaid tuition payment fund account	164A.707(3)
	Wrongful death recoveries for person you depended on, needed for support	427.150(2)(b)
public benefits	Aid to blind, aged, disabled; public assistance, includes earned income tax credit if eligible for Kentucky benefits (*In re Beltz*, 263 B.R. 525 (Bankr. W.D. Ky. 2001))	205.220(c)
	Crime victims' compensation	427.150(2)(a)
	Unemployment compensation	341.470(4)
	Workers' compensation	342.180
tools of trade	Library, office equipment, instruments & furnishings of minister, attorney, physician, surgeon, chiropractor, veterinarian, or dentist to $1,000	427.040
	Motor vehicle of auto mechanic, mechanical, or electrical equipment servicer, minister, attorney, physician, surgeon, chiropractor, veterinarian, or dentist to $2,500	427.030
	Tools, equipment, livestock & poultry of farmer to $3,000	427.010(1)
	Tools of nonfarmer to $300	427.030
wages	Minimum 75% of disposable weekly earnings or 30 times the federal minimum hourly wage per week, whichever is greater; bankruptcy judge may authorize more for low-income debtors	427.010(2), (3)
wildcard	$1,000 of any property	427.160

Louisiana

Federal bankruptcy exemptions not available. All law references are to Louisiana Revised Statutes Annotated unless otherwise noted.

ASSET	EXEMPTION	LAW
homestead	Property you occupy to $35,000 (if debt is result of catastrophic or terminal illness or injury, limit is full value of property as of 1 year before filing); cannot exceed 5 acres in city or town, 200 acres elsewhere (spouses may not double)	20:1(A)(1),(2),(3)
	Spouse or child of deceased owner may claim homestead exemption; spouse given home in divorce gets homestead	20:1(B)

insurance	Annuity contract proceeds & avails	22:912
	Fraternal benefit society benefits	22:298
	Group insurance policies or proceeds	22:944
	Health, accident, or disability proceeds or avails	22:1015
	Life insurance proceeds or avails; if policy issued within 9 months of filing, exempt only to $35,000	22:912
miscellaneous	Property of minor child	13:3881(A)(3); Civil Code Art. 223
pensions	Tax-exempt retirement accounts, including 401(k)s, 403(b)s, profit-sharing and money purchase plans, SEP and SIMPLE IRAs, and defined-benefit plans	11 U.S.C. § 522(b)(3)(C)
	Traditional and Roth IRAs to $1,283,025 per person	11 U.S.C. § 522(b)(3)(C); (n)
	Assessors	11:1403
	Court clerks	11:1526
	District attorneys	11:1583
	ERISA-qualified benefits, including IRAs, Roth IRAs & Keoghs, if contributions made over 1 year before filing for bankruptcy	13:3881; 20:33(1)
	Firefighters	11:2263
	Gift or bonus payments from employer to employee or heirs whenever paid	20:33(2)
	Judges	11:1378
	Louisiana University employees	11:952.3
	Municipal employees	11:1735
	Parochial employees	11:1905
	Police officers	11:3513
	School employees	11:1003
	Sheriffs	11:2182
	State employees	11:405
	Teachers	11:704
	Voting registrars	11:2033
personal property	Military accoutrements; bedding; dishes, glassware, utensils, silverware (nonsterling); clothing, family portraits, musical instruments; bedroom, living room & dining room furniture; poultry, 1 cow, household pets; heating & cooling equipment, refrigerator, freezer, stove, washer & dryer, iron, sewing machine	13:3881(A)(4)
	Firearms, arms, and ammunition for any purpose to $2,500	13:3881(A)(4)(g)
	Cemetery plot, monuments	8:313
	Disaster relief insurance proceeds	13:3881(A)(7)
	Engagement & wedding rings to $5,000	13:3881(A)(5)
	Motor vehicle to $7,500	13:3881(A)(7)
	Motor vehicle modified for disability to $7,500	13:3881(A)(8)
	Spendthrift trusts	9:2004
public benefits	Aid to blind, aged, disabled; public assistance	46:111
	Crime victims' compensation	46:1811
	Earned income tax credit	13:3881(A)(6)
	Unemployment compensation	23:1693
	Workers' compensation	23:1205
tools of trade	Tools, instruments, books, $7,500 of equity in a motor vehicle, one firearm to $500, needed to work	13:3881(A)(2)

wages	Minimum 75% of disposable weekly earnings or 30 times the federal minimum hourly wage per week, whichever is greater; bankruptcy judge may authorize more for low-income debtors	13:3881(A)(1)
wildcard	None	

Maine

Federal bankruptcy exemptions not available. All law references are to Maine Revised Statutes Annotated, in the form "title number-section number," unless otherwise noted.

ASSET	EXEMPTION	LAW
homestead	Real or personal property (including cooperative) used as residence to $47,500; if debtor has minor dependents in residence, to $95,000; if debtor over age 60 or physically or mentally disabled, $95,000; proceeds of sale exempt for six months	14-4422(1)
insurance	Annuity proceeds to $450 per month	24-A-2431
	Death benefit for police, fire, or emergency medical personnel who die in the line of duty	25-1612
	Disability or health proceeds, benefits, or avails	14-4422(13)(A), (C); 24-A-2429
	Fraternal benefit society benefits	24-A-4118
	Group health or life policy or proceeds	24-A-2430
	Life, endowment, annuity, or accident policy, proceeds or avails	14-4422(14)(C); 24-A-2428
	Life insurance policy, interest, loan value, or accrued dividends for policy from person you depended on, to $4,000	14-4422(11)
	Unmatured life insurance policy, except credit insurance policy	14-4422(10)
miscellaneous	Alimony & child support needed for support	14-4422(13)(D)
pensions	Tax-exempt retirement accounts, including 401(k)s, 403(b)s, profit-sharing and money purchase plans, SEP and SIMPLE IRAs, and defined-benefit plans	11 U.S.C. § 522(b)(3)(C)
	Traditional and Roth IRAs to $1,283,025 per person	11 U.S.C. § 522(b)(3)(C); (n)
	ERISA-qualified benefits needed for support	14-4422(13)(E)
	Judges	4-1203
	Legislators	3-703
	State employees	5-17054
personal property	Animals, crops, musical instruments, books, clothing, furnishings, household goods, appliances to $200 per item	14-4422(3)
	Balance due on repossessed goods; total amount financed can't exceed $2,000	9-A-5-103
	Burial plot in lieu of homestead exemption	14-4422(1)
	Cooking stove; furnaces & stoves for heat	14-4422(6)(A), (B)
	Food to last 6 months	14-4422(7)(A)
	Fuel not to exceed 10 cords of wood, 5 tons of coal, or 1,000 gal. of heating oil	14-4422(6)(C)
	Health aids	14-4422(12)
	Jewelry to $750	14-4422(4)
	Lost earnings payments needed for support	14-4422(14)(E)
	Military clothes, arms & equipment	37-B-262
	Motor vehicle to $5,000	14-4422(2)
	Personal injury recoveries to $12,500	14-4422(14)(D)
	Seeds, fertilizers & feed to raise & harvest food for 1 season	14-4422(7)(B)
	Tools & equipment to raise & harvest food	14-4422(7)(C)
	Wrongful death recoveries needed for support	14-4422(14)(B)

public benefits	Maintenance under the Rehabilitation Act	26-1411-H
	Crime victims' compensation	14-4422(14)(A)
	Federal, state, or local public assistance benefits; earned income and child tax credits (but see *In re Tetrault*, No. 12-21373 (Bankr. D. Maine 2013) (child tax credit not exempt if no refund))	14-4422(13)(A); 22-3180, 22-3766
	Social Security	14-4422(13)(A)
	Unemployment compensation	14-4422(13)(A), (C)
	Veterans benefits	14-4422(13)(B)
	Workers' compensation	39-A-106
tools of trade	Books, materials & stock to $5,000	14-4422(5)
	Commercial fishing boat, 5-ton limit	14-4422(9)
	One of each farm implement (& its maintenance equipment needed to harvest & raise crops)	14-4422(8)
wages	None	
wildcard	Unused portion of exemption in homestead to $6,000; to be used for animals, crops, musical instruments, books, clothing, furnishings, household goods, appliances, jewelry, tools of the trade & personal injury recoveries	14-4422(16)
	$400 of any property	14-4422(15)

Maryland

Federal bankruptcy exemptions not available. All law references are to Maryland Code of Courts & Judicial Proceedings unless otherwise noted. New Maryland homestead exemption is indexed for inflation by matching the federal homestead amount.

ASSET	EXEMPTION	LAW
homestead	Owner-occupied residential property or co-op or condo to $22,975 (spouses may double). Includes manufactured home that has been converted to real property pursuant to Real Property Art. 8B-201. Property held as tenancy by the entirety is exempt against debts owed by only one spouse	11-504(f); *In re Birney*, 200 F.3d 225 (4th Cir. 1999)
insurance	Disability or health benefits, including court awards, arbitrations & settlements	11-504(b)(2)
	Fraternal benefit society benefits	Ins. 8-431; Estates & Trusts 8-115
	Life insurance or annuity contract proceeds or avails if beneficiary is insured's dependent, child, or spouse	Ins. 16-111(a); Estates & Trusts 8-115
	Medical insurance benefits deducted from wages plus medical insurance payments to $145 per week or 75% of disposable wages	Commercial Law 15-601.1(3)
miscellaneous	Child support	11-504(b)(6)
	Alimony to same extent wages are exempt	11-504(b)(7)
pensions	Tax-exempt retirement accounts, including 401(k)s, 403(b)s, profit-sharing and money purchase plans, SEP and SIMPLE IRAs, and defined-benefit plans	11 U.S.C. § 522(b)(3)(C)
	Traditional and Roth IRAs to $1,283,025 per person	11 U.S.C. § 522(b)(3)(C); (n)
	ERISA-qualified benefits, including IRAs, Roth IRAs & Keoghs	11-504(h)(1), (4)
	State employees	State Pers. & Pen. 21-502

personal property	Appliances, furnishings, household goods, books, pets & clothing to $1,000 total	11-504(b)(4)
	Burial plot	Bus. Reg. 5-503
	Health aids	11-504(b)(3)
	Perpetual care trust funds	Bus. Reg. 5-603
	Prepaid college trust funds	Educ. 18-1913
	Lost future earnings recoveries	11-504(b)(2)
public benefits	Baltimore Police death benefits	Code of 1957 art. 24, 16-103
	Crime victims' compensation	Crim. Proc. 11-816(b)
	Public assistance benefits	Human Services § 5-407(a) (1), (2)
	Unemployment compensation	Labor & Employment 8-106
	Workers' compensation	Labor & Employment 9-732
tools of trade	Clothing, books, tools, instruments & appliances to $5,000	11-504(b)(1)
wages	Earned but unpaid wages, the greater of 75% or $145 per week; in Kent, Caroline, Queen Anne's & Worcester Counties, the greater of 75% or 30 times federal minimum hourly wage. *In re Stine*, 360 F.3d 455 (4th Cir. 2004); *Bank of America v. Stine*, 379 Md. 76, 839 A.2d 727, 729 (2003)	Commercial Law 15-601.1
wildcard	$6,000 in cash or any property	11-504(b)(5)
	An additional $5,000 personal property	11-504(f)

Massachusetts

Federal bankruptcy exemptions available. All law references are to Massachusetts General Laws Annotated, in the form "title number-section number," unless otherwise noted.

ASSET	EXEMPTION	LAW
homestead	Property held as tenancy by the entirety may be exempt against debt for nonnecessity owed by only one spouse	209-1
	Automatic homestead for principal residence (including mobile home) to $125,000; to $500,000 if homestead declaration is recorded and complies with Massachusetts law; spouses may not double; trust beneficiaries are eligible for exemption; owners with a disability or 62 or older may each exempt up to $500,000, but aggregate cannot be more than $1,000,000. *In re Peirce*, 467 B.R. 260 (Bankr. D. Mass.)	188-1, 2, 5
	Spouse or children of deceased owner may claim homestead exemption	188-2
insurance	Disability benefits to $400 per week	175-110A, 175-36B
	Fraternal benefit society benefits	176-22
	Group annuity policy or proceeds	175-132C
	Group life insurance policy	175-135; 175-36
	Life insurance or annuity contract proceeds if clause prohibits proceeds from being used to pay beneficiary's creditors. *In re Sloss*, 279 B.R. 6 (Bankr. D. Mass. 2002)	175-119A
	Life insurance policy if beneficiary is a married woman. *In re Sloss*, 279 B.R. 6 (Bankr. D. Mass. 2002)	175-126
	Life or endowment policy, proceeds, or cash value. *In re Sloss*, 279 B.R. 6 (Bankr. D. Mass. 2002)	175-125
	Medical malpractice self-insurance	175F-15

miscellaneous	Property of business partnership	108A-25
pensions *see also wages*	Tax-exempt retirement accounts, including 401(k)s, 403(b)s, profit-sharing and money purchase plans, SEP and SIMPLE IRAs, and defined-benefit plans	11 U.S.C. § 522(b)(3)(C)
	Traditional and Roth IRAs to $1,283,025 per person	11 U.S.C. § 522(b)(3)(C); (n)
	Credit union employees	171-84
	ERISA-qualified benefits, including IRAs & Keoghs to specified limits	235-34A; 246-28
	Private retirement benefits	32-41
	Public employees	32-19
	Savings bank employees	168-41; 168-44
personal property	2 cows, 12 sheep, 2 swine, 4 tons of hay	235-34(4)
	Beds & bedding; heating unit, stove, refrigerator, freezer & hot water heater; clothing	235-34(1)
	Bibles & books to $500 total	235-34(3)
	Burial plots, tombs & church pew	235-34(11),(8)
	Cash for fuel, heat, water, or light to $500 per month	235-34(1)
	Cash to $2,500/month for rent, in lieu of homestead	235-34(14)
	Cooperative association shares to $100	235-34(13)
	Food or cash for food to $600	235-34(7)
	Household furnishings to $15,000	235-34(2)
	Jewelry to $1,225	235-34(18)
	Motor vehicle to $7,500; to $15,000 if used by elderly or disabled debtor	235-34(16)
	Moving expenses for eminent domain	79-6A
	Sewing machine, computer, TV to $300	235-34(12)
	Trust company, bank, or credit union deposits to $2,500	235-34(15); 235-28A
public benefits	Public assistance	235-34(15)
	Temporary assistance for needy families	118-10
	Unemployment compensation	151A-36
	Veterans benefits	115-5
	Workers' compensation	152-47
tools of trade	Arms, accoutrements & uniforms required	235-34(10)
	Fishing boats, tackle & nets to $1,500	235-34(9)
	Materials you designed & procured to $5,000	235-34(6)
	Tools, implements & fixtures to $5,000 total	235-34(5)
wages	Earned but unpaid wages to 85% or 50x minimum wage per week	235-34(15)
wildcard	$1,000 plus up to $5,000 of unused automobile, tools of the trade, and household furniture exemptions	235-34(17)

Michigan

Federal bankruptcy exemptions available. All law references are to Michigan Compiled Laws Annotated unless otherwise noted.

Under Michigan law, bankruptcy exemption amounts are adjusted for inflation every three years (starting in 2005) by the Michigan Department of Treasury. You can find the current amounts at www.michigan.gov/documents/BankruptcyExemptions 2005_141050_7.pdf or by searching Google for "Property Debtor in Bankruptcy May Exempt, Inflation Adjusted Amounts."

ASSET	EXEMPTION	LAW
homestead	Property held as tenancy by the entirety may be exempt against debts owed by only one spouse	600.5451(1)(n)
	Real property including condo to $38,225 ($57,350 if over 65 or disabled); property cannot exceed 1 lot in town, village, city, or 40 acres elsewhere; spouse or children of deceased owner may claim homestead exemption; spouses or unmarried co-owners may not double	600.5451(1)(m); *Vinson v. Dakmak*, 347 B.R. 620 (E.D. Mich. 2006)
insurance	Disability, mutual life, or health benefits	600.5451(1)(j)
	Employer-sponsored life insurance policy or trust fund	500.2210
	Fraternal benefit society benefits	500.8181
	Life, endowment, or annuity proceeds if clause prohibits proceeds from being used to pay beneficiary's creditors	500.4054
	Life insurance	500.2207
miscellaneous	Property of business partnership	449.25
pensions	Tax-exempt retirement accounts, including 401(k)s, 403(b)s, profit-sharing and money purchase plans, SEP and SIMPLE IRAs, and defined-benefit plans	11 U.S.C. § 522(b)(3)(C)
	Traditional and Roth IRAs to $1,283,025 per person	11 U.S.C. § 522(b)(3)(C); (n)
	ERISA-qualified benefits, except contributions within last 120 days	600.5451(1)(l)
	Firefighters, police officers	38.559(6); 38.1683
	IRAs & Roth IRAs, except contributions within last 120 days	600.5451(1)(k)
	Judges and probate judges	38.2308; 38.1683
	Legislators	38.1057; 38.1683
	Public school employees	38.1346; 38.1683
	State employees	38.40; 38.1683
personal property	Appliances, utensils, books, furniture, jewelry & household goods to $600 each, $3,825 total	600.5451(1)(c)
	Burial plots, cemeteries	600.5451(1)(a)(vii)
	Church pew, slip, seat for entire family to $650	600.5451(1)(d)
	Clothing; family pictures	600.5451(1)(a)
	Food & fuel to last family for 6 months	600.5451(1)(b)
	Crops, animals, and feed to $2,550	600.5451(1)(e)
	1 motor vehicle to $3,525	600.5451(1)(g)
	Computer & accessories to $650	600.5451(1)(h)
	Household pets to $650	600.5451(1)(f)
	Professionally prescribed health aids	600.5451(a)
public benefits	Crime victims' compensation	18.362
	Social welfare benefits	400.63
	Unemployment compensation	421.30
	Veterans benefits for Korean War veterans	35.977
	Veterans benefits for Vietnam veterans	35.1027
	Veterans benefits for WWII veterans	35.926
	Workers' compensation	418.821

tools of trade	Arms & accoutrements required	600.6023(1)(a)
	Tools, implements, materials, stock, apparatus, or other things needed to carry on occupation to $2,550 total	600.5451(1)(i)
wages	Head of household may keep 60% of earned but unpaid wages (no less than $15/week), plus $2/week per nonspouse dependent; if not head of household may keep 40% (no less than $10/week)	600.5311
wildcard	None	

Minnesota

Federal bankruptcy exemptions available. All law references are to Minnesota Statutes Annotated, unless otherwise noted.

Note: Section 550.37(4)(a) requires certain exemptions to be adjusted for inflation on July 1 of even-numbered years; this table includes all changes made through July 1, 2018. Exemptions are published on or before the May 1 issue of the Minnesota State Register. Go to http://mn.gov. In the search box, type "dollar amount adjustments."

Note: In cases of suspected fraud, the Minnesota constitution permits courts to cap exemptions that would otherwise be unlimited. (*In re Tveten*, 402 N.W.2d 551 (Minn. 1987); *In re Medill*, 119 B.R. 685 (Bankr. D. Minn. 1990); *In re Sholdan*, 217 F.3d 1006 (8th Cir. 2000).)

ASSET	EXEMPTION	LAW
homestead	Home & land on which it is situated to $390,000; if homestead is used for agricultural purposes, $975,000; cannot exceed ½ acre in city, 160 acres elsewhere (spouses may not double)	510.01; 510.02
	Manufactured home to an unlimited value	550.37 subd. 12
insurance	Accident or disability proceeds	550.39
	Fraternal benefit society benefits	64B.18
	Life insurance proceeds to $46,000 if beneficiary is spouse or child of insured, plus $11,500 per dependent	550.37 subd. 10
	Police, fire, or beneficiary association benefits	550.37 subd. 11
	Unmatured life insurance contract dividends, interest, or loan value to $9,200 if insured is debtor or person debtor depends on	550.37 subd. 23
miscellaneous	Earnings of minor child	550.37 subd. 15
pensions	Tax-exempt retirement accounts, including 401(k)s, 403(b)s, profit-sharing and money purchase plans, SEP and SIMPLE IRAs, and defined-benefit plans	11 U.S.C. § 522(b)(3)(C)
	Traditional and Roth IRAs to $1,283,025 per person	11 U.S.C. § 522(b)(3)(C); (n)
	ERISA-qualified benefits if needed for support, up to $69,000 in present value	550.37 subd. 24
	IRAs or Roth IRAs needed for support, up to $69,000 in present value	550.37 subd. 24
	Public employees	353.15; 356.401
	State employees	352.965 subd. 8; 356.401
	State troopers	352B.071; 356.401
personal property	Appliances, furniture, radio, phonographs & TV to $10,350 total	550.37 subd. 4(b)
	Bible & books	550.37 subd. 2
	Burial plot; church pew or seat	550.37 subd. 3
	Clothing, one watch, food & utensils for family	550.37 subd. 4(a)
	Motor vehicle to $4,600 (up to $46,000 if vehicle has been modified for disability)	550.37 subd. 12(a)
	Personal injury recoveries	550.37 subd. 22
	Proceeds for damaged exempt property	550.37 subds. 9, 16
	Wedding rings to $2,817.50	550.37 subd. 4(c)
	Wrongful death recoveries	550.37 subd. 22

public benefits	Crime victims' compensation	611A.60
	Public benefits, including earned income tax credit, child tax credit, education tax credit (*In re Tomczyk*, 295 B.R. 894 (Bankr. D. Minn. 2003); *In re Dmitruk*, 517 B.R. 921 (Bankr. 8th Cir. 2014))	550.37 subd. 14
	Unemployment compensation	268.192 subd. 2
	Veterans benefits	550.38
	Workers' compensation	176.175
tools of trade *total (except teaching materials) can't exceed $13,000*	Farm machines, implements, livestock, produce & crops	550.37 subd. 5
	Teaching materials of college, university, public school, or public institution teacher	550.37 subd. 8
	Tools, machines, instruments, stock in trade, furniture & library to $11,500 total	550.37 subd. 6
wages	Minimum 75% of weekly disposable earnings or 40 times federal minimum hourly wage, whichever is greater	571.922
	Wages deposited into bank accounts for 20 days after depositing	550.37 subd. 13
	Wages paid within 6 months of returning to work after receiving welfare or after incarceration; includes earnings deposited in a financial institution in the last 60 days	550.37 subd. 14
wildcard	None	

Mississippi

Federal bankruptcy exemptions not available. All law references are to Mississippi Code unless otherwise noted.

ASSET	EXEMPTION	LAW
homestead	May file homestead declaration	85-3-27; 85-3-31
	Mobile home does not qualify as homestead unless you own land on which it is located (see *personal property*)	*In re Cobbins*, 234 B.R. 882 (S.D. Miss. 1999)
	Property you own & occupy to $75,000; if over 60 & married or widowed may claim a former residence; property cannot exceed 160 acres; sale proceeds exempt	85-3-1(b)(i); 85-3-21; 85-3-23
insurance	Disability benefits	85-3-1(b)(ii)
	Fraternal benefit society benefits	83-29-39
	Homeowners' insurance proceeds to $75,000	85-3-23
	Life insurance proceeds if clause prohibits proceeds from being used to pay beneficiary's creditors	83-7-5; 85-3-11; 85-3-13, 85-3-15
pensions	Tax-exempt retirement accounts, including 401(k)s, 403(b)s, profit-sharing and money purchase plans, SEP and SIMPLE IRAs, and defined-benefit plans	11 U.S.C. § 522(b)(3)(C)
	Traditional and Roth IRAs to $1,283,025 per person	11 U.S.C. § 522(b)(3)(C); (n)
	ERISA-qualified benefits, IRAs, Keoghs deposited over 1 year before filing bankruptcy	85-3-1(e)
	Firefighters (includes death benefits)	21-29-257; 45-2-1
	Highway patrol officers	25-13-31
	Law enforcement officers' death benefits	45-2-1
	Police officers (includes death benefits)	21-29-257; 45-2-1
	Private retirement benefits to extent tax deferred	71-1-43
	Public employees retirement & disability benefits	25-11-129
	State employees	25-14-5
	Teachers	25-11-201(1)(d)
	Volunteer firefighters' death benefits	45-2-1

personal property	Mobile home to $30,000	85-3-1(d)
	Personal injury judgments to $10,000	85-3-17
	Sale or insurance proceeds for exempt property	85-3-1(b)(i)
	State health savings accounts	85-3-1(g)
	Tangible personal property to $10,000: any items worth less than $200 each; furniture, dishes, kitchenware, household goods, appliances, 1 radio, 1 TV, 1 firearm, 1 lawnmower, clothing, wedding rings, motor vehicles, tools of the trade, books, crops, health aids, domestic animals, cash on hand (does not include works of art, antiques, jewelry, or electronic entertainment equipment)	85-3-1(a)
	Tax-qualified § 529 education savings plans, including those under the Mississippi Prepaid Affordable College Tuition Program	85-3-1(f)
public benefits	Assistance to aged	43-9-19
	Assistance to blind	43-3-71
	Assistance to disabled	43-29-15
	Crime victims' compensation	99-41-23(7)
	Federal income tax refund to $5,000; earned income tax credit to $5,000; state tax refunds to $5,000	85-3-1(h); (i); (j); (k)
	Social Security	25-11-129
	Unemployment compensation	71-5-539
	Workers' compensation	71-3-43
tools of trade	*See personal property*	
wages	Earned but unpaid wages owed for 30 days; after 30 days, minimum 75% of earned but unpaid weekly disposable earnings or 30 times the federal hourly minimum wage, whichever is greater; bankruptcy judge may authorize more for low-income debtors	85-3-4
wildcard	$50,000 of any property, including deposits of money, available to Mississippi resident who is at least 70 years old; *also see personal property*	85-3-1(h)

Missouri

Federal bankruptcy exemptions not available. All law references are to Annotated Missouri Statutes unless otherwise noted.

Note: Federal bankruptcy courts have held that under *Benn v. Cole (In re Benn)*, 491 F.3d 811, 814 (8th Cir. 2007) exemption statutes in Missouri must use the word "exempt" for property to be exempt in bankruptcy. Lower courts have interpreted this to mean that the words "not subject to execution or attachment" do *not* create an exemption for bankruptcy purposes.

Many pension exemption statutes in Missouri do not have the words required to create an exemption in bankruptcy. However, Missouri courts, interpreting the same law, point out that Missouri has long held otherwise—that such Missouri statutes do create an exemption in bankruptcy. See *Russell v. Healthmont of Missouri, LLC*, 348 S.W. 3d 784 (Missouri Court of Appeals, Western District 2011).

The Missouri wage garnishment statute may not be a valid bankruptcy exemption under *In re Benn*, because the word "exempt" does not appear in the wage garnishment statute. See *In re Parsons*, 437 B.R. 854 (Bankr. E.D. Mo. 2010).

ASSET	EXEMPTION	LAW
homestead	Property held as tenancy by the entirety may be exempt against debts owed by only one spouse	*In re Eads*, 271 B.R. 371 (Bankr. W.D. Mo. 2002)
	Real property to $15,000 or mobile home to $5,000 (joint owners may not double)	513.430(6); 513.475; *In re Smith*, 254 B.R. 751 (Bankr. W.D. Mo. 2000)

insurance	Assessment plan or life insurance proceeds	377.090
	Disability or illness benefits	513.430(10)(c)
	Fraternal benefit society benefits to $5,000, bought over 6 months before filing	513.430(8)
	Life insurance dividends, loan value, or interest to $150,000, bought over 6 months before filing	513.430(8)
	Stipulated insurance premiums	377.330
	Unmatured life insurance policy	513.430(7)
miscellaneous	Alimony, child support to $750 per month	513.430(10)(d)
	Property of business partnership	358.250
pensions	Tax-exempt retirement accounts, including 401(k)s, 403(b)s, profit-sharing and money purchase plans, SEP and SIMPLE IRAs, and defined-benefit plans	11 U.S.C. § 522(b)(3)(C)
	Traditional and Roth IRAs to $1,283,025 per person	11 U.S.C. § 522(b)(3)(C); (n)
	Employee benefit spendthrift trust	456.014
	Employees of cities with 100,000 or more people	71.207
	ERISA-qualified benefits, IRAs, Roth IRAs & other retirement accounts needed for support	513.430(10)(e), (f)
	Firefighters	87.090; 87.365; 87.485
	Highway & transportation employees	104.250
	Inherited retirement accounts	513.040(f)
	Police department employees	86.190; 86.353; 86.1430
	Public officers & employees	70.695; 70.755
	State employees	104.540
	Teachers. But see *In re Smith*, 10-60388 (W.D. Mo. 2010). See note at beginning of Missouri chart	169.090
personal property	Appliances, household goods, furnishings, clothing, books, crops, animals & musical instruments to $3,000 total	513.430(1)
	Burial grounds to 1 acre or $100	214.190
	Health aids	513.430(9)
	Health savings accounts	513.040(10)(f)
	Motor vehicles to $3,000 in aggregate	513.430(5)
	Wedding or engagement ring to $1,500 & other jewelry to $500. *In re Urie*, 2006 WL 533514 (Bankr. W.D. Mo. 2006)	513.430(2)
	Wrongful death recoveries for person you depended on	513.430(11)
	Firearms, including accessories and ammunition to $1,500	513.430(12)
public benefits	Crime victims' compensation	595.025
	Public assistance, including earned income tax credit, but not child tax credit (*In re Corbett*, No. 13–60042 (Bankr. W.D. Mo. 2013); *In re Hardy*, 495 BR 440 (Bankr. W.D. Mo. 2013))	513.430(10)(a)
	Social Security	513.430(10)(a)
	Unemployment compensation	288.380(10)(l); 513.430(10)(c)
	Veterans benefits	513.430(10)b)
	Workers' compensation	287.260
tools of trade	Implements, books & tools of trade to $3,000	513.430(4)

wages	Minimum 75% of weekly earnings (90% of weekly earnings for head of family), or 30 times the federal minimum hourly wage, whichever is more; bankruptcy judge may authorize more for low-income debtors. See note at beginning of Missouri chart.	525.030
	See note at beginning of Missouri chart. Wages of servant or common laborer to $90	513.470
wildcard	$600 of any property; an additional $1,250 if head of family, plus another $350 per child under age 21	513.430(3); 513.440

Montana

Federal bankruptcy exemptions not available. All law references are to Montana Code Annotated unless otherwise noted.

ASSET	EXEMPTION	LAW
homestead	Must record homestead declaration before filing for bankruptcy	70-32-105
	Real property or mobile home you occupy to $250,000; sale, condemnation, or insurance proceeds exempt for 18 months	70-32-104; 70-32-201; 70-32-213
insurance	Annuity contract proceeds to $350 per month	33-15-514
	Disability or illness proceeds, avails, or benefits	25-13-608(1)(d); 33-15-513
	Fraternal benefit society benefits	33-7-522
	Group life insurance policy or proceeds	33-15-512
	Hail insurance benefits	80-2-245
	Life insurance proceeds if clause prohibits proceeds from being used to pay beneficiary's creditors	33-20-120
	Medical, surgical, or hospital care benefits	25-13-608(1)(f)
	Unmatured life insurance contracts	25-13-608(1)(k)
miscellaneous	Alimony, child support	25-13-608(1)(g)
pensions	Tax-exempt retirement accounts, including 401(k)s, 403(b)s, profit-sharing and money purchase plans, SEP and SIMPLE IRAs, and defined-benefit plans	11 U.S.C. § 522(b)(3)(C)
	Traditional and Roth IRAs to $1,283,025 per person	11 U.S.C. § 522(b)(3)(C); (n)
	IRAs & ERISA-qualified benefits deposited over 1 year before filing bankruptcy or up to 15% of debtor's gross annual income	31-2-106
	Firefighters	19-18-612(1)
	IRA & Roth IRA contributions & earnings made before judgment filed	25-13-608(1)(e)
	Police officers	19-19-504(1)
	Public employees	19-2-1004; 25-13-608(i)
	Teachers	19-20-706(2); 25-13-608(j)
	University system employees	19-21-212
personal property	Appliances, household furnishings, goods, animals with feed, crops, musical instruments, books, firearms, sporting goods, clothing & jewelry to $600 per item, $4,500 total	25-13-609(1)
	Burial plot	25-13-608(1)(h)
	Cooperative association shares to $500 value	35-15-404
	Health aids	25-13-608(1)(a)
	Motor vehicle to $2,500	25-13-609(2)
	Proceeds from sale or for damage or loss of exempt property for 6 months after received	25-13-610

public benefits	Aid to aged, disabled needy persons	53-2-607
	Crime victims' compensation	53-9-129
	Local public assistance	25-13-608(1)(b)
	Silicosis benefits	39-73-110
	Social Security	25-13-608(1)(b)
	Subsidized adoption payments to needy persons	53-2-607
	Unemployment compensation	31-2-106(2); 39-51-3105
	Veterans benefits	25-13-608(1)(c)
	Vocational rehabilitation to blind needy persons	53-2-607
	Workers' compensation	39-71-743
tools of trade	Implements, books & tools of trade to $3,000	25-13-609(3)
	Uniforms, arms & accoutrements needed to carry out government functions	25-13-613(b)
wages	Minimum 75% of earned but unpaid weekly disposable earnings, or 30 times the federal hourly minimum wage, whichever is greater; bankruptcy judge may authorize more for low-income debtors	25-13-614
wildcard	None	

Nebraska

Federal bankruptcy exemptions not available. All law references are to Revised Statutes of Nebraska unless otherwise noted.

ASSET	EXEMPTION	LAW
homestead	$60,000 for head of family or an unmarried person age 65 or older; cannot exceed 2 lots in city or village, 160 acres elsewhere; sale proceeds exempt 6 months after sale (spouses may not double)	40-101; 40-111; 40-113
	May record homestead declaration	40-105
insurance	Fraternal benefit society benefits to $100,000 loan value unless beneficiary convicted of a crime related to benefits	44-1089
	Life insurance proceeds and avails to $100,000	44-371
pensions *see also wages*	Tax-exempt retirement accounts, including 401(k)s, 403(b)s, profit-sharing and money purchase plans, SEP and SIMPLE IRAs, and defined-benefit plans	11 U.S.C. § 522(b)(3)(C)
	Traditional and Roth IRAs to $1,283,025 per person	11 U.S.C. § 522(b)(3)(C); (n)
	County employees	23-2322
	Deferred compensation of public employees	48-1401
	ERISA-qualified benefits including IRAs & Roth IRAs needed for support	25-1563.01
	Military disability benefits	25-1559
	School employees	79-948
	State employees	84-1324
personal property	Burial plot	12-517
	Clothing	25-1556(2)
	Crypts, lots, tombs, niches, vaults	12-605
	Furniture, household goods & appliances, household electronics, personal computers, books & musical instruments to $1,500	25-1556(3)
	Health aids	25-1556(5)
	Medical or health savings accounts to $25,000	8-1, 131(2)(b)
	Perpetual care funds	12-511
	Personal injury recoveries	25-1563.02
	Personal possessions	25-1556

public benefits	Aid to disabled, blind, aged; public assistance	68-1013
	Earned income tax credit	25-1553
	General assistance to poor persons	68-148
	Unemployment compensation	48-647
	Workers' compensation	48-149
tools of trade	Equipment or tools including a vehicle used in or for commuting to principal place of business to $2,400 (husband & wife may double)	25-1556(4); *In re Keller,* 50 B.R. 23 (D. Neb. 1985)
wages	Minimum 85% of earned but unpaid weekly disposable earnings or pension payments for head of family; minimum 75% of earned but unpaid weekly disposable earnings or 30 times the federal hourly minimum wage, whichever is greater, for all others; bankruptcy judge may authorize more for low-income debtors	25-1558
wildcard	$2,500 of any personal property except wages	25-1552

Nevada

Federal bankruptcy exemptions not available. All law references are to Nevada Revised Statutes Annotated unless otherwise noted.

ASSET	EXEMPTION	LAW
homestead	Must record homestead declaration before filing for bankruptcy	115.020
	Real property or mobile home to $550,000. Spouses may not double	115.010; 21.090(1)(m)
insurance	Annuity contract proceeds	687B.290
	Fraternal benefit society benefits	695A.220
	Group life or health policy or proceeds	687B.280
	Health proceeds or avails	687B.270
	Life insurance policy or proceeds	21.090(1)(k); *In re Bower,* 234 B.R. 109 (Nev. 1999)
	Life insurance proceeds if you're not the insured	687B.260
	Private disability insurance proceeds	21.090(1)(ee)
miscellaneous	Alimony & child support	21.090(1)(s)
	Property of some business partnerships	87.250
	Security deposits for a rental residence, except landlord may enforce terms of lease or rental agreement	21.090(1)(n)
pensions	Tax-exempt retirement accounts, including 401(k)s, 403(b)s, profit-sharing and money purchase plans, SEP and SIMPLE IRAs, and defined-benefit plans	11 U.S.C. § 522(b)(3)(C)
	Traditional and Roth IRAs to $1,283,025 per person	11 U.S.C. § 522(b)(3)(C); (n)
	ERISA-qualified benefits, deferred compensation, SEP IRA, Roth IRA, or IRA to $500,000	21.090(1)(r)
	Public employees	286.670; 21.090(1)(ii)

personal property	Appliances, household goods, furniture, wearing apparel, home & yard equipment to $12,000 total	21.090(1)(b)
	Books, works of art, musical instruments & jewelry to $5,000	21.090(1)(a)
	Burial plot purchase money held in trust	689.700; 21.090(1)(ff)
	Funeral service contract money held in trust	689.700
	Health aids	21.090(1)(q)
	Interests in qualifying trusts	21.090(1)(cc)
	Keepsakes & pictures	21.090(1)(a)
	Metal-bearing ores, geological specimens, art curiosities, or paleontological remains; must be arranged, classified, cataloged & numbered in reference books	21.100
	Mortgage impound accounts	645B.180
	Motor vehicle to $15,000; no limit on vehicle equipped for disabled person	21.090(1)(f), (o)
	1 gun	21.090(1)(i)
	Personal injury compensation to $16,150	21.090(1)(u)
	Restitution received for criminal act	21.090(1)(x)
	Stock in certain closely held corporations	21.090(1)(bb); 78.764
	Tax refunds derived from the state or federal earned income credit	21.090(1)(aa)
	Wrongful death awards to survivors	21.090(1)(v)
public benefits	Aid to blind, aged, disabled; public assistance	422.291; 21.090(1)(kk); 422A.325
	Crime victims' compensation	21.090
	Earned income tax credit (state or federal)	21.090(1)(bb)
	Industrial insurance (workers' compensation)	616C.205; 21.090(1)(gg)
	Public assistance for children	432.036; 21.090(1)(ll)
	Social Security retirement, disability, SSI, survivor benefits	21.090(1)(y)
	Unemployment compensation	612.710; 21.090(1)(hh)
	Vocational rehabilitation benefits	615.270; 21.090(1)(jj)
tools of trade	Arms, uniforms & accoutrements you're required to keep	21.090(1)(j)
	Cabin or dwelling of miner or prospector; mining claim, cars, implements & appliances to $4,500 total (for working claim only)	21.090(1)(e)
	Farm trucks, stock, tools, equipment & seed to $4,500	21.090(1)(c)
	Library, equipment, supplies, tools, inventory & materials to $10,000	21.090(1)(d)
wages	Minimum 75% of disposable weekly earnings or 50 times the federal minimum hourly wage per week, whichever is more; bankruptcy judge may authorize more for low-income debtors. *In re Christensen*, 149 P.3d 40 (2006)	21.090(1)(g)
wildcard	$10,000 of any personal property	21.090(1)(z)

New Hampshire

Federal bankruptcy exemptions available. All law references are to New Hampshire Revised Statutes Annotated unless otherwise noted.

ASSET	EXEMPTION	LAW
homestead	Real property or manufactured housing (& the land it's on if you own it) to $120,000	480:1

insurance	Firefighters' aid insurance	402:69
	Fraternal benefit society benefits	418:17
	Homeowners' insurance proceeds to $5,000	512:21(VIII)
miscellaneous	Jury, witness fees	512:21(VI)
	Property of business partnership	304-A:25
	Wages of minor child	512:21(III)
pensions	Tax-exempt retirement accounts, including 401(k)s, 403(b)s, profit-sharing and money purchase plans, SEP and SIMPLE IRAs, and defined-benefit plans	11 U.S.C. § 522(b)(3)(C)
	Traditional and Roth IRAs to $1,283,025 per person	11 U.S.C. § 522(b)(3)(C); (n)
	ERISA-qualified retirement accounts including IRAs & Roth IRAs	512:2 (XIX)
	Federally created pension (only benefits building up)	512:21(IV)
	Firefighters	102:23
	Police officers	103:18
	Public employees	100-A:26
personal property	Beds, bedding & cooking utensils	511:2(II)
	Bibles & books to $800	511:2(VIII)
	Burial plot, lot	511:2(XIV)
	Church pew	511:2(XV)
	Clothing	511:2(I)
	Cooking & heating stoves, refrigerator	511:2(IV)
	Domestic fowl to $300	511:2(XIII)
	Food & fuel to $400	511:2(VI)
	Furniture to $3,500	511:2(III)
	Jewelry to $500	511:2(XVII)
	Motor vehicle to $4,000	511:2(XVI)
	Proceeds for lost or destroyed exempt property	512:21(VIII)
	Sewing machine	511:2(V)
	1 cow, 6 sheep & their fleece, 4 tons of hay	511:2(XI); (XII)
	1 hog or pig or its meat (if slaughtered)	511:2(X)
public benefits	Aid to blind, aged, disabled; public assistance	167:25
	Unemployment compensation	282-A:159
	Workers' compensation	281-A:52
tools of trade	Tools of your occupation to $5,000	511:2(IX)
	Uniforms, arms & equipment of military member	511:2(VII)
	Yoke of oxen or horse needed for farming or teaming	511:2(XII)
wages	50 times the federal minimum hourly wage per week	512:21(II)
	Deposits in any account designated a payroll account	512:21(XI)
	Earned but unpaid wages of spouse	512:21(III)
	Note: Wage exemptions cannot be used in bankruptcy. See *In re Damast*, 136 B.R. 11 (Bankr. D. N.H. 1991)	
wildcard	$1,000 of any property	511:2(XVIII)
	Unused portion of bibles & books, food & fuel, furniture, jewelry, motor vehicle & tools of trade exemptions to $7,000	511:2(XVIII)

New Jersey

Federal bankruptcy exemptions available. All law references are to New Jersey Statutes Annotated unless otherwise noted.

ASSET	EXEMPTION	LAW
homestead	None, but survivorship interest of a spouse in property held as tenancy by the entirety is exempt from creditors of a single spouse	*Freda v. Commercial Trust Co. of New Jersey,* 570 A.2d 409 (N.J. 1990)
insurance	Annuity contract proceeds to $500 per month	17B:24-7
	Disability benefits	17:18-12
	Disability, death, medical, or hospital benefits for civil defense workers	App. A:9-57.6
	Disability or death benefits for military member	38A:4-8
	Group life or health policy or proceeds	17B:24-9
	Health or disability benefits	17:18-12; 17B:24-8
	Life insurance proceeds if clause prohibits proceeds from being used to pay beneficiary's creditors	17B:24-10
	Life insurance proceeds or avails if you're not the insured	17B:24-6b
pensions	Tax-exempt retirement accounts, including 401(k)s, 403(b)s, profit-sharing and money purchase plans, SEP and SIMPLE IRAs, and defined-benefit plans	11 U.S.C. § 522(b)(3)(C)
	Traditional and Roth IRAs to $1,283,025 per person	11 U.S.C. § 522(b)(3)(C); (n)
	Alcohol beverage control officers	43:8A-20
	City boards of health employees	43:18-12
	Civil defense workers	App. A:9-57.6
	County employees	43:10-57; 43:10-105
	ERISA-qualified benefits for city employees	43:13-9
	Firefighters, police officers, traffic officers	43:16-7; 43:16A-17
	IRAs	*In re Yuhas,* 104 F.3d 612 (3d Cir. 1997)
	Judges	43:6A-41
	Municipal employees	43:13-44
	Prison employees	43:7-13
	Public employees	43:15A-53
	School district employees	18A:66-116
	State police	53:5A-45
	Street & water department employees	43:19-17
	Teachers	18A:66-51
	Trust containing personal property created pursuant to federal tax law, including 401(k) plans, IRAs, Roth IRAs & higher education (529) savings plans	25:2-1; *In re Yuhas,* 104 F.3d 612 (3d Cir. 1997)
personal property	Burial plots	45:27-21
	Clothing	2A:17-19
	Furniture & household goods to $1,000	2A:26-4
	Personal property & possessions of any kind, stock or interest in corporations to $1,000 total	2A:17-19

public benefits	Old age, permanent disability assistance	44:7-35
	Unemployment compensation	43:21-53
	Workers' compensation	34:15-29
tools of trade	None	
wages	90% of earned but unpaid wages if annual income is less than 250% of federal poverty level; 75% if annual income is higher	2A:17-56
	Wages or allowances received by military personnel	38A:4-8
wildcard	None	

New Mexico

Federal bankruptcy exemptions available. All law references are to New Mexico Statutes Annotated unless otherwise noted.

ASSET	EXEMPTION	LAW
homestead	$60,000	42-10-9
insurance	Benevolent association benefits to $5,000	42-10-4
	Fraternal benefit society benefits	59A-44-18
	Life, accident, health, or annuity benefits, withdrawal or cash value, if beneficiary is a New Mexico resident	42-10-3
	Life insurance proceeds	42-10-5
miscellaneous	Ownership interest in unincorporated association	53-10-2
	Property of business partnership	54-1A-501
pensions	Tax-exempt retirement accounts, including 401(k)s, 403(b)s, profit-sharing and money purchase plans, SEP and SIMPLE IRAs, and defined-benefit plans	11 U.S.C. § 522(b)(3)(C)
	Traditional and Roth IRAs to $1,283,025 per person	11 U.S.C. § 522(b)(3)(C); (n)
	Pension or retirement benefits	42-10-1; 42-10-2
	Public school employees	22-11-42A
personal property	Books & furniture	42-10-1; 42-10-2
	Building materials	48-2-15
	Clothing	42-10-1; 42-10-2
	Cooperative association shares, minimum amount needed to be member	53-4-28
	Health aids	42-10-1; 42-10-2
	Jewelry to $2,500	42-10-1; 42-10-2
	Materials, tools & machinery to dig, drill, complete, operate, or repair oil line, gas well, or pipeline	70-4-12
	Motor vehicle to $4,000	42-10-1; 42-10-2
public benefits	Crime victims' compensation	31-22-15
	General assistance	27-2-21
	Occupational disease disablement benefits	52-3-37
	Unemployment compensation	51-1-37
	Workers' compensation	52-1-52
tools of trade	$1,500	42-10-1; 42-10-2
wages	Minimum 75% of disposable earnings or 40 times the federal hourly minimum wage, whichever is more; bankruptcy judge may authorize more for low-income debtors	35-12-7
wildcard	$500 of any personal property	42-10-1
	$5,000 of any real or personal property, in lieu of homestead	42-10-10

New York

Federal bankruptcy exemptions are available. All references are to Consolidated Laws of New York unless otherwise noted; Civil Practice Law & Rules are abbreviated C.P.L.R.

ASSET	EXEMPTION	LAW
homestead	Real property including co-op, condo, or mobile home, to $82,775, $137,950, or $165,550, depending on the county	C.P.L.R. 5206(a); *In re Pearl*, 723 F.2d 193 (2nd Cir. 1983)
insurance	Annuity contract benefits due the debtor, if debtor paid for the contract; $5,000 limit if purchased within 6 months prior to filing & not tax deferred	Ins. 3212(d); Debt. & Cred. 283(1)
	Disability or illness benefits to $400 per month	Ins. 3212(c)
	Life insurance proceeds & avails if the beneficiary is not the debtor, or if debtor's spouse has taken out policy	Ins. 3212(b)
	Life insurance proceeds left at death with the insurance company, if clause prohibits proceeds from being used to pay beneficiary's creditors	Est. Powers & Trusts 7-1.5(a)(2)
miscellaneous	Alimony, child support	C.P.L.R. 5205 (d)(3); Debt. & Cred. 282(2)(d)
	Property of business partnership	Partnership 51
pensions	Tax-exempt retirement accounts, including 401(k)s, 403(b)s, profit-sharing and money purchase plans, SEP and SIMPLE IRAs, and defined-benefit plans	11 U.S.C. § 522(b)(3)(C)
	Traditional and Roth IRAs to $1,283,025 per person	11 U.S.C. § 522(b)(3)(C); (n)
	ERISA-qualified benefits, IRAs, Roth IRAs & Keoghs & income needed for support	C.P.L.R. 5205(c); Debt. & Cred. 282(2)(e)
	Public retirement benefits	Ins. 4607
	State employees	Ret. & Soc. Sec. 10
	Teachers	Educ. 524
	Village police officers	Unconsolidated 5711-o
	Volunteer ambulance workers' benefits	Vol. Amb. Wkr. Ben. 23
	Volunteer firefighters' benefits	Vol. Firefighter Ben. 23
personal property	Religious texts, schoolbooks, other books to $550; pictures; clothing; church pew or seat; sewing machine, refrigerator, TV, radio; furniture, cooking utensils & tableware, dishes; food to last 120 days; stoves with fuel to last 120 days; domestic animal with food to last 120 days, to $1,100; wedding ring; watch, jewelry, art to $1,100; exemptions may not exceed $11,025 total (including tools of trade & limited annuity)	C.P.L.R. 5205(a)(1)-(6); Debt. & Cred. 283(1)
	Burial plot without structure to ¼ acre	C.P.L.R. 5206(f)
	Cash (including savings bonds, tax refunds, bank & credit union deposits) to $5,525, or to $11,050 after exemptions for personal property taken, whichever amount is less (for debtors who do not claim homestead)	Debt. & Cred. 283(2)
	College tuition savings program trust fund	C.P.L.R. 5205(j)
	Electronic deposits of exempt property into bank account in last 45 days	C.P.L.R. 5205(l)(1)
	Health aids, including service animals with food	C.P.L.R. 5205(h)
	Lost future earnings recoveries needed for support	Debt. & Cred. 282(3)(iv)
	Motor vehicle to $4,425; $11,025 if equipped for disabled person (except if municipality is creditor)	Debt. & Cred. 282(1); *In re Miller*, 167 B.R. 782 (S.D. N.Y. 1994)

personal property (continued)	Personal injury recoveries up to 1 year after receiving	Debt. & Cred. 282(3)(iii)
	Recovery for injury to exempt property up to 1 year after receiving	C.P.L.R. 5205(b)
	Savings & loan savings to $600	Banking 407
	Security deposit to landlord, utility company	C.P.L.R. 5205(g)
	Spendthrift trust fund principal, 90% of income if not created by debtor	C.P.L.R. 5205(c), (d)
	Wrongful death to $8,275 recoveries for person you depended on	Debt. & Cred. 282(3)(ii)
public benefits	Aid to blind, aged, disabled	Debt. & Cred. 282(2)(c)
	Crime victims' compensation	Debt. & Cred. 282(3)(i)
	Home relief, local public assistance	Debt. & Cred. 282(2)(a)
	Public assistance, does not include earned income tax credit (*In re Fasarakis*, 423 B.R. 34 (E.D.N.Y. 2010)) but might include rent-controlled lease (*In re Santiago-Monteverde*, 2014 N.Y. Slip Op. 08051 (Ct. App. N.Y. 2014))	Soc. Serv. 137
	Social Security	Debt. & Cred. 282(2)(a)
	Unemployment compensation	Debt. & Cred. 282(2)(a)
	Veterans benefits	Debt. & Cred. 282(2)(b)
	Workers' compensation	Debt. & Cred. 282(2)(c); Work. Comp. 33, 218
tools of trade	Farm machinery, team & food for 60 days; professional furniture, books & instruments to $3,300 total	C.P.L.R. 5205(a),(b)
	Uniforms, medal, emblem, equipment, horse, arms & sword of member of military	C.P.L.R. 5205(e)
wages	90% of earned but unpaid wages received within 60 days before & anytime after filing	C.P.L.R. 5205(d); 5231
	90% of earnings from dairy farmer's sales to milk dealers	C.P.L.R. 5205(f)
	100% of pay of noncommissioned officer, private, or musician in U.S. or N.Y. state armed forces. *In re Wiltsie*, 443 B.R. 223 (Bankr. N.D. N.Y. 2011)	C.P.L.R. 5205(e)
wildcard	$1,100 of personal property, bank account, or cash in lieu of homestead	C.P.L.R. 5205(a)(9)

North Carolina

Federal bankruptcy exemptions not available. All law references are to General Statutes of North Carolina unless otherwise noted.

ASSET	EXEMPTION	LAW
homestead	Property held as tenancy by the entirety may be exempt against debts owed by only one spouse	*In re Chandler*, 148 B.R. 13 (E.D. N.C. 1992)
	Real or personal property, including co-op, used as residence to $35,000; $60,000 if 65 or older; property owned with spouse as tenants by the entirety or joint tenants with right of survivorship, and spouse has died; up to $5,000 of unused portion of homestead may be applied to any property	1C-1601(a)(1),(2)
insurance	Employee group life policy or proceeds	58-58-165
	Fraternal benefit society benefits	58-24-85
	Life insurance on spouse or children	1C-1601(a)(6); Const. Art. X § 5
miscellaneous	Alimony, support, separate maintenance, and child support necessary for support of debtor and dependents	1C-1601(a)(12)
	Property of business partnership	59-55
	Support received by a surviving spouse for 1 year, up to $10,000	30-15

pensions	Tax-exempt retirement accounts, including 401(k)s, 403(b)s, profit-sharing and money purchase plans, SEP and SIMPLE IRAs, and defined-benefit plans	11 U.S.C. § 522(b)(3)(C)
	Traditional and Roth IRAs to $1,283,025 per person	11 U.S.C. § 522(b)(3)(C); (n)
	Firefighters & rescue squad workers	58-86-90
	IRAs & Roth IRAs	1C-1601(a)(9)
	Law enforcement officers	143-166.30(g)
	Legislators	120-4.29
	Municipal, city & county employees	128-31
	Retirement benefits from another state to extent exempt in that state	1C-1601(a)(11)
	Teachers & state employees	135-9; 135-95
personal property	Animals, crops, musical instruments, books, wearing apparel, appliances, household goods & furnishings to $5,000 total; may add $1,000 per dependent, up to $4,000 total additional (all property must have been purchased at least 90 days before filing)	1C-1601(a)(4)
	Burial plot to $18,500, in lieu of homestead	1C-1601(a)(1)
	College savings account established under 26 U.S.C. § 529 to $25,000, excluding certain contributions within prior year	1C-1601(a)(10)
	Health aids	1C-1601(a)(7)
	Motor vehicle to $3,500	1C-1601(a)(3)
	Personal injury & wrongful death recoveries for person you depended on	1C-1601(a)(8)
public benefits	Aid to blind	111-18
	Crime victims' compensation	15B-17
	Public adult assistance under work first program	108A-36
	Unemployment compensation	96-17
	Workers' compensation	97-21
tools of trade	Implements, books & tools of trade to $2,000	1C-1601(a)(5)
wages	Earned but unpaid wages received 60 days before filing for bankruptcy, needed for support	1-362
wildcard	$5,000 of unused homestead or burial exemption	1C-1601(a)(2)
	$500 of any personal property	Constitution Art. X § 1

North Dakota

Federal bankruptcy exemptions not available. All law references are to North Dakota Century Code unless otherwise noted.

ASSET	EXEMPTION	LAW
homestead	Real property, house trailer, or mobile home to $100,000 (spouses may not double)	28-22-02(10); 47-18-01
insurance	Fraternal benefit society benefits Any unmatured life insurance contract, other than credit life insurance	26.1-15.1-18; 26.1-33-40; 28-22-03.1(4)
	Life insurance proceeds payable to deceased's estate, not to a specific beneficiary	26.1-33-40
	Life insurance surrender value to $8,000 per policy, if beneficiary Is insured's dependent & policy was owned over 1 year before filing for bankruptcy; limit does not apply if more needed for support	28-22-03.1(5)
miscellaneous	Child support payments	14-09-09.31; 28-22-03.1(8)(d)

pensions	Tax-exempt retirement accounts, including 401(k)s, 403(b)s, profit-sharing and money purchase plans, SEP and SIMPLE IRAs, and defined-benefit plans	11 U.S.C. § 522(b)(3)(C)
	Traditional and Roth IRAs to $1,283,025 per person	11 U.S.C. § 522(b)(3)(C); (n)
	Disabled veterans' benefits, except military retirement pay	28-22-03.1(4)(d)
	ERISA-qualified benefits, IRAs, Roth IRAs & Keoghs to $100,000 per plan; no limit if more needed for support; total of all accounts cannot exceed $200,000	28-22-03.1(7)
	Public employees' deferred compensation	54-52.2-06
	Public employees' pensions	28-22-19(1)
personal property	One Bible or other religious text; schoolbooks; other books	28-22-02(4)
	Burial plots, church pew	28-22-02(2), (3)
	Wearing apparel to $5,000 and all clothing & family pictures	28-22-02(1), (5)
	Crops or grain raised by debtor on 160 acres where debtor resides	28-22-02(8)
	Food & fuel to last 1 year	28-22-02(6)
	Health aids	28-22-03.1(6)
	Insurance proceeds for exempt property	28-22-02(9)
	One motor vehicle to $2,950 (or $32,000 for vehicle that has been modified to accommodate owner's disability)	28-22-03.1(2)
	Personal injury recoveries to $15,000	28-22-03.1(4)(b)
	Wrongful death recoveries to $15,000	28-22-03.1(4)(a)
public benefits	Crime victims' compensation	28-22-03.1(4); 28-22-19(2)
	Old age & survivor insurance program benefits	52-09-22
	Public assistance	28-22-19(3)
	Social Security	28-22-03.1(8)(a)
	Unemployment compensation	52-06-30
	Veterans disability benefits	28-22-03.1(8)(b)
	Workers' compensation	65-05-29
tools of trade	Books, tools & implements of trade to $1,500	28-22-03.1(3)
wages	Minimum 75% of disposable weekly earnings or 40 times the federal minimum wage, whichever is more; bankruptcy judge may authorize more for low-income debtors. Note: Wage exemption cannot be used in bankruptcy.	32-09.1-03
wildcard	$10,000 of any property in lieu of homestead	28-22-03.1(1)
	Head of household not claiming crops or grain may claim $7,500 of any personal property	28-22-03
	Unmarried with no dependents not claiming crops or grain may claim $3,750 of any personal property	28-22-05

Ohio

Federal bankruptcy exemptions not available. All law references are to Ohio Revised Code unless otherwise noted. Amounts are adjusted for inflation by tracking federal exemption amounts.

ASSET	EXEMPTION	LAW
homestead	Property held as tenancy by the entirety may be exempt against debts owed by only one spouse	*In re Pernus*, 143 B.R. 856 (N.D. Ohio 1992)
	Real or personal property used as residence to $136,925	2329.66(A)(1)(b)
insurance	Benevolent society benefits to $5,000	2329.63; 2329.66(A)(6)(a)
	Disability benefits needed for support	2329.66(A)(6)(e); 3923.19
	Fraternal benefit society benefits	2329.66(A)(6)(d); 3921.18
	Group life insurance policy or proceeds	2329.66(A)(6)(c); 3917.05

insurance (continued)	Life, endowment, or annuity contract avails for your spouse, child, or dependent	2329.66(A)(6)(b); 3911.10
	Life insurance proceeds for a spouse	3911.12
	Life insurance proceeds if clause prohibits proceeds from being used to pay beneficiary's creditors	3911.14
miscellaneous	Alimony, child support needed for support	2329.66(A)(11)
	Property of business partnership	1775.24; 2329.66(A)(14)
pensions	Tax-exempt retirement accounts, including 401(k)s, 403(b)s, profit-sharing and money purchase plans, SEP and SIMPLE IRAs, and defined-benefit plans	11 U.S.C. § 522(b)(3)(C)
	Traditional and Roth IRAs to $1,283,025 per person	11 U.S.C. § 522(b)(3)(C); (n)
	ERISA-qualified benefits needed for support	2329.66(A)(10)(b)
	Firefighters, police officers	742.47
	IRAs, Roth IRAs & Keoghs needed for support	2329.66(A)(10)(c), (a)
	Public employees	145.56
	Public safety officers' death benefit	2329.66(A)(10)(a)
	Public school employees	3309.66
	State highway patrol employees	5505.22
	Volunteer firefighters' dependents	146.13
personal property	Animals, crops, books, musical instruments, appliances, household goods, furnishings, wearing apparel, firearms, hunting & fishing equipment to $600 per item; jewelry to $1,600 in the aggregate; $12,625 total	2329.66(A)(4)(b), (c), (d); *In re Szydlowski*, 186 B.R. 907 (N.D. Ohio 1995)
	Burial plot	517.09; 2329.66(A)(8)
	Cash, money due within 90 days, tax refund, bank, security & utility deposits to $475	2329.66(A)(3); *In re Szydlowski*, 186 B.R. 907 (N.D. Ohio 1995)
	Compensation for lost future earnings needed for support, received during 12 months before filing	2329.66(A)(12)(d)
	Health aids (professionally prescribed)	2329.66(A)(7)
	Motor vehicle to $3,775	2329.66(A)(2)(b)
	Personal injury recoveries to $23,700, received during 12 months before filing	2329.66(A)(12)(c)
	Tuition credit or payment	2329.66(A)(16)
	Wrongful death recoveries for person debtor depended on, needed for support, received during 12 months before filing	2329.66(A)(12)(b)
public benefits	Crime victims' compensation, received during 12 months before filing	2329.66(A)(12)(a); 2743.66(D)
	Disability assistance payments	2329.66(A)(9)(f); 5115.07
	Child tax credit and earned income tax credit	2329.66(A)(9)(g)
	Public assistance	2329.66(A)(9)(d), (e); 5107.75; 5108.08
	Unemployment compensation	2329.66(A)(9)(c); 4141.32
	Vocational rehabilitation benefits	2329.66(A)(9)(a); 3304.19
	Workers' compensation	2329.66(A)(9)(b); 4123.67
tools of trade	Implements, books & tools of trade to $2,400	2329.66(A)(5)
wages	Minimum 75% of disposable weekly earnings or 30 times the federal hourly minimum wage, whichever is higher; bankruptcy judge may authorize more for low-income debtors. *In re Jones*, 318 B.R. 841 (Bankr. S.D. Ohio 2005)	2329.66(A)(13)
wildcard	$1,250 of any property	2329.66(A)(18)

Oklahoma

Federal bankruptcy exemptions not available. All law references are to Oklahoma Statutes Annotated (in the form "title number-section number"), unless otherwise noted.

ASSET	EXEMPTION	LAW
homestead	Real property or manufactured home to unlimited value; property cannot exceed 1 acre in city, town, or village, or 160 acres elsewhere; $5,000 limit if more than 25% of total sq. ft. area used for business purposes; okay to rent homestead as long as no other residence is acquired	31-1(A)(1); 31-1(A)(2); 31-2
insurance	Annuity benefits & cash value	36-3631.1
	Assessment or mutual benefits	36-2410
	Fraternal benefit society benefits	36-2718.1
	Funeral benefits prepaid & placed in trust	36-6125
	Group life policy or proceeds	36-3632
	Life, health, accident & mutual benefit insurance proceeds & cash value, if clause prohibits proceeds from being used to pay beneficiary's creditors	36-3631.1
	Limited stock insurance benefits	36-2510
miscellaneous	Alimony, child support	31-1(A)(19)
	Beneficiary's interest in a statutory support trust	6-3010
	Liquor license	37-532
	Property of business partnership	54-1-504
pensions	Tax-exempt retirement accounts, including 401(k)s, 403(b)s, profit-sharing and money purchase plans, SEP and SIMPLE IRAs, and defined-benefit plans	11 U.S.C. § 522(b)(3)(C)
	Traditional and Roth IRAs to $1,283,025 per person	11 U.S.C. § 522(b)(3)(C); (n)
	County employees	19-959
	Disabled veterans	31-7
	ERISA-qualified benefits, IRAs, Roth IRAs, Education IRAs & Keoghs	31-1(A)(20), (24)
	Firefighters	11-49-126
	Judges	20-1111
	Law enforcement employees	47-2-303.3
	Police officers	11-50-124
	Public employees	74-923
	Tax-exempt benefits	60-328
	Teachers	70-17-109
personal property	Books, portraits & pictures	31-1(A)(6)
	Burial plots	31-1(A)(4); 8-7
	Clothing to $4,000	31-1(A)(7)
	College savings plan interest	31-1A(24)
	Deposits in an IDA (Individual Development Account)	31-1A(22)
	Food & seed for growing to last 1 year	31-1(A)(17)
	Guns for household use to $2,000	31-1A(14)
	Health aids (professionally prescribed)	31-1(A)(9)
	Household & kitchen furniture; personal computer and related equipment	31-1(A)(3)
	Livestock for personal or family use: 5 dairy cows & calves under 6 months; 100 chickens; 20 sheep; 10 hogs; 2 horses, bridles & saddles; forage & feed to last 1 year	31-1(A)(10), (11), (12), (15), (16), (17)
	Motor vehicle to $7,500	31-1(A)(13)
	Personal injury & wrongful death recoveries to $50,000	31-1(A)(21)

personal property (continued)	Prepaid funeral benefits	36-6125(H)
	War bond payroll savings account	51-42
	Wedding and anniversary rings to $3,000	31-1(A)(8)
public benefits	Crime victims' compensation	21-142.13
	Public assistance	56-173
	Federal earned income tax credit	31-1(A)(23)
	Social Security	56-173
	Unemployment compensation	40-2-303
	Workers' compensation	85-48
tools of trade	Implements needed to farm homestead; tools, books & apparatus to $10,000 total	31-1(A)(5); 31-1(C)
wages	75% of wages earned in 90 days before filing bankruptcy; bankruptcy judge may allow more if you show hardship	12-1171.1; 31-1(A) (18); 31-1.1
wildcard	None	

Oregon

Federal bankruptcy exemptions available. All law references are to Oregon Revised Statutes unless otherwise noted.

ASSET	EXEMPTION	LAW
homestead	Prepaid rent & security deposit for renter's dwelling	*In re Casserino*, 379 F.3d 1069 (9th Cir. 2004)
	Real property of a soldier or sailor during time of war	408.440
	Real property you occupy or intend to occupy to $40,000 ($50,000 for joint owners); property cannot exceed 1 block in town or city or 160 acres elsewhere; sale proceeds exempt 1 year from sale if you intend to purchase another home or use sale proceeds for rent	18.395; 18.402; *In re Wynn*, 369 B.R. 605 (D. Or. 2007)
	Tenancy by entirety not exempt, but subject to survivorship rights of nondebtor spouse	*In re Pletz*, 225 B.R. 206 (D. Or. 1997)
insurance	Annuity contract benefits to $500 per month	743.049
	Fraternal benefit society benefits to $7,500	748.207; 18.348
	Group life policy or proceeds not payable to insured	743.047
	Health or disability proceeds or avails	743.050
	Life insurance proceeds or cash value if you are not the insured	743.046; 743.047
miscellaneous	Alimony, child support needed for support	18.345(1)(i)
	Liquor licenses	471.292 (1)
pensions	Tax-exempt retirement accounts, including 401(k)s, 403(b)s, profit-sharing and money purchase plans, SEP and SIMPLE IRAs, and defined-benefit plans	11 U.S.C. § 522(b)(3)(C)
	Traditional and Roth IRAs to $1,283,025 per person	11 U.S.C. § 522(b)(3)(C); (n)
	ERISA-qualified benefits, including IRAs & SEPs & payments to $7,500	18.358; 18.348
	Public officers', employees' pension payments to $7,500	237.980; 238.445; 18.348(2)
personal property	Books, pictures & musical instruments to $600 total	18.345(1)(a)
	Building materials for construction of an improvement	87.075
	Burial plot	65.870
	Clothing, jewelry & other personal items to $1,800 total	18.345(1)(b)
	Compensation for lost earnings payments for debtor or someone debtor depended on, to extent needed	18.345(1)(L),(3)

personal property (continued)	Books, pictures & musical instruments to $600 total	18.345(1)(a)
	Building materials for construction of an improvement	87.075
	Burial plot	65.870
	Clothing, jewelry & other personal items to $1,800 total	18.345(1)(b)
	Compensation for lost earnings payments for debtor or someone debtor depended on, to extent needed	18.345(1)(L),(3)
	Domestic animals, poultry & pets to $1,000 plus food to last 60 days (no doubling)	18.345(1)(e)
	Food & fuel to last 60 days if debtor is householder	18.345(1)(f)
	Furniture, household items, utensils, radios & TVs to $3,000 total (no doubling)	18.345(1)(f)
	Health aids	18.345(1)(h)
	Health savings accounts & medical savings accounts	18.345(1)(o)
	Higher education savings account to $7,500	348.863; 18.348(1)
	Motor vehicle to $3,000	18.345(1)(d),(3)
	Personal injury recoveries to $10,000	18.345(1)(k),(3)
	Pistol, rifle or shotgun (owned by person over 16) to $1,000	18.362
	Wages deposited into a bank account to $7,500; cash for sold exempt property	18.348; 18.385
public benefits	Aid to blind to $7,500	411.706; 411.760; 18.348
	Aid to disabled to $7,500	411.706; 411.760; 18.348
	Civil defense & disaster relief to $7,500	18.348
	Crime victims' compensation	18.345(1)(j),(3); 147.325
	Federal earned income tax credit	18.345(1)(n)
	General assistance to $7,500	411.760; 18.348
	Injured inmates' benefits to $7,500	655.530; 18.348
	Medical assistance to $7,500	414.095; 18.348
	Old-age assistance to $7,500	411.706; 411.760; 18.348
	Unemployment compensation to $7,500	657.855; 18.348
	Veterans benefits & proceeds of Veterans loans	407.125; 407.595; 18.348(m)
	Vocational rehabilitation to $7,500	344.580; 18.348
	Workers' compensation to $7,500	656.234; 18.348
tools of trade	Tools, library, team with food to last 60 days, to $5,000	18.345(1)(c), (3)
wages	75% of disposable wages or $170 per week, whichever is greater; bankruptcy judge may authorize more for low-income debtors	18.385
	Wages withheld in state employee's bond savings accounts. *In re Robinson*, 241 B.R. 447 (9th Cir. B.A.P. 1999)	292.070
wildcard	$400 of any personal property not already covered by existing exemption	18.345(1)(p)

Pennsylvania

Federal bankruptcy exemptions available. All law references are to Pennsylvania Consolidated Statutes Annotated unless otherwise noted.

ASSET	EXEMPTION	LAW
homestead	None; however, property held as tenancy by the entirety may be exempt against debts owed by only one spouse	*In re Martin*, 269 B.R. 119 (M.D. Pa. 2001)

insurance	Accident or disability benefits	42-8124(c)(7)
	Fraternal benefit society benefits	42-8124(c)(1), (8)
	Group life policy or proceeds	42-8124(c)(5)
	Insurance policy or annuity contract payments where insured is the beneficiary, cash value or proceeds to $100 per month	42-8124(c)(3)
	Life insurance & annuity proceeds if clause prohibits proceeds from being used to pay beneficiary's creditors	42-8214(c)(4)
	Life insurance annuity policy cash value or proceeds if beneficiary is insured's dependent, child or spouse	42-8124(c)(6)
	No-fault automobile insurance proceeds	42-8124(c)(9)
miscellaneous	Property of business partnership	15-8342
pensions	Tax-exempt retirement accounts, including 401(k)s, 403(b)s, profit-sharing and money purchase plans, SEP and SIMPLE IRAs, and defined-benefit plans	11 U.S.C. § 522(b)(3)(C)
	Traditional and Roth IRAs to $1,283,025 per person	11 U.S.C. § 522(b)(3)(C); (n)
	City employees	53-13445; 53-23572; 53-39383; 42-8124(b)(1)(iv)
	County employees	16-4716
	Municipal employees	53-881.115; 42-8124(b)(1)(vi)
	Police officers	53-764; 53-776; 53-23666; 42-8124(b)(1)(iii)
	Private retirement benefits to extent tax-deferred, if clause prohibits proceeds from being used to pay beneficiary's creditors; exemption limited to deposits of $15,000 per year made at least 1 year before filing (limit does not apply to rollovers from other exempt funds or accounts)	42-8124(b)(1)(vii), (viii), (ix)
	Public school employees	24-8533; 42-8124(b)(1)(i)
	State employees	71-5953; 42-8124(b)(1)(ii)
personal property	Bibles & schoolbooks	42-8124(a)(2)
	Clothing	42-8124(a)(1)
	Military uniforms & accoutrements	42-8124(a)(4); 51-4103
	Sewing machines	42-8124(a)(3)
public benefits	Crime victims' compensation	18-11.708
	Korean conflict veterans benefits	51-20098
	Unemployment compensation	42-8124(a)(10); 43-863
	Veterans benefits	51-20012; 20048; 20098; 20127
	Workers' compensation	42-8124(c)(2)
tools of trade	Seamstress's sewing machine	42-8124(a)(3)
wages	Earned but unpaid wages	42-8127
	Wages of victims of abuse	42-8127(f)
wildcard	$300 of any property, including cash, real property, securities, or proceeds from sale of exempt property	42-8123

Rhode Island

Federal bankruptcy exemptions available. All law references are to General Laws of Rhode Island unless otherwise noted.

ASSET	EXEMPTION	LAW
homestead	$500,000 in land & buildings you occupy or intend to occupy as a principal residence (spouse may not double)	9-26-4.1
insurance	Accident or sickness proceeds, avails, or benefits	27-18-24
	Fraternal benefit society benefits	27-25-18
	Life insurance proceeds if clause prohibits proceeds from being used to pay beneficiary's creditors	27-4-12
	Temporary disability insurance	28-41-32
miscellaneous	Earnings of a minor child	9-26-4(9)
	Property of business partnership	7-12-36
pensions	Tax-exempt retirement accounts, including 401(k)s, 403(b)s, profit-sharing and money purchase plans, SEP and SIMPLE IRAs, and defined-benefit plans	11 U.S.C. § 522(b)(3)(C)
	Traditional and Roth IRAs to $1,283,025 per person	11 U.S.C. § 522(b)(3)(C); (n)
	ERISA-qualified benefits	9-26-4(12)
	Firefighters	9-26-5
	IRAs & Roth IRAs	9-26-4(11)
	Police officers	9-26-5
	Private employees	28-17-4
	State & municipal employees	36-10-34
personal property	Beds, bedding, furniture, household goods & supplies, to $9,600 total (spouses may not double)	9-26-4(3); *In re Petrozella*, 247 B.R. 591 (R.I. 2000)
	Bibles & books to $300	9-26-4(4)
	Burial plot	9-26-4(5)
	Clothing	9-26-4(1)
	Consumer cooperative association holdings to $50	7-8-25
	Debt secured by promissory note or bill of exchange	9-26-4(7)
	Jewelry to $2,000	9-26-4 (14)
	Motor vehicles to $12,000	9-26-4 (13)
	Prepaid tuition program or tuition savings account	9-26-4 (15)
public benefits	Aid to blind, aged, disabled; general assistance	40-6-14
	Crime victims' compensation	12-25.1-3(b)(2)
	State disability benefits	28-41-32
	Unemployment compensation	28-44-58
	Veterans disability or survivors death benefits	30-7-9
	Workers' compensation	28-33-27
tools of trade	Library of practicing professional	9-26-4(2)
	Working tools to $2,000	9-26-4(2)
wages	Earned but unpaid wages due military member on active duty	30-7-9
	Earned but unpaid wages due seaman	9-26-4(6)
	Earned but unpaid wages to $50	9-26-4(8)(iii)
	Wages of any person who had been receiving public assistance are exempt for 1 year after going off of relief	9-26-4(8)(ii)
	Wages of spouse & minor children	9-26-4(9)
	Wages paid by charitable organization or fund providing relief to the poor	9-26-4(8)(i)
wildcard	$6,500 in any assets	9-26-4(16)

South Carolina

Federal bankruptcy exemptions not available. All law references are to Code of Laws of South Carolina unless otherwise noted. (Amounts adjusted for inflation in 2016 (15-41-30(B)).)

ASSET	EXEMPTION	LAW
homestead	Real property, including co-op, to $59,100 (single owner); $118,200 (multiple owners)	15-41-30(A)(1)
insurance	Accident & disability benefits	38-63-40(D)
	Benefits accruing under life insurance policy after death of insured, where proceeds left with insurance company pursuant to agreement; benefits not exempt from action to recover necessaries if parties agree	38-63-50
	Disability or illness benefits	15-41-30(A)(11)(C)
	Dividend, interest/loan value of unmatured life insurance contract to $4,725	15-41-30(A)(9)
	Fraternal benefit society benefits	38-38-330
	Group life insurance proceeds; cash value to $50,000	38-63-40(C); 38-65-90
	Life insurance avails from policy for person you depended on to $4,725	15-41-30(A)(9)
	Life insurance proceeds from policy for person you depended on, needed for support	15-41-30(A)(12)(c)
	Proceeds & cash surrender value of life insurance payable to beneficiary other than insured's estate & for the express benefit of insured's spouse, children, or dependents (must be purchased 2 years before filing) to $50,000	38-63-90
	Proceeds of life insurance or annuity contract	38-63-40(B)
	Unmatured life insurance contract, except credit insurance policy	15-41-30(A)(8)
miscellaneous	Alimony, child support	15-41-30(A)(11)(d)
	Property of business partnership	33-41-720
pensions	Tax-exempt retirement accounts, including 401(k)s, 403(b)s, profit-sharing and money purchase plans, SEP and SIMPLE IRAs, and defined-benefit plans	11 U.S.C. § 522(b)(3)(C)
	Traditional and Roth IRAs to $1,283,025 per person	11 U.S.C. § 522(b)(3)(C); (n)
	ERISA-qualified benefits; your share of the pension plan fund	15-41-30(10)(E), (14)
	Firefighters	9-13-230
	General assembly members	9-9-180
	IRAs & Roth IRAs	15-41-30(A)(13)
	Judges, solicitors	9-8-190
	Police officers	9-11-270
	Public employees	9-1-1680
personal property	Animals, crops, appliances, books, clothing, household goods, furnishings, musical instruments to $4,725 total	15-41-30(A)(3)
	Burial plot to $59,100, in lieu of homestead	15-41-30(1)
	Cash & other liquid assets to $5,900, in lieu of burial or homestead exemption	15-41-30(A)(5)
	College investment program trust fund	59-2-140
	Health aids	15-41-30(A)(10)
	Jewelry to $1,175	15-41-30(A)(4)
	Motor vehicle to $5,900	15-41-30(A)(2)
	Personal injury & wrongful death recoveries for person you depended on for support	15-41-30(A)(12)

public benefits	Crime victims' compensation	15-41-30(A)(12); 16-3-1300
	General relief; aid to aged, blind, disabled	43-5-190
	Local public assistance	15-41-30(A)(11)
	Social Security	15-41-30(A)(11)
	Unemployment compensation	15-41-30(A)(11)
	Veterans benefits	15-41-30(A)(11)
	Workers' compensation	42-9-360
tools of trade	Implements, books & tools of trade to $1,775	15-41-30(A)(6)
wages	None (use federal nonbankruptcy wage exemption)	15-41-30(A)(7)
wildcard	Up to $5,900 for any property from unused exemption amounts	15-41-30(A)(7)

South Dakota

Federal bankruptcy exemptions not available. All law references are to South Dakota Codified Law unless otherwise noted.

ASSET	EXEMPTION	LAW
homestead	Gold or silver mine, mill, or smelter not exempt	43-31-5
	May file homestead declaration	43-31-6
	Real property to unlimited value or mobile home (larger than 240 sq. ft. at its base & registered in state at least 6 months before filing) to unlimited value; property cannot exceed 1 acre in town or 160 acres elsewhere; sale proceeds to $60,000 ($170,000 if over age 70 or widow or widower who hasn't remarried) exempt for 1 year after sale (spouses may not double)	43-31-1; 43-31-2; 43-31-3; 43-31-4; 43-45-3
	Spouse or child of deceased owner may claim homestead exemption	43-31-13
insurance	Annuity contract proceeds to $250 per month	58-12-6; 58-12-8
	Endowment, life insurance, policy proceeds to $20,000; if policy issued by mutual aid or benevolent society, cash value to $20,000	58-12-4
	Fraternal benefit society benefits	58-37A-18
	Health benefits to $20,000	58-12-4
	Life insurance proceeds, if clause prohibits proceeds from being used to pay beneficiary's creditors	58-15-70
	Life insurance proceeds to $10,000, if beneficiary is surviving spouse or child	43-45-6
miscellaneous	Court-ordered alimony or support if not lump sum, up to $750 per month	43-45-2(9)
pensions	Tax-exempt retirement accounts, including 401(k)s, 403(b)s, profit-sharing and money purchase plans, SEP and SIMPLE IRAs, and defined-benefit plans	11 U.S.C. § 522(b)(3)(C)
	Traditional and Roth IRAs to $1,283,025 per person	11 U.S.C. § 522(b)(3)(C); (n)
	City employees	9-16-47
	ERISA-qualified benefits, limited to income & distribution on $1,000,000	43-45-16
	Public employees	3-12-115
personal property	Bible, schoolbooks; other books to $200	43-45-2(4)
	Burial plots, church pew	43-45-2(2), (3)
	Cemetery association property	47-29-25
	Clothing	43-45-2(5)
	Family pictures	43-45-2(1)
	Food & fuel to last 1 year	43-45-2(6)
	Health aids professionally prescribed	43-45-2(8)

public benefits	Crime victims' compensation	23A-28B-24
	Public assistance	28-7A-18
	Unemployment compensation	61-6-28
	Workers' compensation	62-4-42
tools of trade	None	
wages	Earned wages owed 60 days before filing bankruptcy, needed for support of family	15-20-12
	Wages of prisoners in work programs	24-8-10
wildcard	Head of family may claim $7,000, or nonhead of family may claim $5,000 of any personal property	43-45-4

Tennessee

Federal bankruptcy exemptions not available. All law references are to Tennessee Code Annotated unless otherwise noted.

ASSET	EXEMPTION	LAW
homestead	$5,000; $7,500 for joint owners; $25,000 if at least one dependent is a minor child (if 62 or older, $12,500 if single; $20,000 if married; $25,000 if spouse is also 62 or older)	26-2-301
	2–15-year lease	26-2-303
	Life estate	26-2-302
	Property held as tenancy by the entirety may be exempt against debts owed by only one spouse, but survivorship right is not exempt	*In re Arango*, 136 B.R. 740 aff'd, 992 F.2d 611 (6th Cir. 1993); *In re Arwood*, 289 B.R. 889 (Bankr. E.D. Tenn. 2003)
	Spouse or child of deceased owner may claim homestead exemption	26-2-301
insurance	Accident, health, or disability benefits for resident & citizen of Tennessee	26-2-110
	Disability or illness benefits	26-2-111(1)(C)
	Fraternal benefit society benefits	56-25-1403
	Life insurance or annuity	56-7-203
miscellaneous	Alimony, child support owed for 30 days before filing for bankruptcy	26-2-111(1)(E)
	Educational scholarship trust funds & prepayment plans	49-4-108; 49-7-822
pensions	Tax-exempt retirement accounts, including 401(k)s, 403(b)s, profit-sharing and money purchase plans, SEP and SIMPLE IRAs, and defined-benefit plans	11 U.S.C. § 522(b)(3)(C)
	Traditional and Roth IRAs to $1,283,025 per person	11 U.S.C. § 522(b)(3)(C); (n)
	ERISA-qualified benefits, IRAs & Roth IRAs	26-2-111(1)(D)
	Public employees	8-36-111
	State & local government employees	26-2-105
	Teachers	49-5-909
personal property	Bible, schoolbooks, family pictures & portraits	26-2-104
	Burial plot to 1 acre	26-2-305; 46-2-102
	Clothing & storage containers	26-2-104
	Health aids	26-2-111(5)
	Health savings accounts	26-2-105
	Lost future earnings payments for you or person you depended on	26-2-111(3)
	Personal injury recoveries to $7,500; wrongful death recoveries to $10,000 ($15,000 total for personal injury, wrongful death & crime victims' compensation)	26-2-111(2)(B), (C)
	Wages of debtor deserting family, in hands of family	26-2-109

public benefits	Aid to blind	71-4-117
	Aid to disabled	71-4-1112
	Crime victims' compensation to $5,000 (*see personal property*)	26-2-111(2)(A); 29-13-111
	Local public assistance	26-2-111(1)(A)
	Old-age assistance	71-2-216
	Relocation assistance payments	13-11-115
	Social Security	26-2-111(1)(A)
	Unemployment compensation	26-2-111(1)(A)
	Veterans benefits	26-2-111(1)(B)
	Workers' compensation	50-6-223
tools of trade	Implements, books & tools of trade to $1,900	26-2-111(4)
wages	Minimum 75% of disposable weekly earnings or 30 times the federal minimum hourly wage, whichever is more, plus $2.50 per week per child; bankruptcy judge may authorize more for low-income debtors. Note: *In re Lawrence*, 219 B.R. 786 (E.D. Tenn. 1998) ruled that wage garnishment is not an exemption in bankruptcy.	26-2-106, 107
wildcard	$10,000 of any personal property including deposits on account with any bank or financial institution	26-2-103

Texas

Federal bankruptcy exemptions available. All law references are to Texas Revised Civil Statutes Annotated unless otherwise noted.

ASSET	EXEMPTION	LAW
homestead	Unlimited; property cannot exceed 10 acres in town, village, city or 100 acres (200 for families) elsewhere; sale proceeds exempt for 6 months after sale (renting okay if another home not acquired, Prop. 41.003)	Prop. 41.001; 41.002; Const. Art. 16 §§ 50, 51
	If property acreage is larger than what is covered by homestead exemption, may have to file homestead declaration	Prop. 41.005; 41.021 to 41.023
insurance	Fraternal benefit society benefits	Ins. 885.316
	Life, health, accident, or annuity benefits, monies, policy proceeds & cash values due or paid to beneficiary or insured	Ins. 1108.051
	Texas employee uniform group insurance	Ins. 1551.011
	Texas public school employees group insurance	Ins. 1575.006
	Texas state college or university employee benefits	Ins. 1601.008
miscellaneous	Alimony & child support	Prop. 42.001(b)(3)
	Higher education savings plan trust account	Educ. 54.709(e)
	Liquor licenses & permits	Alco. Bev. Code 11.03
	Prepaid tuition plans	Educ. 54.639
pensions	Tax-exempt retirement accounts, including 401(k)s, 403(b)s, profit-sharing and money purchase plans, SEP and SIMPLE IRAs, and defined-benefit plans	11 U.S.C. § 522(b)(3)(C)
	Traditional and Roth IRAs to $1,283,025 per person	11 U.S.C. § 522(b)(3)(C); (n)
	County & district employees	Gov't. 811.006
	ERISA-qualified government or church benefits, including Keoghs, IRAs, & Roth IRAs	Prop. 42.0021
	Firefighters	6243e(5); 6243a-1(8.03); 6243b(15); 6243e(5); 6243e.1(1.04)

pensions (continued)	Judges	Gov't. 831.004
	Law enforcement officers, firefighters, emergency medical personnel survivors	Gov't. 615.005
	Municipal employees & elected officials, state employees	6243h(22); Gov't. 811.005
	Police officers	6243d-1(17); 6243j(20); 6243a-1(8.03); 6243b(15); 6243d-1(17)
	Retirement benefits to extent tax-deferred	Prop. 42.0021
	Teachers	Gov't. 821.005
personal property *to $100,000 total for family, $50,000 for single adult (include tools of trade in these aggregate limits)*	Athletic & sporting equipment, including bicycles	Prop. 42.002(a)(8)
	Bible or other book containing sacred writings of a religion (doesn't count toward $30,000 or $60,000 total)	Prop. 42.001(b)(4)
	Burial plots (exempt from total)	Prop. 41.001
	Clothing & food	Prop. 42.002(a)(2), (5)
	Health aids (exempt from total)	Prop. 42.001(b)(2)
	Health savings accounts	Prop. 42.0021
	Home furnishings including family heirlooms	Prop. 42.002(a)(1)
	Jewelry (limited to 25% of total exemption)	Prop. 42.002(a)(6)
	Pets & domestic animals plus their food: 2 horses, mules, or donkeys & tack; 12 head of cattle; 60 head of other livestock; 120 fowl	Prop. 42.002(a)(10), (11)
	1 two-, three- or four-wheeled motor vehicle per family member or per single adult who holds a driver's license; or, if not licensed, who relies on someone else to operate vehicle	Prop. 42.002(a)(9)
	2 firearms	Prop. 42.002(a)(7)
public benefits	Crime victims' compensation	Crim. Proc. 56.49
	Medical assistance	Hum. Res. 32.036
	Public assistance	Hum. Res. 31.040
	Unemployment compensation	Labor 207.075
	Workers' compensation	Labor 408.201
tools of trade *included in aggregate dollar limits for personal property*	Farming or ranching vehicles & implements	Prop. 42.002(a)(3)
	Tools, equipment (includes boat & motor vehicles used in trade) & books	Prop. 42.002(a)(4)
wages	Earned but unpaid wages	Prop. 42.001(b)(1)
	Unpaid commissions not to exceed 25% of total personal property exemptions	Prop. 42.001(d)
wildcard	None	

Utah

Federal bankruptcy exemptions not available. All law references are to Utah Code unless otherwise noted.

ASSET	EXEMPTION	LAW
homestead	Must file homestead declaration before attempted sale of home	78B-5-504
	Real property, mobile home, or water rights to $30,000 if primary residence; $5,000 if not primary residence	78B-5-504
	Sale proceeds exempt for 1 year	78B-5-503(5)(b)

insurance	Disability, illness, medical, or hospital benefits	78B-5-505(1)(a)(iii)
	Fraternal benefit society benefits	31A-9-603
	Life insurance policy cash surrender value, excluding payments made on the contract within the prior year	78B-5-505(i)(a)(xiii)
	Life insurance proceeds if beneficiary is insured's spouse or dependent, as needed for support	78B-5-505(i)(a)(xi)
	Medical, surgical & hospital benefits	78B-5-505(1)(a)(iv)
miscellaneous	Alimony needed for support	78B-5-505(a)(vi), (vii)
	Child support	78B-5-505(1) (f), (k)
pensions	Tax-exempt retirement accounts, including 401(k)s, 403(b)s, profit-sharing and money purchase plans, SEP and SIMPLE IRAs, and defined-benefit plans	11 U.S.C. § 522(b)(3)(C)
	Traditional and Roth IRAs to $1,283,025 per person	11 U.S.C. § 522(b)(3)(C); (n)
	ERISA-qualified benefits, IRAs, Roth IRAs & Keoghs (benefits that have accrued & contributions that have been made at least 1 year prior to filing)	78B-5-505(1)(a)(xiv)
	Other pensions & annuities needed for support	78-23-6(3)
	Public employees	49-11-612
personal property	Animals, books & musical instruments to $1,000	78B-5-506(1)(c)
	Artwork depicting, or done by, a family member	78B-5-505(1)(a)(ix)
	Bed, bedding, carpets	78B-5-505(1)(a)(viii)
	Burial plot	78B-5-505(1)(a)(i)
	Clothing (cannot claim furs or jewelry)	78B-5-505(1)(a)(viii)
	Dining & kitchen tables & chairs to $1,000	78B-5-505(1)(b)
	Firearms to $250	78B-5-506(1)(e)
	Food to last 12 months	78B-5-505(1)(a)(viii)
	Health aids	78B-5-505(1)(a)(ii)
	Heirlooms to $1,000	78B-5-506(1)(d)
	Motor vehicle to $3,000	78B-5-506(3)
	Personal injury, wrongful death recoveries for you or person you depended on	78B-5-505(1)(a)(x)
	Proceeds for sold, lost, or damaged exempt property	78B-5-507
	Refrigerator, freezer, microwave, stove, sewing machine, washer & dryer	78B-5-505(1)(a)(viii)
	Sofas, chairs & related furnishings to $1,000	78B-5-506(1)(a)
public benefits	Crime victims' compensation	63-25a-421(4)
	General assistance	35A-3-112
	Occupational disease disability benefits	34A-3-107
	Unemployment compensation	35A-4-103(4)(b)
	Veterans benefits	78B-5-505(1)(a)(v)
	Workers' compensation	34A-2-422
tools of trade	Implements, books & tools of trade to $5,000	78B-5-506(2)
	Military property of National Guard member	39-1-47
wages	Unpaid earnings due as of the bankruptcy filing date in an amount equal to $1/24$ of the median Utah annual income if paid more than once per month and $1/12$ if paid monthly	78B-5-505(1)(a)(xvi)
wildcard	None	

Vermont

Federal bankruptcy exemptions available. All law references are to Vermont Statutes Annotated unless otherwise noted.

ASSET	EXEMPTION	LAW
homestead	Property held as tenancy by the entirety may be exempt against debts owed by only one spouse	*In re McQueen*, 21 B.R. 736 (D. Ver. 1982)
	Real property or mobile home to $125,000; may also claim rents, issues, profits & outbuildings (spouses may not double); *D'Avignon v. Palmisano*, 34 B.R. 796 (D.Vt. 1982)	27-101
	Spouse of deceased owner may claim homestead exemption	27-105
insurance	Annuity contract benefits to $350 per month	8-3709
	Disability benefits that supplement life insurance or annuity contract	8-3707
	Disability or illness benefits needed for support	12-2740(19)(C)
	Fraternal benefit society benefits	8-4478
	Group life or health benefits	8-3708
	Health benefits to $200 per month	8-4086
	Life insurance proceeds for person you depended on	12-2740(19)(H)
	Life insurance proceeds if clause prohibits proceeds from being used to pay beneficiary's creditors	8-3705
	Life insurance proceeds if beneficiary is not the insured	8-3706
	Unmatured life insurance contract other than credit	12-2740(18)
miscellaneous	Alimony, child support	12-2740(19)(D)
pensions	Tax-exempt retirement accounts, including 401(k)s, 403(b)s, profit-sharing and money purchase plans, SEP and SIMPLE IRAs, and defined-benefit plans	11 U.S.C. § 522(b)(3)(C)
	Traditional and Roth IRAs to $1,283,025 per person	11 U.S.C. § 522(b)(3)(C); (n)
	Municipal employees	24-5066
	Other pensions	12-2740(19)(J)
	Self-directed accounts (IRAs, Roth IRAs, Keoghs); contributions must be made 1 year before filing	12-2740(16)
	State employees	3-476
	Teachers	16-1946
personal property	Appliances, furnishings, goods, clothing, books, crops, animals, musical instruments to $2,500 total	12-2740(5)
	Bank deposits to $700	12-2740(15)
	Cow, 2 goats, 10 sheep, 10 chickens & feed to last 1 winter; 3 swarms of bees plus honey; 5 tons coal or 500 gal. heating oil; 10 cords of firewood; 500 gal. bottled gas; growing crops to $5,000; yoke of oxen or steers, plow & ox yoke; 2 horses with harnesses, halters & chains	12-2740(6), (9)–(14)
	Health aids	12-2740(17)
	Jewelry to $500; wedding ring unlimited	12-2740(3), (4)
	Motor vehicles to $2,500	12-2740(1)
	Personal injury, lost future earnings, wrongful death recoveries for you or person you depended on	12-2740(19)(F), (G), (I)
	Stove, heating unit, refrigerator, freezer, water heater & sewing machines	12-2740(8)
public benefits	Aid to blind, aged, disabled; general assistance	33-124
	Crime victims' compensation needed for support	12-2740(19)(E)
	Social Security needed for support	12-2740(19)(A)
	Unemployment compensation	21-1367
	Veterans benefits needed for support	12-2740(19)(B)
	Workers' compensation	21-681

tools of trade	Books & tools of trade to $5,000	12-2740(2)
wages	Entire wages, if you received welfare during 2 months before filing	12-3170
	Minimum 75% of weekly disposable earnings or 30 times the federal minimum hourly wage, whichever is greater; bankruptcy judge may authorize more for low-income debtors. Note: The court in *In re Riendeau*, 293 B.R. 832 (D. Vt. 2002) held that Vermont's wage garnishment law does not create an exemption that can be used in bankruptcy.	12-3170
wildcard	Unused exemptions for motor vehicle, tools of trade, jewelry, household furniture, appliances, clothing & crops to $7,000	12-2740(7)
	$400 of any property	12-2740(7)

Virginia

Federal bankruptcy exemptions not available. All law references are to Code of Virginia unless otherwise noted.

ASSET	EXEMPTION	LAW
homestead	$5,000 plus $500 per dependent; rents & profits; sale proceeds exempt to $5,000 (unused portion of homestead may be applied to any personal property); exemption is $10,000 if over 65	*Cheeseman v. Nachman*, 656 F.2d 60 (4th Cir. 1981); 34-4; 34-18; 34-20
	May include mobile home	*In re Goad*, 161 B.R. 161 (W.D. Va. 1993)
	Must file homestead declaration before filing for bankruptcy	34-6
	Property held as tenancy by the entirety may be exempt against debts owed by only one spouse	*In re Bunker*, 312 F.3d 145 (4th Cir. 2002)
	Surviving spouse may claim $20,000; if no surviving spouse, minor children may claim exemption	64.2-311
insurance	Accident or sickness benefits	38.2-3406
	Burial society benefits	38.2-4021
	Cooperative life insurance benefits	38.2-3811
	Fraternal benefit society benefits	38.2-4118
	Group life or accident insurance for government officials	51.1-510
	Group life insurance policy or proceeds	38.2-3339
	Industrial sick benefits	38.2-3549
	Life insurance proceeds	38.2-3122
miscellaneous	Property of business partnership	50-73.108
	Unpaid spousal or child support	34-26(10)
pensions *see also wages*	Tax-exempt retirement accounts, including 401(k)s, 403(b)s, profit-sharing and money purchase plans, SEP and SIMPLE IRAs, and defined-benefit plans	11 U.S.C. § 522(b)(3)(C)
	Traditional and Roth IRAs to $1,283,025 per person	11 U.S.C. § 522(b)(3)(C); (n)
	City, town & county employees	51.1-802
	ERISA-qualified benefits to same extent permitted by federal bankruptcy law	34-34
	Judges	51.1-300
	State employees	51.1-124.4(A)
	State police officers	51.1-200

personal property	Bible	34-26(1)
	Burial plot	34-26(3)
	Clothing to $1,000	34-26(4)
	Family portraits & heirlooms to $5,000 total	34-26(2)
	Firearms to $3,000	34-26(4b)
	Health aids	34-26(6)
	Health savings accounts & medical savings accounts	38.2-5604
	Household furnishings to $5,000	34-26(4a)
	Motor vehicles to $6,000	34-26(8)
	Personal injury causes of action & recoveries	34-28.1
	Pets	34-26(5)
	Prepaid tuition contracts	23-38.81(E)
	Wedding & engagement rings	34-26(1a)
public benefits	Aid to blind, aged, disabled; general relief	63.2-506
	Crime victims' compensation unless seeking to discharge debt for treatment of injury incurred during crime	19.2-368.12
	Earned income tax credit or child tax credit	34-26(9)
	Payments to tobacco farmers	3.1-1111.1
	Unemployment compensation	60.2-600
	Workers' compensation	65.2-531
tools of trade	For farmer, pair of horses, or mules with gear; one wagon or cart, one tractor to $3,000; 2 plows & wedges; one drag, harvest cradle, pitchfork, rake; fertilizer to $1,000	34-27
	Tools, books & instruments of trade, including motor vehicles, to $10,000, needed in your occupation or education	34-26(7)
	Uniforms, arms, equipment of military member	44-96
wages	Minimum 75% of weekly disposable earnings or 40 times the federal minimum hourly wage, whichever is greater; bankruptcy judge may authorize more for low-income debtors	34-29
wildcard	Unused portion of homestead exemption	34-13
	$10,000 of any property for disabled veterans	34-4.1

Washington

Federal bankruptcy exemptions available. All law references are to Revised Code of Washington Annotated unless otherwise noted.

ASSET	EXEMPTION	LAW
homestead	Must record homestead declaration before sale of home if property unimproved or home unoccupied	6.15.040
	Real property or manufactured home to $125,000; unimproved property intended for residence to $15,000 (spouses may not double)	6.13.010; 6.13.030
insurance	Annuity contract proceeds to $2,500 per month	48.18.430
	Disability proceeds, avails, or benefits	48.36A.180
	Fraternal benefit society benefits	48.18.400
	Group life insurance policy or proceeds	48.18.420
	Life insurance proceeds or avails if beneficiary is not the insured	48.18.410

miscellaneous	Child support payments	6.15.010(1)(c)(iv)
pensions	Tax-exempt retirement accounts, including 401(k)s, 403(b)s, profit-sharing and money purchase plans, SEP and SIMPLE IRAs, and defined-benefit plans	11 U.S.C. § 522(b)(3)(C)
	Traditional and Roth IRAs to $1,283,025 per person	11 U.S.C. § 522(b)(3)(C); (n)
	City employees	41.28.200; 41.44.240
	ERISA-qualified benefits, IRAs, Roth IRAs & Keoghs	6.15.020
	Judges	2.10.180; 2.12.090
	Law enforcement officials & firefighters	41.26.053
	Police officers	41.20.180
	Public & state employees	41.40.052
	State patrol officers	43.43.310
	Teachers	41.32.052
	Volunteer firefighters	41.24.240
personal property	Appliances, furniture, household goods, home & yard equipment to $6,500 total for individual ($13,000 for community)	6.15.010(1)(c)(i)
	Books and electronic media to $3,500	6.15.010(1)(b)
	Burial ground	68.24.220
	Burial plots sold by nonprofit cemetery association	68.20.120
	Clothing, but no more than $3,500 in furs, jewelry, ornaments	6.15.010(1)(a)
	Fire insurance proceeds for lost, stolen, or destroyed exempt property	6.15.030
	Food & fuel for comfortable maintenance	6.15.010(1)(c)(i)
	Health aids prescribed	6.15.010(1)(c)(v)
	Health savings account & medical savings account deposits	6.15.020
	Keepsakes & family pictures	6.15.010(1)(b)
	Motor vehicle to $3,250 total for individual (two vehicles to $6,500 for community)	6.15.010(1)(c)(iii)
	Personal injury recoveries to $20,000	6.15.010(1)(c)(vi)
	Tuition units purchased more than 2 years before	6.15.010(1)(e)
public benefits	Child welfare	74.13.070
	Crime victims' compensation	7.68.070(10)
	General assistance	74.04.280
	Industrial insurance (workers' compensation)	51.32.040
	Old-age assistance	74.08.210
	Unemployment compensation	50.40.020
tools of trade	Farmer's trucks, stock, tools, seed, equipment & supplies to $10,000 total	6.15.010(1)(d)(i)
	Library, office furniture, office equipment & supplies of physician, surgeon, attorney, clergy, or other professional to $10,000 total	6.15.010(1)(d)(ii)
	Tools & materials used in any other trade to $10,000	6.15.010(1)(d)(iii)
wages	Minimum 75% of weekly disposable earnings or 30 times the federal minimum hourly wage, whichever is greater; bankruptcy judge may authorize more for low-income debtors	6.27.150
wildcard	$3,000 of any personal property (no more than $1,500 in cash, bank deposits, bonds, stocks & securities)	6.15.010(1)(c)(ii)

West Virginia

Federal bankruptcy exemptions not available. All law references are to West Virginia Code unless otherwise noted.

ASSET	EXEMPTION	LAW
homestead	Real or personal property used as residence to $25,000; unused portion of homestead may be applied to any property	38-10-4(a)
insurance	Fraternal benefit society benefits	33-23-21
	Group life insurance policy or proceeds	33-6-28
	Health or disability benefits	38-10-4(j)(3)
	Life insurance payments from policy for person you depended on, needed for support	38-10-4(k)(3)
	Unmatured life insurance contract, except credit insurance policy	38-10-4(g)
	Unmatured life insurance contract's accrued dividend, interest, or loan value to $8,000, if debtor owns contract & insured is either debtor or a person on whom debtor is dependent	38-10-4(h)
miscellaneous	Alimony, child support needed for support	38-10-4(j)(4)
pensions	Tax-exempt retirement accounts, including 401(k)s, 403(b)s, profit-sharing and money purchase plans, SEP and SIMPLE IRAs, and defined-benefit plans	11 U.S.C. § 522(b)(3)(C)
	Traditional and Roth IRAs to $1,283,025 per person	11 U.S.C. § 522(b)(3)(C); (n)
	ERISA-qualified benefits, IRAs needed for support	38-10-4(j)(5)
	Public employees	5-10-46
	Teachers	18-7A-30
personal property	Animals, crops, clothing, appliances, books, household goods, furnishings, musical instruments to $400 per item, $8,000 total	38-10-4(c)
	Burial plot to $25,000, in lieu of homestead	38-10-4(a)
	Health aids	38-10-4(i)
	Jewelry to $1,000	38-10-4(d)
	Lost earnings payments needed for support	38-10-4(k)(5)
	Motor vehicle to $2,400	38-10-4(b)
	Personal injury recoveries to $15,000	38-10-4(k)(4)
	Prepaid higher education tuition trust fund & savings plan payments	38-10-4(k)(6)
	Wrongful death recoveries for person you depended on, needed for support	38-10-4(k)(2)
public benefits	Aid to blind, aged, disabled; general assistance	9-5-1
	Crime victims' compensation	38-10-4(k)(1)
	Social Security	38-10-4(j)(1)
	Unemployment compensation	38-10-4(j)(1)
	Veterans benefits	38-10-4(j)(2)
	Workers' compensation	23-4-18
tools of trade	Implements, books & tools of trade to $1,500	38-10-4(f)
wages	Minimum 30 times the federal minimum hourly wage per week; bankruptcy judge may authorize more for low-income debtors	38-5A-3
wildcard	$800 plus unused portion of homestead or burial exemption, of any property	38-10-4(e)

Wisconsin

Federal bankruptcy exemptions available. All law references are to Wisconsin Statutes Annotated unless otherwise noted.

ASSET	EXEMPTION	LAW
homestead	Property you occupy or intend to occupy to $75,000; $150,000 for married couples filing jointly; sale proceeds exempt for 2 years if you intend to purchase another home (spouses may not double)	815.20
insurance	Federal disability insurance benefits	815.18(3)(ds)
	Fire and casualty insurance (2 years from receipt)	815.18(e)
	Fraternal benefit society benefits	614.96
	Life insurance proceeds for someone debtor depended on, needed for support	815.18(3)(i)(a)
	Life insurance proceeds held in trust by insurer, if clause prohibits proceeds from being used to pay beneficiary's creditors	632.42
	Unmatured life insurance contract (except credit insurance contract) if debtor owns contract & insured is debtor or dependents, or someone debtor is dependent on	815.18(3)(f)
	Unmatured life insurance contract's accrued dividends, interest, or loan value to $150,000 total, if debtor owns contract & insured is debtor or dependents, or someone debtor is dependent on (to $4,000 if issued less than 2 years prior)	815.18(3)(f)
miscellaneous	Alimony, child support needed for support	815.18(3)(c)
	Property of business partnership	178.21(3)(c)
pensions	Tax-exempt retirement accounts, including 401(k)s, 403(b)s, profit-sharing and money purchase plans, SEP and SIMPLE IRAs, and defined-benefit plans	11 U.S.C. § 522(b)(3)(C)
	Traditional and Roth IRAs to $1,283,025 per person	11 U.S.C. § 522 (b)(3)(C); (n)
	Certain municipal employees	62.63(4)
	Firefighters, police officers who worked in city with population over 100,000	815.18(3)(ef)
	Military pensions	815.18(3)(n)
	Private or public retirement benefits	815.18(3)(j)
	Public employees	40.08(1)
personal property	Burial plot, tombstone, coffin	815.18(3)(a)
	College savings account or tuition trust fund	815.18(3)(o)(p)
	Deposit accounts to $5,000	815.18(3)(o)(p)
	Fire & casualty proceeds for destroyed exempt property for 2 years from receiving	815.18(3)(e)
	Household goods & furnishings, clothing, keepsakes, jewelry, appliances, books, musical instruments, firearms, sporting goods, animals & other tangible personal property to $12,000 total	815.18(3)(d)
	Lost future earnings recoveries, needed for support	815.18(3)(i)(d)
	Motor vehicles to $4,000; unused portion of $12,000 personal property exemption may be added	815.18(3)(g)
	Personal injury recoveries to $50,000	815.18(3)(i)(c)
	Tenant's lease or stock interest in housing co-op, to homestead amount	182.004(6)
	Wages used to purchase savings bonds	20.921(1)(e)
	Wrongful death recoveries, needed for support	815.18(3)(i)(b)

public benefits	Crime victims' compensation	949.07
	Social services payments	49.96
	Unemployment compensation	108.13
	Veterans benefits	45.03(8)(b)
	Workers' compensation	102.27
tools of trade	Equipment, inventory, farm products, books & tools of trade to $15,000 total	815.18(3)(b)
wages	75% of weekly net income or 30 times the greater of the federal or state minimum hourly wage; bankruptcy judge may authorize more for low-income debtors	815.18(3)(h)
	Wages of county jail prisoners	303.08(3)
	Wages of county work camp prisoners	303.10(7)
	Wages of inmates under work-release plan	303.065(4)(b)
wildcard	None	

Wyoming

Federal bankruptcy exemptions not available. All law references are to Wyoming Statutes Annotated unless otherwise noted.

ASSET	EXEMPTION	LAW
homestead	Property held as tenancy by the entirety may be exempt against debts owed by only one spouse	*In re Anselmi*, 52 B.R. 479 (D. Wy. 1985)
	Real property or a house trailer you occupy to $20,000	1-20-101; 102; 104
	Spouse or child of deceased owner may claim homestead exemption	1-20-103
insurance	Annuity contract proceeds to $350 per month	26-15-132
	Disability benefits if clause prohibits proceeds from being used to pay beneficiary's creditors	26-15-130
	Fraternal benefit society benefits	26-29-218
	Group life or disability policy or proceeds, cash surrender & loan values, premiums waived & dividends	26-15-131
	Individual life insurance policy proceeds, cash surrender & loan values, premiums waived & dividends	26-15-129
	Life insurance proceeds held by insurer, if clause prohibits proceeds from being used to pay beneficiary's creditors	26-15-133
miscellaneous	Liquor licenses & malt beverage permits	12-4-604
pensions	Tax-exempt retirement accounts, including 401(k)s, 403(b)s, profit-sharing and money purchase plans, SEP and SIMPLE IRAs, and defined-benefit plans	11 U.S.C. § 522(b)(3)(C)
	Traditional and Roth IRAs to $1,283,025 per person	11 U.S.C. § 522 (b)(3)(C); (n)
	Criminal investigators, highway officers	9-3-620
	Firefighters' death benefits	15-5-209
	Game & fish wardens	9-3-620
	Police officers	15-5-313(c)
	Private or public retirement funds & accounts including IRAs, Roth IRAs and SEP IRAs	1-20-110
	Public employees	9-3-426

personal property	Bedding, furniture, household articles & food to $4,000 per person in the home	1-20-106(a)(iii)
	Bible, schoolbooks & pictures	1-20-106(a)(i)
	Burial plot	1-20-106(a)(ii)
	Clothing & wedding rings to $2,000	1-20-105
	Medical savings account contributions	1-20-111
	Motor vehicle to $5,000	1-20-106(a)(iv)
	3 firearms and ammunition (1,000 rounds per firearm) to $3,000	1-20-106(a)(v)
	Prepaid funeral contracts	26-32-102
public benefits	Crime victims' compensation	1-40-113
	General assistance	42-2-113(b)
	Unemployment compensation	27-3-319
	Workers' compensation	27-14-702
tools of trade	Library & implements of profession to $4,000 or tools, motor vehicle, implements, team & stock in trade to $4,000	1-20-106(b)
wages	Earnings of National Guard members	19-9-401
	Minimum 75% of disposable weekly earnings or 30 times the federal hourly minimum wage, whichever is more	1-15-511; 1-15-408; 40-14-505
	Wages of inmates in adult community corrections program	7-18-114
	Wages of inmates in correctional industries program	25-13-107
	Wages of inmates on work release	7-16-308
wildcard	None	

Federal Bankruptcy Exemptions

Spouses filing jointly may double all exemptions. All references are to 11 U.S.C. § 522. These exemptions were last adjusted in 2016. Every three years ending on April 1, these amounts will be adjusted to reflect changes in the Consumer Price Index. Debtors in the following states may select the federal bankruptcy exemptions:

Alaska	Hawaii	Minnesota	New York	Texas
Arkansas	Kentucky	New Hampshire	Oregon	Vermont
Connecticut	Massachusetts	New Jersey	Pennsylvania	Washington
District of Columbia	Michigan	New Mexico	Rhode Island	Wisconsin

ASSET	EXEMPTION	SUBSECTION
homestead	Real property, including co-op or mobile home, or burial plot to $23,675; unused portion of homestead to $11,850 may be applied to any property	(d)(1); (d)(5)
insurance	Disability, illness, or unemployment benefits	(d)(10)(C)
	Life insurance payments from policy for person you depended on, needed for support	(d)(11)(C)
	Life insurance policy with loan value, in accrued dividends or interest, to $12,625	(d)(8)
	Unmatured life insurance contract, except credit insurance policy	(d)(7)
miscellaneous	Alimony, child support needed for support	(d)(10)(D)
pensions	Tax exempt retirement accounts (including 401(k)s, 403(b)s, profit-sharing and money purchase plans, SEP and SIMPLE IRAs, and defined-benefit plans)	(b)(3)(C)
	IRAs and Roth IRAs to $1,283,025 per person	(b)(3)(C)(n)
personal property	Animals, crops, clothing, appliances, books, furnishings, household goods, musical instruments to $600 per item, $12,625 total	(d)(3)
	Health aids	(d)(9)
	Jewelry to $1,600	(d)(4)
	Lost earnings payments	(d)(11)(E)

personal property (continued)	Motor vehicle to $3,775	(d)(2)
	Personal injury recoveries to $23,675 (not to include pain & suffering or pecuniary loss)	(d)(11)(D)
	Wrongful death recoveries for person you depended on	(d)(11)(B)
public benefits	Crime victims' compensation	(d)(11)(A)
	Public assistance	(d)(10)(A)
	Social Security	(d)(10)(A)
	Unemployment compensation	(d)(10)(A)
	Veterans benefits	(d)(10)(A)
tools of trade	Implements, books & tools of trade to $2,375	(d)(6)
wages	None	
wildcard	$1,250 of any property	(d)(5)
	Up to $11,850 of unused homestead exemption amount, for any property	(d)(5)

Federal Nonbankruptcy Exemptions

These exemptions are available only if you select your state exemptions. You may use them for any exemptions in addition to those allowed by your state, but they cannot be claimed if you file using federal bankruptcy exemptions. All law references are to the United States Code.

ASSET	EXEMPTION	LAW
death & disability benefits	Government employees	5 § 8130
	Longshoremen & harbor workers	33 § 916
	War risk, hazard, death, or injury compensation	42 § 1717
miscellaneous	Debts of seaman incurred while on a voyage	46 § 11111
	Indian lands or homestead sales or lease proceeds	25 § 410; 412a
	Klamath Indian tribe benefits for Indians residing in Oregon; agricultural or grazing lands to $5,000	25 §§ 543; 545
	Life insurance benefits for serviceman's Group Life Ins. or Veteran's Group Life Ins.	38 § 1970(g)
	Military deposits in savings accounts while on permanent duty outside U.S.	10 § 1035
	Military group life insurance	38 § 1970(g)
	Railroad workers' unemployment insurance	45 § 352(e)
	Seamen's clothing	46 § 11110
	Seamen's wages (except for spousal and child support)	46 § 11109
	Minimum 75% of disposable weekly earnings or 30 times the federal minimum hourly wage, whichever is more; bankruptcy judge may authorize more for low-income debtors	15 § 1673
retirement	CIA employees	50 § 403
	Civil service employees	5 § 8346
	Foreign Service employees	22 § 4060
	Military Medal of Honor roll pensions	38 § 1562(c)
	Military service employees	10 § 1440
	Railroad workers	45 § 231m
	Social Security	42 § 407
	Veterans benefits	38 § 5301
survivors benefits	Judges, U.S. court & judicial center directors, administrative assistants to U.S. Supreme Court Chief Justice	28 § 376
	Lighthouse workers	33 § 775
	Military service	10 § 1450

Chart and Sample Forms

Median Family Income Chart (as of November 1, 2017)

State	Family Size				State	Family Size			
	1 Earner	2 People	3 People	4 People*		1 Earner	2 People	3 People	4 People*
Alabama	$45,432	$53,206	$60,739	$75,978	Montana	$48,210	$60,691	$71,942	$82,460
Alaska	$62,199	$85,915	$85,915	$102,997	Nebraska	$45,837	$67,535	$76,648	$85,885
Arizona	$47,360	$60,761	$62,013	$74,317	Nevada	$48,144	$60,906	$65,701	$75,783
Arkansas	$41,164	$50,594	$57,426	$69,807	New Hampshire	$63,185	$74,274	$90,338	$113,508
California	$53,644	$71,636	$77,412	$89,444	New Jersey	$64,901	$79,363	$96,126	$118,697
Colorado	$56,698	$74,305	$83,180	$94,472	New Mexico	$42,010	$56,497	$56,497	$62,509
Connecticut	$62,814	$82,253	$96,608	$117,344	New York	$52,024	$66,667	$79,154	$96,527
Delaware	$51,797	$64,826	$77,345	$90,892	North Carolina	$45,469	$56,742	$64,977	$76,382
DC	$55,330	$107,097	$107,097	$107,097	North Dakota	$50,622	$72,105	$78,599	$95,893
Florida	$45,703	$56,759	$61,600	$72,958	Ohio	$47,582	$59,565	$69,058	$83,515
Georgia	$45,142	$58,363	$65,900	$78,368	Oklahoma	$45,206	$57,207	$63,622	$70,144
Hawaii	$63,137	$72,867	$88,706	$97,849	Oregon	$52,385	$63,830	$75,005	$88,448
Idaho	$49,096	$57,984	$64,889	$72,299	Pennsylvania	$51,960	$62,359	$77,306	$91,692
Illinois	$51,317	$67,254	$78,559	$94,472	Rhode Island	$50,602	$67,649	$80,509	$105,447
Indiana	$46,802	$59,392	$69,235	$79,296	South Carolina	$44,786	$57,131	$60,191	$75,946
Iowa	$49,158	$64,221	$74,895	$91,006	South Dakota	$44,992	$62,984	$73,988	$86,452
Kansas	$49,630	$63,754	$72,221	$83,723	Tennessee	$44,886	$54,596	$62,533	$73,604
Kentucky	$42,808	$52,202	$61,388	$75,416	Texas	$46,253	$61,831	$67,849	$76,933
Louisiana	$42,341	$50,732	$58,757	$76,237	Utah	$57,771	$63,480	$74,479	$81,794
Maine	$49,805	$60,191	$77,047	$91,184	Vermont	$52,414	$66,109	$79,385	$89,657
Maryland	$64,352	$84,268	$96,105	$115,826	Virginia	$58,759	$72,749	$85,194	$101,389
Massachusetts	$61,353	$78,508	$96,698	$121,280	Washington	$62,054	$73,447	$84,823	$100,282
Michigan	$48,626	$59,541	$70,579	$87,070	West Virginia	$44,849	$50,948	$60,409	$72,767
Minnesota	$53,474	$72,734	$85,979	$105,651	Wisconsin	$48,521	$63,739	$76,378	$93,500
Mississippi	$39,231	$48,931	$53,476	$62,564	Wyoming	$55,831	$68,533	$70,868	$90,270
Missouri	$45,518	$57,570	$68,627	$81,445	* Add $8,400 for each individual in excess of 4.				

Median Family Income Chart (as of November 1, 2017) (continued)				
Commonwealth or U.S. Territory	Family Size			
	1 Earner	2 People	3 People	4 People*
Guam	$40,152	$48,008	$54,708	$66,204
Northern Mariana Islands	$26,964	$26,964	$31,370	$46,139
Puerto Rico	$23,945	$23,945	$24,043	$32,338
Virgin Islands	$31,857	$38,288	$40,824	$44,725

* Add $8,400 for each individual in excess of 4.

Schedule J: Your Expenses

Check if this is:

☐ An amended filing
☐ A supplement showing postpetition chapter 13
   expenses as of the following date:

_____
MM / DD / YYYY

Official Form 106J

Schedule J: Your Expenses

12/15

Be as complete and accurate as possible. If two married people are filing together, both are equally responsible for supplying correct information. If more space is needed, attach another sheet to this form. On the top of any additional pages, write your name and case number (if known). Answer every question.

Part 1: Describe Your Household

1. **Is this a joint case?**

   ☐ No. Go to line 2.
   ☐ Yes. **Does Debtor 2 live in a separate household?**

      ☐ No
      ☐ Yes. Debtor 2 must file Official Form 106J-2, *Expenses for Separate Household of Debtor 2.*

2. **Do you have dependents?**

   Do not list Debtor 1 and Debtor 2.

   Do not state the dependents' names

   ☐ No
   ☐ Yes. Fill out this information for each dependent..........

Dependent's relationship to Debtor 1 or Debtor 2	Dependent's age	Does dependent live with you?
_____	_____	☐ No ☐ Yes
_____	_____	☐ No ☐ Yes
_____	_____	☐ No ☐ Yes
_____	_____	☐ No ☐ Yes
_____	_____	☐ No ☐ Yes

3. **Do your expenses include expenses of people other than yourself and your dependents?**

   ☐ No
   ☐ Yes

Part 2: Estimate Your Ongoing Monthly Expenses

Estimate your expenses as of your bankruptcy filing date unless you are using this form as a supplement in a Chapter 13 case to report expenses as of a date after the bankruptcy is filed. If this is a supplemental *Schedule J*, check the box at the top of the form and fill in the applicable date.

Include expenses paid for with non-cash government assistance if you know the value of such assistance and have included it on *Schedule I: Your Income* (Official Form 106I.)

Your expenses

4. **The rental or home ownership expenses for your residence.** Include first mortgage payments and any rent for the ground or lot.   4. $_____

   If not included in line 4:

   4a. Real estate taxes   4a. $_____

   4b. Property, homeowner's, or renter's insurance   4b. $_____

   4c. Home maintenance, repair, and upkeep expenses   4c. $_____

   4d. Homeowner's association or condominium dues   4d. $_____

Schedule J: Your Expenses (page 2)

Debtor 1 _____   Case number *(If known)*_____
First Name   Middle Name   Last Name

		Your expenses

5. **Additional mortgage payments for your residence,** such as home equity loans   5. $_____

6. **Utilities:**
   6a. Electricity, heat, natural gas   6a. $_____
   6b. Water, sewer, garbage collection   6b. $_____
   6c. Telephone, cell phone, Internet, satellite, and cable services   6c. $_____
   6d. Other. Specify: _____   6d. $_____

7. **Food and housekeeping supplies**   7. $_____
8. **Childcare and children's education costs**   8. $_____
9. **Clothing, laundry, and dry cleaning**   9. $_____
10. **Personal care products and services**   10. $_____
11. **Medical and dental expenses**   11. $_____
12. **Transportation.** Include gas, maintenance, bus or train fare. Do not include car payments.   12. $_____
13. **Entertainment, clubs, recreation, newspapers, magazines, and books**   13. $_____
14. **Charitable contributions and religious donations**   14. $_____
15. **Insurance.** Do not include insurance deducted from your pay or included in lines 4 or 20.
   15a. Life insurance   15a. $_____
   15b. Health insurance   15b. $_____
   15c. Vehicle insurance   15c. $_____
   15d. Other insurance. Specify:_____   15d. $_____

16. **Taxes.** Do not include taxes deducted from your pay or included in lines 4 or 20.
   Specify: _____   16. $_____

17. **Installment or lease payments:**
   17a. Car payments for Vehicle 1   17a. $_____
   17b. Car payments for Vehicle 2   17b. $_____
   17c. Other. Specify:_____   17c. $_____
   17d. Other. Specify:_____   17d. $_____

18. **Your payments of alimony, maintenance, and support that you did not report as deducted from your pay on line 5, *Schedule I, Your Income* (Official Form 106I).**   18. $_____

19. **Other payments you make to support others who do not live with you.**
   Specify:_____   19. $_____

20. **Other real property expenses not included in lines 4 or 5 of this form or on *Schedule I: Your Income.***
   20a. Mortgages on other property   20a. $_____
   20b. Real estate taxes   20b. $_____
   20c. Property, homeowner's, or renter's insurance   20c. $_____
   20d. Maintenance, repair, and upkeep expenses   20d. $_____
   20e. Homeowner's association or condominium dues   20e. $_____

Schedule J: Your Expenses (page 3)

Debtor 1 _____

First Name   Middle Name   Last Name

Case number *(if known)*_____

21. **Other**. Specify: _____   21.   **+$**_____

22. **Calculate your monthly expenses.**

    22a. Add lines 4 through 21.   22a. $_____

    22b. Copy line 22 (monthly expenses for Debtor 2), if any, from Official Form 106J-2   22b. $_____

    22c. Add line 22a and 22b. The result is your monthly expenses.   22c. $_____

23. **Calculate your monthly net income.**

    23a. Copy line 12 (*your combined monthly income*) from *Schedule I.*   23a. $_____

    23b. Copy your monthly expenses from line 22c above.   23b.   **–** $_____

    23c. Subtract your monthly expenses from your monthly income.
The result is your *monthly net income*.   23c. $_____

24. **Do you expect an increase or decrease in your expenses within the year after you file this form?**

For example, do you expect to finish paying for your car loan within the year or do you expect your mortgage payment to increase or decrease because of a modification to the terms of your mortgage?

❑ No.

❑ Yes.   Explain here:

Form 122A-1: *Chapter 7 Statement of Your Current Monthly Income*

Fill in this information to identify your case:	Check one box only as directed in this form and in Form 122A-1Supp:

Fill in this information to identify your case:

Debtor 1 _____
       First Name   Middle Name   Last Name

Debtor 2 _____
(Spouse, if filing) First Name   Middle Name   Last Name

United States Bankruptcy Court for the: _____ District of _____

Case number _____
(If known)

Check one box only as directed in this form and in Form 122A-1Supp:

❑ 1. There is no presumption of abuse.

❑ 2. The calculation to determine if a presumption of abuse applies will be made under *Chapter 7 Means Test Calculation* (Official Form 122A–2).

❑ 3. The Means Test does not apply now because of qualified military service but it could apply later.

❑ Check if this is an amended filing

Official Form 122A—1

Chapter 7 Statement of Your Current Monthly Income

12/15

Be as complete and accurate as possible. If two married people are filing together, both are equally responsible for being accurate. If more space is needed, attach a separate sheet to this form. Include the line number to which the additional information applies. On the top of any additional pages, write your name and case number (if known). If you believe that you are exempted from a presumption of abuse because you do not have primarily consumer debts or because of qualifying military service, complete and file *Statement of Exemption from Presumption of Abuse Under § 707(b)(2)* (Official Form 122A-1Supp) with this form.

Part 1:	Calculate Your Current Monthly Income

1. **What is your marital and filing status?** Check one only.

   ❑ **Not married.** Fill out Column A, lines 2-11.

   ❑ **Married and your spouse is filing with you.** Fill out both Columns A and B, lines 2-11.

   ❑ **Married and your spouse is NOT filing with you.** You and your spouse are:

       ❑ **Living in the same household and are not legally separated.** Fill out both Columns A and B, lines 2-11.

       ❑ **Living separately or are legally separated.** Fill out Column A, lines 2-11; do not fill out Column B. By checking this box, you declare under penalty of perjury that you and your spouse are legally separated under nonbankruptcy law that applies or that you and your spouse are living apart for reasons that do not include evading the Means Test requirements. 11 U.S.C. § 707(b)(7)(B).

Fill in the average monthly income that you received from all sources, derived during the 6 full months before you file this bankruptcy case. 11 U.S.C. § 101(10A). For example, if you are filing on September 15, the 6-month period would be March 1 through August 31. If the amount of your monthly income varied during the 6 months, add the income for all 6 months and divide the total by 6. Fill in the result. Do not include any income amount more than once. For example, if both spouses own the same rental property, put the income from that property in one column only. If you have nothing to report for any line, write $0 in the space.

		Column A Debtor 1	Column B Debtor 2 or non-filing spouse
2.	**Your gross wages, salary, tips, bonuses, overtime, and commissions** (before all payroll deductions).	$ _____	$ _____
3.	**Alimony and maintenance payments.** Do not include payments from a spouse if Column B is filled in.	$ _____	$ _____
4.	**All amounts from any source which are regularly paid for household expenses of you or your dependents, including child support.** Include regular contributions from an unmarried partner, members of your household, your dependents, parents, and roommates. Include regular contributions from a spouse only if Column B is not filled in. Do not include payments you listed on line 3.	$ _____	$ _____

5. **Net income from operating a business, profession, or farm**

	Debtor 1	Debtor 2			
Gross receipts (before all deductions)	$ _____	$ _____			
Ordinary and necessary operating expenses	– $ _____	– $ _____			
Net monthly income from a business, profession, or farm	$ _____	$ _____	Copy here ➔	$ _____	$ _____

6. **Net income from rental and other real property**

	Debtor 1	Debtor 2			
Gross receipts (before all deductions)	$ _____	$ _____			
Ordinary and necessary operating expenses	– $ _____	– $ _____			
Net monthly income from rental or other real property	$ _____	$ _____	Copy here ➔	$ _____	$ _____

7.	**Interest, dividends, and royalties**	$ _____	$ _____

Form 122A-1: *Chapter 7 Statement of Your Current Monthly Income* (page 2)

Debtor 1 _____   Case number *(if known)* _____
       First Name   Middle Name   Last Name

	Column A Debtor 1	Column B Debtor 2 or non-filing spouse

8. **Unemployment compensation** $_____ $_____

    Do not enter the amount if you contend that the amount received was a benefit
    under the Social Security Act. Instead, list it here: .... ↓

        For you .... $_____

        For your spouse... $_____

9. **Pension or retirement income.** Do not include any amount received that was a
    benefit under the Social Security Act. $_____ $_____

10. **Income from all other sources not listed above.** Specify the source and amount.
    Do not include any benefits received under the Social Security Act or payments received
    as a victim of a war crime, a crime against humanity, or international or domestic
    terrorism. If necessary, list other sources on a separate page and put the total below.

    _____ $_____ $_____

    _____ $_____ $_____

    Total amounts from separate pages, if any.   + $_____   + $_____

11. **Calculate your total current monthly income.** Add lines 2 through 10 for each
    column. Then add the total for Column A to the total for Column B. $_____   + $_____   = $_____
                                                                                        Total current
                                                                                       monthly income

Part 2:   Determine Whether the Means Test Applies to You

12. **Calculate your current monthly income for the year.** Follow these steps:

    12a.   Copy your total current monthly income from line 11. .... **Copy line 11 here** → $_____

            Multiply by 12 (the number of months in a year).   **x 12**

    12b.   The result is your annual income for this part of the form.   12b. $_____

13. **Calculate the median family income that applies to you.** Follow these steps:

    Fill in the state in which you live.   [_____]

    Fill in the number of people in your household.   [_____]

    Fill in the median family income for your state and size of household. .... 13. $_____
    To find a list of applicable median income amounts, go online using the link specified in the separate
    instructions for this form. This list may also be available at the bankruptcy clerk's office.

14. **How do the lines compare?**

    14a. ☐   Line 12b is less than or equal to line 13. On the top of page 1, check box 1, *There is no presumption of abuse.*
               Go to Part 3.

    14b. ☐   Line 12b is more than line 13. On the top of page 1, check box 2, *The presumption of abuse is determined by Form 122A-2.*
               Go to Part 3 and fill out Form 122A–2.

Part 3:   Sign Below

    By signing here, I declare under penalty of perjury that the information on this statement and in any attachments is true and correct.

✗ _____   ✗ _____
   Signature of Debtor 1   Signature of Debtor 2

   Date _____   Date _____
      MM / DD / YYYY   MM / DD / YYYY

    If you checked line 14a, do NOT fill out or file Form 122A–2.

    If you checked line 14b, fill out Form 122A–2 and file it with this form.

Form 122A-2: *Chapter 7 Means Test Calculation*

Fill in this information to identify your case:

Debtor 1 _____
First Name   Middle Name   Last Name

Debtor 2 _____
(Spouse, if filing) First Name   Middle Name   Last Name

United States Bankruptcy Court for the: _____ District of _____

Case number _____
(If known)

Check the appropriate box as directed in lines 40 or 42:

According to the calculations required by this Statement:

☐ 1. There is no presumption of abuse.

☐ 2. There is a presumption of abuse.

☐ Check if this is an amended filing

Official Form 122A–2

Chapter 7 Means Test Calculation

04/16

To fill out this form, you will need your completed copy of *Chapter 7 Statement of Your Current Monthly Income* (Official Form 122A-1).

Be as complete and accurate as possible. If two married people are filing together, both are equally responsible for being accurate. If more space is needed, attach a separate sheet to this form. Include the line number to which the additional information applies. On the top of any additional pages, write your name and case number (if known).

Part 1: Determine Your Adjusted Income

1. Copy your total current monthly income..Copy line 11 from Official Form 122A-1 here ➔ .... $_____

2. **Did you fill out Column B in Part 1 of Form 122A–1?**

☐ No. Fill in $0 for the total on line 3

☐ Yes. Is your spouse filing with you?

☐ No. Go to line 3.

☐ Yes. Fill in $0 for the total on line 3.

3. **Adjust your current monthly income by subtracting any part of your spouse's income not used to pay for the household expenses of you or your dependents.** Follow these steps:

On line 11, Column B of Form 122A–1, was any amount of the income you reported for your spouse NOT regularly used for the household expenses of you or your dependents?

☐ No. Fill in 0 for the total on line 3.

☐ Yes. Fill in the information below:

State each purpose for which the income was used For example, the income is used to pay your spouse's tax debt or to support people other than you or your dependents	Fill in the amount you are subtracting from your spouse's income
_____	$_____
_____	$_____
_____	+ $_____
Total.	$_____ Copy total here .... ➔ – $_____

4. **Adjust your current monthly income.** Subtract the total on line 3 from line 1.

$_____

Form 122A-2: *Chapter 7 Means Test Calculation* (page 2)

Debtor 1 _____ Case number *(if known)* _____
First Name   Middle Name   Last Name

Part 2: Calculate Your Deductions from Your Income

The Internal Revenue Service (IRS) issues National and Local Standards for certain expense amounts. Use these amounts to answer the questions in lines 6-15. To find the IRS standards, go online using the link specified in the separate instructions for this form. This information may also be available at the bankruptcy clerk's office.

Deduct the expense amounts set out in lines 6-15 regardless of your actual expense. In later parts of the form, you will use some of your actual expenses if they are higher than the standards. Do not deduct any amounts that you subtracted from your spouse's income in line 3 and do not deduct any operating expenses that you subtracted from income in lines 5 and 6 of Form 122A–1.

If your expenses differ from month to month, enter the average expense.

Whenever this part of the form refers to *you*, it means both you and your spouse if Column B of Form 122A–1 is filled in.

5. **The number of people used in determining your deductions from income**

   Fill in the number of people who could be claimed as exemptions on your federal income tax return, plus the number of any additional dependents whom you support. This number may be different from the number of people in your household.

National Standards You must use the IRS National Standards to answer the questions in lines 6-7.

6. **Food, clothing, and other items:** Using the number of people you entered in line 5 and the IRS National Standards, fill in the dollar amount for food, clothing, and other items. $_____

7. **Out-of-pocket health care allowance:** Using the number of people you entered in line 5 and the IRS National Standards, fill in the dollar amount for out-of-pocket health care. The number of people is split into two categories—people who are under 65 and people who are 65 or older—because older people have a higher IRS allowance for health care costs. If your actual expenses are higher than this IRS amount, you may deduct the additional amount on line 22.

   People who are under 65 years of age

   7a. Out-of-pocket health care allowance per person $_____

   7b. Number of people who are under 65 X _____

   7c. **Subtotal.** Multiply line 7a by line 7b. $_____ Copy here➔ $_____

   People who are 65 years of age or older

   7d. Out-of-pocket health care allowance per person $_____

   7e. Number of people who are 65 or older X _____

   7f. **Subtotal.** Multiply line 7d by line 7e. $_____ Copy here➔ + $_____

   7g. **Total.** Add lines 7c and 7f.. $_____ Copy total here➔ $_____

Form 122A-2: *Chapter 7 Means Test Calculation* (page 3)

Debtor 1 _____   Case number *(if known)*_____
　　　　　First Name　　Middle Name　　Last Name

Local Standards	You must use the IRS Local Standards to answer the questions in lines 8-15.

Based on information from the IRS, the U.S. Trustee Program has divided the IRS Local Standard for housing for bankruptcy purposes into two parts:

■ **Housing and utilities – Insurance and operating expenses**
■ **Housing and utilities – Mortgage or rent expenses**

To answer the questions in lines 8-9, use the U.S. Trustee Program chart.

To find the chart, go online using the link specified in the separate instructions for this form. This chart may also be available at the bankruptcy clerk's office.

8. **Housing and utilities – Insurance and operating expenses:** Using the number of people you entered in line 5, fill in the dollar amount listed for your county for insurance and operating expenses. .... $_____

9. **Housing and utilities – Mortgage or rent expenses:**

   9a. Using the number of people you entered in line 5, fill in the dollar amount listed for your county for mortgage or rent expenses.. $_____

   9b. Total average monthly payment for all mortgages and other debts secured by your home.

   To calculate the total average monthly payment, add all amounts that are contractually due to each secured creditor in the 60 months after you file for bankruptcy. Then divide by 60.

Name of the creditor	Average monthly payment
_____	$_____
_____	$_____
_____	+ $_____
Total average monthly payment	$_____

Copy here ➔   − $_____   Repeat this amount on line 33a.

   9c. Net mortgage or rent expense.

   Subtract line 9b (*total average monthly payment*) from line 9a (*mortgage or rent expense*). If this amount is less than $0, enter $0. .... $_____   Copy here ➔ $_____

10. If you claim that the U.S. Trustee Program's division of the IRS Local Standard for housing is incorrect and affects the calculation of your monthly expenses, fill in any additional amount you claim. $_____

   Explain why: _____
   _____

11. **Local transportation expenses:** Check the number of vehicles for which you claim an ownership or operating expense.

   ☐ 0. Go to line 14.
   ☐ 1. Go to line 12.
   ☐ 2 or more. Go to line 12.

12. **Vehicle operation expense:** Using the IRS Local Standards and the number of vehicles for which you claim the operating expenses, fill in the *Operating Costs* that apply for your Census region or metropolitan statistical area. $_____

Form 122A-2: *Chapter 7 Means Test Calculation* (page 4)

Debtor 1 _____   Case number *(if known)*_____
        First Name   Middle Name   Last Name

13. **Vehicle ownership or lease expense:** Using the IRS Local Standards, calculate the net ownership or lease expense for each vehicle below. You may not claim the expense if you do not make any loan or lease payments on the vehicle. In addition, you may not claim the expense for more than two vehicles.

    Vehicle 1   **Describe Vehicle 1:** _____
    _____

13a. Ownership or leasing costs using IRS Local Standard. .... $_____

13b. Average monthly payment for all debts secured by Vehicle 1.
Do not include costs for leased vehicles.

To calculate the average monthly payment here and on line 13e, add all amounts that are contractually due to each secured creditor in the 60 months after you filed for bankruptcy. Then divide by 60.

Name of each creditor for Vehicle 1	Average monthly payment
_____	$_____
_____	**+** $_____
Total average monthly payment	$_____

Copy here ➔   — $_____   Repeat this amount on line 33b.

13c. Net Vehicle 1 ownership or lease expense
Subtract line 13b from line 13a. If this amount is less than $0, enter $0. .... $_____   Copy net Vehicle 1 expense here ..... ➔ $_____

    Vehicle 2   **Describe Vehicle 2:** _____
    _____

13d. Ownership or leasing costs using IRS Local Standard. .... $_____

13e. Average monthly payment for all debts secured by Vehicle 2.
Do not include costs for leased vehicles.

Name of each creditor for Vehicle 2	Average monthly payment
_____	$_____
_____	**+** $_____
Total average monthly payment	$_____

Copy here ➔   — $_____   Repeat this amount on line 33c.

13f. Net Vehicle 2 ownership or lease expense
Subtract line 13e from 13d. If this amount is less than $0, enter $0. .... $_____   Copy net Vehicle 2 expense here ... ➔ $_____

14. **Public transportation expense**: If you claimed 0 vehicles in line 11, using the IRS Local Standards, fill in the *Public Transportation* expense allowance regardless of whether you use public transportation. $_____

15. **Additional public transportation expense**: If you claimed 1 or more vehicles in line 11 and if you claim that you may also deduct a public transportation expense, you may fill in what you believe is the appropriate expense, but you may not claim more than the IRS Local Standard for *Public Transportation*. $_____

Form 122A-2: *Chapter 7 Means Test Calculation* (page 5)

Debtor 1 _____ Case number *(if known)*_____
    First Name   Middle Name   Last Name

Other Necessary Expenses	In addition to the expense deductions listed above, you are allowed your monthly expenses for the following IRS categories.

16. **Taxes:** The total monthly amount that you will actually owe for federal, state and local taxes, such as income taxes, self-employment taxes, Social Security taxes, and Medicare taxes. You may include the monthly amount withheld from your pay for these taxes. However, if you expect to receive a tax refund, you must divide the expected refund by 12 and subtract that number from the total monthly amount that is withheld to pay for taxes. $_____

    Do not include real estate, sales, or use taxes.

17. **Involuntary deductions:** The total monthly payroll deductions that your job requires, such as retirement contributions, union dues, and uniform costs.

    Do not include amounts that are not required by your job, such as voluntary 401(k) contributions or payroll savings. $_____

18. **Life insurance:** The total monthly premiums that you pay for your own term life insurance. If two married people are filing together, include payments that you make for your spouse's term life insurance. Do not include premiums for life insurance on your dependents, for a non-filing spouse's life insurance, or for any form of life insurance other than term. $_____

19. **Court-ordered payments:** The total monthly amount that you pay as required by the order of a court or administrative agency, such as spousal or child support payments.

    Do not include payments on past due obligations for spousal or child support. You will list these obligations in line 35. $_____

20. **Education:** The total monthly amount that you pay for education that is either required:

    ■ as a condition for your job, or

    ■ for your physically or mentally challenged dependent child if no public education is available for similar services. $_____

21. **Childcare:** The total monthly amount that you pay for childcare, such as babysitting, daycare, nursery, and preschool.

    Do not include payments for any elementary or secondary school education. $_____

22. **Additional health care expenses, excluding insurance costs:** The monthly amount that you pay for health care that is required for the health and welfare of you or your dependents and that is not reimbursed by insurance or paid by a health savings account. Include only the amount that is more than the total entered in line 7.
    Payments for health insurance or health savings accounts should be listed only in line 25. $_____

23. **Optional telephones and telephone services:** The total monthly amount that you pay for telecommunication services for you and your dependents, such as pagers, call waiting, caller identification, special long distance, or business cell phone service, to the extent necessary for your health and welfare or that of your dependents or for the production of income, if it is not reimbursed by your employer.   + $_____

    Do not include payments for basic home telephone, internet and cell phone service. Do not include self-employment expenses, such as those reported on line 5 of Official Form 122A-1, or any amount you previously deducted.

24. **Add all of the expenses allowed under the IRS expense allowances.**
    Add lines 6 through 23. $_____

Form 122A-2: *Chapter 7 Means Test Calculation* (page 6)

Debtor 1 _____ Case number *(if known)*_____
First Name   Middle Name   Last Name

Additional Expense Deductions	These are additional deductions allowed by the Means Test.
	Note: Do not include any expense allowances listed in lines 6-24.

25. **Health insurance, disability insurance, and health savings account expenses.** The monthly expenses for health insurance, disability insurance, and health savings accounts that are reasonably necessary for yourself, your spouse, or your dependents.

    Health insurance $_____

    Disability insurance $_____

    Health savings account   + $_____

    Total $_____   Copy total here➜ .... $_____

    Do you actually spend this total amount?

    ☐ No. How much do you actually spend? $_____
    ☐ Yes

26. **Continuing contributions to the care of household or family members.** The actual monthly expenses that you will continue to pay for the reasonable and necessary care and support of an elderly, chronically ill, or disabled member of your household or member of your immediate family who is unable to pay for such expenses. These expenses may include contributions to an account of a qualified ABLE program. 26 U.S.C. § 529A(b). $_____

27. **Protection against family violence.** The reasonably necessary monthly expenses that you incur to maintain the safety of you and your family under the Family Violence Prevention and Services Act or other federal laws that apply. $_____

    By law, the court must keep the nature of these expenses confidential.

28. **Additional home energy costs.** Your home energy costs are included in your insurance and operating expenses on line 8.

    If you believe that you have home energy costs that are more than the home energy costs included in expenses on line 8, then fill in the excess amount of home energy costs. $_____

    You must give your case trustee documentation of your actual expenses, and you must show that the additional amount claimed is reasonable and necessary.

29. **Education expenses for dependent children who are younger than 18.** The monthly expenses (not more than $160.42* per child) that you pay for your dependent children who are younger than 18 years old to attend a private or public elementary or secondary school.

    You must give your case trustee documentation of your actual expenses, and you must explain why the amount claimed is reasonable and necessary and not already accounted for in lines 6-23. $_____

    * Subject to adjustment on 4/01/19, and every 3 years after that for cases begun on or after the date of adjustment.

30. **Additional food and clothing expense.** The monthly amount by which your actual food and clothing expenses are higher than the combined food and clothing allowances in the IRS National Standards. That amount cannot be more than 5% of the food and clothing allowances in the IRS National Standards. $_____

    To find a chart showing the maximum additional allowance, go online using the link specified in the separate instructions for this form. This chart may also be available at the bankruptcy clerk's office.

    You must show that the additional amount claimed is reasonable and necessary.

31. **Continuing charitable contributions.** The amount that you will continue to contribute in the form of cash or financial instruments to a religious or charitable organization. 26 U.S.C. § 170(c)(1)-(2).   + $_____

32. **Add all of the additional expense deductions.**
    Add lines 25 through 31. $_____

Form 122A-2: *Chapter 7 Means Test Calculation* (page 7)

Debtor 1 _____
First Name   Middle Name   Last Name

Case number *(if known)*_____

Deductions for Debt Payment

33. **For debts that are secured by an interest in property that you own, including home mortgages, vehicle loans, and other secured debt, fill in lines 33a through 33e.**

    To calculate the total average monthly payment, add all amounts that are contractually due to each secured creditor in the 60 months after you file for bankruptcy. Then divide by 60.

	Average monthly payment

    Mortgages on your home:

    33a. Copy line 9b here .... ➔ $_____

    Loans on your first two vehicles:

    33b. Copy line 13b here. .... ➔ $_____

    33c. Copy line 13e here. .... ➔ $_____

    33d. List other secured debts:

Name of each creditor for other secured debt	Identify property that secures the debt	Does payment include taxes or insurance?	
_____	_____	☐ No ☐ Yes	$_____
_____	_____	☐ No ☐ Yes	$_____
_____	_____	☐ No ☐ Yes	+ $_____

    33e. Total average monthly payment. Add lines 33a through 33d................... $_____   Copy total here ➔ $_____

34. **Are any debts that you listed in line 33 secured by your primary residence, a vehicle, or other property necessary for your support or the support of your dependents?**

    ☐ No. Go to line 35.

    ☐ Yes. State any amount that you must pay to a creditor, in addition to the payments listed in line 33, to keep possession of your property (called the *cure amount*). Next, divide by 60 and fill in the information below.

Name of the creditor	Identify property that secures the debt	Total cure amount		Monthly cure amount
_____	_____	$_____	÷ 60 =	$_____
_____	_____	$_____	÷ 60 =	$_____
_____	_____	$_____	÷ 60 =	+ $_____
		Total		$_____ Copy total here ➔ $_____

35. **Do you owe any priority claims such as a priority tax, child support, or alimony — that are past due as of the filing date of your bankruptcy case?** 11 U.S.C. § 507.

    ☐ No. Go to line 36.

    ☐ Yes. Fill in the total amount of all of these priority claims. Do not include current or ongoing priority claims, such as those you listed in line 19.

    Total amount of all past-due priority claims .... $_____   ÷ 60 = $_____

Form 122A-2: *Chapter 7 Means Test Calculation* (page 8)

Debtor 1 _____   Case number *(if known)*_____
First Name   Middle Name   Last Name

36. **Are you eligible to file a case under Chapter 13?** 11 U.S.C. § 109(e).
For more information, go online using the link for *Bankruptcy Basics* specified in the separate
instructions for this form. *Bankruptcy Basics* may also be available at the bankruptcy clerk's office.

   ☐ No. Go to line 37.

   ☐ Yes. Fill in the following information.

   Projected monthly plan payment if you were filing under Chapter 13 $_____

   Current multiplier for your district as stated on the list issued by the
   Administrative Office of the United States Courts (for districts in Alabama and
   North Carolina) or by the Executive Office for United States Trustees (for all
   other districts).   x _____

   To find a list of district multipliers that includes your district, go online using the
   link specified in the separate instructions for this form. This list may also be
   available at the bankruptcy clerk's office.

   Average monthly administrative expense if you were filing under Chapter 13 $_____ Copy total here➔ $_____

37. **Add all of the deductions for debt payment.**
Add lines 33e through 36. .... $_____

Total Deductions from Income

38. **Add all of the allowed deductions.**

   Copy line 24, *All of the expenses allowed under IRS
   expense allowances* .... $_____

   Copy line 32, *All of the additional expense deductions*.......... $_____

   Copy line 37, *All of the deductions for debt payment*............. **+** $_____

   Total deductions $_____   Copy total here ....➔ $_____

Part 3:   Determine Whether There Is a Presumption of Abuse

39. **Calculate monthly disposable income for 60 months**

   39a. Copy line 4, *adjusted current monthly income* ..... $_____

   39b. Copy line 38, *Total deductions*..........   **−** $_____

   39c. Monthly disposable income. 11 U.S.C. § 707(b)(2).
   Subtract line 39b from line 39a. $_____   Copy here➔ $_____

   For the next 60 months (5 years)...   x 60

   39d. **Total**. Multiply line 39c by 60. .... $_____   Copy here➔ $_____

40. **Find out whether there is a presumption of abuse.** Check the box that applies:

   ☐ **The line 39d is less than $7,700*.** On the top of page 1 of this form, check box 1, *There is no presumption of abuse*. Go
   to Part 5.

   ☐ **The line 39d is more than $12,850*.** On the top of page 1 of this form, check box 2, *There is a presumption of abuse*. You
   may fill out Part 4 if you claim special circumstances. Then go to Part 5.

   ☐ **The line 39d is at least $7,700*, but not more than $12,850*.** Go to line 41.

   * Subject to adjustment on 4/01/19, and every 3 years after that for cases filed on or after the date of adjustment.

Official Form 122A–2   **Chapter 7 Means Test Calculation**   page **8**

Form 122A-2: *Chapter 7 Means Test Calculation* (page 9)

Debtor 1 _____   Case number *(if known)*_____
First Name   Middle Name   Last Name

41. 41a. **Fill in the amount of your total nonpriority unsecured debt.** If you filled out *A Summary of Your Assets and Liabilities and Certain Statistical Information Schedules* (Official Form 106Sum), you may refer to line 3b on that form.. $_____

x .25

41b. **25% of your total nonpriority unsecured debt.** 11 U.S.C. § 707(b)(2)(A)(i)(I).
Multiply line 41a by 0.25. .... $_____ Copy here➜ $_____

42. **Determine whether the income you have left over after subtracting all allowed deductions is enough to pay 25% of your unsecured, nonpriority debt.**
Check the box that applies:

❑ **Line 39d is less than line 41b.** On the top of page 1 of this form, check box 1, *There is no presumption of abuse.* Go to Part 5.

❑ **Line 39d is equal to or more than line 41b.** On the top of page 1 of this form, check box 2, *There is a presumption of abuse.* You may fill out Part 4 if you claim special circumstances. Then go to Part 5.

Part 4:   **Give Details About Special Circumstances**

43. **Do you have any special circumstances that justify additional expenses or adjustments of current monthly income for which there is no reasonable alternative?** 11 U.S.C. § 707(b)(2)(B).

❑ No. Go to Part 5.
❑ Yes. Fill in the following information. All figures should reflect your average monthly expense or income adjustment for each item. You may include expenses you listed in line 25.

You must give a detailed explanation of the special circumstances that make the expenses or income adjustments necessary and reasonable. You must also give your case trustee documentation of your actual expenses or income adjustments.

Give a detailed explanation of the special circumstances	Average monthly expense or income adjustment
_____	$_____
_____	$_____
_____	$_____
_____	$_____

Part 5:   **Sign Below**

By signing here, I declare under penalty of perjury that the information on this statement and in any attachments is true and correct.

✘ _____   ✘ _____
Signature of Debtor 1   Signature of Debtor 2

Date _____   Date _____
     MM / DD / YYYY   MM / DD / YYYY

Form 122A-1Supp: *Statement of Exemption from Presumption of Abuse Under § 707(b)(2)*

Fill in this information to identify your case:

Debtor 1 _____
First Name   Middle Name   Last Name

Debtor 2 _____
(Spouse, if filing) First Name   Middle Name   Last Name

United States Bankruptcy Court for the: _____ District of _____

Case number _____
(If known)

☐ Check if this is an amended filing

Official Form 122A—1Supp

Statement of Exemption from Presumption of Abuse Under § 707(b)(2) 12/15

File this supplement together with *Chapter 7 Statement of Your Current Monthly Income* (Official Form 122A-1), if you believe that you are exempted from a presumption of abuse. Be as complete and accurate as possible. If two married people are filing together, and any of the exclusions In this statement applies to only one of you, the other person should complete a separate Form 122A-1 if you believe that this is required by 11 U.S.C. § 707(b)(2)(C).

Part 1: **Identify the Kind of Debts You Have**

1. **Are your debts primarily consumer debts?** *Consumer debts* are defined in 11 U.S.C. § 101(8) as "incurred by an individual primarily for a personal, family, or household purpose." Make sure that your answer is consistent with the answer you gave at line 16 of the *Voluntary Petition for Individuals Filing for Bankruptcy* (Official Form 101).

     ☐ No. Go to Form 122A-1; on the top of page 1 of that form, check box 1, *There is no presumption of abuse,* and sign Part 3. Then submit this supplement with the signed Form 122A-1.

     ☐ Yes. Go to Part 2.

Part 2: **Determine Whether Military Service Provisions Apply to You**

2. **Are you a disabled veteran** (as defined in 38 U.S.C. § 3741(1))**?**

     ☐ No. Go to line 3.

     ☐ Yes. Did you incur debts mostly while you were on active duty or while you were performing a homeland defense activity?
     10 U.S.C. § 101(d)(1); 32 U.S.C. § 901(1).

          ☐ No. Go to line 3.

          ☐ Yes. Go to Form 122A-1; on the top of page 1 of that form, check box 1, *There is no presumption of abuse,* and sign Part 3. Then submit this supplement with the signed Form 122A-1.

3. **Are you or have you been a Reservist or member of the National Guard?**
     ☐ No. Complete Form 122A-1. Do not submit this supplement.
     ☐ Yes. Were you called to active duty or did you perform a homeland defense activity? 10 U.S.C. § 101(d)(1); 32 U.S.C. § 901(1).

          ☐ No. Complete Form 122A-1. Do not submit this supplement.
          ☐ Yes. Check any one of the following categories that applies:

               ☐ **I was called to active duty after September 11, 2001,** for at least 90 days and remain on active duty.

               ☐ **I was called to active duty after September 11, 2001,** for at least 90 days and was released from active duty on _____, which is fewer than 540 days before I file this bankruptcy case.

               ☐ **I am performing a homeland defense activity for at least 90 days.**

               ☐ **I performed a homeland defense activity for at least 90 days,** ending on _____, which is fewer than 540 days before I file this bankruptcy case.

If you checked one of the categories to the left, go to Form 122A-1. On the top of page 1 of Form 122A-1, check box 3, *The Means Test does not apply now,* and sign Part 3. Then submit this supplement with the signed Form 122A-1. You are not required to fill out the rest of Official Form 122A-1 during the exclusion period. The *exclusion period* means the time you are on active duty or are performing a homeland defense activity, and for 540 days afterward. 11 U.S.C. § 707(b)(2)(D)(ii).

If your exclusion period ends before your case is closed, you may have to file an amended form later.

Form 122C-1: *Chapter 13 Statement of Your Current Monthly Income and Calculation of Commitment Period*

Fill in this information to identify your case:

Debtor 1 _____
First Name   Middle Name   Last Name

Debtor 2 _____
(Spouse, if filing) First Name   Middle Name   Last Name

United States Bankruptcy Court for the: _____ District of _____
(State)

Case number _____
(If known)

Check as directed in lines 17 and 21:

According to the calculations required by this Statement:

☐ 1. Disposable income is not determined under 11 U.S.C. § 1325(b)(3).

☐ 2. Disposable income is determined under 11 U.S.C. § 1325(b)(3).

☐ 3. The commitment period is 3 years.

☐ 4. The commitment period is 5 years.

☐ Check if this is an amended filing

Official Form 122C–1

Chapter 13 Statement of Your Current Monthly Income and Calculation of Commitment Period

12/15

Be as complete and accurate as possible. If two married people are filing together, both are equally responsible for being accurate. If more space is needed, attach a separate sheet to this form. Include the line number to which the additional information applies. On the top of any additional pages, write your name and case number (if known).

Part 1: **Calculate Your Average Monthly Income**

1. **What is your marital and filing status?** Check one only.

   ☐ **Not married.** Fill out Column A, lines 2-11.

   ☐ **Married.** Fill out both Columns A and B, lines 2-11.

   Fill in the average monthly income that you received from all sources, derived during the 6 full months before you file this bankruptcy case. 11 U.S.C. § 101(10A). For example, if you are filing on September 15, the 6-month period would be March 1 through August 31. If the amount of your monthly income varied during the 6 months, add the income for all 6 months and divide the total by 6. Fill in the result. Do not include any income amount more than once. For example, if both spouses own the same rental property, put the income from that property in one column only. If you have nothing to report for any line, write $0 in the space.

	Column A Debtor 1	Column B Debtor 2 or non-filing spouse
2. **Your gross wages, salary, tips, bonuses, overtime, and commissions** (before all payroll deductions).	$_____	$_____
3. **Alimony and maintenance payments.** Do not include payments from a spouse.	$_____	$_____
4. **All amounts from any source which are regularly paid for household expenses of you or your dependents, including child support.** Include regular contributions from an unmarried partner, members of your household, your dependents, parents, and roommates. Include regular contributions from a spouse only if Column B is not filled in. Do not include payments you listed on line 3.	$_____	$_____

5. **Net income from operating a business, profession, or farm**

   Gross receipts (before all deductions) $_____

   Ordinary and necessary operating expenses   – $_____

   Net monthly income from a business, profession, or farm $_____ Copy here ➔ $_____ $_____

6. **Net income from rental and other real property**

   Gross receipts (before all deductions) $_____

   Ordinary and necessary operating expenses   – $_____

   Net monthly income from rental or other real property $_____ Copy here ➔ $_____ $_____

Form 122C-1: *Chapter 13 Statement of Your Current Monthly Income and Calculation of Commitment Period* (page 2)

Debtor 1 _____
First Name   Middle Name   Last Name

Case number *(if known)*_____

	Column A Debtor 1	Column B Debtor 2 or non-filing spouse
7. **Interest, dividends, and royalties**	$_____	$_____
8. **Unemployment compensation**	$_____	$_____

Do not enter the amount if you contend that the amount received was a benefit under the Social Security Act. Instead, list it here: .... ↓

For you... $_____

For your spouse .... $_____

9. **Pension or retirement income.** Do not include any amount received that was a benefit under the Social Security Act.

$_____ $_____

10. **Income from all other sources not listed above.** Specify the source and amount. Do not include any benefits received under the Social Security Act or payments received as a victim of a war crime, a crime against humanity, or international or domestic terrorism. If necessary, list other sources on a separate page and put the total below.

_____ $_____ $_____

_____ $_____ $_____

Total amounts from separate pages, if any.   + $_____   + $_____

11. **Calculate your total average monthly income.** Add lines 2 through 10 for each column. Then add the total for Column A to the total for Column B.

$_____ + $_____ = $_____

**Total average
monthly income**

Part 2:   Determine How to Measure Your Deductions from Income

12. **Copy your total average monthly income from line 11.** .... $_____

13. **Calculate the marital adjustment.** Check one:

☐ You are not married. Fill in 0 below.

☐ You are married and your spouse is filing with you. Fill in 0 below.

☐ You are married and your spouse is not filing with you.

Fill in the amount of the income listed in line 11, Column B, that was NOT regularly paid for the household expenses of you or your dependents, such as payment of the spouse's tax liability or the spouse's support of someone other than you or your dependents.

Below, specify the basis for excluding this income and the amount of income devoted to each purpose. If necessary, list additional adjustments on a separate page.

If this adjustment does not apply, enter 0 below.

_____ $_____

_____ $_____

_____   + $_____

Total... $_____   Copy here ➔   − _____

14. **Your current monthly income.** Subtract the total in line 13 from line 12. $_____

15. **Calculate your current monthly income for the year.** Follow these steps:

15a. Copy line 14 here ➔ .... $_____

Multiply line 15a by 12 (the number of months in a year).   x 12

15b. The result is your current monthly income for the year for this part of the form. .... $_____

Form 122C-1: *Chapter 13 Statement of Your Current Monthly Income and Calculation of Commitment Period* (page 3)

Debtor 1 _____   Case number *(if known)*_____
           First Name   Middle Name   Last Name

16. **Calculate the median family income that applies to you.** Follow these steps:

  16a. Fill in the state in which you live.   _____

  16b. Fill in the number of people in your household.   _____

  16c. Fill in the median family income for your state and size of household. .... $_____
       To find a list of applicable median income amounts, go online using the link specified in the separate
       instructions for this form. This list may also be available at the bankruptcy clerk's office.

17. **How do the lines compare?**

  17a. ☐ Line 15b is less than or equal to line 16c. On the top of page 1 of this form, check box 1, *Disposable income is not determined under*
       11 U.S.C. § 1325(b)(3). **Go to Part 3.** Do NOT fill out *Calculation of Your Disposable Income (Official Form 122C–2).*

  17b. ☐ Line 15b is more than line 16c. On the top of page 1 of this form, check box 2, *Disposable income is determined under*
       11 U.S.C. § 1325(b)(3). **Go to Part 3 and fill out Calculation of Your Disposable Income (Official Form 122C–2).**
       On line 39 of that form, copy your current monthly income from line 14 above.

Part 3:   Calculate Your Commitment Period Under 11 U.S.C. § 1325(b)(4)

---

18. **Copy your total average monthly income from line 11.** .... $_____

19. **Deduct the marital adjustment if it applies.** If you are married, your spouse is not filing with you, and you contend that
    calculating the commitment period under 11 U.S.C. § 1325(b)(4) allows you to deduct part of your spouse's income, copy
    the amount from line 13.
    19a. If the marital adjustment does not apply, fill in 0 on line 19a. .... − $_____

  19b. **Subtract line 19a from line 18.** $_____

20. **Calculate your current monthly income for the year.** Follow these steps:

  20a. Copy line 19b. .... $_____

       Multiply by 12 (the number of months in a year).   **x 12**

  20b. The result is your current monthly income for the year for this part of the form. $_____

  20c. Copy the median family income for your state and size of household from line 16c. .... $_____

21. **How do the lines compare?**

  ☐ Line 20b is less than line 20c. Unless otherwise ordered by the court, on the top of page 1 of this form, check box 3,
    The commitment period is 3 years. Go to Part 4.

  ☐ Line 20b is more than or equal to line 20c. Unless otherwise ordered by the court, on the top of page 1 of this form,
    check box 4, *The commitment period is 5 years.* Go to Part 4.

Part 4:   Sign Below

By signing here, under penalty of perjury I declare that the information on this statement and in any attachments is true and correct.

✗ _____   ✗ _____
   Signature of Debtor 1   Signature of Debtor 2

  Date _____   Date _____
      MM / DD / YYYY   MM / DD   / YYYY

  If you checked 17a, do NOT fill out or file Form 122C–2.
  If you checked 17b, fill out Form 122C–2 and file it with this form. On line 39 of that form, copy your current monthly income from line 14 above.

Official Form 122C-1   Chapter 13 Statement of Your Current Monthly Income and Calculation of Commitment Period   page 3

Form 122C-2: *Chapter 13 Calculation of Your Disposable Income*

Fill in this information to identify your case:

Debtor 1 _____
　　　　　First Name　　　　　　Middle Name　　　　　　Last Name

Debtor 2 _____
(Spouse, if filing)　First Name　　　Middle Name　　　　　Last Name

United States Bankruptcy Court for the: _____ District of _____

Case number _____
(If known)

☐ Check if this is an amended filing

Official Form 122C-2

Chapter 13 Calculation of Your Disposable Income

04/16

To fill out this form, you will need your completed copy of *Chapter 13 Statement of Your Current Monthly Income and Calculation of Commitment Period* (Official Form 122C–1).

Be as complete and accurate as possible. If two married people are filing together, both are equally responsible for being accurate. If more space is needed, attach a separate sheet to this form. Include the line number to which the additional information applies. On the top of any additional pages, write your name and case number (if known).

Part 1: **Calculate Your Deductions from Your Income**

The Internal Revenue Service (IRS) issues National and Local Standards for certain expense amounts. Use these amounts to answer the questions in lines 6-15. To find the IRS standards, go online using the link specified in the separate instructions for this form. This information may also be available at the bankruptcy clerk's office.

Deduct the expense amounts set out in lines 6-15 regardless of your actual expense. In later parts of the form, you will use some of your actual expenses if they are higher than the standards. Do not include any operating expenses that you subtracted from income in lines 5 and 6 of Form 122C–1, and do not deduct any amounts that you subtracted from your spouse's income in line 13 of Form 122C–1.

If your expenses differ from month to month, enter the average expense.

Note: Line numbers 1-4 are not used in this form. These numbers apply to information required by a similar form used in chapter 7 cases.

5. **The number of people used in determining your deductions from income**

    Fill in the number of people who could be claimed as exemptions on your federal income tax return, plus the number of any additional dependents whom you support. This number may be different from the number of people in your household.

    ☐

National Standards　　You must use the IRS National Standards to answer the questions in lines 6-7.

6. **Food, clothing, and other items:** Using the number of people you entered in line 5 and the IRS National Standards, fill in the dollar amount for food, clothing, and other items.

    $_____

7. **Out-of-pocket health care allowance:** Using the number of people you entered in line 5 and the IRS National Standards, fill in the dollar amount for out-of-pocket health care. The number of people is split into two categories—people who are under 65 and people who are 65 or older—because older people have a higher IRS allowance for health care costs. If your actual expenses are higher than this IRS amount, you may deduct the additional amount on line 22.

Form 122C-2: *Chapter 13 Calculation of Your Disposable Income* (page 2)

Debtor 1 _____   Case number (*if known*)_____
First Name   Middle Name   Last Name

People who are under 65 years of age

7a. Out-of-pocket health care allowance per person $_____

7b. Number of people who are under 65   X _____

7c. Subtotal. Multiply line 7a by line 7b. $_____   Copy here ➔ $_____

People who are 65 years of age or older

7d. Out-of-pocket health care allowance per person $_____

7e. Number of people who are 65 or older   X _____

7f. Subtotal. Multiply line 7d by line 7e. $_____   Copy here ➔   + $_____

7g. **Total**. Add lines 7c and 7f. .... $_____   Copy here ➔ .... $_____

Local Standards   You must use the IRS Local Standards to answer the questions in lines 8-15.

Based on information from the IRS, the U.S. Trustee Program has divided the IRS Local Standard for housing for bankruptcy purposes into two parts:

■ **Housing and utilities – Insurance and operating expenses**
■ **Housing and utilities – Mortgage or rent expenses**

To answer the questions in lines 8-9, use the U.S. Trustee Program chart. To find the chart, go online using the link specified in the separate instructions for this form. This chart may also be available at the bankruptcy clerk's office.

8. **Housing and utilities – Insurance and operating expenses:** Using the number of people you entered in line 5, fill in the dollar amount listed for your county for insurance and operating expenses. $_____

9. **Housing and utilities – Mortgage or rent expenses:**

9a. Using the number of people you entered in line 5, fill in the dollar amount listed for your county for mortgage or rent expenses. $_____

9b. Total average monthly payment for all mortgages and other debts secured by your home.

To calculate the total average monthly payment, add all amounts that are contractually due to each secured creditor in the 60 months after you file for bankruptcy. Next divide by 60.

Name of the creditor	Average monthly payment
_____	$_____
_____	$_____
_____	+ $_____

9b. Total average monthly payment $_____   Copy here ➔   – $_____   Repeat this amount on line 33a.

9c. Net mortgage or rent expense.

Subtract line 9b (*total average monthly payment*) from line 9a (*mortgage or rent expense*). If this number is less than $0, enter $0. $_____   Copy here ➔ .... $_____

10. **If you claim that the U.S. Trustee Program's division of the IRS Local Standard for housing is incorrect and affects the calculation of your monthly expenses, fill in any additional amount you claim.** $_____

Explain why: _____
_____

Form 122C-2: *Chapter 13 Calculation of Your Disposable Income* (page 3)

Debtor 1 _____   Case number *(if known)* _____
First Name   Middle Name   Last Name

11. **Local transportation expenses:** Check the number of vehicles for which you claim an ownership or operating expense.

☐ 0. Go to line 14.
☐ 1. Go to line 12.
☐ 2 or more. Go to line 12.

12. **Vehicle operation expense:** Using the IRS Local Standards and the number of vehicles for which you claim the operating expenses, fill in the *Operating Costs* that apply for your Census region or metropolitan statistical area. $_____

13. **Vehicle ownership or lease expense:** Using the IRS Local Standards, calculate the net ownership or lease expense for each vehicle below. You may not claim the expense if you do not make any loan or lease payments on the vehicle. In addition, you may not claim the expense for more than two vehicles.

Vehicle 1   **Describe Vehicle 1:** _____
                                       _____

13a. Ownership or leasing costs using IRS Local Standard .... $_____

13b. Average monthly payment for all debts secured by Vehicle 1.
Do not include costs for leased vehicles.

To calculate the average monthly payment here and on line 13e, add all amounts that are contractually due to each secured creditor in the 60 months after you file for bankruptcy. Then divide by 60.

Name of each creditor for Vehicle 1	Average monthly payment
_____	$_____
_____	+ $_____

Total average monthly payment $_____   Copy here➔   — $_____   Repeat this amount on line 33b.

13c. Net Vehicle 1 ownership or lease expense
Subtract line 13b from line 13a. If this number is less than $0, enter $0. .... $_____   **Copy net Vehicle 1 expense here**➔ $_____

Vehicle 2   **Describe Vehicle 2:** _____
                                       _____

13d. Ownership or leasing costs using IRS Local Standard .... $_____

13e. Average monthly payment for all debts secured by Vehicle 2.
Do not include costs for leased vehicles.

Name of each creditor for Vehicle 2	Average monthly payment
_____	$_____
_____	+ $_____

Total average monthly payment $_____   Copy here➔   — $_____   Repeat this amount on line 33c.

13f. Net Vehicle 2 ownership or lease expense
Subtract line 13e from line 13d. If this number is less than $0, enter $0. .... $_____   **Copy net Vehicle 2 expense here** ➔ $_____

14. **Public transportation expense:** If you claimed 0 vehicles in line 11, using the IRS Local Standards, fill in the *Public Transportation* expense allowance regardless of whether you use public transportation. $_____

15. **Additional public transportation expense:** If you claimed 1 or more vehicles in line 11 and if you claim that you may also deduct a public transportation expense, you may fill in what you believe is the appropriate expense, but you may not claim more than the IRS Local Standard for *Public Transportation*. $_____

Form 122C-2: *Chapter 13 Calculation of Your Disposable Income* (page 4)

Debtor 1 _____   Case number *(if known)*_____
      First Name   Middle Name   Last Name

Other Necessary Expenses	In addition to the expense deductions listed above, you are allowed your monthly expenses for the following IRS categories.

16. **Taxes:** The total monthly amount that you actually pay for federal, state and local taxes, such as income taxes, self-employment taxes, social security taxes, and Medicare taxes. You may include the monthly amount withheld from your pay for these taxes. However, if you expect to receive a tax refund, you must divide the expected refund by 12 and subtract that number from the total monthly amount that is withheld to pay for taxes. Do not include real estate, sales, or use taxes. $_____

17. **Involuntary deductions:** The total monthly payroll deductions that your job requires, such as retirement contributions, union dues, and uniform costs.

    Do not include amounts that are not required by your job, such as voluntary 401(k) contributions or payroll savings. $_____

18. **Life insurance:** The total monthly premiums that you pay for your own term life insurance. If two married people are filing together, include payments that you make for your spouse's term life insurance.

    Do not include premiums for life insurance on your dependents, for a non-filing spouse's life insurance, or for any form of life insurance other than term. $_____

19. **Court-ordered payments:** The total monthly amount that you pay as required by the order of a court or administrative agency, such as spousal or child support payments.

    Do not include payments on past due obligations for spousal or child support. You will list these obligations in line 35. $_____

20. **Education:** The total monthly amount that you pay for education that is either required:
    - as a condition for your job, or
    - for your physically or mentally challenged dependent child if no public education is available for similar services. $_____

21. **Childcare:** The total monthly amount that you pay for childcare, such as babysitting, daycare, nursery, and preschool. Do not include payments for any elementary or secondary school education. $_____

22. **Additional health care expenses, excluding insurance costs:** The monthly amount that you pay for health care that is required for the health and welfare of you or your dependents and that is not reimbursed by insurance or paid by a health savings account. Include only the amount that is more than the total entered in line 7.

    Payments for health insurance or health savings accounts should be listed only in line 25. $_____

23. **Optional telephones and telephone services:** The total monthly amount that you pay for telecommunication services for you and your dependents, such as pagers, call waiting, caller identification, special long distance, or business cell phone service, to the extent necessary for your health and welfare or that of your dependents or for the production of income, if it is not reimbursed by your employer.   + $_____

    Do not include payments for basic home telephone, internet or cell phone service. Do not include self-employment expenses, such as those reported on line 5 of Form 122C-1, or any amount you previously deducted.

24. **Add all of the expenses allowed under the IRS expense allowances.**
    Add lines 6 through 23. $_____

Additional Expense Deductions	These are additional deductions allowed by the Means Test. *Note:* Do not include any expense allowances listed in lines 6-24.

25. **Health insurance, disability insurance, and health savings account expenses.** The monthly expenses for health insurance, disability insurance, and health savings accounts that are reasonably necessary for yourself, your spouse, or your dependents.

    Health insurance $_____

    Disability insurance $_____

    Health savings account   + $_____

    Total $_____ Copy total here➜ .... $_____

    Do you actually spend this total amount?

    ☐ No. How much do you actually spend? $_____

    ☐ Yes

26. **Continuing contributions to the care of household or family members.** The actual monthly expenses that you will continue to pay for the reasonable and necessary care and support of an elderly, chronically ill, or disabled member of your household or member of your immediate family who is unable to pay for such expenses. These expenses may include contributions to an account of a qualified ABLE program. 26 U.S.C. § 529A(b). $_____

27. **Protection against family violence.** The reasonably necessary monthly expenses that you incur to maintain the safety of you and your family under the Family Violence Prevention and Services Act or other federal laws that apply.

    By law, the court must keep the nature of these expenses confidential. $_____

Form 122C-2: *Chapter 13 Calculation of Your Disposable Income* (page 5)

Debtor 1 _____   Case number *(if known)*_____
First Name   Middle Name   Last Name

28. **Additional home energy costs.** Your home energy costs are included in your insurance and operating expenses on line 8.

If you believe that you have home energy costs that are more than the home energy costs included in expenses on line 8, then fill in the excess amount of home energy costs. $_____

You must give your case trustee documentation of your actual expenses, and you must show that the additional amount claimed is reasonable and necessary.

29. **Education expenses for dependent children who are younger than 18.** The monthly expenses (not more than $160.42* per child) that you pay for your dependent children who are younger than 18 years old to attend a private or public elementary or secondary school. $_____

You must give your case trustee documentation of your actual expenses, and you must explain why the amount claimed is reasonable and necessary and not already accounted for in lines 6-23.

* Subject to adjustment on 4/01/19, and every 3 years after that for cases begun on or after the date of adjustment.

30. **Additional food and clothing expense.** The monthly amount by which your actual food and clothing expenses are higher than the combined food and clothing allowances in the IRS National Standards. That amount cannot be more than 5% of the food and clothing allowances in the IRS National Standards. $_____

To find a chart showing the maximum additional allowance, go online using the link specified in the separate instructions for this form. This chart may also be available at the bankruptcy clerk's office.

You must show that the additional amount claimed is reasonable and necessary.

31. **Continuing charitable contributions.** The amount that you will continue to contribute in the form of cash or financial instruments to a religious or charitable organization. 11 U.S.C. § 548(d)(3) and (4).   + $_____

Do not include any amount more than 15% of your gross monthly income.

32. **Add all of the additional expense deductions.**
Add lines 25 through 31. $_____

Deductions for Debt Payment

33. **For debts that are secured by an interest in property that you own, including home mortgages, vehicle loans, and other secured debt, fill in lines 33a through 33e.**

To calculate the total average monthly payment, add all amounts that are contractually due to each secured creditor in the 60 months after you file for bankruptcy. Then divide by 60.

	Average monthly payment
Mortgages on your home	
33a. Copy line 9b here .... ➔	$_____
Loans on your first two vehicles	
33b. Copy line 13b here. .... ➔	$_____
33c. Copy line 13e here. .... ➔	$_____

33d. List other secured debts:

Name of each creditor for other secured debt	Identify property that secures the debt	Does payment include taxes or insurance?	
_____	_____	☐ No ☐ Yes	$_____
_____	_____	☐ No ☐ Yes	$_____
_____	_____	☐ No ☐ Yes	+ $_____

| 33e. Total average monthly payment. Add lines 33a through 33d. .... | $_____ | Copy total here ➔ | $_____ |

Form 122C-2: *Chapter 13 Calculation of Your Disposable Income* (page 6)

Debtor 1 _____ Case number *(if known)*_____
First Name   Middle Name   Last Name

34. **Are any debts that you listed in line 33 secured by your primary residence, a vehicle, or other property necessary for your support or the support of your dependents?**

☐ No. Go to line 35.

☐ Yes. State any amount that you must pay to a creditor, in addition to the payments listed in line 33, to keep possession of your property (called the *cure amount*). Next, divide by 60 and fill in the information below.

Name of the creditor	Identify property that secures the debt	Total cure amount		Monthly cure amount
_____	_____	$_____ ÷ 60 =		$_____
_____	_____	$_____ ÷ 60 =		$_____
_____	_____	$_____ ÷ 60 = +		$_____

Total $_____   Copy total here ➜ $_____

35. **Do you owe any priority claims—such as a priority tax, child support, or alimony— that are past due as of the filing date of your bankruptcy case?** 11 U.S.C. § 507.

☐ No. Go to line 36.

☐ Yes. Fill in the total amount of all of these priority claims. Do not include current or ongoing priority claims, such as those you listed in line 19.

Total amount of all past-due priority claims. .... $_____ ÷ 60 $_____

36. **Projected monthly Chapter 13 plan payment** $_____

Current multiplier for your district as stated on the list issued by the Administrative Office of the United States Courts (for districts in Alabama and North Carolina) or by the Executive Office for United States Trustees (for all other districts).

To find a list of district multipliers that includes your district, go online using the link specified in the separate instructions for this form. This list may also be available at the bankruptcy clerk's office.   x _____

Average monthly administrative expense $_____   Copy total here ➜ $_____

37. **Add all of the deductions for debt payment.** Add lines 33e through 36. $_____

Total Deductions from Income

38. **Add all of the allowed deductions.**

Copy line 24, *All of the expenses allowed under IRS expense allowances* .... $_____

Copy line 32, *All of the additional expense deductions* .... $_____

Copy line 37, *All of the deductions for debt payment* .... + $_____

Total deductions .... $_____   Copy total here ➜ $_____

Form 122C-2: *Chapter 13 Calculation of Your Disposable Income* (page 7)

Debtor 1 _____ Case number *(if known)* _____

First Name   Middle Name   Last Name

Part 2: Determine Your Disposable Income Under 11 U.S.C. § 1325(b)(2)

39. **Copy your total current monthly income** from line 14 of Form 122C-1, *Chapter 13 Statement of Your Current Monthly Income and Calculation of Commitment Period.* .... $_____

40. **Fill in any reasonably necessary income you receive for support for dependent children.** The monthly average of any child support payments, foster care payments, or disability payments for a dependent child, reported in Part I of Form 122C-1, that you received in accordance with applicable nonbankruptcy law to the extent reasonably necessary to be expended for such child. $_____

41. **Fill in all qualified retirement deductions.** The monthly total of all amounts that your employer withheld from wages as contributions for qualified retirement plans, as specified in 11 U.S.C. § 541(b)(7) plus all required repayments of loans from retirement plans, as specified in 11 U.S.C. § 362(b)(19). $_____

42. **Total of all deductions allowed under 11 U.S.C. § 707(b)(2)(A).** Copy line 38 here ....➔ $_____

43. **Deduction for special circumstances.** If special circumstances justify additional expenses and you have no reasonable alternative, describe the special circumstances and their expenses. You must give your case trustee a detailed explanation of the special circumstances and documentation for the expenses.

Describe the special circumstances	Amount of expense
_____	$_____
_____	$_____
_____	+ $_____
Total	$_____

Copy here ➔ + $_____

44. **Total adjustments.** Add lines 40 through 43. .... $_____ Copy here ➔ − $_____

45. **Calculate your monthly disposable income under § 1325(b)(2).** Subtract line 44 from line 39. $_____

Part 3: Change in Income or Expenses

46. **Change in income or expenses.** If the income in Form 122C-1 or the expenses you reported in this form have changed or are virtually certain to change after the date you filed your bankruptcy petition and during the time your case will be open, fill in the information below. For example, if the wages reported increased after you filed your petition, check 122C-1 in the first column, enter line 2 in the second column, explain why the wages increased, fill in when the increase occurred, and fill in the amount of the increase.

Form	Line	Reason for change	Date of change	Increase or decrease?	Amount of change
☐ 122C–1 ☐ 122C–2	___	_____	_____	☐ Increase ☐ Decrease	$_____
☐ 122C–1 ☐ 122C–2	___	_____	_____	☐ Increase ☐ Decrease	$_____
☐ 122O–1 ☐ 122C–2	___	_____	_____	☐ Increase ☐ Decrease	$_____
☐ 122C–1 ☐ 122C–2	___	_____	_____	☐ Increase ☐ Decrease	$_____

Form 122C-2: *Chapter 13 Calculation of Your Disposable Income* (page 8)

Debtor 1 _____
       First Name   Middle Name   Last Name

Case number *(if known)*_____

Part 4:	Sign Below

By signing here, under penalty of perjury you declare that the information on this statement and in any attachments is true and correct.

✗ _____

✗ _____

Signature of Debtor 1   Signature of Debtor 2

Date _____
     MM / DD / YYYY

Date _____
     MM / DD / YYYY

Print	Save As...	Add Attachment		Reset

Index

△△ NOLO *Online Legal Forms*

Nolo offers a large library of legal solutions and forms, created by Nolo's in-house legal staff. These reliable documents can be prepared in minutes.

Create a Document

- **Incorporation.** Incorporate your business in any state.
- **LLC Formations.** Gain asset protection and pass-through tax status in any state.
- **Wills.** Nolo has helped people make over 2 million wills. Is it time to make or revise yours?
- **Living Trust (avoid probate).** Plan now to save your family the cost, delays, and hassle of probate.
- **Trademark.** Protect the name of your business or product.
- **Provisional Patent.** Preserve your rights under patent law and claim "patent pending" status.

Download a Legal Form

Nolo.com has hundreds of top quality legal forms available for download—bills of sale, promissory notes, nondisclosure agreements, LLC operating agreements, corporate minutes, commercial lease and sublease, motor vehicle bill of sale, consignment agreements and many, many more.

Review Your Documents

Many lawyers in Nolo's consumer-friendly lawyer directory will review Nolo documents for a very reasonable fee. Check their detailed profiles at **Nolo.com/lawyers**.

Nolo's Bestselling Books

Credit Repair
Make a Plan, Improve Your Credit, Avoid Scams
$24.99

The New Bankruptcy
Will It Work for You?
$24.99

Solve Your Money Troubles
$24.99

How to File for Chapter 7 Bankruptcy
$39.99

Legal Research
How to Find & Understand the Law
$49.99

Every Nolo title is available in print and for download at Nolo.com.

NOLO

Save 15% *off your next order*

Register your Nolo purchase, and we'll send you a **coupon for 15% off** your next Nolo.com order!

Nolo.com/customer-support/productregistration

On Nolo.com you'll also find:

Books & Software

Nolo publishes hundreds of great books and software programs for consumers and business owners. Order a copy, or download an ebook version instantly, at Nolo.com.

Online Legal Documents

You can quickly and easily make a will or living trust, form an LLC or corporation, apply for a trademark or provisional patent, or make hundreds of other forms—online.

Free Legal Information

Thousands of articles answer common questions about everyday legal issues including wills, bankruptcy, small business formation, divorce, patents, employment, and much more.

Plain-English Legal Dictionary

Stumped by jargon? Look it up in America's most up-to-date source for definitions of legal terms, free at nolo.com.

Lawyer Directory

Nolo's consumer-friendly lawyer directory provides in-depth profiles of lawyers all over America. You'll find all the information you need to choose the right lawyer.

CHB14